D0154134

"If I were to make a list of scholars who we should hire to assemble current thinking on human resource management in the nonprofit sector, Sowa and Word would be at the top of my list. Lo, it seems that these two have been doing just that. They have organized an impressive panoply of both young and established nonprofit sector scholars who represent our best current thinking on strategic human resource management. Interested readers will be able to pick and choose among its offerings. Some teachers will assign the entire volume in their college courses on nonprofit HRM."

Mark Hager, *Arizona State University, USA*

"Sowa and Word have contributed an outstanding new guide for both nonprofit managers and scholars, in *The Nonprofit Resource Management Handbook*. This book offers an impressive collection of thoughtfully-written and practical pieces by leading voices in the field. Comprehensive in scope, Sowa and Word cover critical topics ranging from how to attract the best and brightest employees and volunteers into the sector, to managing and cultivating diversity, to applications of technology in human resource management, and everything in between. This book serves as a valuable resource that I look forward to sharing with my students undertaking careers in the nonprofit sector."

Kelly LaRoux, *The University of Chicago at Illinois, USA*

"*The Nonprofit Human Resource Management Handbook* is an excellent confluence of the state-of-art research on human resources in nonprofit organizations and the practical matters confronting nonprofit managers seeking to effectively deploy their human capital. Sowa and Word and their outstanding colleagues have compiled an accessible, yet rigorous, resource that benefits both scholars and practitioners by highlighting critical issues that nonprofit organizations must successfully navigate to recruit and retain talented workers in the current environment. This will certainly be a much-used textbook in nonprofit management courses. I wish I would have had this book when I was a student!"

Rebecca Nesbit, *University of Georgia, USA*

The Nonprofit Human Resource Management Handbook

As an increasing number of individuals go to work in the nonprofit sector, nonprofit managers need support on how best to build their human resource management (HRM) capacity. They need to know which systems to examine, what questions to ask, and how to ensure they are managing people in a legal manner and as effectively as possible, given their particular resource constraints. Important questions include: Do we have a clear philosophy, one that aligns with our nonprofit mission and values and allows us to treat our employees as the professionals they are? How do we select, develop, and retain the best people who will produce high-value, high performance work, and how do we do so with limited resources? How do we effectively manage our mix of volunteers and paid staff? What do we need to consider to ensure diverse people work together in a harmonious fashion? With all-new chapters written by the top scholars in the field of nonprofit HRM, these are but a few of the many questions that are addressed in this timely volume.

These scholars delve into their particular areas of expertise, offering a comprehensive look at theories and trends; legal and ethical issues; how to build HRM from recruitment, management, labor relations, to training and appraisal; as well as topics in diversity, technology, and paid versus volunteer workforce management. This essential handbook offers all core topic coverage as well as countless insider insights, additional resource lists, and tool sets for practical application. With chapters grounded in existing research, but also connecting research to practice for those in the field, *The Nonprofit Human Resource Management Handbook* will be required reading for a generation of scholars, students, and practitioners of nonprofit human resource management.

Jessica K. A. Word is an Associate Professor in the School of Public Policy and Leadership at the University of Nevada, Las Vegas, USA.

Jessica E. Sowa is an Associate Professor in the School of Public and International Affairs in the College of Public Affairs at the University of Baltimore, USA.

PUBLIC ADMINISTRATION AND PUBLIC POLICY
A Comprehensive Publication Program

EDITOR-IN-CHIEF

DAVID H. ROSENBLOOM
Distinguished Professor of Public Administration
American University, Washington, DC

Founding Editor
JACK RABIN

RECENTLY PUBLISHED BOOKS

The Nonprofit Human Resource Management Handbook: From Theory to Practice, edited by Jessica K. A. Word and Jessica E. Sowa

Cost and Optimization in Government: An Introduction to Cost Accounting, Operations Management, and Quality Control, Second Edition, by Aman Khan

The Constitutional School of American Public Administration, edited by Stephanie P. Newbold and David H. Rosenbloom

Contracting for Services in State and Local Government Agencies, Second Edition, William Sims Curry

Democracy and Civil Society in a Global Era, Scott Nicholas Romaniuk and Marguerite Marlin

Development and the Politics of Human Rights, Scott Nicholas Romaniuk and Marguerite Marlin

Public Administration and Policy in the Caribbean, Indianna D. Minto-Coy and Evan Berman

The Economic Survival of America's Isolated Small Towns, Gerald L. Gordon

Sustainable Development and Human Security in Africa: Governance as the Missing Link, Louis A. Picard, Terry F. Buss, Taylor B. Seybolt, and Macrina C. Lelei

Information and Communication Technologies in Public Administration: Innovations from Developed Countries, Christopher G. Reddick and Leonidas Anthopoulos

Creating Public Value in Practice: Advancing the Common Good in a Multi-Sector, Shared-Power, No-One-Wholly-in-Charge World, edited by John M. Bryson, Barbara C. Crosby, and Laura Bloomberg

Digital Divides: The New Challenges and Opportunities of e-Inclusion, Kim Andreasson

Living Legends and Full Agency: Implications of Repealing the Combat Exclusion Policy, G.L.A. Harris

Politics of Preference: India, United States, and South Africa, Krishna K. Tummala

Crisis and Emergency Management: Theory and Practice, Second Edition, Ali Farazmand

Labor Relations in the Public Sector, Fifth Edition, Richard C. Kearney and Patrice M. Mareschal

Democracy and Public Administration in Pakistan, Amna Imam and Eazaz A. Dar

The Economic Viability of Micropolitan America, Gerald L. Gordon

The Nonprofit Human Resource Management Handbook

From Theory to Practice

Edited by Jessica K. A. Word and Jessica E. Sowa

Routledge
Taylor & Francis Group

NEW YORK AND LONDON

First published 2017
by Routledge
711 Third Avenue, New York, NY 10017

and by Routledge
2 Park Square, Milton Park, Abingdon, Oxon OX14 4RN

Routledge is an imprint of the Taylor & Francis Group, an informa business

Library of Congress Cataloging in Publication Data
Names: Sowa, Jessica E., 1975– editor. | Word, Jessica K.A., 1977– editor.
Title: The nonprofit human resource management handbook : from theory to practice / edited by Jessica E. Sowa and Jessica K.A. Word.
Description: New York : Routledge, 2017. | Includes bibliographical references and index.
Identifiers: LCCN 2016054950 | ISBN 9781498738170 (hbk : alk. paper) | ISBN 9781315181585 (ebk)
Subjects: LCSH: Nonprofit organizations—Management. | Personnel management.
Classification: LCC HD62.6 .N656 2017 | DDC 658.3—dc23
LC record available at https://lccn.loc.gov/2016054950

ISBN: 978-1-4987-3817-0 (hbk)
ISBN: 978-1-315-18158-5 (ebk)

Typeset in Bembo
by Keystroke, Neville Lodge, Tettenhall, Wolverhampton

Contents

Figures

Tables

Notes on Contributors

About the Editors

Jessica E. Sowa is an Associate Professor in the School of Public and International Affairs in the College of Public Affairs at the University of Baltimore, USA. She currently serves as Director of the M.S. in Nonprofit Management and Social Entrepreneurship program. Her research focuses on public and nonprofit management, with an emphasis on organizational effectiveness, leadership, and the management of human resources in public and nonprofit organizations. Dr. Sowa's work has been published in *Public Management Review, Administration and Society, Public Personnel Management American Review of Public Administration, Journal of Public Administration Research and Theory, Nonprofit and Voluntary Sector Quarterly,* and the *Review of Public Personnel Administration.* Her current research on high performance work systems in nonprofit human service organizations was funded by a grant from the Society for Human Resource Management (SHRM) Foundation. She serves on the editorial board of a number of journals in public administration and human resource management.

Jessica K. A. Word is an Associate Professor in the School of Public Policy and Leadership at the University of Nevada, Las Vegas, USA. She currently serves as Director of the Nonprofit, Community, and Leadership Initiative and Graduate Coordinator for the School. She received her doctorate from the Rueben Askew School of Public Administration and Policy at Florida State University in 2006. Her research focuses on capacity building in the public and nonprofit sector. Her work has been published in *Public Administration Review, Review of Public Personnel Administration, Public Personnel Management, Journal for Nonprofit Management, Journal of Management, Spirituality and Religion,* and *The Innovation Journal.* She currently serves as the book review editor for the *International Journal of Public Administration.* She has worked with notable national nonprofits such as the Girl Scouts of the USA, Volunteers of America, and Opportunity Knocks on issues related to employee engagement and burnout.

About the Contributors

Rikki Abzug (PhD, Yale University), is a Professor and Convener of Management, Anisfield School of Business, Ramapo College, USA. A prolific researcher of organizational governance, sector theory, social purpose organizations, and neo-institutionalism in organizations, Dr. Abzug is co-author (with Jeffrey Simonoff) of *Nonprofit Trusteeship in Different Contexts*; as well as the author/co-author of a myriad of scholarly peer-reviewed articles in journals including: *Organization Science, The Academy of Management Journal, Nonprofit and Voluntary Sector Quarterly, Nonprofit Management & Leadership, Voluntas: International Journal of Voluntary and Non-Profit Organisations,* and *Sexualities*. Before coming to Ramapo, Dr. Abzug was the Chair of the Nonprofit Management Program at The New School for Social Research in NYC and before that, the Associate Director of Yale University's Program on Nonprofit Organizations.

Kunle Akingbola is an Associate Professor in the Faculty of Business Administration at Lakehead University, Canada. His research focuses on the interactions in human resource management and strategic management in nonprofit and healthcare organizations. He is a certified HR professional with industry experience and a consultant to nonprofit organizations. He is the author of *Managing Human Resources for Nonprofits*, published in 2015 by Routledge.

Alina McCandless Baluch is Lecturer in Management at the University of St Andrews, Scotland, and Associate Director of the Centre for the Study of Philanthropy and Public Good. Her research looks at employment relations in nonprofit organizations with a particular focus on implementation gaps in HRM, employee-line manager relations, and employee well-being. Alina's research has been published in several nonprofit, HRM, and management journals.

Jeffrey L. Brudney, Ph.D., is the Betty and Dan Cameron Family Distinguished Professor of Innovation in the Nonprofit Sector at the University of North Carolina Wilmington. Dr. Brudney has received notable honors and awards for his scholarship and service to the field, including the Award for Distinguished Achievement and Leadership in Nonprofit and Voluntary Action Research (formerly called the Award for Distinguished Lifetime Achievement) from the Association for Research on Nonprofit Organizations and Voluntary Action (ARNOVA), and the Harriet Naylor Distinguished Member Service Award from the Association for Volunteer Administration. His book, *Fostering Volunteer Programs in the Public Sector: Planning, Initiating, and Managing Voluntary Activities*, earned the John Grenzebach Award for Outstanding Research in Philanthropy for Education. He has served as Editor-in-Chief of *Nonprofit and Voluntary Sector Quarterly*, the leading academic journal in nonprofit and voluntary sector studies world-wide.

Heather L. Carpenter is Assistant Professor and Program Coordinator of the MA in Nonprofit Management in the Business Department at Notre Dame of Maryland University, USA. She is co-author of the book, *The Talent Development Platform: Putting People First in Social Change Organizations*. Heather's research interests include nonprofit employment, professional development, and nonprofit management education.

Ida Drury is a doctoral student in the School of Public Affairs at the University of Colorado Denver and a Sr. Instructor at the Kempe Center for the Prevention and Treatment of Child Abuse and Neglect on the University of Colorado Anschutz Medical Campus. She has almost twenty years of practical experience in human services nonprofits and government organizations. Her research centers on citizen engagement and emotional labor performance by street-level bureaucrats.

Toby Egan, Ph.D., is Associate Professor and Senior Executive Fellow in the School of Public Policy and the Robert H. Smith School of Business at the University of Maryland, USA. He is former vice-president of a US-based consulting firm now merged with Korn-Ferry International (the world's largest talent management organization). Dr. Egan researches learning organizations, nonprofit/private/public management, dyadic development, and creativity/innovation. He has received international, national, state and university level awards for his leadership, research, teaching and service.

Anne-Meike Fechter is Senior Lecturer in the Department of Anthropology at the University of Sussex, UK. Her research focuses on migration processes, including mobile professionals, with a regional emphasis on Southeast Asia. Her work has examined corporate expatriates (*Transnational Lives: Expatriates in Indonesia*, Routledge, 2007), and international development workers (*The Personal and the Professional in Aid Work*, Routledge, 2013). She is currently researching forms of 'Do-it-yourself Aid' in Cambodia.

Eric Franklin Amarante earned his B.A. from the University of Texas at Austin and his J.D. from Cornell Law School. He is an Assistant Professor of Law at the University of Tennessee where he directs the Community Economic Development Clinic. Prior to joining UT, he directed the Small Business & Nonprofit Legal Clinic UNLV's William S. Boyd School of Law and was the inaugural Whiting Fellow at the University of Denver Sturm College of Law. Before entering academia, Eric spent over five years in transactional private practice in Palo Alto and Seattle.

Beth Gazley is Professor of Public and Environmental Affairs at Indiana University-Bloomington, USA. She teaches public and nonprofit management, and directs IU's Master of Public Affairs program. Her research addresses nonprofit management and governance, volunteerism, nonprofit participation in public service delivery, and intersectoral collaboration. Before entering academia, she had a career in nonprofit fundraising and management consulting.

Femida Handy is Professor at the School of Social Policy and Practice at the University of Pennsylvania and currently the Director of the Ph.D. program in Social Welfare. She has served as the Editor-in-Chief of *Nonprofit and Voluntary Sector Quarterly*. Her research and teaching focus on the economics of the nonprofit sector, volunteering, and philanthropy.

Jasmine McGinnis Johnson is an Assistant Professor at The George Washington University in the Trachtenberg School of Public Policy and Public Administration, USA. Her research interests include the implications of variations in nonprofit governance, within the context of foundation, how nonprofit organizations are shaped by the philanthropic market, and the causes and consequences of how nonprofits shape their human resource practices for Millennials' public service commitments. She worked in development and evaluation for several human service organizations prior to beginning graduate school.

Jennifer A. Jones, Ph.D., is an Assistant Professor of nonprofit leadership and management at the University of Florida. She holds a Ph.D. in Leadership Studies (nonprofit specialization) and an M.A. in Nonprofit Management and Leadership from the University of San Diego. She is a member of the Nu Lambda Mu international honor society for nonprofit scholars, has received an Emerging Scholar Award in 2015 from the Association for Research on Nonprofit Organizations and Voluntary Action, and has more than a decade of experience as a nonprofit practitioner.

Troy Kennedy is a Graduate Assistant at the School of Public and Environmental Affairs at Indiana University-Purdue University Indianapolis, USA. He is currently finishing his Master of Public Affairs with a concentration in Public Management. Previously, Troy completed his Bachelor of Science majoring in Policy Studies at Indiana University-Purdue University Indianapolis.

Yeonsoo Kim, Ph.D., SPHR, has been in HR field both professionally and academically for more than 15 years. She is an assistant professor in School of Public Policy and Leadership at University of Nevada Las Vegas. In that capacity, she teaches and conducts research in the field of Human Resource Management and Development. Her research interests include human resource development, strategic human resource management, talent management, organization development in both public and private sector.

Ishbel McWha-Hermann is an Early Career Fellow in international human resource management at the University of Edinburgh Business School, Scotland. Her research focuses broadly on issues of social justice and diversity at work. She has a particular interest in the people management practices of international NGOs and their impact on both organizations and their employees, including, for example, through motivation, performance, commitment, and teamwork. Ishbel has a Ph.D. in psychology from Massey University, New Zealand.

Annie Miller is a Research Assistant Professor in the Graduate School of Professional Psychology at the University of Denver and a social change consultant, senior project manager and researcher at the Spark Policy Institute. Annie has authored chapters on public engagement in higher education, immigrant threat and national salience, non-profit network membership and network effectiveness. Her current research focuses on management of public networks, combating human trafficking, preventing acts of mass and ideological violence, and social service provision through multi-sector networks.

Laurie Mook is Associate Professor in the School of Community Resources and Development at Arizona State University, USA. She is also a research associate at the ASU-Lodestar Center for Philanthropy and Nonprofit Innovation. Her research focuses on social accounting, the social economy, and volunteering.

Eddy Ng is a Professor of Organizational Behaviour and the F.C. Manning Chair in Economics and Business at Dalhousie University. His research focuses on managing diversity for organizational competitiveness, the changing nature of work and organizations, and managing an intergenerational workforce. He is Editor-in-Chief of *Equality, Diversity and Inclusion*, and Associate Editor of *Personnel Review*, and he serves on the Editorial Boards of *Cross-cultural and Strategic Management*, *Employee Relations*, *Management Communication Quarterly*, and *Public Personnel Management*.

Carrie R. Oelberger is an Assistant Professor of Management at the University of Minnesota's Humphrey School of Public Affairs. Her research examines how working in nonprofit organizations influences the private lives of their staff. In particular, she studies how various social identities—especially gender, sexual orientation, and family status—influence how employees navigate careers in deeply meaningful work settings that compromise meaningful private lives. She also studies how the private interests, needs, and desires of nonprofit employees and trustees shape organizations and fields, with an empirical focus on how philanthropy shapes social movements and organizational fields. She received her Ph.D. in organization studies from Stanford University.

Jaclyn Schede Piatak is an Assistant Professor in the Department of Political Science and Public Administration at the University of North Carolina at Charlotte, USA. Her research examines how organizations interact to deliver public services, how job sector relates to individual outcomes and behaviors, and how society influences employment and volunteering. Her professional experience includes working in the federal government at the U.S. Department of Labor and the Corporation for National and Community Service.

Joan E. Pynes is Professor of Public Administration at the University of South Florida. She is the author or co-author of five books including *Human Resources Management: A Strategic Approach*, 4th ed. (Jossey-Bass, 2013), co-author of *Human Resources Management for Health Care Organizations: A Strategic Approach* (Jossey-Bass, 2012), and *Nonprofit Management: Context and Environment* (M. E. Sharpe, 2012); *Public Sector Labor Relations: A Guide for Public Administrators* (Quorum Books, 1993); and *Nursing Home Management: A People Oriented Perspective* (Charles C. Thomas, 1988). She is the author or co-author of more than 50 academic articles, book chapters, technical reports, and encyclopedia entries about public and non-profit human resources management.

Hans-Gerd Ridder holds the Chair in Human Resource Management at the Leibniz Universität Hannover, Germany. His research focuses on strategic HRM in for-profit and nonprofit organizations. He is the former editor of the German Journal of HRM (*Zeitschrift für Personalforschung*) and his work appears in leading HRM, nonprofit, and public management journals.

John C. Ronquillo is Assistant Professor of Nonprofit and Public Management in the School of Public Affairs at the University of Colorado Denver, USA. His research focuses on issues related to organizational and social innovation, indigenous leadership and governance, and leadership of nonprofit and public organizations, in general.

Allison R. Russell is a Ph.D. student at the School of Social Policy and Practice at the University of Pennsylvania. She has served as the Managing Editor of *Nonprofit and Voluntary Sector Quarterly*. Her research interests focus on volunteering, civil society, nonprofit management, and related issues.

Sally Coleman Selden is Vice President and Dean for Academic Affairs and Professor of Management at Lynchburg College, USA. She is the author of a number of articles on human resource management and public administration. She is the author of two books, *The Promise of a Representative Bureaucracy* and *Human Capital: Tools and Strategies for the Public Sector*, both of which won book awards. Dr. Selden is currently involved in two research projects: a study of High Performance Work Systems in Nonprofit Organization funded by the SHRM Foundation and the State Government Workforce Project, which is a collaborative project with the National Association of State Personnel Executives.

Hayley K. Sink, M.P.A., is a practitioner in the nonprofit field in Wilmington, North Carolina, USA. Her research interests include volunteer management and volunteering, with particular interest in the impact of volunteering on special populations, such as those with disabilities, and the aging population. She received a Master of Public Administration with a concentration in Nonprofit Management at the University of North Carolina Wilmington and a Bachelor of Science in Sociology with a minor in Political Science from Virginia Tech. She has served as a Graduate Research Assistant, as well as Editorial Assistant to Dr. Jeffrey L. Brudney for the academic journal *Nonprofit and Voluntary Sector Quarterly*. Hayley wishes to acknowledge Dr. Brudney for his invaluable mentorship and support.

Marlene Walk is Assistant Professor of Nonprofit Management at the School of Public and Environmental Affairs at Indiana University-Purdue University Indianapolis. Marlene holds a Ph.D. in Social Welfare from the University of

Pennsylvania, School of Social Policy and Practice. She researches and publishes on human resource management, volunteering, and volunteer management in nonprofit organizations as well as on organizational change and the effects of change on employees in public and nonprofit organizations. Her work has earned awards from numerous institutions, including the Academy of Management, Organization Development and Change Division's Best Paper based on a Dissertation Award in 2015 and the Association for Research on Nonprofit and Voluntary Action's Emerging Scholar Award in 2013.

Judith Y. Weisinger, Ph.D., is Visiting Associate Professor of Management at Bucknell University in Lewisburg, PA, USA. Her research examines diversity and inclusion in nonprofit organizations, with interests in the role of organizational structuring for diversity/inclusion and the role of social capital. Dr. Weisinger's work has appeared in the *Nonprofit & Voluntary Sector Quarterly*, *Nonprofit Management & Leadership*, and the *Journal of Nonprofit Education and Leadership*, among others.

Acknowledgements

The editors would like to thank the generous contributions of our colleagues to this volume. We are honored that so many of our wonderful colleagues agreed to participate in this project and we look forward to continuing the conversation on how to build better human resource management in the nonprofit sector. We also are grateful to our students and colleagues in the nonprofit sector, for doing the hard work to make the world a better place.

Jessica Word would like to acknowledge her family for their patience and support through many busy days and nights. In particular, I want to thank my daughter Lela Spilman for reminding me playtime is important and to always keep smiling.

Jessica Sowa would like to acknowledge her family for their unending support and Sally Coleman Selden for being such a great mentor and building my love for all things human resource management.

1

Introduction

Jessica E. Sowa and Jessica K. A. Word

Over the past thirty years, the role of nonprofit and non-governmental organizations has changed dramatically, both in the United States and globally (Salamon, 2015; Tschirhart & Bielefeld, 2012). The nonprofit sector, as a component of the economy and as a critical player in serving the public, has grown in importance, depth, and breadth. In the United States, as of 2013, there are an estimated 1.4 million registered nonprofits operating, with this number not including religious organizations and smaller, largely unregistered nonprofits that are hard to track (McKeever, 2015). Globally, it is incredibly difficult to get estimates on the full scope of nonprofits, but nonprofits operate across numerous continents and in a wide variety of forms (Salamon et al., 2012). Nonprofits play a critical role globally in strengthening societies, assisting governments, and promoting the well-being of citizens along a number of crucial dimensions (Smith, 2008; Weisbrod, 1988).

There are few areas of life, society, government, and governance not influenced by nonprofit organizations. Nonprofits feed the hungry (Feeding America™, Share Our Strength), help homeless youth (Stand Up For Kids, Covenant House), fight, treat, and cure diseases (St. Jude Children's Hospital, Leukemia and Lymphoma Society), advocate for the environment (Greenpeace, the Nature Conservancy), aid the poor in starting their own businesses through microloans (Grameen Bank of Bangladesh, Kiva), educate children (Harlem Children's Zone, Communities in Schools), seek to prevent war and protect human security around the globe (Amnesty International, Carnegie Endowment for International Peace), and countless other actions that attempt to make the world a better place and improve the well-being of individuals and communities. Nonprofit and nongovernmental organizations (NGOs) impact major social, economic, and environmental issues, especially intractable or "wicked problems," which require multifaceted solutions including advocating for changes to public policy or simply shining a light on the plight of others. While operating on a global scale, nonprofits are also incredibly important on a local scale. They serve as a catalyst to bring people together by enhancing the identity and cohesion of neighborhoods (e.g. Wyman Park Community Association, Summit Neighborhood Association), connecting people with their favorite type of dog (e.g. Northern New England Westie Rescue, Basset Hound Rescue League, Inc.), fostering connection between people with similar interests (e.g. Knots of Love, Cowee Pottery School), and providing opportunities for socialization and connection (e.g. New Haven Rowing Club, Twin Cities Running Club). Nonprofits change the world and also change individual lives— they create policy change and build social capital bonds to strengthen individuals and communities. Overall, few can ignore the importance of the nonprofit sector in the 21st century.

As the sector has grown, both in the United States and worldwide, more and more people are seeking to pursue their goals and achieve their professional identities through work in the nonprofit sector. In 2010, the nonprofit sector constituted around 10% of private employment in the United States, making it the third largest industry (Salamon, Sokolowski, & Geller, 2012). In 2012, a little more than 11 million people worked in the nonprofit sector, according to the U.S. Bureau of Labor Statistics, with nonprofits in some states employing an even larger percentage of individuals as a percentage of private employment (e.g. New York, 18.1%; North Dakota, 14.7%; Pennsylvania, 15.9%) (Bureau of Labor Statistics, 2014). The 2016 Nonprofit Employment Practices Survey™, conducted by Nonprofit HR, documented the continued growth of the sector and reported that over half of the nonprofits surveyed anticipate taking on new staff in 2016 (as opposed to around 36% in the private sector) (Nonprofit HR, 2016). Therefore, in the United States in particular, nonprofit organizations represent a major employer, make a strong contribution to the economic well-being of the country, and are a critical player in a strong society. While perhaps not quite as plentiful in other countries, scholars have documented the importance of and continuing growth of nonprofits worldwide, even countries previously considered state-centered in terms of programs for their citizens, such as China (Hu & Guo, 2016; Salamon et al., 2012). Nonprofits and their foreign counterparts' non-governmental organizations (NGOs) are often even credited with being key to the development and maintenance of democracy both in the USA and abroad (Fukuyama, 2001; Putnam, 1995). Nonprofits are a major force and their importance and influence is only expected to grow as we move further into the 21st century.

Associated with the growth in the nonprofit sector and nonprofit employment, there has been an increase in the number of education programs focused specifically on nonprofit management, including separate degree programs in nonprofit management and specializations or concentrations within existing professional degree programs (such as Master of Public Administration, Master of Social Work, and Master of Business Administration programs). Mirabella (2007) documented the growth in nonprofit education programs. Her work observed a 10-year-long expansion in universities offering some form of nonprofit education, a growth rate of around 50%, with this increase occurring at both the undergraduate and graduate levels. The Network of Schools of Public Policy, Affairs, and Administration (NASPAA), the accrediting body for public affairs programs, now has a section specifically devoted to nonprofit management education and nonprofit management is one of the subfields tracked and ranked by U.S. News and World Report for graduate programs in public affairs (Morse, 2016).

While some choose the public sector, more and more students and workers interested in making a difference increasingly seek out the nonprofit sector as their venue to operate and make professional contributions (Lee & Wilkins, 2011; Mesch, 2010). Scholars have examined where public service-inclined individuals (those who express an interest in public service work or demonstrate high levels of public service motivation) pursue their professional opportunities (Brewer, Selden & Facer, 2000; Mann, 2006; Park & Word, 2012; Taylor, 2010; Park & Word, 2012). For those who teach in programs geared toward public and non-profit management, there has been an operating assumption that our students move between sectors, seeking different ways to make an impact and improve their professional capabilities. However, research has demonstrated that sector preferences and sector shifting are more complicated in practice (Su & Bozeman, 2009; Tschirhart, Reed, Freeman, & Anker, 2008). Students with expressed preferences and early experiences in nonprofit work are more likely to pursue work in that sector, but research has demonstrated that attraction to the sector and the missions of organizations within it can be difficult to sustain. Nonprofit employees are likely to leave if the organizational capacity fails to provide for sufficient com-pensation (McGinnis Johnson & Ng, 2015), human resource management (HRM) practices, career advancement opportunities, and training and development in order to maintain and refresh that connection over time (Kim & Lee, 2007; Word & Carpenter, 2013). If the nonprofit sector is increasingly the venue in which public service-focused individuals seek to carve out their professional identities, the time has come to have larger discussions about how well the sector supports those professional identities—how well the nonprofit sector manages its human resources. Therefore, this book seeks to add to the work of scholars before us who have explored the benefits of working in the nonprofit sector and the particular challenges of managing people in the nonprofit sector (e.g. Akingbola, 2015; Pynes, 2013), bringing together the current research across the whole of the human resource management function to explore what we know today and what are some of the continuing questions for the nonprofit workforce.

Human Resource Management in the Nonprofit Sector

In order to understand what it means to manage people in the nonprofit sector, it is first important to explore what human resource management (HRM) is and why this is an important field of study and practice, in particular for those concerned with and working in nonprofits. Formally defined, human resource management is "the design of formal systems in an organization to ensure the effective use of employees' knowledge, skills, abilities, and other characteristics (KSAOCs) to accomplish organizational goals" (Pynes, 2013, p. 3). Effective HRM involves considering what systems are in place for every step of the employment relationship, from the design of jobs, recruitment, and selection of individuals to fill those jobs, training, development, and evaluation of the performance of the individuals within those jobs, and, sadly, to the occasional termination of people when they are not a good fit for those jobs. While some nonprofits like hospitals and universities may have well-developed HRM infrastructures, for many nonprofits, this has been a challenging area for building management capacity, with many nonprofit executive directors often handling the primary responsibility for HRM practices (Selden & Sowa, 2014). Managing people effectively is one of the toughest skill sets out there—for the executive director who is balancing finances, operations, and HRM, good HR practices may often fall by the wayside, with fingers crossed that no problems occur. In addition, simply holding a management position does not mean one holds the necessary knowledge and skills to manage people effectively. This takes training and study—this book is designed to help fill that need.

While we are not advocating for every smaller nonprofit organization to immediately invest in new expensive HRM systems across the board, as more individuals go to work in the nonprofit sector as their primary professional venue, nonprofit managers need support on how best to build their HRM capacity. They need to know which systems to examine, what questions to ask, and how to ensure they are managing people in a legal manner and as effectively as possible given their particular resource constraints. Therefore, a systematic treatment of HRM in the nonprofit sector examines such questions as:

- What is our approach to managing people in our nonprofit? Do we have a clear philosophy for human resource management, one that aligns with our nonprofit mission and values and allows us to treat our employees as the professionals they are?
- We want to hire and retain the best people for our nonprofit. How do we go about this? How do we select the right people and develop them over time so they remain with our organization and produce high value, high performance work?
- As a nonprofit, our budget is tight and generating new resources can be challenging. How do we design a compensation system that rewards our employees fairly but does not strain the resources of our nonprofit or threaten our financial sustainability?
- Our nonprofit uses a mix of volunteers and paid staff. How do we effectively manage those volunteers? How do we blend those two sets of human capital in a way that promotes the mission of our nonprofit?

- We are employing individuals from many different backgrounds and many different age groups or generations in our nonprofit. What do we need to consider to ensure these diverse people work together in a harmonious fashion?

These are but a few of the many questions that are addressed by the chapters contained within this volume.

While HRM involves many systems, policies, and procedures, with these often being transferable across settings and sectors, effective HRM also involves developing an overall philosophy toward how an organization views its people and their role in the organization, a philosophy that underpins those systems, policies, and procedures (Akingbola, 2012, 2013; Pfeffer, 1998; Ridder & McCandless, 2010). Scholars studying HRM practices considered to be the most effective, what are known as high performance work systems, emphasize a philosophy toward managing people known as the resource-based view (RBV) of human capital (Colbert, 2004; Ridder, Piening, & Baluch, 2012; Selden & Sowa, 2015; Way, 2002; Wright et al., 2001). Holding a resource-based view of one's staff, an organization (in the case of this book, nonprofit organizations) recognizes the crucial role of people in accomplishing the mission of the organization and performing at a high level. Much like an organization can have other forms of capital (e.g. financial capital, capital investments) to aid in working toward the mission of an organization and help it maintain a competitive advantage, so too does the human capital of an organization (Boxall, 1996; Combs et al., 2006; Pfeffer, 1998). Therefore, this human capital needs to be viewed as a valuable asset, an asset that requires investment and maintenance over time for it to continue to contribute value to the organization. The vital role of an overall strategic approach or philosophy to HRM is discussed in more detail in Chapter 5 in this volume. However, it is important to highlight why nonprofits need to consider their approach to managing their people, both for the good of the nonprofit and for the people that work within the nonprofit. People are the critical ingredient in how nonprofits make a difference—those people are the ones interacting with the clients to improve their well-being, knocking on doors to educate people about environmental challenges, reading to children during story time at the library. Human capital is the main input used by a nonprofit to accomplish their mission. While financial capital helps reward those people and helps the organization keep its lights on, the people are the difference in a good versus great nonprofit and therefore need to be managed accordingly. Your personnel in your nonprofit are not your largest expenditure—they are your greatest asset. Manage them accordingly.

This is easier said than done, as anyone who has worked in the nonprofit sector knows, there are some particular challenges that can make effective HRM a challenge. Therefore, in addition to understanding what is human resource management and what is our overall philosophy to managing people in the nonprofit sector, it is important to understand some of the contextual differences in the nonprofit sector and how this may influence the operation of HRM in this sector.

What are some of the particular constraints that affect managing people in the nonprofit sector? First, nonprofit organizations face significant challenges in terms of their financial management and fiscal resources (Chikoto & Neely, 2014; Froelich, 1999; Greenlee & Trussel, 2000). While this is discussed in more detail in Chapters 2 and 3 in this volume, we want to briefly introduce those issues here.

In nonprofit organizations, the ability to generate funding is more challenging than in the private sector or government. That money needs to be found somewhere—nonprofits cannot just raise the price of the product (as many of their clients may not be able to pay) or pass a new tax. Generating revenue requires human capital and human resource management capacity—one needs to have a strong case for support, staff, or volunteers to raise money from donations, and/or staff or volunteers to help secure government or foundation grants or contracts. However, gaining that human capital generally requires a certain level of revenue, otherwise a nonprofit may struggle to acquire and sustain that staff or support those volunteers. Therefore, for many nonprofits, this becomes a chicken or the egg problem. As will be addressed later in this volume, many nonprofits are very small, operating with few paid staff members and relying on volunteers to help fill their human capital stock. As explored in Chapters 12 and 15, managing volunteers on their own and balancing the management of volunteers alongside paid staff requires careful attention to HRM policies in practice in order to support and maintain that human capital stock, regardless of whether it is donated or paid labor. However, we recognize that building HRM capacity has been a challenge for many smaller nonprofit organizations.

In addition, nonprofits often face pressures from various stakeholders, including funders, donors, and other groups reviewing nonprofit operations, to keep "overhead" or administrative costs down or low (Bowman, 2006; Gregory & Howard, 2009; Hager et al., 2004). While we would argue spending on good human resource management is not in any way, shape, or form wasteful and in fact is directly tied to the effective operation and performance of nonprofits, this pressure is real for many nonprofits. Donors and other stakeholders want to know where money is going—if that money is being spent on programs. However, for nonprofits, there are no programs without staff—volunteer or paid. We as scholars and practitioners of nonprofit management need to change the discussion around investing in our human resource management, the policies and practices and the people. This is not money wasted—well-managed staff are happier staff, who should perform better and leave the organization at a lower rate (Selden & Sowa, 2015). Good human resource management is a good investment for the nonprofit sector and this book is designed to explore how to make that investment work for those in the field in nonprofits.

The Purpose and Scope of This Book

While research has been growing on nonprofit HRM and there have been several comprehensive examinations from some leading scholars (e.g. Akingbola,

2015; Baluch, 2012; Pynes, 2013; Ridder & McCandless, 2010; Ridder et al., 2012), we are adding to this conversation and area of study by bringing together many of the top scholars to reflect on the state of research and the field. These scholars are diving into their particular areas of expertise in human resource management, in the chapters contained in this volume, exploring where we have progressed in studying and understanding nonprofit HRM and also charting a course for future areas of research and practice. This book is for scholars, students, and practitioners. The chapters are grounded in existing research, but also connect research to practice to demonstrate the usefulness of research in nonprofit studies for those in the field directly managing people (or human resources). Therefore, the primary utility of the book is to provide an up-to-date and comprehensive picture of the state of research on the management of human resources in nonprofit organizations and to inform practice in the nonprofit sector. Overall, the book is meant to do the following:

- Provide a solid grounding in existing research on nonprofit human resource management, encompassing the core components of the HRM process along with special topics and areas of consideration in managing the paid and volunteer human capital that populates the nonprofit sector.
- Raise questions on how this research connects to practice, including considerations of what we know about how to strengthen practice and what are some continuing questions on how to improve the HRM process in nonprofit organizations.

Overview of the Chapters

The chapters in this handbook cover a wide spectrum of topics on human resource management in the nonprofit sector, ranging from foundational issues of the sector and the workforce within it, the core HRM functions, from recruitment and selection, to compensation, performance evaluation, and training and development. In addition, the scholars included in this volume raise new and emerging questions for how we understand the workforce in the nonprofit sector and how best to manage it. This includes questions of what a strategic approach is to managing people that fits the nonprofit sector, how we engage our employees in the nonprofit sector so they remain committed to the missions of their organizations, and what it means for nonprofits as their workforces become more complex demographically, including different age groups, backgrounds, countries, and cultural understandings.

The handbook is divided into three Parts. Part I, Working in the Sector, provides a critical background of the nonprofit sector, its workforce, and the legal environment for effectively managing people in the nonprofit sector.

In Chapter 2, Beth Gazley provides an overview on the nonprofit sector, including foundational theories on why the nonprofit sector exists and what this means for working in the sector and managing its employees.

In Chapter 3, John Ronquillo, Annie Miller, and Ida Drury deliver an overview on employment in the nonprofit sector in the United States. Drawing on data from the U.S. federal government and several major nonprofit research groups, this chapter examines patterns of employment and some of the challenges facing nonprofits as they seek to grow their human capital stock.

In Chapter 4, Eric Franklin Amarante provides a primer on employment law for nonprofits. While this subject alone could be a multi-volume set, this chapter highlights some of the main laws and policies nonprofits need to review to ensure they are in compliance with federal and state laws as they build and manage their workforces.

In Part II, Building an HRM Infrastructure in a Nonprofit Organization, this handbook then comprehensively explores the HRM function, from the overall philosophy or approach nonprofits should consider to effectively managing their people through recruitment and selection, compensation, labor relations, training and talent development, evaluation, and employee motivation and engagement.

In Chapter 5, Hans-Gerd Ridder and Alina McCandless Baluch explore strategic human resource management (SHRM) in nonprofit organizations, focusing on the core principles underlying this approach and on what SHRM means for nonprofits, with lessons from the construction of and examination of a model of nonprofit-focused HR architectures.

In Chapter 6 by Rikki Abzug, the process of staffing a nonprofit is examined, from what kinds of workers are attracted to the nonprofit sector to how to adopt a strategic approach to recruitment and selection to maximize the value of your nonprofit's human capital.

Chapter 7 by Yeonsoo Kim aligns with recruitment and selection, but with a focus on the challenge of ensuring a steady flow of leaders through succession planning and management. Effective nonprofit human resource management requires an overall strategic approach to making sure key positions are filled in a timely and effective manner.

In Chapter 8 by Heather Carpenter, the question of how to invest in employees is examined with a discussion of talent development and talent management in nonprofit organizations. This chapter explores various models of talent management, highlighting how to apply these in nonprofit organizations.

Chapter 9 by Sally Coleman Selden adds to the discussion of how to strategically manage human resources in nonprofits, with the focus being compensation systems. Compensation can be a key component of developing a high performance approach to managing human resources in nonprofits, but requires attention and careful design on the part of nonprofit managers.

Chapter 10 by Joan Pynes considers the employment relationship in the nonprofit sector from the perspective of labor relations, examining how unions operate in the nonprofit sector and the legal environment associated with labor relations in the sector. In addition, she examines the role of unions for workers in the sector and worker rights.

In Chapter 11, Kunle Akingbola shows that human resource management is not only about programs and policies. How we engage employees in our nonprofit organizations can have a significant impact on the motivation of these employees over time and their job satisfaction.

Chapter 12 by Jeffrey Brudney and Hayley Sink considers how we manage our donated human capital in the nonprofit sector, the valuable resource of volunteer labor that helps many nonprofits accomplish their missions. They propose a "ratchet" model of volunteer management that allows for tailoring effective volunteer management practices for particular nonprofit organizational contexts.

In Chapter 13, Toby Egan highlights the role that human resource management plays in maintaining the quality and performance of human capital in nonprofits, discussing training and development in the nonprofit sector, including the history, role, and particular needs of training and development for nonprofits.

Chapter 14 by Marlene Walk and Troy Kennedy continues this examination with a focus on performance management and appraisals. Grounding their analysis in a comprehensive review of the existing research on performance appraisal and performance management, they propose a comprehensive model of performance management and appraisal for nonprofit organizations.

The final section of this handbook, Part III, Emergent Challenges in Nonprofit Human Resource Management, focuses on some emergent issues that are affecting how we understand managing people working in nonprofits today, such as new technology and demographic changes, and the overall increasing complexity in our workforce and some of the unique challenges faced by nonprofits, including balancing paid and volunteer human capital and the particular challenges of managing people in international nongovernmental organizations (INGOs), which often operate across national borders and contexts.

Chapter 15 by Allison Russell, Laurie Mook, and Femida Handy builds on many of the previous chapters by examining the question of how to manage effectively together the two forms of human capital prevalent in the nonprofit sector—paid and donated human capital. They review the research on managing volunteers and paid staff together, what is known as the inter-changeability of labor, addressing the conditions and challenges associated with a blended staffing structure in nonprofits.

In Chapter 16, Carrie R. Oelberger, Anne-Meike Fechter, and Ishbel McWha-Hermann provide a comprehensive examination of the particularly challenging HR issues that arise in international non-governmental organizations (INGOs), including multiple different approaches to staffing these organizations, where differences in contracts, compensation, and designation as in-country staff and/or central staff can lead to tensions. They also explore some of the unique pressures and motivational challenges for those who work in nonprofits on the international stage.

Chapters 17 and 18 together consider the opportunities and challenges associated with the changing demographics in the nonprofit workforce today. In

Chapter 17, Jasmine McGinnis Johnson, Jaclyn Schede Piatak, and Eddy Ng tackle the issue of the multiple generations present in today's workforce and what that means for effective human resource management. They specifically address the question of bringing younger generations into the nonprofit workforce and present a strategic approach for managing multiple generations. Chapter 18 by Judith Weisinger dives deeper into the question of diversity, reviewing traditional approaches to diversity and inclusion and addressing how current models of diversity management need to be tailored to capture the true complexity of the workforce in today's nonprofit and be improved to be truly inclusive.

Chapter 19 by Jennifer Jones tackles the question of technology and its relationship to human resource management in nonprofit organizations. Technology has changed how we carry out a lot of HR practices, but has also raised new questions and concerns that must be addressed by nonprofit managers.

We conclude in Chapter 20 by considering what we know and the areas we still need to explore in terms of HRM in the nonprofit sector. We are so grateful for the wonderful contributions of the scholars in this volume and hope that this collection represents an important step forward in building the human resource management capacity of the nonprofit sector. We want to ensure that those who choose to dedicate their professional careers toward service of the greater good in the nonprofit sector are provided with every opportunity to have a well-developed and rewarding career path.

References

Akingbola, K. (2012). Context and nonprofit human resource management. *Administration & Society*, *45*(8), 974–1004.

Akingbola, K. (2013). Contingency, fit and flexibility of HRM in nonprofit organizations. *Employee Relations*, *35*(5), 479–494.

Akingbola, K. (2015). *Managing human resources for nonprofits*. London: Routledge.

Baluch, A. (2012). *Human resource management in nonprofit organizations*. New York: Routledge.

Bowman, W. (2006). Should donors care about overhead costs? Do they care? *Nonprofit and Voluntary Sector Quarterly*, *35*(2), 288–310.

Boxall, P. (1996). The strategic HRM debate and the resource-based view of the firm. *Human Resource Management Journal*, *6*(3), 59–75.

Brewer, G., Selden, S., & Facer II, R. (2000). Individual conceptions of public service motivation. *Public Administration Review*, *60*(3), 254–264.

Bureau of Labor Statistics, U.S. Department of Labor. (2014). Nonprofits account for 11.4 million jobs, 10.3 percent of all private sector employment. *The Economics Daily*. Available at: www.bls.gov/opub/ted/2014/ted_20141021.htm (accessed October 26, 2016).

Chikoto, G. & Neely, D. (2014). Building nonprofit financial capacity: The impact of revenue concentration and overhead costs. *Nonprofit and Voluntary Sector Quarterly*, *43*(3), 570–588.

Colbert, B. (2004). The complex resource-based view: Implications for theory and practice in strategic human resource management. *The Academy of Management Review*, *29*(3), 341.

Combs, J., Liu, Y., Hall, A., & Ketchen, D. (2006). How much do high performance work practices matter? A meta-analysis of their effects on organizational performance. *Personnel Psychology, 59*(3), 501–528.

Froelich, K. (1999). Diversification of revenue strategies: Evolving resource dependence in nonprofit organizations. *Nonprofit and Voluntary Sector Quarterly, 28*(3), 246–268.

Fukuyama, F. (2001). Social capital, civil society and development. *Third World Quarterly, 22*(1), 7–20.

Greenlee, J. & Trussel, J. (2000). Predicting the financial vulnerability of charitable organizations. *Nonprofit Management & Leadership, 11*(2), 199–210.

Gregory, A. G. & Howard, D. (2009). The nonprofit starvation cycle. *Stanford Social Innovation Review*, Fall 2009, 48–53.

Hager, M., Pollak, T., Wing, K., & Rooney, P.M. (2004). Getting what we pay for: Low overhead limits nonprofit effectiveness. Nonprofit Overhead Cost Project, 3. Available at: http://nccsdataweb.urban.org/knowledgebase/detail.php?linkID=311&category=51&xrefID=1659

Hu, M. & Guo, C. (2016). Fundraising policy reform and its impact on nonprofits in China: A view from the trenches. *Nonprofit Policy Forum, 7*(2), 213–236.

Kim, S. E. & Lee, J. V. (2007). Is mission attachment an effective management tool for employee retention? An empirical analysis of a nonprofit human services agency. *Review of Public Personnel Administration, 27*(3), 227–248.

Lee, Y. & Wilkins, V. (2011). More similarities or more differences? Comparing public and nonprofit managers' job motivations. *Public Administration Review, 71*(1), 45–56.

Mann, G. A. (2006). A motive to serve: Public service motivation in human resource management and the role of PSM in the nonprofit Sector. *Public Personnel Management, 35*(1), 33–48.

McGinnis Johnson, J. M. & Ng, E. S. (2015). Money talks or millennials walk: The effect of compensation on nonprofit millennial workers' sector-switching intentions. *Review of Public Personnel Administration*, doi: 0734371X15587980.

McKeever, B. S. (2015). The nonprofit sector in brief 2015: Public charities, giving, and volunteering. Washington, DC: The Urban Institute. Available at: www.urban.org/sites/default/files/alfresco/publication-pdfs/2000497-The-Nonprofit-Sector-in-Brief-2015-Public-Charities-Giving-and-Volunteering.pdf (accessed October 1, 2016).

Mesch, D. (2010). Management of human resources in 2020: The outlook for nonprofit organizations. *Public Administration Review, 70*, s173–s174.

Mirabella, R. (2007). University-based educational programs in nonprofit management and philanthropic studies: A 10-year review and projections of future trends. *Nonprofit and Voluntary Sector Quarterly, 36*(4 suppl.), 11S–27S.

Morse, R. (2016). Methodology: Best public affairs schools rankings. Available at: www.usnews.com/education/best-graduate-schools/articles/public-affairs-schools-methodology

Nonprofit HR. (2016). The 2016 Nonprofit Employment Practices Survey™. Washington, DC. Available at: www.nonprofithr.com (accessed October 1, 2016).

Park, S. M. & Word, J. (2012). Driven to service: Intrinsic and extrinsic motivation for public and nonprofit managers. *Public Personnel Management, 41*(4), 705–734.

Pfeffer, J. (1998). *The human equation.* Boston: Harvard Business School Press.

Putnam, R. (1995). Bowling alone: America's declining social capital. *Journal of Democracy, 6*(1), 65–78.

Pynes, J. (2013). *Human resources management for public and nonprofit organizations: A strategic approach* (4th ed.). Chichester: John Wiley & Sons, Ltd.

Ridder, H. & McCandless, A. (2010). Influences on the architecture of human resource management in nonprofit organizations: An analytical framework. *Nonprofit and Voluntary Sector Quarterly, 39*(1), 124–141.

Ridder, H., Piening, E., & Baluch, A. (2012). The third way reconfigured: How and why nonprofit organizations are shifting their human resource management. *Voluntas: International Journal of Voluntary and Nonprofit Organizations, 23*(3), 605–635.

Salamon, L. M. (2015). *The resilient sector revisited: The new challenge to nonprofit America.* Washington, DC: The Brookings Institution Press.

Salamon, L. M., Sokolowski, S. W., & Geller, S. L. (2012). Holding the fort: Nonprofit employment during a decade of turmoil. *Nonprofit Employment Bulletin, 39*, Johns Hopkins University. January 2012. Available at: www.thenonprofitpartnership.org/files/ned_national_2012.pdf

Salamon, L. M., Sokolowski, S. W., Haddock, M. A. & Tice, H. S. (2012). The state of global civil society and volunteering: Latest findings from the implementation of the UN *Nonprofit Handbook.* Working Paper No. 49. Baltimore, MD: Johns Hopkins Center for Civil Society Studies.

Selden, S. C. & Sowa, J. E. (2014). High performance work systems in nonprofit organizations: Surfacing better practices to improve nonprofit HRM capacity. Final Report for the Society for Human Resource Management Foundation. Available at: www.shrm.org/about/foundation/research/Documents/FinalReportSelden%20Sowa.pdf

Selden, S. C. & Sowa, J. E. (2015). Voluntary turnover in nonprofit human service organizations: The impact of high performance work practices. *Human Service Organizations: Management, Leadership & Governance, 39*(3), 182–207.

Smith, S. (2008). The challenge of strengthening nonprofits and civil society. *Public Administration Review, 68*, S132–S145.

Su, X. & Bozeman, B. (2009). Dynamics of sector switching: Hazard models predicting changes from private sector jobs to public and nonprofit sector jobs. *Public Administration Review, 69*(6), 1106–1114.

Taylor, J. (2010). Public service motivation, civic attitudes and actions of public, nonprofit and private sector employees. *Public Administration, 88*(4), 1083–1098.

Tschirhart, M. & Bielefeld, W. (2012). *Managing nonprofit organizations.* San Francisco: Jossey-Bass.

Tschirhart, M., Reed, K. K., Freeman, S. J., & Anker, A. L. (2008). Is the grass greener? Sector shifting and choice of sector by MPA and MBA graduates. *Nonprofit and Voluntary Sector Quarterly, 37*(4), 668–688.

Way, S. (2002). High performance work systems and intermediate indicators of firm performance within the US small business sector. *Journal of Management, 28*(6), 765–785.

Weisbrod, B. (1988). *The nonprofit economy.* Cambridge, MA: Harvard University Press.

Word, J. & Carpenter, H. (2013). The new public service? Applying the public service motivation model to nonprofit employees. *Public Personnel Management, 42*(3), 315–336.

Wright, P. M., Dunford, B. B., & Snell, S. A. (2001). Human resources and the resource based view of the firm. *Journal of Management, 27*(6), 701–721.

Part I
Working in the Sector

2

Theories of the Nonprofit Sector

Beth Gazley

Introduction

In keeping with the aim of *The Nonprofit Human Resource Management Handbook* to connect research to practice, this introductory chapter focuses on nonprofit theories of particular interest to the study and practice of nonprofit human resource management (HRM). Each chapter author in this book will have made his or her own choices about the conceptual landscape considered worthy of coverage. As a consequence, we may vary in the groundwork we cover, but that strategy overall should be considered an exciting rather than confusing aspect of nonprofit HRM study and practice, since all chapter authors would agree that this field of research and practice is still in development and moving in rapid and sometimes unexpected directions.

With this book's interest in using research to inform the practice of nonprofit human resource management, and also in offering students as future nonprofit managers a current picture of the state of the field, this chapter also attempts to ground its introduction of major nonprofit theoretical concepts with plenty of concrete examples to help readers envision how these ideas play out at the forefront of managerial action. Given the relative youth of nonprofit HRM research (reflected in part by the paucity of nonprofit HRM textbooks), most HR professionals working within the nonprofit sector will have had limited exposure to general nonprofit theory, except for those few who have obtained a specialized degree in nonprofit management or closely related fields such as public affairs. Thus, these general theories of nonprofit behavior at the sectoral or organizational level may still be unfamiliar and therefore useful to frontline professionals.

Another aim of this chapter is to avoid making the requisite discussion of "theories" at the start of a management book dry, inaccessible, or irrelevant to its readers. The poor authors of "theory chapters" must sometimes feel like a sadly paraphrased parody of the 1970 Edwin Starr song (i.e., "Theory, yeah! What is it good for? Absolutely nothing . . ."). The problem arises when theories themselves are widely misunderstood by the public as simple guesses about what happens in the real world, especially outside the natural sciences. Applied to the workplace, theories may be considered too abstract to be of much value to the practitioner. Theories vary considerably in their descriptive and predictive powers. And in a world that values intellectual and situational diversity, not all theories make sense in all circumstances.

Good management theories, however, can be fairly reliable and helpful predictors of organizational phenomena. The best offer a logical and ordered set of arguments about how people and organizations behave (DiMaggio, 1995; Sutton & Staw, 1995; Weick, 1995). The reader should pay careful attention, however, to the strong role that "normative" theory plays in managerial decision-making. Normative theories are easy to find: they tend to be accompanied by the statement that nonprofits *should* behave a certain way. Such directions can be both powerful and problematic to nonprofit decision-making. They can certainly steer managers in the wrong direction when attempts to mimic the prescriptive advice fail to account for differences in organizational context such as mission, age, culture (of course, predictive theories can, as well). But normative theories do help to connect managerial decisions to potentially valuable philosophical and moral underpinnings about how nonprofits *should* behave (for example, that it is better to be honest and open in sharing information with stakeholders than it is to withhold information).

While they vary in the clarity with which they make sense of the world, and while new paradigms pop up unexpectedly, strong theories help a manager identify the crucial aspects of an event and sideline the less relevant factors (Kuhn, 1970). Theories, therefore, support managerial efficiency. Weick (1995) put it charmingly when he wrote that "good" theory "explains, predicts, and delights." Certainly, HR managers deserve to be delighted when theories help them make sense of a challenging personnel problem.

Structure of the Chapter

To introduce readers to this broad theoretical field in the brief confines of a single chapter, this chapter is organized to cover nonprofit theories at two conceptual levels: first, a set of economic and legal theories that address sectoral-wide behavior, followed by a selection of organizational theories from many other disciplines that excel at helping the HR manager understand distinct workplace settings. The emphasis is on economic theories over organizational theories following the rationale that these are fundamental to understanding what plays out in the front lines of employee and employer behavior in the nonprofit sector, yet less likely to have been incorporated into the following chapters. All theories should be understood as complementary to one another, to offer just one of many possible lenses, perspectives, or frameworks by which to understand workplace behavior. No discipline alone can capture the complexity of human and organizational behavior. Thus, nonprofit scholars are taking an increasingly multidimensional and multi-disciplinary perspective to pull together our understanding of the sector and its human capital (see, for example, Nesbit et al., 2011).

Nonprofit Sectoral Theories

Why study human resource management within the context of nonprofit sectoral theory, rather than using a broader, non-sector-specific perspective? Aren't employees more alike in terms of their common characteristics (e.g., age, seniority) than they are distinct across the nonprofit, for-profit, and governmental sectors? The answer rests in the important ways that each sector has created certain economic incentives and legal conditions for human resource management. The distinct legal status of U.S. nonprofit organizations under state and federal law results in a related set of legal circumstances respecting nonprofit employment discrimination, volunteer management, governance, compensation, labor relations, and a host of additional HR concerns. These circumstances sometimes impose legal constraints on nonprofit employers but they often offer greater legal freedoms as well.

"Three Failures" Theory and Implications for Human Resource Management

Economic theories have made essential contributions to explanations of sectoral distinctiveness, which in turn impacts employment practices and obligations. Theories of market failure, government failure, and voluntary or philanthropic failure were developed to explain why market-driven economies can produce a vibrant third sector, and why even in a state-controlled economy (such as China) nonprofits can still achieve a foothold (Hansmann, 1980; Salamon, 1987; Steinberg, 2006). Each "failure" describes the circumstances where a lack of perfect market conditions makes any sector unable to produce an independent, efficient solution to a human need (Anheier, 2005). For example, market failures might occur where consumers of a service that is widely desired ("demand homogeneity") consider the charitable organization the more trustworthy provider because it is less likely to cheat the consumer ("contract failure"; Anheier, 2005; Steinberg, 2006; Weisbrod, 1988).

Circumstances of both market and government failures encourage voluntary organizational activity (Salamon, 1987; Weisbrod, 1977). They explain why the U.S. healthcare industry spans all three sectors in that it can take for-profit, nonprofit, or public form. Not only are hospitals expensive to build, discouraging open competition, but the nonprofit form can signal greater trustworthiness to consumers and less likelihood of skimping on quality ("contract failure"). As a consequence, six out of ten U.S. hospitals have taken the legal status of a charitable nonprofit. Healthcare, incidentally, is also responsible for more than half of all nonprofit wages (Roeger et al., 2012).

Even then, the charitable sector is not immune to concerns about opportunistic behavior and transparency of information. The U.S. Congress and Internal Revenue Service carefully scrutinize 501(c)(3) hospitals for assurance of a balance between profit motive and charitable mission. The research of Brickley and Van Horn (2002) suggests nonprofit hospitals maintain a tenuous hold on sectoral distinctiveness since hospital executives are incentivized mainly by the same things across sectors, i.e., performance rather than charitable behavior. Meanwhile, healthcare "conversions" occur frequently, as business investors continue to find new ways to make healthcare profitable, and acquire the assets of nonprofit hospitals to do so.

Given copious examples of nonprofit activity despite the absence of market and government failures, and also the evidence of centuries-long historical cooperation between U.S. governments and nonprofits to deliver public services, Salamon (1987) argued the sector's behavior was better viewed through the lens of "voluntary failure." This third concept has been joined with the others to comprise a set of "three failures theories" but its original conceptualization was as an alternative or prequel to "market" and "government" failures (see Steinberg, 2006, for an explanation).

Voluntary failure can also occur for several overlapping reasons described by Salamon (1987; 1990). Insufficient financial resources can make the nonprofit response too weak to meet demand for services, or can increase the cost of raising money ("philanthropic insufficiency"). That circumstance explains why Fund Development is one of the most highly paid jobs in the sector. It also explains why an estimated three out of four U.S. volunteers is providing free labor to a nonprofit organization, giving rise to another crucial but less generously compensated profession, that of Volunteer Management (Gazley, 2009). It also explains the variations in dependence on volunteers, with some subsectors heavily dependent on them but others much less so. And it has given rise to additional scholarly discussion over the implications for the quality and sustainability of volunteer resources (Brudney & Meijs, 2009; see Chapter 12 in this volume).

The obvious fact that many nonprofit organizations lack both the profit-making opportunities that attract capital investment and the overwhelming public demand that attracts stable governmental grants and contracts means that many struggle financially. The HR manager must be fully aware of these potentially challenging circumstances given the nonprofit sector's status as much more human capital-intensive than either the business or government sectors (i.e., the majority of nonprofit expenditures are invested in personnel rather than infrastructure; Roeger et al., 2012). Various forms of voluntary failure may also explain why employee turnover is higher in the nonprofit sector when compared to business or government sectors, and why nonprofit employers express considerable concern about employee retention (Gazley, 2009).

"Philanthropic insufficiency" can create, in turn, circumstances of financial volatility that lead to "philanthropic amateurism" where service provision is insufficiently professionalized (Salamon, 1990). It would be unfair to assume "amateur" care is of lesser quality, but it may certainly be of lower consistency and therefore less attractive to consumers or donors. For that reason, employee and volunteer professional development, certification, and other means of professionalizing service roles are of great interest to HR management.

Another reason for voluntary failure is "philanthropic particularism," the ability of nonprofits to form themselves to serve only individuals who share select characteristics or preferences (e.g., religion, gender identity, ideology, geography; Salamon, 1987). Since associational rights in the U.S. derive from the First Amendment to the U.S. Constitution, this circumstance first explains why so many nonprofits are free to provide overlapping services in a region (e.g., multiple clubs, after-school programs, animal welfare organizations). This situation seems to the casual eye to be inefficient and redundant, but it also creates a unique and somewhat opportunistic labor market for the paid and volunteer nonprofit workforce. For example, the situation allows for greater donor choice based on mission attraction: a volunteer or employee could choose between an animal shelter that euthanizes and a "no-kill" shelter based on their personal values and preference for each mission. And if they don't like either organization, they have government support for creating a third option.

This circumstance of "particularism" also explains why it is possible to hire employees based on certain select characteristics and exclude others from consideration. Even when such a decision appears to violate employment discrimination laws under Title VII of the Civil Rights Act, selective hiring is legally permitted *provided* (a key point, and the focus of many lawsuits) that the preferred characteristic is necessary to maintain the "essence" and normal operation of the business or mission (Berman, 2000). This necessary qualification then becomes, in legal terms, a "*bona fide* occupational qualification" (BFOQ) of the job. An example that seems fairly straightforward is the requirement that a spiritual leader (such as a priest, imam, or minister) practice the religion of the sponsoring faith-based nonprofit organization. Indeed, Civil Rights laws have been written to provide strong protection for such intentional faith-based discrimination, in the form of a general "religious exemption" doctrine.

Three failures theory has other implications for human resource management. The opportunity for market conditions to support the provision of some services (e.g., healthcare, education, childcare, musical performances) across the three sectors increases the diversity of many industries. An employee in most professions (e.g., an engineer, a nurse, a firefighter, even a trombonist) can span the for-profit, nonprofit, and public sectors in a single career. Those responsible for the nonprofit HRM function will be responsible for ensuring employees recruited from other sectors are prepared to navigate the new legal environment and interact successfully with a new set of stakeholders (e.g., donors, regulators).

Even when capably described according to its predominant characteristics, the nonprofit sector harbors subsidiary features that can confuse both internal and external stakeholders attempting to understand the organization's responsibilities. For example, the sector's predominant characteristics as "private, voluntary, and for public benefit" (Anheier, 2005, p. 11) mask its still considerable *public* obligations with respect to transparent reporting, its *non-voluntary* dimensions (for example, when a publicly chartered nonprofit such as the American Red Cross must petition the U.S. Congress to change its bylaws) and its *mutual benefit* activities (where most legal forms such as c(6) business leagues, c(7) social clubs, are engaged in distinctly private, member-serving, and exclusionary activities).

Further, the blurred and evolving borders of the three sectors, in addition to fostering an enormous amount of nonprofit policy research, mean that it is not easy to characterize the nonprofit workplace environment, nor the incentives that will motivate nonprofit employees. An example is the creation of new hybrid legal forms that operate at the borders of the nonprofit sector, such as low-profit limited liability corporations (L3Cs), which in turn introduce new employment opportunities and dilemmas. Entrepreneurial behavior within the sector is widespread, although not always understood or trusted. Many scholars have argued for a closer examination of nonprofit behavior through the lens of entrepreneurship theory, and a better understanding of its implications for management (see, for example, Badelt, 2003; Young, 2003). Unfortunately, the study of these hybrid enterprises is very new and not yet focused on human resource management questions. When the scholarship advances, it will be fascinating to see how it changes our understanding of employee motivation since most of the new public benefit entrepreneurs come from the millennial and post-millennial generations and therefore are important to the future of the nonprofit sector generally.

The Non-Distribution Constraint and Implications for Compensation

Ending the last section on the topic of employee motivation reminds us that a central concern of many nonprofits is their ability to offer competitive compensation packages. Here, public law puts some brakes on that ability. In many countries (e.g., the USA, Canada), public laws for charitable organizations restrict how the profits are used. The "non-distribution constraint" encoded in tax law is a fundamental although widely misunderstood legal condition that allows nonprofits to make a financial surplus ("profit") but requires those in control of the organization to retain or reinvest the surplus in public benefit activities (Hansmann, 1980). This non-distribution constraint is intended to discourage insider self-dealing and private benefit transactions among those in control of the organization. Steinberg (2006, p. 118) observes how fundamental a distinction this restriction on self-dealing has been for human resource management, since the non-distribution constraint on nonprofits "affects how the organization obtains resources, how it is controlled, how it behaves in the marketplace, how it is perceived by donors and clients, and how its employees are motivated."

One of the more visible aspects of the non-distribution constraint is reflected in compensation policies. Nonprofits must follow stringent laws respecting how those leaders with even a hint of control over organizational assets are compensated. The transparency of this information under federal law and the amount of public concern over self-dealing have resulted in many *normative* expectations respecting compensation levels in the charitable sector. The State of New Jersey, for example, began capping executive salaries for all charities with state contracts. Another normative expectation is that charitable board members should serve voluntarily (see, for example, the Panel on the Nonprofit Sector, 2007). However, legally, compensation of board member labor is allowed, provided procedures are in place to prevent self-dealing. As a result, while nearly all board members of 501(c)(3) public charities now serve without pay, compensation is still widespread in 501(c)(3) private foundations (Schambra, 2008). But the cultural backlash against board compensation is strong, as evidenced by recent news stories addressing hospital board stipends (see, for example, McCambridge, 2016).

Some implications of the non-distribution constraint, however, are at odds with others. The theory also suggests that since all surplus profits are reinvested in a nonprofit organization rather than being redistributed, as they are in the for-profit firm, nonprofit employees will benefit from the reinvested profit in the form of marginally higher wages. Yet, the "donative labor hypothesis" suggests the opposite: that mission-driven nonprofits can attract employees who are willing to work for less. In her review of the theory-testing that has been undertaken in this area, Leete (2006) observes that neither the causes for wage differentials across the sectors nor their consequences are entirely understood. While job-seeking behavior in the absence of a profit motive does cause employee self-selection within the nonprofit sector (see, for example, Brown & Yoshioka, 2003), wages are more likely to be based on a unique combination of market pressures, labor supply and demand, geography, and factors unique to each industry (Gazley, 2016).

Implications of Theories for Third Sector Employment Law

The blurry lines between sectors extend to implications for employment law. Public law is still somewhat ambivalently carving out a distinct third sector when it comes to employment practice. Nonprofits are, to some extent, deliberately protected from the obligations of for-profit firms in order to encourage a robust civil society. As examples, many state Civil Rights Acts exclude smaller nonprofits from compliance, and the federal Volunteer Protection Act of 1995 deliberately protects a large portion of the nonprofit workforce from groundless lawsuits. Volunteers, as uncompensated workers, generally have few employment rights or protections. Exceptions do exist, such as instances where nonprofits operating under government contracts have stronger obligations to employees. And public laws requiring "interns," whether paid or unpaid, to receive a true educational experience apply equally to nonprofits. But for the most part, U.S. state and federal law continues to recognize nonprofits as private sector actors, enjoying most of the free agency of the for-profit sector with respect to employment (such as the euphemistically labeled "right-to-work" laws, which facilitate job termination and apply to both for-profit and nonprofit organizations) (see Chapter 4 for a discussion of the legal environment of nonprofit human resource management).

Implications of Theories for Nonprofit Accountability

The unique status of nonprofits as *private* organizations from the perspective of employment law but with some *public* privileges as well as public obligations from the perspective of tax law amounts to a simple and problematic fact: the public is interested in more details of nonprofit activity (e.g., salaries, programmatic efficiency) than it can access. A current example is the public controversy over 501(c)(4) social welfare nonprofits that, since the 2010 U.S. Supreme Court *Citizens United v. FEC* decision, may influence public elections without disclosing the sources of the money.

This gap between what the public expects of nonprofits and what nonprofits are legally obligated to deliver amounts to what many describe as a "crisis" or "paradox" of accountability (Ebrahim, 2010; Salamon, 1990; Sidel, 2005). The concern partly focuses on the risks of opportunistic behavior by a few bad actors within the sector, since the imbalanced coverage of these events by the media certainly reduces public trust in charities generally. But as the term "paradox" suggests, the greater concern is theoretical—that the more complex economic and legal status of the sector makes developing clear accountability expectations not simply more difficult but impossible.

In the face of public confusion as to what can be expected of nonprofit organization leaders and their employees, the question of to whom and for what nonprofits are accountable is central to managerial practice (Schatteman, 2013). The research is too young to explain very well the implications of this ambivalent status for HRM, but Ebrahim's (2010) helpful list of possible accountability mechanisms (e.g. disclosure statements, performance assessment, codes of conduct, citizen participation in nonprofit decision-making) makes it clear that HR managers are centrally involved in creating and implementing the employee systems that support a healthy sectoral environment for accountability. Some on Ebrahim's list, in fact, are at the forefront of employment best practice, such as adaptive learning and critical reflection to help employees capably identify stakeholders and learn how to communicate effectiveness to them.

All organizations, whether for-profit or not-for-profit, face competing accountability demands (e.g., Ebrahim's "upward, downward, inward, outward" accountabilities). A commercial business has multiple accountabilities—to regulators, stockholders, employees—but (at the risk of oversimplifying business science) has a relatively efficient means of reconciling them. A nonprofit organization that operates in a "double" or "triple bottom line" world (responsible for social value, fiscal, and environmental sustainability—i.e., "profit, people, planet") faces multiple accountabilities—to regulators, stakeholders, donors, employees, volunteers, taxpayers, not to mention all self-appointed proxies for the public interest such as "watchdog" organizations, and the media.

Ebrahim (2010) and Sidel (2005) are among the many who argue nonprofits should reconcile themselves to operating within a world of multiple accountabilities and should simply be vigilant in pursuing the "splendid diversity" of self-regulation options at their disposal (Sidel, 2005, p. 835). HR managers are in a position to provide valuable guidance to employers about how the multiple accountability frameworks that employees face should be navigated, and most especially about how the hard choices should be made respecting priorities. Stakeholder theory covers the field of inquiry interested in understanding who really counts, and what mechanisms are most helpful in remaining responsive to them (Freeman, 1984). When conducting a stakeholder analysis, the lens is still complex regarding the factors that matter (e.g., power, legitimacy, urgency) but the practice is sufficiently advanced to provide helpful decision-making tools to the manager (Mitchell, Agle, & Wood, 1997).

Organizational Theories

As this chapter has argued so far, human resource managers who are focused on public accountability have their hands full addressing the legal incentives and disincentives to nonprofit work, sometimes with limited empirical evidence to guide them. Fortunately, however, the internal management of the nonprofit enterprise can rely on a much older and broader theoretical understanding of the work environment. The second section of this chapter introduces a selection of *organizational* theories that explain some of the key dynamics of workplace behavior.

The term itself belies the fact that organizational theories have a keen interest in *human* and not simply organizational behavior (see, for example, Nahavandi et al., 2014). The eponymous Hawthorne Studies of the 1930s were, after all, studies of the effect of workplace environments on the productivity of individual employees. And because of their well-known finding that worker productivity depends on much more than the controlled work environment, these early studies helped researchers to understand how complex and unpredictable the study of employee motivation could be.

Most of the functional stages of strategic human resource management, after all, are about finding, motivating, training, evaluating, and retaining good people. On days that don't go so well in the HR office, managers are disciplining, firing, and resolving conflicts. The modern view grounds organizational theories in many social science disciplines that excel at explaining human behavior, such as psychology, political science, sociology, anthropology, and communications (Denhardt et al., 2013; Rainey, 2009). These fields, in turn, have created distinct sub-disciplines that a scholar or practitioner of nonprofit HRM would be wise to explore further (the well-developed discipline of sociology has more than 40 subfields, psychology has more than 20, and many have applications to HRM). Comparing their value to his field of economics, Meier (2006) comments that it is somewhat of an understatement that economic theories offer a limited ability to predict pro-social behavior since the "*institutional environment* might significantly interact with pro-social preferences" [emphasis added] to explain observed variations in an individual's behavior.

In social psychology, for example—the discipline closely related to the Hawthorne Studies—we discover a range of theories (e.g., social cognition, equity) helpful in explaining current nonprofit employee and volunteer behavior. Chief among them is social role theory, which explains why individuals of different sexes and gender identities pursue different jobs, volunteer at different rates, make different ethical decisions, assume different workplace roles, and donate money in different ways. The theory of pro-social behavior is one micro-theory emerging from this field, and helps the HR manager to understand the value in shaping incentives and workplace culture to attract individuals who are strongly oriented toward public benefit missions (Eagly & Crowley, 1986).

Certain motivational theories are also especially useful in explaining why people are attracted to nonprofit work, as well as why they stay. This knowledge is important, given that the more complex economic and legal incentives of nonprofit work, layered on top of an enormously diverse field of nonprofit industries, mean that assumptions about nonprofit employees' intentions can easily be misconstrued. For example, a popular perception is that nonprofit employees are motivated by "mission, not money." This statement not only grossly over-generalizes a complex sector, it is wrong since most employees are motivated by both goals at the same time (Gazley, 2016). Theuvsen (2004, p. 125) observes that "most [employee] actions are . . . extrinsically as well as intrinsically motivated." Employees perform their work for both psychological and self-determined needs (intrinsic) and for instrumental reasons and externally derived rewards (extrinsic) (Ryan & Deci, 2000). An over-emphasis on the extrinsic rewards of a position, such as pay and benefits, praise, even the corner office, can cause an employer to overlook important intrinsic benefits inherent to nonprofit work, such as the ability to produce work of social value, to serve others, to improve the environment, and to effect change. But an over-emphasis on the intrinsic nature of a job can lead to burnout and harm workplace morale if it makes employees feel undervalued. The solution for most employers appears to rest in good internal data collection to understand how to balance the benefits package. For nonprofits specifically, however, the value in understanding how to help employees achieve the personal benefits of a mission-driven job cannot be overstated, given this is an area where nonprofit organizations may enjoy an enormous competitive advantage.

Organizational theories are also strongly based on the discipline of sociology. It has produced, for example, resource dependency theory, which has consistently and predictably linked nonprofit organizational behavior to the expectations of donors and other revenue sources (Grønbjerg, 1993). A seminal contribution to organizational theory generally was made by sociologists DiMaggio and Powell (1991) in the form of a group of neo-institutional theories that explain why organizations do not always appear to behave in the same (assumedly rational) manner within industries or subsectors. Rather, they adapt to mimetic, normative, and coercive pressures unique to their individual circumstances. For example, two similarly sized nonprofits with similar missions could end up creating very different work environments due to differences in accreditation, certification, and regulation (coercive isomorphism), differences in training, ethics, and rules (normative isomorphism), and differences in the techniques they borrow from their industry and others (mimetic isomorphism).

The application of neo-institutional theories to the accountability concerns described above should be clear. Nonprofits are likely to look for the means of responding to stakeholder demands from many places, and apply them in different ways. Mitchell (2016) describes this impetus as a central "managerial logic" of nonprofit decision-making, given the strong normative culture of the sector. How to choose the right path remains an open question. For human resources managers, it will seem tempting and time-saving to rely on "normative" practices by looking for guidance from similar organizations (for example, borrowing boilerplate policy documents or adopting generic job descriptions). However, by doing so, a manager may lose opportunities to achieve workplace success based on more evidentiary grounds, the "instrumentalist" side of the managerial mind.

Conclusion

Economic theories help to explain a basic fact: The existence of a third sector, with distinct legal requirements in the United States, as in many other parts of the world. These distinctions explain, in turn, why a book focused on *nonprofit* human resource management has value. But as Anheier (2005, p. 148) has observed, economic theories put the emphasis on rational action and simple rules, so they benefit from being balanced with organizational theories that emphasize sociological and cognitive processes to better capture the complex nature of organizational and human action. When combining the two, HR managers are better equipped to navigate both the blurry edges of the nonprofit sector and its enormous internal diversity as they locate, recruit, motivate, and reward an equally diverse nonprofit workforce. But they must also understand when theoretical blurriness gives way to the nonprofit sector's clear-cut legal distinctions, whose legal responsibilities must in turn be communicated to employees.

Discussion Questions

1   How many professions can you identify that are exclusive to one sector?
2   Is it a misplaced assumption that nonprofit services are less "professional" than those in other sectors?

3   What examples of "philanthropic particularism" can you find in your community? In addition to those discussed in this chapter, what are the possible implications for HR management?

4   How many "stakeholders" can you identify who care about nonprofit accountability and performance?

5   Think about a time when you preferred to take a certain role in the workplace (at a meeting, on a team, etc.). Do you know why you chose the role? How could social psychology explain your choice?

6   What would a nonprofit workplace look like if the HR office thought workers were motivated by "mission, not money"?

References

Anheier, H. K. (2005). *Nonprofit organizations: Theory, management, policy*. New York, NY: Routledge.

Badelt, C. (2003). Entrepreneurship in nonprofit organizations: Its role in theory and in the real world nonprofit sector. In H. K. Anheier & A. Ben-Ner (Eds.), *The study of the nonprofit enterprise: Theories and approaches* (pp. 139–168). New Yok: Springer.

Berman, J. B. (2000). Defining the "essence of the business": An analysis of Title VII's Privacy BFOQ after Johnson Controls. *The University of Chicago Law Review, 67,* 749–775.

Brickley, J. A. & Van Horn, R. L. (2002). Managerial incentives in nonprofit organizations: Evidence from hospitals. *The Journal of Law & Economics, 45,* 227–249.

Brown, W. A. & Yoshioka, C. F. (2003). Mission attachment and satisfaction as factors in employee retention. *Nonprofit Management & Leadership, 14,* 5–18.

Brudney, J. L. & Meijs, L. C. (2009). It ain't natural: Toward a new (natural) resource conceptualization for volunteer management. *Nonprofit and Voluntary Sector Quarterly, 38,* 564–581.

Denhardt, R. B., Denhardt, J. V., & Aristigueta, M. P. (2013). *Managing human behavior in public and nonprofit organizations* (3rd ed.). Thousand Oaks, CA: Sage Publications.

DiMaggio, P. J. (1995). Comments on "what theory is not." *Administrative Science Quarterly, 40,* 391–397.

DiMaggio, P. J. & Powell, W. W. (Eds.). (1991). *The new institutionalism in organizational analysis* (vol. 17). Chicago: University of Chicago Press.

Eagly, A. H. & Crowley, M. (1986). Gender and helping behavior: A meta-analytic review of the social psychology literature. *Psychological Bulletin, 100,* 287–308.

Ebrahim, A. (2010). The many faces of nonprofit accountability. In D. O. Renz (Ed.). *The Jossey-Bass handbook of nonprofit leadership and management* (3rd ed.; pp. 101–124). San Francisco: Jossey-Bass.

Freeman, R. E. (1984). *Strategic management: A stakeholder approach*. Boston: Pitman.

Gazley, B. (2009). Personnel recruitment and retention in the nonprofit sector. In S. W. Hays, R. C. Kearney, & J. Coggburn (Eds.), *Public human resource management: Problems and prospects* (5th ed.; pp. 79–92). Upper Saddle River, NJ: Prentice-Hall.

Gazley, B. (2016). The nonprofit sector labor force. In R. C. Kearney & J. Coggburn (Eds.), *Public human resource management: Problems and prospects* (6th ed.; pp. 90–103). Thousand Oaks, CA: SAGE/CQ Press.

Grønbjerg, K. A. (1993). *Understanding nonprofit funding: Managing revenues in social services and community development organizations*. San Francisco, CA: Jossey-Bass.

Hansmann, H. B. (1980). The role of nonprofit enterprise. *The Yale Law Journal, 89,* 835–901.

Kuhn, T. S. (1970). *The structure of scientific revolutions* (2nd ed.). Chicago: University of Chicago Press.

Leete, L. (2006). Work in the nonprofit sector. In W. W. Powell & R. Steinberg (Eds.), *The nonprofit sector: A research handbook* (2nd ed.; pp. 159–179). New Haven, CT: Yale University Press.

McCambridge, R. (March 10, 2016). Tampa General Hospital board votes to pay itself. *Nonprofit Quarterly*. Available at: https://nonprofitquarterly.org/2016/03/10/tampa-general-hospital-board-votes-to-pay-itself/

Meier, S. (2006). A survey of economic theories and field evidence on pro-social behavior, Federal Reserve Bank of Boston Working Paper No. 06-6. Available at; http://papers.ssrn.com/sol3/Papers.cfm?abstract_id=917187

Mitchell, G. E. (2016). Modalities of managerialism: The "Double Bind" of normative and instrumental nonprofit management imperatives. *Administration & Society*, doi: 10-1177/0095399716664832.

Mitchell, R. K., Agle, B. R., & Wood, D. J. (1997). Toward a theory of stakeholder identification and salience: Defining the principle of who and what really counts. *Academy of Management Review, 22,* 853–886.

Nahavandi, A., Denhardt, R. B., Denhardt, J. V., & Aristigueta, M. P. (2014). *Organizational behavior.* Thousand Oaks, CA: Sage Publications.

Nesbit, R., Moulton, S., DeHart-Davis, L., Feeney, M., Gazley, B., Hou, Y., et al. (2011). Wrestling with intellectual diversity in public administration. *Journal of Public Administration Research and Theory, 21*(Supplement 1), i13–i28.

Panel on the Nonprofit Sector. (2007). *Principles for good governance and ethical practice: A guide for charities and foundations.* Available at: www.independentsector.org/principles

Piliavin, J. A. & Charng, H.-W. (1990). Altruism: A review of recent theory and research. *Annual Review of Sociology, 16,* 27–65. Available at: www.jstor.org/stable/2083262

Rainey, H. G. (2009). *Understanding and managing public organizations* (3rd ed.). Hoboken, NJ: John Wiley & Sons, Inc.

Roeger, K. L., Blackwood, A. S., & Pettijohn, S. L. (2012). *The nonprofit almanac 2012.* Washington, DC: The Urban Institute Press.

Ryan, R. M. & Deci, E. L. (2000). Intrinsic and extrinsic motivations: Classic definitions and new directions. *Contemporary Educational Psychology, 25,* 54–67.

Theuvsen, L. (2004). Doing better while doing good: Motivational aspects of pay-for-performance effectiveness in nonprofit organizations. *Voluntas: International Journal of Voluntary and Nonprofit Organizations, 15,* 117–136.

Salamon, L. M. (1987). Of market failure, voluntary failure, and third-party government: Toward a theory of government–nonprofit relations in the modern welfare state. *Nonprofit and Voluntary Sector Quarterly, 16,* 29–49.

Salamon, L. M. (1990). The nonprofit sector and government: The American experience in theory and practice. In H. K. Anheier & W. Seibel (Eds.), *The third sector: Comparative studies of nonprofit organizations* (pp. 219–239). New York: De Gruyter.

Schambra, W. (Winter 2008). Board compensation: To pay or not to pay? *Philanthropy Roundtable.* Available at: www.philanthropyroundtable.org/topic/philanthropic_freedom/compensating_foundation_directors1

Schatteman, A. (2013). Nonprofit accountability: To whom and for what? An introduction to the Special Issue. *International Review of Public Administration, 18,* 1–6.

Sidel, M. (2005). Guardians guarding themselves: A comparative perspective on nonprofit self-regulation. *The Chicago-Kent Law Review, 80,* 803–835.

Steinberg, R. (2006). Economic theories of nonprofit organizations. In W. W. Powell and R. Steinberg (Eds.), *The nonprofit sector: A research handbook* (2nd ed.; pp. 117–139). New Haven, CT: Yale University Press.

Sutton, R. I. & Staw, B. M. (1995). What theory is not. *Administrative Science Quarterly, 40,* 371–384.

Weick, K. E. (1995). "Definition of 'theory.'" In N. Nicholson (Ed.), *Blackwell dictionary of organizational behavior* (p. xxx). Oxford: Blackwell. Available at: www.blackwellreference.com/subscriber/uid=326/tocnode?id=g9780631233176_chunk_g978063123536124_ss3-6

Weisbrod, B. A. (Ed.). (1977). *The voluntary nonprofit sector.* Lexington, MA: Lexington Books.

Weisbrod, B. A. (1988). *The nonprofit economy.* Cambridge, MA: Harvard University Press.

Young, D. R. (2003). Entrepreneurs, managers, and the nonprofit enterprise. In H. K. Anheier & A. Ben-Ner (Eds.), *The study of the nonprofit enterprise: Theories and approaches* (pp. 161–168). New York: Springer.

3

Trends in Nonprofit Employment

John C. Ronquillo, Annie Miller, and Ida Drury

Introduction

Nonprofits face a variety of challenges that necessitate distinct labor and management skills, including the ability to work with stakeholders in government and the private sector, but also skills that accommodate the diverse industries in which nonprofits operate. While many perceive the nonprofit sector to be focused exclusively on the charitable sector, other industries, including energy and technology, for example, are seeing expansion among their nonprofit counterparts. Recent studies show the nonprofit sector employs the third largest number of paid workers in United States, with almost 1.5 million nonprofit organizations employing nearly 11 million people (Salamon, 2012; Salamon, Sokolowski & Geller 2012). The industry produces revenue that totals over $2 trillion and constitutes 5.4% of the U.S. gross domestic product (GDP) (McKeever, 2015; Nonprofit HR, 2016). As the nonprofit sector has expanded in size and scope over the past several decades, so has its share in the labor market. Diversification of the sector merits ongoing monitoring of how employment and human resource management (HRM) is evolving. This sector is often misunderstood, yet is dynamic in its composition and scope of work as well as providing a sufficient number of challenges with regard to high-quality data collection practices across the sector, leading to difficulties in analyzing employment trends. One such challenge includes the diversity of organizations included in this sector, from very small, community-based agencies to large, internationally recognized agencies with a global scope. As such, the HRM needs will vary greatly and may have very different implications for each type of employer. This chapter provides some insights on current issues and trends in nonprofit employment.

Assessing the State of the Sector: Size and Employment

The Bureau of Labor Statistics has compiled data on nonprofits in past years as part of its Research Data on the Nonprofit Sector series. These data contain observations on employment, wages, and establishment figures for nonprofit organizations, and illuminate the sector's economic footprint. However, there are certain limitations of these data, including a fairly limited time series (2007–2012) and no data updates since 2012. The data include observations on only 501(c)3 public charities, and are pulled based on the existence of unemployment insurance. As these data come from states and territories with different laws and rules governing this insurance, researchers had to rely on varied data cleaning by jurisdiction. However, what currently exists provides insight on where the charitable sector has grown, especially in the years immediately preceding and following the economic recession of the late 2000s (Bureau of Labor Statistics, 2015).

Figure 3.1 details the number of registered 501(c)(3) charitable organizations from the year 2007 to 2012. In 2007, just over 1.02 million organizations were registered, steadily climbing to 1.16 million in 2010, then dropping to 1.06 million in 2011. This drop is reflective of the 279,599 organizations across the sector that lost their tax-exempt status with the Internal Revenue Service over the preceding three years (Blackwood & Roeger, 2011; Cyr, 2011). While that number may seem alarmingly high, it is likely most of those nonprofits had already ceased operations prior to their tax-exempt revocation. Blackwood and Roeger (2011) attribute these revocations largely to the implementation of the Pension Protection Act of 2006, which mandated nonprofits with less than $25,000 in annual gross receipts to file the "e-Postcard," or Form 990-N. The number of revocations represented 16% of nonprofits nationwide, with human

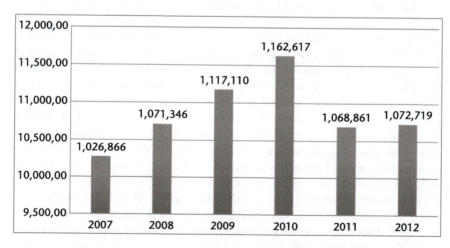

Figure 3.1 Number of registered 501(c)(3) organizations

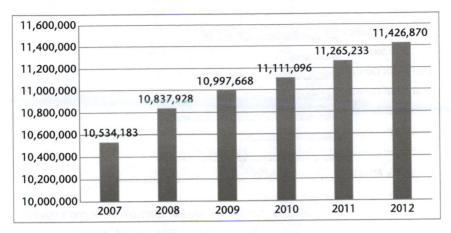

Figure 3.2 Average annual employment in 501(c)(3) organizations (millions)

service organizations seeing the largest share, followed by public and societal benefit organizations and arts organizations as the next largest groups (Blackwood & Roeger, 2011).

Despite the number of nonprofit organizations that lost their tax-exempt status, the average annual employment (at least in 501(c)(3) organizations) continued to climb steadily from 2007 to 2012. In 2007, there were just over 10.5 million people employed in 501(c)(3) organizations, climbing to 10.8 million in 2008, 10.9 million in 2009, and 11.1 million in 2010 (Figure 3.2). One might assume with a drop in the number of registered 501(c)(3) organizations in 2011, the average annual employment would also drop. Employment grew, however, to 11.2 million in 2011, and further to 11.4 million in 2012, suggesting steady job creation over that span of six years. Regional employment, of course, has risen concomitantly with the national numbers between 2007 and 2012, as well, as seen in Figure 3.3. Middle Atlantic states (New York, New Jersey, and Pennsylvania) had the largest share of employees in the nonprofit sector, followed by the East North Central (Illinois, Indiana, Michigan, Ohio, and Wisconsin), South Atlantic (Delaware, Florida, Georgia, Maryland, North Carolina, South Carolina, Virginia, Washington, D.C., and West Virginia), and Pacific (Alaska, California, Hawaii, Oregon, and Washington) regions, respectively.

Current Trends and Challenges in Nonprofit Employment

Four key areas present challenges for human resources managers within the nonprofit sector. Market pressures, retention, talent acquisition, and workforce needs remain prevalent issues to consider when projecting and exploring trends in nonprofit employment. This section provides an overview of each of these four challenge areas and connects each to key trends emerging in nonprofit sector human resources.

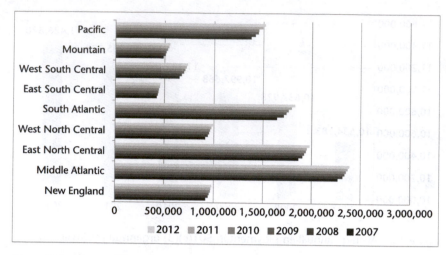

Figure 3.3 Nonprofit employment by census region (millions)

Shrinking government budgets appear to increase financial pressures on nonprofits while the same decreases in public spending require greater services to be provided from the nonprofit sector. The additional pressure of social enterprise (for-profit) agencies recruiting and retaining employees who historically may have opted for mission-driven nonprofit employment creates additional market pressure challenges for the nonprofit sector.

Retention, the ability of nonprofit organizations to retain high-quality, competent, and well-trained employees, is generally considered to be correlated with the personal connection to the mission of the organization, how well the employee fits with the organizational culture, and effective supervision (Brown & Yoshioka, 2003; Rycraft, 1994). Alongside retention, as agencies grow or when employees inevitably leave, talent acquisition of qualified staff rises to the forefront of challenges for human resources. Current trends in sector growth play into this need, as well as the associated challenges of diversity and inclusiveness for agency talent.

Workforce needs include the skills, supply, demand, and overall 'goodness' of fit in employment across the nonprofit sector. Several of the trends identified below suggest a rise in skills that few nonprofit or social science bachelor's or master's level programs appear to be meeting. Specifically, quantitative and qualitative skills are requirements for many jobs in this sector and will be a workforce need with potentially low supply. This will likely drive up the cost to employ methods-trained employees and increasing competition across the marketplace.

Market Pressures

Nonprofit organizations face two simultaneous market-based trends that have a direct impact on HRM. As a result of the new public management movement

(Hood, 1995), many government agencies have reduced or changed the nature of public goods. Fundamentally this reduction in grant making and funding for social services has increased the demand for nonprofit services.

Additionally, the rise of social enterprise organizations creeping into the third sector space primarily reserved for nonprofits challenges nonprofits in new ways that have direct impacts on HRM (Dees, 1998; Defourny & Nyssens, 2007; Kerlin, 2006). This shift to a market-driven focus may challenge important values such as equitable access to public goods, the democratized nature of service provision networks, or the overall goal of strengthening civil society as an important externality of third sector organizations (Dart, 2004; Eikenberry & Kluver, 2004). The pressure from these organizations results in talented, entrepreneurial potential employees leaving nonprofits to be compensated at levels similar to for-profit organizations while attracting individuals who desire mission-driven or socially beneficial workplaces. Some evidence suggests that as a result of the rise of charitable giving following the "great recession" in the United States, there may be increases in staff sizes and perhaps the creation of new positions, bolstering the nonprofit sector as a viable area of employment (Nonprofit HR, 2016). The Nonprofit HR survey reports approximately 57% of nonprofits that responded (n = 443) expect to create new positions in the very near future. Organizations were assessed based on the size of their respective annual operating budgets: Over 50% of small ($0–$5 million), medium ($5.1–$15 million), and large ($15.1 million and above). However, this survey does not distinguish clearly between social enterprise and nonprofits, with the possible new positions in the very near future created by the nonprofits.

Turnover and Retention

Alongside sector growth, nonprofit rates of turnover remain constant, between 17–19%. Turnover as a whole can be divided into three groups: voluntary, involuntary, or retirement (Selden & Moynihan, 2000). According to the 2016 Nonprofit Employment Practices Survey™, involuntary turnover (where an employee is terminated or laid off) remains low, while voluntary turnover (where an employee quits) has remained between 11 and 13% (Nonprofit HR, 2016). The costs of turnover are well known to human resources in many sectors, including the need for recruitment and retraining, as well as additional strain on employees remaining with the organization who must take on the work of the vacant position. In nonprofits, direct service employees are the hardest to retain and have the highest rates of turnover. This staff churn can directly impact both the continuity and quality of care for service recipients, which in turn may negatively influence the desired service outcomes (Chester, Hughes, & Challis, 2014; Nonprofit HR, 2016). Selden and Sowa (2015) specifically examine voluntary turnover and the deleterious effects it can have on nonprofit human service organizations, including reductions in performance and threats to overall sustainability.

The reasons for turnover in the public sector may be generally grouped into three areas: environmental, individual, and organizational (Selden & Moynihan, 2000). Similarly, a meta-analysis of human services turnover (which may closely mirror or represent direct service turnover in nonprofits) pointed to the relationship between burnout and stress and increases in employee turnover intent, whereas social support, fairness in management practices, and job satisfaction were related to decreases in turnover intent and actual turnover (Barak, Nissly, & Levin, 2001). Retention strategies must target these areas specifically. Little can be done about environmental effects (such as a bustling economy that encourages mobility of employees), but opportunities for human resources targeting individual experiences and organizational realities may create promise for nonprofit sector employee retention. As an example, high performance work practices including effective onboarding practices, active leadership succession programs, high-performance compensation programs, and solid employee relations are likely to reduce voluntary turnover (Selden & Sowa, 2015). Researchers and practitioners seem to be acknowledging these turnover antecedents more often, focusing on issues of professionalization and examining individual needs through strategic human resource management (Akingbola, 2012), as well as talent development and empowerment of employees through a "people first" approach (Carpenter & Qualls, 2015). Issues of turnover and retention have also seen increasing coverage in the research literature through topics such as mission attachment (Brown & Yoshioka, 2003; Kim & Lee, 2007), and work-life balance and job choice motivation (Word & Park, 2015). Despite the challenges of turnover and retention for nonprofit stability and the extant empirical research on solutions, 84% of respondents to the 2016 Nonprofit Employment Practices Survey™ report they do not have a formal retention strategy, and most (76%) will either not create a formal retention strategy, or are unsure of whether or not that is something they will undertake in the future (Nonprofit HR, 2016).

While employees may have varying levels of discretion and authority in nonprofits, executive directors provide leadership and report to organizations' boards of directors. They also may be partially or solely in charge of fundraising, depending on the size of the nonprofit. This is a unique position in a nonprofit agency and warrants specific attention, particularly when discussing retention and turnover. Turnover intent for this group has been consistently monitored, and in a 2011 survey it was estimated that 67% of current nonprofit executive directors would leave their positions in the subsequent five years (Cornelius, Moyers, & Bell, 2011). The transition at this pinnacle may be fraught with many issues, such as organizational instability and disruption in funding streams due to relationship loss (Stewart, 2016). In smaller nonprofits, the transition may necessitate a period of time where the board of directors must take a more active role in daily operations. The importance of succession planning is well understood in the sector, but not well practiced, according to disclosures from boards and executives alike (Froelich, McKee, & Rathge, 2011; Nonprofit HR, 2016).

In the interest of retaining executives, the characteristics of environment, individuals, and organizations are again at play. According to a survey of nonprofit executive directors by Peters and Wolfred in 2001, controlling for the size of organizations, fundraising and low compensation were the most stressful factors for small nonprofits with an annual budget of less than $499,999. Mid-sized nonprofits with a budget size between $500,000 and $999,999 experienced HR management as the most challenging, while the large agencies reported a high level of stress and lack of support at the top. They concluded managing these stressors could decrease executive turnover rates. Further, when executives are replaced in nonprofits, they come from outside the organization at a rate of almost 3 to 1 (Nonprofit HR, 2016). Based on a survey of emerging leaders in the sector, potential executives fear lack of development, mentorship, and support from incumbent leaders (Cornelius, Corvington, & Ruesga, 2008). Legitimately, networks in the organization can play a strong role in retention (Moynihan & Pandey, 2007), making it imperative for executive tenure to develop this network early and not watch relationships leave with the old director.

Diverse and Inclusive Talent Acquisition

When turnover occurs, regardless of magnitude, recruiting qualified, diverse, and talented staff requires resources. Currently, the demonstrated expansion of jobs in the nonprofit sector and the expected continued growth create a clear market demand for job seekers. At the same time, turnover rates persist, even in times of growth. Looking to the Nonprofit Employment Practices Survey™, 33% of respondents reported the most difficult challenge was hiring qualified staff under the current budget constraints. This challenge has remained constant since 2012, whereas the 23% who report finding qualified staff as the biggest challenge has grown since 2012 (Nonprofit HR, 2016). Some 73% of small nonprofits report they do not have a formal talent acquisition strategy, while 49% of medium nonprofits, and 41% of large nonprofits report the same (Nonprofit HR, 2016). Some 91% of small nonprofits report they do not have a formal talent acquisition budget, while 64% of medium organizations and 59% of large organizations report the same. Fifty-six percent of those surveyed state they have no plans to change how they recruit talent, while 20% report they are considering making changes, and 14% affirm they will be making changes; and 75% of the nonprofits surveyed state they do not have an employment branding strategy (Nonprofit HR, 2016).

Nonprofits have directed a fair amount of attention to diversity and inclusion efforts in recent years. It is necessary to distinguish different types of goal related to diversity and hiring strategies within the nonprofit, as different organizations likely to seek different results from hiring practices. According to Kossek, Lobel, and Brown (2006), there are three key considerations in regard to understanding strategies for diverse hiring practices: (1) organizations may seek to increase the number of individuals hired who represent marginalized, underrepresented, or protected class identities; (2) organizations may seek specific types of outcome as a result of diversity or inclusion hiring practices (i.e. increase number of Spanish-speaking employees to more effectively serve the client population); or (3) organizations may recognize that one level of the organization has a great deal of diversity but at the mid and upper levels of management, for example, a lack of diversity may occur. This section outlines implications for hiring and retention challenges that may arise as a result of trends in the three different types of organizational goals for inclusion and diversity efforts. Many different types of diversity are considered below.

A generational difference among employees has been and continues to be of interest to researchers and practitioners alike (Kunreuther, 2003; McGinnis, 2011a; 2011b). The Nonprofit Employment Practices Survey™ (2016) highlights the struggle of retaining staff under the age of 30 as a challenge, noting these staff want to engage in meaningful work, and tend to seek more responsibility and leadership. They tend to look for cultures focused on innovation, as many perceive the nonprofit sector to be more innovative, or at least have a culture that values innovation (Ronquillo, 2013). As Millennials surpass Generation X as the largest generation in the workforce, along with steadily decreasing numbers of Baby Boomers, nonprofits will need to find ways to better incorporate Millennials into the workplace. As is the case with many nonprofit organizations, resource dependency is a factor, and one that is often tied to the ability to adequately compensate future generations, and Millennials appear to prefer higher compensation over other types of benefit when considering workplace choices (McGinnis Johnson & Ng, 2015). The values held by this emerging generation in the workforce will require nonprofit leaders to examine hiring practices that allow Millennials to act autonomously, provide opportunity for leadership and personal development as a part of compensation packages, and find innovative ways to balance work experience and Millennial zeal in mid and upper management roles and responsibilities.

The 2014 national survey of Board Source of 846 nonprofit chief executives found more than 80% of leadership positions including chairs, board members, and CEOs are white, which is higher than the 64% of White Americans reported in the 2010 U.S. census. The responding organizations show an even greater gender gap when controlling for the size: more than half of females are in leader positions in small and medium-sized agencies while only 37% of large agencies account for female leaders. Ruhm and Borkoski's (2003) study demonstrated that females had a 70% share of employment in nonprofit sector jobs, compared to about 46% of jobs across all sectors. Conversely, women encounter the glass ceiling even in this sector, with fewer women executive directors and board members (Pynes, 2000). This gap is not accounted for by education or experience levels among women (Peters & Wolfred, 2001).

Compensation and Equity

Compensation of both employees and executives in the nonprofit sector is complicated by both the financial constraints facing many nonprofit agencies as well as the public perception tied to tax-exempt status. Compensation is often linked to the available labor supply and demand paradigms, and nonprofits often serve areas of "market failure," where the goods and services offered are not lucrative for the private sector, or "government failure," where governments cannot publicly provide these goods and services in an efficient or cost-effective manner (Salamon & Anahier, 1998). Traditionally, the nonprofit sector has also been characterized by value and mission-driven work, where the "spoils" are delivered in kind, not in financial gain. As sectoral boundaries continue to be blurred, and as organizations of differing sectors continue to partner, nonprofits often find themselves in an increasingly competitive labor market, and in order to remain competitive with public and private sectors, the nonprofit sector must offer incentives to attract potential employees and provide advantages over competitors (Ruhm & Borkoski, 2003; Twombly, 2009). The need to remain fiscally salient coupled with the need to recruit and retain talented employees pulls nonprofits from two sides in a manner that Kellner, Townsend, and Wilkinson (2016) observed as "the balance between the mission and the margin" (p. 1).

Previous studies on nonprofit compensation have varied in results over the past decade, making generalized assumptions about pay differentials in the public and private sectors difficult to ascertain. A prevailing thought among many is that individuals are attracted to work in the nonprofit sector for altruistic reasons, and that individuals will forsake higher wages and benefits for the sake of creating impact (Handy & Katz, 1998; Leete, 2006; Tschirhart et al., 2008; Word, 2011; Word & Park, 2015). For example, Johnston and Rudney (1987) found the average annual earnings of nonprofit workers are more than 20% less than those employed in for-profit companies. A more recent study by Leete (2001) demonstrated there was no wage differential after controlling for industry and occupation. The setting of hospitals, as an example, offers a look into similar industries and occupations across the nonprofit and for-profit divide, as both are relatively common. Ruhm and Borkoski (2003) demonstrated that nonprofit weekly earnings were an average of 2.7% lower than for-profit counterparts, though also showing variation within industry and occupation. Social services, hospitals, and other health services, along with education and nursing or personal care facilities, were all better compensated in the nonprofit sector than in the for-profit sector. In terms of occupation, those who worked in nonprofit health and education were likely to have a higher weekly take-home than for-profit counterparts, while administrative support, other management, and non–health service workers took home more in the for-profit sector (Ruhm & Borkoski, 2003). This discrepancy may be associated with altruistic value prescribed more to direct care as opposed to indirect service (Ruhm & Borkoski, 2003).

Apart from sectoral distinctions in pay, there is also the issue of compensation equity within the nonprofit sector when it comes to protected classes such as sex, gender, education, and race or ethnicity. The nonprofit sector tends to be predominantly female in terms of gender identity, and yet questions still emerge about pay equity, as in other sectors (see, for example, Faulk et al., 2012; Mesch and Rooney, 2008). The salary gender pay gap is 6% for CEOs in organizations with an annual budget size of less than $250,000, while nonprofits with budgets of $2.5 million to $5 million report a gender gap of 23% (GuideStar, 2015). These data indicate a gendered pay gap persists in the nonprofit sector, and while some analyses find this gap lower than in the for-profit sector, recent research argues this may be an artifact of greater numbers of traditionally female-occupied positions available in nonprofits and in industries where nonprofits have a greater share of the market than for-profits (Faulk et al., 2012). With regard to race and ethnicity, the representation of Whites is similar when examining all jobs (86% White) versus nonprofit jobs (87% White), while Blacks and Hispanics are largely underrepresented across the board. Blacks had both a 10% share in employment across all sectors and in nonprofit jobs, while Hispanics had a 9% share in employment across all jobs, and a 4% share of employment in nonprofit jobs (Ruhm & Borkoski, 2003). Beyond the issues of wage equity among varying populations who work in the nonprofit sector, other dynamics factor into the debate, as well. Resource availability and the fiscal health of nonprofit organizations will always be considerations, and more research on the relationship between compensation and organizational financial performance is emerging (see Grasse et al., 2014; Yan & Sloan, 2016).

In addition to the general discourse on wages paid to employees in the nonprofit sector is a focus on the compensation of nonprofit executives. Oster (1998) found that organizational size is a strong predictor of compensation, but also that the size effect varies considerably within the sector. Like other studies that touch on this topic, the type of organization (e.g. hospitals, educational institutions, and foundations) is a significant factor (Ruhm & Borkoski, 2003). Grasse et al. (2014) found a bit of variation based on their hypotheses and industry, when it comes to executive compensation. Across all nonprofits, however, they found support for executive compensation being positively associated with organizational efficiency, support from nongovernmental grant-making organizations, total expenditures, total number of employees, and total number of expert staff or management employees (Grasse et al., 2014).

While the public at large often misunderstands certain aspects of the nonprofit sector, executive compensation is an issue that can often find itself in the spotlight, as press attention has given more exposure to it in recent years. One example of such controversy is the Wounded Warrior Project, which made national news for elaborate meetings, expensive marketing strategies, and higher than average executive compensation. Organization director Steve Natuzzi was paid $473,000 in 2014 (Phillips, 2016). This revelation, along with other, relatively large nonprofit executive salaries, has been the source of intense public backlash, despite services provided by these nonprofits. This salary is an outlier, of course. For a more representative illustration of nonprofit compensation levels, see Figure 3.4. Nonetheless, public demand for financial constraint may force some nonprofits to find other methods of reward and non-monetary compensation in order to adequately retain talent (Akingbola, 2012; Selden & Sowa, 2015).

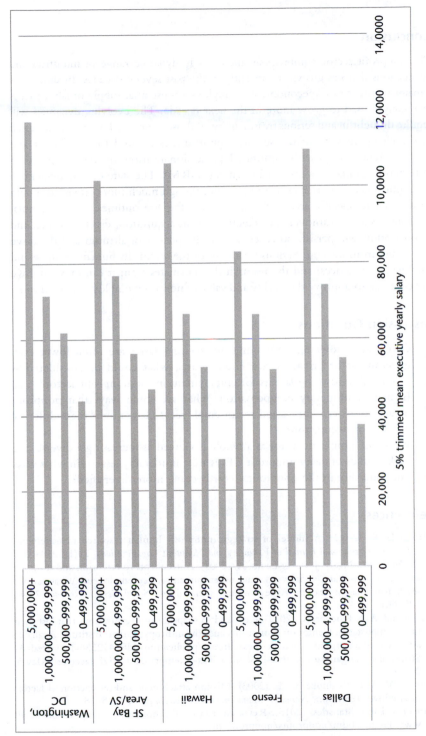

Figure 3.4 Mean executive compensation level by region and budget size

Conclusion

The nonprofit sector comprises an increasingly dynamic range of industries and occupations that has grown significantly in the past several decades. In short, it is a major segment of the economy and employs a substantial supply of labor that is seemingly poised to grow more in the next decade. The evolving dynamics will require thoughtful and serious treatment by all those concerned with and interested in the changing state of the sector. Opportunities abound for assessment and improvement, along with continued professionalization of various practices in nonprofit human resources management (HRM). The state of employment in nonprofit organizations appears to be sound, though much more attention should be devoted to specific areas, of which only a few are outlined here. Perennial challenges, such as turnover and retention, talent acquisition, diversity issues, and compensation will persist, however, as will the pursuit of altruism and the drive that comes from mission. Serious treatment of the sector, its human resource and employment practices, and the research that emanates from it can only improve and continue to improve the quality and value of nonprofit employment over time.

Discussion Questions

1   Given the knowledge that nonprofit sector salaries are often lower than government or private sector counterparts, what could be considered as additional motivating factors for employment in the nonprofit sector?
2   In lieu of monetary compensation, what are some ways that nonprofit organizations can attract and retain employees? How might these differ by industry or occupation?
3   While the nonprofit sector as a whole is viewed as increasingly diverse, the backgrounds of many nonprofit CEOs are considerably less so. In what ways can leadership in the nonprofit sector become more diversified?

References

Akingbola, K. (2012). A model of strategic nonprofit human resource management. *Voluntas: International Journal of Voluntary and Nonprofit Organizations, 24*(1), 214–240.
Barak, M. E. M., Nissly, J. A., & Levin, A. (2001). Antecedents to retention and turnover among child welfare, social work, and other human service employees: What can we learn from past research? A review and metanalysis. *Social Service Review, 75*(4), 625–661.
Blackwood, A. & Roeger, K. (2011). Revoked: A snapshot of organizations that lost their tax-exempt status. Center on Nonprofits and Philanthropy, Urban Institute. Available at: www.urban.org/sites/default/files/alfresco/publication-pdfs/412386-Revoked-A-Snapshot-of-Organizations-that-Lost-their-Tax-Exempt-Status.PDF (accessed May 5, 2016).
Brown, W. A. & Yoshioka, C. F. (2003). Mission attachment and satisfaction as factors in employee retention. *Nonprofit Management & Leadership, 14*(1), 5–18.
Bureau of Labor Statistics. (2015). Research data on the nonprofit sector. Available at: www.bls.gov/bdm/nonprofits/nonprofits.htm

Carpenter, H. L. & Qualls, T. W. (2015). *The talent development platform: Putting people first in social change organizations*. San Francisco: Jossey-Bass.

Chester, H., Hughes, J., & Challis, D. (2014). Commissioning social care for older people: Influencing the quality of direct care. *Ageing and Society, 34*(06), 930–950.

Cornelius, M., Corvington, P., & Ruesga, A. (2008). *Ready to lead? Next generation leaders speak out*. Washington, DC: CompassPoint Nonprofit Services, the Annie E. Casey Foundation, the Meyer Foundation, and Idealist.org.

Cornelius, M., Moyers, R., & Bell, J. (2011). *Daring to lead*. Washington, DC: Compass Point Nonprofit Services and the Meyer Foundation.

Cyr, S. (2011). Staff report: Over 279,000 nonprofits lose tax exempt status. *Philanthropy Journal*. Available at: http://pj.news.chass.ncsu.edu/2011/09/12/over-279000-nonprofits-lose-tax-exempt-status/ (accessed May 5, 2016).

Dart, R. (2004). The legitimacy of social enterprise. *Nonprofit Management & Leadership, 14*(4), 411–424.

Deesk, J. G. (1998). Enterprising nonprofits. *Harvard Business Review, 76*, 54–67.

Defourny, J. & Nyssens, M. (2007). Defining social enterprise. In M. Nyssens (Ed), *Social enterprise: At the crossroads of market, public policies and civil societies*, ed. M. Nyssens, (pp. 3–26). New York: Routledge.

Eikenberry, A. M. & Kluver, J. D. (2004). The marketization of the nonprofit sector: Civil society at risk? *Public Administration Review, 64*(2), 132–140.

Faulk, L., Edwards, L. H., Lewis, G. B., & McGinnis, J. (2012). An analysis of gender pay disparity in the nonprofit sector: An outcome of labor motivation or gendered jobs? *Nonprofit and Voluntary Sector Quarterly, 42*(6), 1268–1287.

Froelich, K., McKee, G., & Rathge, R. (2011). Succession planning in nonprofit organizations. *Nonprofit Management & Leadership, 22*(1), 3–20.

Grasse, N., Davis, T., & Ihrke, D. (2014). Understanding the compensation of nonprofit executive directors: Examining the influence of performance and organizational characteristics. *Nonprofit Management & Leadership, 24*(3), 377–398.

GuideStar USA, Inc. (2015). 2015 GuideStar Nonprofit Compensation Report. www.guidestar.org. (Accessed May 20, 2016).

Handy, F. & Katz, E. (1998). The wage differential between nonprofit institutions and corporations: Getting more by paying less? *Journal of Comparative Economics, 26*(2), 246–261.

Hood, C. (1995). The "New Public Management" in the 1980s: Variations on a theme. *Accounting, Organizations and Society, 20*(2), 93–109.

Johnston, D. & Rudney, G. (1987). Characteristics of workers in nonprofit organizations. *Monthly Labor Review, 110*(7), 28–33.

Kerlin, J. A. (2006). Social enterprise in the United States and Europe: Understanding and learning from the differences. *Voluntas: International Journal of Voluntary and Nonprofit Organizations, 17*(3), 246–262.

Kim, S. E., & Lee, J. W. (2007). Is mission attachment an effective management tool for employee retention? An empirical analysis of a nonprofit human services agency. *Review of Public Personnel Administration, 27*(3), 227–48.

Kossek, E., Lobel, S., & Brown, J. (2006). Human resource strategies to manage workforce diversity. In A. M. Konrad, P. Prasad, & J. Pringle (Eds.), *Handbook of workplace diversity* (pp. 53–74). Thousand Oaks, CA: Sage.

Kunreuther, F. (2003). The changing of the guard: What generational differences tell us about social-change organizations. *Nonprofit and Voluntary Sector Quarterly, 32*(3), 450–457.

Leete, L. (2001). Whither the nonprofit wage differential estimates from the 1990 census? *Journal of Labor Economics, 19*(1), 136–170.

Leete, L. (2006). Work in the nonprofit sector. In W. W. Powell & R. Steinberg (Eds.), *The nonprofit sector: A research handbook* (pp. 159–179). New Haven, CT: Yale University Press.

McGinnis, J. (2011a). The young and restless: Generation Y in the nonprofit workforce. *Public Administration Quarterly, 35*(3), 342–362.

McGinnis, J. (2011b). Making the case for nonprofit workforce diversity. In K. A. Agard (Ed.), *Leadership in nonprofit organizations* (pp. 871–877). Thousand Oaks, CA: Sage.

McGinnis Johnson, J. & Ng, E. S. (2015). Money talks or Millennials walk: The effect of compensation on nonprofit Millennial workers' sector-switching intentions. *Review of Public Personnel Administration*. Published online before print June 1, 2015, doi: 10.1177/0734371X15587980. Available at: http://rop.sagepub.com/content/early/2015/05/29/0734371X15587980.abstract (accessed June 6, 2016).

McKeever, B. S. (2015). *The nonprofit sector in brief 2015: Public charities, giving, and volunteering.* Washington, DC: The Urban Institute. Available at: www.urban.org/sites/default/files/alfresco/publication-pdfs/2000497-The-Nonprofit-Sector-in-Brief-2015-Public-Charities-Giving-and-Volunteering.pdf (accessed May 5, 2016).

Mesch, D. J. & Rooney, P. M. (2008). Determinants of compensation: A study of pay, performance, and gender differences for fundraising professionals. *Nonprofit Management & Leadership, 18*(4), 43–63.

Moynihan, D. P. & Pandey, S. K. (2007). The ties that bind: Social networks, person-organization value fit, and turnover intention. *Journal of Public Administration Research and Theory, 18*, 205–227.

Nonprofit HR. (2016). The 2016 Nonprofit Employment Practices Survey™. Washington, DC Available at: www.nonprofithr.com (accessed May 20, 2016).

Oster, S. M. (1998). Executive compensation in the nonprofit sector. *Nonprofit Management & Leadership, 8*(3), 207–221.

Peters, J. & Wolfred, T. (2001). *Daring to lead: Nonprofit executive directors and their work experience.* San Francisco, CA: CompassPoint Nonprofit Services.

Phillips, D. (2016). Wounded Warrior project spends lavishly on itself, insiders say. *New York Times*, January 27, 2016.

Pynes, J. E. (2000). Are women underrepresented as leaders of nonprofit organizations? *Review of Public Personnel Administration, 20*(2), 35–49.

Ronquillo, J. C. (2013). Conceptualizing the climate for innovation in public and nonprofit organizations. In B. L. Kedia & S. C. Jain (Eds.), *Restoring America's global competitiveness through Innovation* (pp. 126–147). Cheltenham: Edward Elgar.

Ruhm, C. J. & Borkoski, C. (2003). Compensation in the nonprofit sector. *Journal of Human Resources, 38*(4), 992–1021.

Rycraft, J. R. (1994). The party isn't over: The agency role in the retention of public child welfare caseworkers. *Social Work, 39*(1), 75–80.

Salamon, L. M. (2012). *America's nonprofit sector* (3rd ed.). New York: The Foundation Center.

Salamon, L. M. & Anheier, H. K. (1998). Social origins of civil society: Explaining the nonprofit sector cross-nationally. *Voluntas: International Journal of Voluntary and Nonprofit Organizations, 9*(3), 213–248.

Salamon, L. M., Sokolowski, S. W., & Geller S. L. (2012). Holding the fort: Nonprofit employment during a decade of turmoil. *Nonprofit Employment Bulletin, 39*, Johns Hopkins University. Available at: www.thenonprofitpartnership.org/files/ned_national_2012.pdf (accessed May 5, 2016).

Selden, S. C. & Moynihan, D. P. (2000). A model of voluntary turnover in state government. *Review of Public Personnel Administration, 20*(2), 63–74.

Selden, S. C. & Sowa, J. E. (2015). Voluntary turnover in nonprofit human service organizations: The impact of high performance work practices. *Human Service Organizations: Management, Leadership & Governance, 39*(3), 182–207.

Stewart, A. J. (2016). Exploring nonprofit executive turnover. *Nonprofit Management & Leadership, 27*(1): 43–58.

Tschirhart, M., Reed, K. K., Freeman, S. J., & Anker, A. L. (2008). Is the grass greener? Sector shifting and choice of sector by MPA and MBA graduates. *Nonprofit and Voluntary Sector Quarterly, 37*(4), 668–688.

Twombly, E. C. (2009). Nonprofit labor: current trends and future directions. In J. J. Cordes & C. E. Steuerle (Eds.), *Nonprofits and business* (pp. 217–237). Washington, DC: The Urban Institute Press.

Word, J. (2011). Human resource leadership and management. In K. A. Agard (Ed.), *Leadership in nonprofit organizations* (pp. 395–401). Thousand Oaks, CA: Sage.

Word, J. & Park, S. M. (2015). The new public service? Empirical research on job choice motivation in the nonprofit sector. *Personnel Review, 44*(1), 91–118.

Yan, W. & Sloan, M. F. (2016). The impact of employee compensation and financial performance on nonprofit organization donations. *The American Review of Public Administration, 46*(2), 243–258.

4

Legal Aspects of Nonprofit Employment

Eric Franklin Amarante

Introduction

Employment law as applied to nonprofit organizations is not easily summarized. It has local, state, and federal components, with overlapping requirements that can appear contradictory and impossibly complex. To illustrate this complexity, consider the federal minimum wage law. The Fair Labor Standards Act sets the minimum hourly wage for certain employees at $7.25. This may be the final word in your state. But more likely, your state imposes a higher minimum and your city or locality may impose a separate minimum wage for certain industries. The only way to be certain is to ensure familiarity with federal, state, and local statutes. This simple example is repeated across the employment law spectrum, creating an increasingly intricate regime with numerous interactions among federal, state, and local laws that need to be followed by nonprofits.

In addition to its complexity, employment law is not static. Laws are amended, new laws are adopted, and courts and agencies issue new interpretations of employment regulations and laws on a near-constant basis. Take, for example, the distinction between employees and independent contractors (a discussion of which appears below). Due to cost concerns, many nonprofit employers attempt to classify their workers as independent contractors. However, recent administrative guidance from the U.S. Department of Labor details a new emphasis on this distinction and warns misclassification of workers as independent contractors will be more strictly policed. Employment law constantly evolves in this manner.

Given this state of affairs, it is virtually impossible for a single chapter to incorporate everything a nonprofit organization will need to know in terms of employment law. Indeed, a multi-volume treatise will not likely cover all the nuances of a particular organization's employment law needs. As such, this chapter is not intended to replace the advice of an employment lawyer, and a nonprofit organization is strongly encouraged to engage a lawyer to review its organizational policies and procedures and ensure its legal compliance. Quite simply, this chapter is no substitute for a seasoned legal professional's expertise and judgment.

There are, however, some universal steps a nonprofit organization can take to mitigate its risk, regardless of its size, number of employees, or jurisdiction. This chapter endeavors to cover these areas. By reviewing this chapter, a nonprofit organization will know many areas of potential risk, have the tools to take precautionary measures, and make the job of the organization's employment lawyer much easier (and hopefully cheaper).

Application of Employment Law on Nonprofits

Many nonprofits mistakenly think that charitable organizations are exempt from employment laws. Perhaps this is because many organizations view compliance with employment laws as, at best, a nuisance, and, at worst, a costly intrusion. This is a reasonable assumption. After all, charitable organizations are exempt from most taxes, many business licenses, and countless other local regulations. It is therefore not a stretch to think that nonprofit organizations may be exempt from employment laws. Unfortunately, this is simply not the case.

To understand why, recall that employment laws were put in place to protect employees, not punish employers. This is perhaps best illustrated by a note in the Occupational Safety and Health Act (OSHA). Congress passed OSHA to make workplaces safer for employees. In discussing whether OSHA regulations should apply to nonprofit organizations, the Act states that "any charitable or non-profit organization which employs one or more employees is covered under [OSHA] and is required to comply with its provisions" because "[t]he basic purpose of [OSHA] is to improve working environments in the sense that they impair, or could impair, the lives and health of employees."

It is difficult to argue with this logic. Why shouldn't an individual enjoy the benefits of federal protections simply because his or her employer is a nonprofit organization? Indeed, because employment law's primary aim is to protect employees from poor treatment by employers, there is little room to argue exemption for any entities.

Due to the differences among the states and localities, this chapter primarily focuses on federal law. In a few cases, state law is consistent enough to be summarized, and this chapter addresses such areas. However, this chapter cannot offer a state-by-state catalog of employment law, and it is important for a nonprofit organization to engage a lawyer familiar with the nonprofit's jurisdiction-specific legal requirements.

This chapter begins by discussing the hiring process, including how to classify workers (i.e., as employees or independent contractors), before discussing important practices to maintain at the beginning of the employment relation-ship, including having detailed job descriptions, the importance of maintain-ing an employee handbook, and the potential liability for damages caused by workers. Next, this chapter discusses federal anti-discrimination laws, describing the steps employers must take to avoid discrimination. This chapter then discusses termination of employees and how organizations can avoid potential lawsuits from terminated employees before discussing some best practices regarding how to manage employees, including conducting regular employee performance reviews.

Are We Hiring an Employee or an Independent Contractor?

Before discussing the process of actually hiring employees, it is important to identify whether the person you are hiring is an employee or an independent con-tractor. The distinction is important. If the individual is an independent contrac-tor, the nonprofit will have fewer obligations and responsibilities regarding the relationship. More specifically, if an individual is an employee, the employer must withhold income, Social Security, and Medicare taxes as well as pay unemployment taxes ("Independent Contractor (Self-Employed) or Employee?," n.d.). None of this is required for an organization hiring an independent contractor.

In addition to taxes, the employee-independent contractor classification also carries important implications regarding potential liability. Generally speaking, an organization is liable if an employee willfully or negligently causes harm while acting within the scope of their employment. In other words, if you hire an employee to drive a delivery truck and the employee negligently causes an accident during a delivery, your organization may be responsible for the damages. This concept is known as *vicarious liability*, and it does not apply to independent contractors.

Thus, it is reasonable to expect organizations to do all they can to classify their workers as independent contractors. Not only does an organization avoid potential vicarious liability, but if an organization does not have to pay and withhold taxes, the organization also stands to save as much as 40% on a would-be employee's overhead costs (Harris, 2010). However, a nonprofit may not simply declare that an individual is an independent contractor in order to lighten its potential liability. Rather, the determination is based upon the details of the relationship.

An organization must ignore the obvious advantages of the independent contractor classification and honestly engage in the classification process. This is because an incorrect determination may result in significant fines and penalties imposed by both the state and the Internal Revenue Service. Further, regulating agencies are paying closer attention to this distinction. As noted in the introductory section to this chapter, the U.S. Department of Labor (DOL) has made misclassification of workers an enforcement priority. In an official statement, a

DOL administrator emphasized that not only does misclassification rob employees of "important workplace protections," but it also "results in lower tax revenue for government and an uneven playing field for employers who properly classify workers" (Weil, 2015).

Employees vs. Independent Contractors: How to Make the Determination

Given the potential consequences of misclassification, one might reasonably assume there is a clear and bright-line rule to make the appropriate employee-independent contractor determination. Unfortunately, this is not the case. Without any obvious self-awareness, the IRS warns that "[i]t is critical [to] correctly determine whether the individuals providing services are employees or independent contractors," before noting that "[t]here is no 'magic' or set number of factors that 'makes' the worker an employee or an independent contractor, and no one factor stands alone in making this determination" (Weil, 2015, p.5). As if that were not confusing enough, the IRS continues to note that "factors which are relevant in one situation may not be relevant in another" (Weil, 2015, p.5).

Thus, nonprofits must engage in a detailed investigation to determine if an individual providing services is properly classified as an independent contractor or an employee. Traditionally, the determination turned on the amount of *control* the nonprofit had over the individual: the more control the nonprofit enjoyed over the worker, the more likely the worker should be classified as an employee. This common law control test, however, is no longer the determinative factor. Rather, it serves as a single factor in a six-factor test. This test is known as the "economic realities" test, and includes the following factors:

- *The extent to which the work performed is an integral part of the employer's business.* Determining the precise activities that constitute an "integral part" of the nonprofit's activities is not clear. Case law provides some examples, with courts finding that cake decorators are integral to the business of selling customized cakes[1] and pickle pickers are integral to the pickle business.[2] Suffice it to say that if a worker's contributions are integral to an organization's operations, this factor suggests that the worker ought to be classified as an employee.
- *The worker's opportunity for profit or loss depends on the worker's managerial skill.* This factor may be more simply stated as the ability of the worker to make decisions that affect his or her bottom line. If an individual has the autonomy to exercise managerial decision-making that results in savings realized by the worker, then this factor weighs in favor of an independent contractor classification. As an example, imagine two grant writers, Anne and Bob. Anne prepares grant applications as assigned by the nonprofit, does not advertise her services, and does not solicit additional clients. Bob prepares grant applications for clients that he secured through advertising and direct

solicitation. For each such client, Bob negotiates a contract, decides which jobs to perform, when to perform them, and whether or not to hire additional workers. Anne's lack of managerial skill suggests that she is an employee, while Bob's exercise of managerial skill directly affects his opportunity for profit and loss and suggests that he is an independent contractor. Please note that merely working more hours to make more money does not constitute exercise of "managerial" skill.

- *The extent of the relative investments of the employer and the worker.* To be considered an independent contractor, a worker should make some investment in order to prove that the worker is engaged in an independent business. This coincides with the previous factor: an independent investment suggests the possibility of realizing profit and loss based on that investment.

- *Whether the work performed requires special skills and initiative.* On its face, this factor is misleading. The DOL is not interested in the technical skills of the worker in determining the classification of the worker. For example, a highly skilled engineer may be properly classified as an employee while a low-skilled janitor may be properly classified as an independent contractor. Rather than technical skills, this factor focuses on the worker's "business skills, judgment, and initiative" (Weil, 2015, p. 10). To illustrate this, the DOL describes a "highly skilled carpenter" who does not make any independent judgments at the construction site with respect to work sequence, materials necessary, or securing additional jobs. In other words, the carpenter is "simply providing his skilled labor" but is not "demonstrating the skill and initiative of an independent contractor" (Weil, 2015, p. 10). In this case, the carpenter is properly classified as an employee.

- *The permanency of the relationship.* The more permanent or indefinite the work is, the more likely that the worker will be deemed an employee. For this factor, it is important to note that permanency does not necessarily mean forever; If an employee accepts a job and quits after one week, that relationship may still be considered permanent under this factor. Rather than actual time, this factor is more concerned about the nature of the work. The prototypical independent contractor works on a project-by-project basis, skipping from employer to employer. Thus, a person who performs sporadic work for the same employer may be considered an employee under this factor. As an example, the DOL describes an editor who works for the same publishing house for several years, following the publishing house's instructions and editing books provided by the publishing house. Even if the editor's work is sporadic, "[t]his scenario indicates a permanence to the relationship between the editor and the publishing house that is indicative of an employment relationship" (Weil, 2015, p. 13).

- *The degree of control exercised or retained by the employer.* The final factor is the traditional common law question of the amount of control the hiring organization has over the worker. If the control of the hiring organization is at a level such that the worker can no longer be considered an independent businessperson, then this factor weighs in favor of an employee classification (Weil, 2015, pp. 13–14).

Predictably, the DOL's guidance caused quite a stir, with many commentators noting these factors skew toward classification as employees rather than independent contractors. Indeed, the DOL admitted as much in its guidance by stating that "[i]n sum, most workers are employees" (Weil, 2015, p. 15). The key to the classification analysis is to follow the DOL's instructions that "each factor should be considered in light of the ultimate determination of whether the worker is really in business for him or herself (and this is an independent contractor) or is economically dependent on the employer (and this is its employee)" (Weil, 2015, p. 15). As with all areas of employment law, an organization is urged to consult with an experienced attorney to make the employee–independent contractor classification.

Crafting Job Descriptions

Having an adequate job description is a remarkably important step that many nonprofits overlook. A job description is not a legal requirement, but it can be an invaluable tool to prevent potential future liability. A proper job description may include the following: job title and salary range; where the work will be performed and expected hours; how the position fits within the organization's hierarchy (i.e., to whom the individual reports and who the individual supervises); a description of the job's essential functions (e.g., driving, lifting certain weight, standing for certain periods of time, etc.); required credentials and other prerequisites (e.g., experience, education, skills, etc.); and a statement on how the job fits into the organization's mission.

An adequate job description is important because it may help the organization avoid liability. Without a detailed job description, a nonprofit will not have clearly detailed minimum qualifications for a particular job. Such minimum qualifications may be necessary if an applicant claims he or she did not receive a job offer based upon a discriminatory reason. To illustrate the importance of a job description, imagine the following scenarios:

- A job description describes a certain physical activity as a requirement for the position. An applicant with a disability is not hired for a position because the applicant would not be able to engage in the activity, even with reasonable accommodation. Without the job description, the decision not to hire might be construed as an impermissible discrimination based upon the applicant's disability.
- A job description indicates a particular credential required for the position. A female applicant is not hired because she lacks the required credential. The applicant sues, claiming she was not hired solely because of her gender. Because the job description includes a reference to the required credential, the employer has a solid defense against this discrimination claim.

As these examples illustrate, a well-crafted job description may prove to be the best defense an organization has against a claim of discrimination in the hiring process.

Employee Handbook

Similar to the job description, there is no legal requirement for a nonprofit organization to have an employee handbook. However, a nonprofit should strongly consider having and following an updated employee handbook. From a practical perspective, it is an efficient way to communicate expectations and workplace policies to your employees in an efficient and consistent manner. But it also can help mitigate potential liability. It is not an exaggeration to say that the employee handbook is the first place a lawyer will look to defend an employment-related claim.

One of the most important things to include in an employee handbook is clear language stating the employment is at-will. Even though at-will employment is the default in most states, this default status can be frustrated if the employer enters into an employment contract or makes statements that provide an implied contractual right of continued employment. Thus, it is important all documents contain language that reinforces the at-will employment status and refrains from language that contradicts such status. Such language should clearly indicate that all employment contracts must be in writing and all employees are subject to termination at any time for any reason. The employee handbook is an ideal place to include such language. A sample statement follows, but it is important that an attorney review your particular statement to ensure compliance with local laws.

> Employment is on an at-will basis unless otherwise stated in a written individual employment agreement signed by the Executive Director. This means the employee or employer may terminate the employment relationship at any time, for any reason or for no reason, and with or without prior notice. No one has the authority to make any express or implied representations in connection with, or in any way limit, an employee's right to resign or the employer's right to terminate an employee at any time, for any reason or for no reason, with or without prior notice. Nothing in this handbook creates an employment agreement, express or implied, or any other agreement between any employee and the employer. No statement, act, series of acts, or pattern of conduct can change this at-will relationship.
>
> *(adapted from Kearney, 2014)*

In addition to the statement regarding employment at-will, an employee manual may contain one or more of the following:

- *Holidays and vacation policies*. Neither holidays nor vacation time is legally required, however, similarly situated employees must be treated similarly.

- *Drug, alcohol, and smoking policy.* If an employee is expected to refrain from certain activities, an organization should clearly detail the contours of this expectation. In addition, recipients of federal grants in excess of $100,000 must comply with the Drug Free Workplace Act. This law, in part, requires publication of the drug-free expectations and employee notification of the policy. The employee manual represents a perfect means of complying with such requirements. Please note that many states have instituted laws and regulations relating to drugs and alcohol testing, so it is vital that an attorney review your policies to ensure federal and state compliance.

- *Disciplinary procedures.* As noted in the termination section, the documentation of disciplinary procedures is an effective way to defend against employment litigation. An organization may want to include a consistently applied policy that explains the organization's disciplinary procedures. However, any such procedures should be flexible. For example, although it is considered best practice to apply progressive disciplinary measures that give employees adequate notice of their inadequacies and an opportunity to remedy their missteps (e.g., oral warning, followed by a written warning, followed by suspension, followed by termination), it is best not to specifically require such a progressive disciplinary policy. This is because it may serve to restrict an employer from terminating an employee without strict adherence to the progressive policy. Generally speaking, an entity should have the flexibility to immediately terminate an employee in the event of egregious misconduct.

- *Complaint procedures.* An employee handbook ought to detail clear procedures for employees to report any instance of workplace issues. Employees will often be aware of employment issues long before the employer, and expedient notice of potential issues provides the employer with an opportunity to properly address issues in a timely manner.

- *Harassment policy.* State and federal laws require certain employers to institute a harassment policy. Thus, it is important for an organization to consult with a lawyer to determine the proper means of complying with this requirement. However, even if an employer is exempted from this requirement, it is a good idea for all employers to institute a comprehensive harassment policy. The policy will give employees notice that certain behaviors are not tolerated, and provide the procedures for employees to report harassment.

- *Social media.* An employer may consider a robust social media policy to inform employees of the appropriate means of representing the organization on social media platforms. Such a policy might clearly prohibit an employee from speaking for the organization on social media. In any case, social media is a near-ubiquitous aspect of modern life, and a hiring organization would be wise to consider its effect on the organization.

An employee handbook is only useful if you have proof that all the employees have received it. Thus, it is important for every employee to sign a form acknowledging receipt of the handbook.

Hiring and Retention

For nonprofits, it is important to make sure you take certain precautions in hiring and retaining employees. Most organizations are aware that an employee will serve as the organization's *de facto* representative. This is true in a very practical sense, in that employees are often the face of the organization. They wear the organization's t-shirts, solicit donations for the organization, and carry out the charitable works of the organization. But more importantly, the notion of an employee as representative of the organization is true in a legal sense, and an employer may be responsible for harm or damage committed by an employee. As noted above, the doctrine of vicarious liability holds an employer liable for harm and damages committed by an employee in the scope of his or her employment. In addition to vicarious liability, an employer may be liable for an employee's damages under the theory of *negligent hiring* or *negligent retention*. This concept stands for the proposition that an employer may be liable for an employee's actions if the employer knew or should have known the employee represented a threat of harm to third parties. The difference between negligent hiring and negligent retention is timing: if the employer's failure occurred during the hiring process, it is negligent hiring, and if the employer's failure occurred after the employee is engaged, it is negligent retention. In either case, a court will ask two questions: (1) did the employer know or should the employer have known about the employee's potential risk?; and (2) would the employer have discovered the risk through a reasonable investigation?

In many ways, the concepts of negligent hiring and negligent retention make sense. Indeed, the examples of plaintiffs winning such cases are not surprising and do not offend intuitive notions of justice. Although the standards vary from state to state, the prevailing fact patterns are fairly consistent. A prototypical example is an organization that provides childcare hiring a convicted child molester. When such situations end poorly, it is not a surprise that courts find the hiring organizations liable. The law simply asks a hiring organization to take reasonable measures when hiring and retaining employees.

How to Protect Against Negligent Hiring and Negligent Retention Claims

If one of your employees harms a third party, you should expect to be sued. There is no mechanism to prevent those harmed from seeking compensation in court. However, there are steps a hiring organization may take that will help defend against a claim of negligent hiring or negligent retention. As the previous section notes, a nonprofit must prove it acted in a reasonable manner in hiring and retaining an employee. Acting reasonably involves two basic components: screening and taking appropriate action.

To the first component, an organization should incorporate proper screening mechanisms whenever an employee is hired. Such screening mechanisms must be tailored to the employee's job description (the importance of the job description is discussed later in this chapter). For example, if a job description includes significant driving duties, it is reasonable to expect an employer to inquire into the employee's driving history.

One word of warning on conducting the reasonable inquiry in the screening process: many states have laws that govern the extent to which prospective employers may inquire into an applicant's criminal background. Thus, it is important to have a lawyer familiar with your state's laws review your proposed screening procedures. Further, federal law prohibits blanket discrimination against applicants with criminal histories. Under Title VII of the Civil Rights Act of 1964, an employer may not exclude an applicant due to his or her criminal history unless there is a business necessity for the exclusion. In other words, you cannot have a policy that refuses to hire any applicants simply because they have any criminal history.

For the second component, it is imperative an employer act in a reasonable manner as soon as it learns an employee may not be fit for a particular activity. For example, if an employee's job description involves driving duties and the employer learns that the employee was recently cited for reckless driving, the employer should respond appropriately. To ignore this information is to endanger the organization. The following list details some specific steps that will protect your nonprofit from negligent hiring and negligent retention claims:

- *Institute job-specific policies to ensure that employees are properly screened.* This may include criminal background checks, confirming work history, and checking professional references.
- *Carefully document the screening process.* If you are ultimately sued for negligent hiring, you will need to provide proof you properly screened the employee in the hiring process. If you are unable to prove you took such steps, then you may be unable to properly establish a defense against a negligent hiring claim.
- *Supervise employees to ensure appropriate behavior.* The threat of liability for negligent hiring or retention stems not only from facts the employer knew, but also facts the employer should have known. In other words, willful ignorance will not protect you. If an employee repeatedly acts in a reckless manner, the employer should know about this and take appropriate action. Thus, it is important for the employer to institute proper monitoring procedures to arm the employer with the knowledge of how an employee is operating.
- *Take immediate action upon receiving information that an employee engaged in inappropriate activity.* Once an employer knows an employee engaged in inappropriate activity, it is vital the employer act immediately. To do otherwise may be considered unreasonable and may expose the organization to liability.

- *Carefully document any investigation conducted into an employee's activities.* Again, the inquiry in a negligent hiring or negligent retention action will be whether or not the employer acted in a reasonable manner. One of the best ways an employer can prove it acted reasonably is to produce a detailed and thorough investigation into any inappropriate activity committed by an employee. A carefully documented investigation will be the best defense against a negligent retention claim.

Anti-Discrimination Laws

The previous sections detailed how vicarious liability, negligent hiring, and negligent retention could result in liability for a hiring organization. It is therefore important to hire the right people. However, a nonprofit must be careful that the search for the best employees is free from discrimination. The entire hiring process, including the application form, the job interview, and any job advertisement, must comply with anti-discrimination laws. However, this is not as simple as it might seem. There is a comprehensive set of laws that prohibit many forms of discrimination, including discrimination based on a number of characteristics, and it behooves a hiring organization to be familiar with the anti-discrimination legal regime.

Federal law prohibits certain organizations from using an applicant's race, color, sex, age, national origin, religion, disability, pregnancy, military status, or genetic information in the hiring process. The federal restrictions apply to organizations based on the number of individuals they employ. The employee threshold is different for each statute (see Table 4.1 on p. 62). For example, Title VII, which prohibits discrimination based on race, color, religion, sex, or national origin, applies to private employers that have 15 or more employees. However, a hiring organization that employs fewer than 15 employees should also avoid discrimination, and not just because it is the right thing to do. Even if your organization has fewer than 15 employees, your organization may still be subject to anti-discrimination laws. This is because many states have their own anti-discrimination laws with lower thresholds. In addition, states may prohibit discrimination on characteristics not covered by Title VII, such as sexual orientation. Further, if you hope to eventually grow into a larger organization, you may find yourself surpassing the relevant threshold and becoming subject to federal laws. Finally, many foundations require their grantees to have anti-discrimination policies in place. Thus, it is in the best interest of the organization to follow anti-discrimination laws, regardless of the number of individuals employed.

Hopefully, it is no great burden to ask a nonprofit not to discriminate. But even well-intentioned pre-employment inquiries may inadvertently discriminate. Thus, it is important to institute the following policies:

- Avoid asking any pre-employment questions that are intended to discover information about any of the applicant's protected categories.

- Ask all applicants the same questions, to avoid any appearance of disparate treatment.
- Ask objective questions and avoid subjective inquiries.
- Do not ask third parties to engage in impermissible questioning (i.e., you cannot have someone discriminate on your behalf).
- Avoid questions that may inadvertently disclose protected information (e.g., asking an applicant for their high school graduation date may reveal the applicant's age).
- Given expansive definitions of discrimination based upon sex, avoid questions regarding marital status, name changes, and children.
- Avoid asking about criminal convictions unless there is a legitimate business reason for the inquiry.
- Avoid asking about arrest records; because of the disproportionate number of minority arrests, this inquiry may be viewed as an impermissible attempt to exclude minority applicants.
- Avoid using gender-specific terms (e.g., salesman, waiter).

Harassment in the Workplace

Sexual harassment is a form of unlawful discrimination under Title VII. As set forth in the statute,

> [u]nwelcome sexual advances, requests for sexual favors, and other verbal or physical conduct of a sexual nature constitute sexual harassment when this conduct explicitly or implicitly affects an individual's employment, unreasonably interferes with an individual's work performance, or creates an intimidating, hostile, or offensive work environment.
>
> (U.S. Equal Employment Opportunity Commission, 2009)

The first portion of the definition encompasses the obvious cases. Hopefully, there is little question that unwelcome sexual advances and inappropriate requests constitute harassment that should not be tolerated in a workplace. The more subtle distinctions fall within in the latter portion of the definition: what, precisely, constitutes activity that creates an "intimidating, hostile, or offensive work environment" under the statute?

The latitude within the definition is intentional. The point of the definition is to capture the subjective state of the victim, and employers are wise to err on the side of caution in crafting a sexual harassment policy. To emphasize the subjective nature of the definition of a hostile workplace, note the following examples of activities that have been found to constitute sexual harassment:

- persistent gender-based slurs, sexual innuendoes, lewd jokes, or ribbing about gender-specific traits;
- leering, staring, or ogling;

- sharing sexually suggestive material (pictures, calendars, websites, etc.);
- unwelcome touching (rubbing shoulders, pinching, slapping, etc.);
- inappropriate comments about an employee's attire or appearance;
- gender-based jokes or comments that demean one gender.

A sexual harassment policy should make clear such activities are not tolerated, and all complaints of sexual harassment will be vigorously investigated and addressed.

Although sexual harassment is generally the most well-known form of legally actionable workplace-based harassment, harassment on the basis of any protected characteristic may expose the organization to liability. This includes harassment based upon race, religion, national origin, disability, and age. Some examples of behavior that have been found to constitute harassment include: racial epithets or race-based jokes; comments on a person's skin color, hair, or other racially or ethnically identifiable characteristics; negative comments or jokes about certain religions or religious practices; negative comments or jokes based on age (when the employee is over 40 years of age); and negative comments or jokes about a person's physical or mental disability.

The Employer's Responsibility to Address Harassment

As the language of Title VII makes clear, the employer is expected to provide a harassment-free workplace. Once an employer knows (or should have known) about harassment, the employer is subject to liability if it fails to take appropriate action. Generally speaking, an employer ought to have an open-door policy for complaints, and it is wise for any policy to include a detailed mechanism for victims of harassment to report improper behavior in a confidential and sensitive manner. Once a complaint is received, the employer ought to take the complaint seriously and conduct an investigation. If the complaint has merit, disciplinary action must be taken. If the harassment was especially egregious, the disciplinary action may include terminating the employee.

The first step an organization ought to take is to adopt a comprehensive harassment policy and include the policy in the employee handbook, in order to ensure each employee acknowledges receipt of a copy. A harassment policy should contain the following elements:

- a statement that the organization is dedicated to providing a harassment-free workplace;
- a clear and comprehensive definition of harassment, providing examples of inappropriate behavior;
- the process for reporting harassment, identifying the individuals responsible for receiving complaints, and a statement that all complaints will be handled confidentially and with sensitivity;
- a description of the steps the organization will take to investigate the harassment claims;

- a notice that violations of this policy will result in disciplinary action, up to and including termination;
- a statement that employees will not be subject to retaliation for reporting harassment.

If an organization adopts a comprehensive anti-harassment policy and engages in a good faith investigation of all harassment complaints, then the organization is taking steps to protect itself from liability. More important than avoiding liability, however, these steps may help prevent harassment from occurring altogether.

Terminating Employees

At this point, it is clear an organization might have to terminate an employee under certain circumstances. In addition to harassment claims, an organization may have to terminate an employee to avoid potential liability through vicarious liability, negligent retention, and negligent hiring claims. However, it is important to be careful when terminating an employee. Terminating an employee is a sensitive situation and should be treated as such. If an employee is treated fairly and respectfully during termination, the employee is less likely to sue the employer. Thus, it is in an organization's best interest to be honest with the employee, give the employee as much notice as possible, and provide appropriate transition services.

Even if all precautions are taken to make the termination as respectful and fair as possible, a lawsuit is a very real possibility. The following section discusses the facts that might give rise to a wrongful termination claim. For example, if an employee is terminated for a discriminatory purpose (i.e., the termination is based upon the employee's race, gender, religion, etc.), then the employee may have a legal claim against the organization for wrongful termination. However, a terminated employee is not limited to the rights detailed in federal and state statutes. In the absence of a statutory right, an employee may make a claim based upon: (1) breach of contract; (2) breach of the duty of good faith and fair dealing; or (3) violation of public policy.

Wrongful Termination Claims

As stated earlier, the default position of the law in most states is that an employer may terminate an employee for any (or no) reason. Absent an employee contract, employment is considered "at-will." This means that either an employer or an employee may terminate the relationship at any time. This default rule is true in most situations and in most states.

However, the actions and statements of the employer may frustrate the at-will nature of an employment relationship. This is known as the "implied contract" exception. If an employer makes promises to an employee of job security, then a court may determine a contract is in place and the employer may no longer freely terminate the employee. The most common example of an implied contract is when a statement made in an employee handbook establishes an expectation of continued employment (such statements include promises that an employee will only be discharged for "just cause" or similar terms). In many states, an implied contract may be created orally as well. Thus, it is important for employers to take care not to make any promises of continued employment, either orally or in writing, and statements similar to the following should be avoided:

- We have a policy of only terminating employees for just cause.
- As long as you do your job, you will have a position here.
- We have a progressive discipline policy and you won't be terminated without receiving oral and written warnings.
- If you perform well during a six-month probationary period, you will have a job here.

In addition to the implied contract theory of liability, there is the possibility that an employee might sue for breach of the duty of good faith and fair dealing. This common law duty is implied in every contract and requires contracting parties to act fairly with one another, honor commonly understood obligations, and avoid frustrating the other party's understanding of the contract. For employment relationships, a minority of state courts have held this duty requires employers to avoid dealing with their employees in an arbitrary manner[3] (*Equal Employment Opportunity Commission v. Chestnut Hill Hospital*, 1995). In some of the states that recognize this cause of action, there is an implied "just cause" standard in the employment relationship (i.e., an employer must have just cause to terminate an employee) (*Chambers v. Valley National Bank of Arizona*, 1988).[4] In other states, courts have held that employers may not terminate employees for malicious reasons (i.e., the terminations must be in good faith). The quintessential example of malicious termination is when an employer terminates an employee prior to retirement in order to avoid paying retirement benefits. Several state courts have held that this constitutes bad faith and violates the implied duty of good faith and fair dealing (*Stafford v. Purofied Down Products Corporation*, 1992).[5]

In some cases, a court may deem a termination against public policy. This rarely used doctrine is invoked when a court determines an employee's termination would harm the public. Such cases involve an employee refusing to engage in illegal activity, such as terminating an employee for not bribing a public official or refusing to file an inaccurate public document. Other examples include terminations for actions states have determined to be in the public interest. These situations include, for example, a termination as retaliation for an employee filing a workers' compensation claim.

How to Terminate an Employee

Before taking any action, it is important to determine if the employee had an express or implied contract. If there is a written employment agreement, then you must follow any terms of the contract, some of which may limit the circumstances in which an employee may be terminated. Further, an organization should check all other written documents (e.g. employee handbook, documents distributed upon hiring) to ensure there were no written assurances of continued employment. Once an organization has determined there are no written agreements of continued employment, it must make sure there has been no oral statement that might be construed as a promise of continued employment.

Even if an organization has determined it has no legal obligation to continue employment, it is a good idea to have a legitimate reason for the termination. Again, the "at-will" employment doctrine generally means an employer does not need a reason for termination. However, a legitimate reason for firing may help discourage any potential wrongful termination claims. Legitimate reasons may include excessive tardiness, poor performance, use of alcohol or drugs at work, or violating organizational rules. However, a legitimate reason for termination will not provide much protection if the employer does not consistently enforce the rules. For example, if an organization terminates a black employee for violating a particular organizational rule routinely violated by white employees, then a court might uphold a wrongful termination claim.

Finally, it is imperative that an organization carefully documents the termination process. If an employee brings a lawsuit claiming wrongful termination, it is important the organization is able to provide proof of the reasons for the termination.

Consider Securing a Release

An employer may wish to have a departing employee sign a release of claims. By signing a release, a former employee promises not to sue the organization. If properly drafted, a release will protect the organization from future lawsuits. A release is only valid if it is given in exchange for something of value. If an employee signs a release but receives no compensation, it is an unenforceable promise a court may not uphold. Compensation can be anything of value, but it usually comes in the form of severance pay. For example, an employer who does not normally give severance may decide to offer a severance package to a particular employee in exchange for an executed release. This release will be enforceable as long as the severance package is a new consideration. The idea behind this requirement is that the release must be a product of a bargained-for exchange. Thus, if an organization has a policy of providing severance, the organization will have to offer something in addition to the normal severance package to secure an enforceable release.

In addition to an exchange of value, some statutes require any purported releases to specifically list the rights a former employee is giving up. Further, many states have requirements that affect the enforceability of releases. Thus, it is imperative that an organization consults with an attorney before having a departing employee sign a release of claims.

Employee Performance Reviews

Regular employee performance reviews are strongly recommended for all organizations. There are several practical reasons for regular performance reviews. For employees, it provides an opportunity to hear how they are performing and how they might improve. It is also a chance for the employer to point out areas in which employees are excelling and areas that could use some attention. From a legal perspective, regular employee performance reviews provide the documentation necessary to protect the organization against future potential claims. If an organization needs to terminate an employee, the employee's performance reviews should help establish the termination is for a legitimate reason. For example, imagine an employer needs to terminate an employee for poor performance. How would an employer prove the employee's shortcomings without proper documentation? Regular employee performance reviews provide the perfect opportunity not only to discuss the employee's shortcomings, but also to document the issues in the event of future discipline and/or termination.

For the employee review process to be useful, the process should be consistently applied. This means the reviews should occur at regular times throughout the year (or at least annually) and the content of the reviews should be consistent. Ideally, employers will use a form that permits consistent reviews and encourages detailed documentation of the review process. Finally, the review process should ensure the employee has the opportunity to understand the performance review contents.

Paying Employees

The federal law that governs payment of employees is the Fair Labor Standards Act (FLSA), which in part establishes a federal minimum wage and overtime requirements (Elaws: Employment Laws Assistance for Workers & Small Businesses, n.d.).[6] In addition to the FLSA, most states have minimum wage laws that are higher than the federal minimum. Indeed, some localities have their own minimum wage laws. For example, San Francisco has a minimum wage of $14.00 (as of July 2017), Albuquerque has a minimum wage of $8.80 (as of January 1, 2017 if the employer does not provide healthcare benefits), and Chicago is phasing in a minimum wage that will reach $13.00 by 2019. Thus, it is important to understand not only federal minimum wage laws, but also the state and local laws that may affect the minimum payment requirements of your employees.

However, not all employees are subject to all minimum wage laws. Many of the local laws apply to certain sectors (e.g., New York City is raising the minimum wage of fast-food workers to $15.00). In addition, the federal minimum wage requirement does not apply to all employees. Such employees are called "exempt" employees, and it is important to understand how employees are classified under the FLSA.

The minimum wage requirements of the FLSA are complex, but there are certain employees who are always considered exempt and certain employees who are always classified as non-exempt. The former category includes "blue-collar" employees and first responders, who are always subject to the FLSA's minimum wage and overtime requirements. Similarly, the FLSA also describes a category of employees who are always exempt (e.g., employees of seasonal businesses, small circulation newspaper employees, and newspaper deliverers).

Further, there are provisions in the FLSA that permit certain organizations to apply to pay disabled employees less than the minimum wage. Specifically, Section 14(c) of the FLSA allows employers to pay subminimum wages to employees with disabilities directly affecting their job performance. In order to qualify for this exception, employers must obtain a special certification from the DOL. It is important to note that Section 14(c) is somewhat controversial, with some commentators arguing it does more harm than good for the disabled community. Organizations relying upon this exemption should pay careful attention to changes in the law, as there are several organizations attempting to repeal or phase-out the exemption.

Outside of those specific situations, an organization has to look at the FLSA's requirements to determine if a particular employee is exempt or nonexempt. The FLSA lists the following employees as common exemptions on their website ("Compliance Assistance: Wages and the Fair Labor Standards Act (FLSA)," n.d.):[7]

- *Commissioned sales employees.* If more than half of an employee's compensation is derived from commissions and the employee averages at least 1.5 times the minimum wage for each hour worked, such employees are exempt from overtime.
- *Certain well-paid computer professionals.* Certain computer professionals paid an hourly wage of at least $27.63 are exempt from overtime.
- *Certain well-paid white-collar employees.* Those employees who earn a salary of at least $23,660 per year and have executive, administrative, or professional duties are exempt from the overtime and minimum wage requirements of the FLSA.

The foregoing exemptions do not represent all of the exemptions set forth in the law, and this list is not intended to be exhaustive. Rather, this list is provided to show the precision of the federal wage and hour regime and emphasize the need to engage legal help. Given the complexity of the FLSA and its exemptions, it is vital for an organization to consult with an attorney to ensure compliance with federal, state, and local wage and hour laws.

Summary of Federal Laws

As this chapter has shown, there are a number of federal laws that regulate employers. These laws not only regulate harassment claims and wage and hour complaints, but they also cover safety in the workplace and privacy concerns. As noted earlier, although many of the federal laws are only applicable to organizations with a certain number of employees, it is in the best interest of organizations to comply with all federal laws regardless of the thresholds. The list in Table 4.1 is

Table 4.1 Federal regulations and protections

Law	Federal Threshold	Protection
Title VII of the Civil Rights Act of 1964	15 or more employees working for 20 or more weeks during previous or current calendar year	Prohibits discrimination based upon race, color, religion, gender, or national origin
Age Discrimination in Employment Act	20 or more employees	Prohibits discrimination against workers older than 40 years of age (but note that an organization may discriminate in favor of older workers)
Employee Retirement Income Security Program (ERISA)	Applies to most private benefit plans (e.g., health and disability, pension, and retirement)	Imposes protections of benefits, including continuation of coverage (COBRA) and confidentiality requirements (HIPPA)
Fair Labor Standards Act	Employees that engage in interstate commerce Organizations that (i) have annual sales or business of over $500,000 or (ii) are hospitals, businesses that provide medical or nursing care for residents, schools, or government agencies	Establishes minimum wage, overtime pay, recordkeeping, and child labor standards
Equal Pay Act	All employers subject to Fair Labor Standards Act	Prohibits pay discrimination based upon gender for work of equal skill, effort, and responsibility
Family and Medical Leave Act	50 or more employees (within a 50 mile radius)	Employees entitled to a total of 12 work weeks of leave due to birth, adoption, or serious health condition of employee, spouse, child, or parent
Federal Fair Credit Reporting Act	All employers	Requires disclosure of use of investigative consumer reports (e.g., credit reports)

Act	Coverage	Description
Federal Protection of Juror's Employment Act	All employers	Prohibits discharging employees for taking time to serve on a jury
Occupational Safety and Health Act	All employers engaged in interstate commerce (including nonprofits)	Requires employers to provide workplaces free from hazards
Older Workers Benefit Protection Act	20 or more employees for at least 20 weeks a year	Prohibits discriminating against workers over 40 years of age in providing benefits (e.g., lowering life insurance benefits for older employees)
Pregnancy Discrimination Act	15 or more employees	Prohibits discrimination based upon an employee's pregnancy, childbirth, or related condition
Immigration Reform and Control Act of 1986	4 or more employees	Prohibits discrimination against workers who are not U.S. citizens or nationals
Vocational Rehabilitation Act of 1973	Recipients of federal funds	Prohibits discrimination on the basis of disability
Genetic Information Nondiscrimination Act	15 or more employees	Prohibits discrimination on the basis of a person's genetic make-up (e.g., family history of disease)
Americans with Disabilities Act	15 or more employees working for 20 or more weeks during previous or current calendar year	Prohibits discrimination based upon disability. If a person can perform a job (with a reasonable accommodation), such person must be treated the same as others

intended to serve as a general guide to the types of laws that may apply to your organization, and should serve as a starting point in discussing compliance with an attorney. The list is not exhaustive, but it will provide a good idea of the type of federal regulations that may apply to your organization.

Conclusion

This chapter opened with a warning about the breadth and scope of employment law. While every effort has been made to cover the more important steps that nonprofits might take to comply with employment laws, there are many areas that simply could not be addressed. The requirements of OSHA, for example, are too complex to adequately cover in this format. Further, this chapter did not mention obligations to provide continuation of certain health benefits under the Consolidated Omnibus Budget Reconciliation Act (COBRA), the mass layoff notice requirements of the Worker Adjustment and Retraining Notification (WARN) Act, or the anti-discrimination requirements and reasonable accommodation provisions of the Americans with Disabilities Act (ADA). This chapter provides a foundation of employment law, empowering nonprofits to recognize issues and identify areas of concern, but it is absolutely imperative for nonprofits to recognize the need for legal counsel. Only an attorney well versed in your industry and local jurisdictional laws will be able to adequately protect your organization.

Discussion Questions

1   Reflect on your own experience as a worker or job candidate. Have you seen instances where legal guidelines presented in this chapter have been violated? If so, what, if any, negative events or changes occurred?
2   Issues of sexual harassment and discrimination are some of the most often litigated issues for employers. What are some actions your employer or volunteer organization has taken to avoid these issues? If they have not, what actions do you suggest they take?
3   Termination of an employee is also often litigated. Have you ever been fired from a job or do you know of someone fired from a job? If so, in what ways was the termination handled well (in a legally defensible way) and in what ways was it handled poorly?

Notes

1   *Dole v. Snell*, 875 F. 2d 802 (10th Cir. 1989).
2   *Sec'y of Labor v. Lauritzen*, 835 F. 2d 1529 (7th Cir. 1987).
3   *E.E.O.C. v. Chestnut Hill Hosp.*, 874 F. Supp. 92, 96 (1995):

> Pennsylvania has adopted the Restatement (Second) of Contracts § 205, which imposes a duty of good faith and fair dealing in the performance of a contract.

The Superior Court has observed that this duty "does not evaporate merely because the contract is an employment contract, and the employee has been held to be an employee at will."

(citations omitted)

Kankonde v. Richmond Cancer & Blood Disease Center, Inc., 2012 WL 423366 (February 8, 2012) ("[Plaintiff] is correct that, unlike with most other contracts, Indiana law will imply a duty of good faith and fair dealing into employment contracts.").

4   *Chambers v. Valley Nat. Bank of Arizona*, 721 F. Supp. 1128, 1131 (1988):

Arizona recognizes three major exceptions to the employer's right to terminate an employee at will[, including] the "implied-in-fact contract" exception, which relies upon proof of an implied promise of continued employment absent just cause for termination, to protect the legitimate expectations of workers, and which may be established by oral representations, a course of dealing, personnel manuals or memoranda.

5   *Stafford v. Purofied Down Products Corp.*, 801 F. Supp. 130, 135 (1992):

[Plaintiff] argues that [Defendant] terminated his employment in bad faith and for the malicious purpose of depriving him of commissions to which he was and would be entitled. Under Seventh Circuit precedent, an employee at will may bring such a claim, despite the lack of an employment contract.

6   The FLSA also protects against pay discrepancies based upon gender and establishes rules for the employment of minors.

7   See www.dol.gov.

References

Chambers v. Valley National Bank of Arizona, 721 F. Supp. 1128, 1131 (United States District Court, D. Arizona, Phoenix Division October 4, 1988).

Dole v. Snell, 875 F.2d 802 (United States Court of Appeals, Tenth Circuit May 23, 1989).

Elaws: Employment Laws Assistance for Workers & Small Businesses – Fair Labor Standards Act Advisor. (n.d.). elaws – employment laws assistance for workers and small businesses. Available at: webapps.dol.gov/elaws/whd/flsa/screen75.asp

Equal Employment Opportunity Commission v. Chestnut Hill Hospital, 874 F. Supp. 92, 96 (United States District Court, E.D. Pennsylvania. January 26, 1995).

Harris, S. D. (2010). Statement of Seth D. Harris Deputy Secretary U.S. Department of Labor. Address presented at Committee on Health, Education, Labor, and Pensions U.S. Senate, Washington, DC. Available at: www.dol.gov/_sec/media/congress/20100617_Harris.htm

Independent Contractor (Self-Employed) or Employee? (2016, July 7 Available at: www.irs.gov/businesses/small-businesses-self-employed/independent-contractor-self-employed-or-employee

Kearney, B. J. (2014). Lionbridge Technologies Case 19-CA-115285 (Advice Memorandum, pp. 1-6) (United States, National Labor Relations Board, Office of the General Counsel).

Secretary of Labor United States Department of Labor v. Lauritzen, 835 F.2d 1529 (United States Court of Appeals, Seventh Circuit. December 15, 1987).

Stafford v. Purofied Down Products Corp., 801 F. Supp. 130, 135 (United States District Court, N.D. Illinois, E.D. September 2, 1992).

U.S. Department of Labor. (n.d.). Compliance Assistance – Wages and the Fair Labor Standards Act (FLSA) – Wage and Hour Division (WHD). Available at: www.dol.gov/whd/flsa

U.S. Equal Employment Opportunity Commission. Facts about Sexual Harassment. (2009, December 14). Available at: www.eeoc.gov/eeoc/publications/upload/fs-sex.pdf

Weil, D. (2015). Administrator's Interpretation No. 2015-1 (The Application of the Fair Labor Standards Act's "Suffer or Permit" Standard in the Identification of Employees Who Are Misclassified as Independent Contractors) (pp. 1–15). Washington, DC: U.S. Department of Labor.

Part II

Building an HRM Infrastructure in a Nonprofit Organization

5

Strategic Human Resource Management

Hans-Gerd Ridder and Alina McCandless Baluch

Introduction

Ask nonprofit managers and they will likely concur that their employees are their most valuable asset—trumping their mission, reputation, or program of activities in importance. Given that nonprofit organizations (NPOs) often provide services to vulnerable groups in society and their employees are engaged in some form of knowledge work, the value attributed to human resources is hardly surprising. Managing and sustaining the commitment of these employees is therefore a central management function in NPOs.

This human resource (HR) function is often carried out by an HR department, or, if the NPO is a small organization, managers or employees themselves are responsible for selecting, socializing, organizing, developing, rewarding, promoting, and even dismissing employees. These HR practices are often understood as "administrative" if they are not very well connected to the organization's goals. On the other hand, the organizational goals may well be strategic. In this case, the NPO would carefully align its strategic goals with the question: "Which HR practices are most important to achieve these goals?" Instead of having repetitive administrative practices, specific practices are developed or supported, whereas other practices are neglected if they are not important for the outlined goals. Consider, for example, NPOs that believe a strong strategic orientation should be transferred from the top down into the organizational departments. HR practices are then evaluated in terms of how they contribute to achieving the nonprofit mission and organizational strategy. Alternatively, NPOs might believe the careful selection and development of employees are central to adapting to their uncertain environments and responding to these challenges. Again, HR practices will be assessed with regard to these goals. These orientations—whether administrative, strategic or employee-centered—influence an organization's HR architecture in which HR practices are, consciously or not, arranged in a specific manner.

Given the importance of the HR function in NPOs, it remains puzzling that there is so little research on strategic human resource management (SHRM) in the nonprofit field and, in turn, how the aforementioned orientations shape the ways in which NPOs carry out their HR function. Therefore, this chapter aims, first, to provide an overview of SHRM in NPOs. Stemming from these foundations, second, we outline a model of HR architectures in NPOs (Ridder, Baluch, & Piening, 2012; Ridder & McCandless, 2010). Third, we review the empirical support for this model of HRM that considers both strategic and HR orientations when designing and implementing HR practices. Finally, we conclude with some lessons learned, which invite the reader to reflect on the practice of managing employees in NPOs.

Strategic Human Resource Management

There is a long tradition in management theory to define objectives, structures, processes, and outcomes of an organization from its strategic perspective. This strategic view can be subdivided into two dominant streams (Tucker & Parker, 2013). Strategy *content* is concerned with the objectives of an organization: Why does the organization exist? What is the mission of the organization? What are the related goals? What are the products and services? What structures are in place for the organization to achieve these goals? What are the expected outcomes of the strategy? The second stream in the strategic perspective is concerned with *processes*. How are strategies *formulated* (top down, bottom up, or both) and how is the strategy *implemented* (top down or participative)? Needless to say, there are numerous theoretical approaches and empirical findings in all of these domains (for an overview, see Ahearne, Lam, & Kraus, 2014; Canales, 2015; Mirabeau & Maguire, 2014).

SHRM, like other functions of the organization, is expected to contribute to the strategic perspective of the organization. Consequently, SHRM can be defined "as the pattern of planned human resource deployments and activities intended to enable an organization to achieve its goals" (Wright & McMahan, 1992, p. 298). This definition has two implications. On the one hand, there must be a strategic orientation of the organization—either consciously or not—and HR has to have knowledge about this orientation. On the other hand, HR must be able to plan how it systematically contributes to the organizational strategy.

Concerning the first implication, the strategy of the organization and HRM have to be aligned, which is usually termed *vertical fit*. Consider, for example, an NPO in elderly care that has a strategy of growth and plans to expand its services beyond the nursing home to offer individualized at-home care services. HR has to systematically develop plans in which it outlines how HRM will contribute to the strategy of expanding its reach into this market. When planning to hire new care personnel, HRM will dictate where, when, and with what qualifications new personnel will be procured. Accordingly, new organizational structures, changes in work organization, and the division of responsibilities will accompany the increase and diversification of care services. Again, HR plans how these changes will support the strategic orientation of the organization. HRM is, in this perspective, a strategic partner (Ulrich, 1997), as all of these plans have not only to be in sync with the overall strategy, but also with other departments, e.g. finance and marketing.

This vertical fit is accompanied by a *horizontal fit*. A horizontal fit is achieved by reconciling the old and new HR practices into a coherent and consistent system. For example, SHRM may entail reacting to a strategy of expansion by implementing a new recruiting strategy. This HR strategy has to be brought in line with the existing practices of socialization, training, development, and promotion. If there is a professional personnel development system in the organization, the organization might hire young, less experienced workers, and offer training systems and promotion opportunities. If there is not a sophisticated personnel development system or even no system at all, the organization might look for more experienced workers in the labor market who fit the jobs without delay. For the latter, it has to be considered that higher wages are likely to attract this clientele. This example highlights that a new HR strategy will require a set of coherent HR practices for recruiting, training, and retaining employees.

This horizontal fit is largely inspired by research that provides evidence that harmonized *HRM bundles* affect better (performance) results than isolated, often contradicting, single HR practices (for an overview, see Jiang, Lepak, Hu, & Baer, 2012). This concept reflects both organizational experience and research that coherent HRM systems are more likely to have the desired effects (Gooderham, Parry, & Ringdal, 2008). For instance, high performance work systems target the synchronization of HR practices in order to meet high standards of productivity. Control systems aim to bundle HR practices that are focused on achieving pre-specified performance measures. Commitment practices are based on the assumption that bundles promoting identification enhance the quality of work and employee retention. Depending on the organization's HR goals (e.g., high performance, control, or commitment), the impact of HR practices on performance will be greater if these practices are complementary, mutually reinforcing, and introduced simultaneously. Needless to say, organizational performance and financial outcomes are the dominant goals in this strategic perspective (Batt & Banerjee, 2012; Boxall, Ang, & Bartram, 2011). SHRM is seen as a management tool that links HR practices to financial outcomes rather than human or social outcomes (Kramar, 2014).

Although the organizational strategy plays a dominant role in defining and planning SHRM, the relationship between strategy, SHRM, and organizational outcomes is multilayered (Kehoe & Wright, 2013). SHRM is concerned with the formulation and implementation of the strategy. In *strategy formulation*, issues have to be considered which might constrain strategic options, such as the labor market, employment laws, or important stakeholders, such as workers' representatives or unions' activities. As a result, the intended HR practices are an amalgamation of the organization's strategic plans and SHRM considerations. In *strategy implementation*, numerous studies demonstrate the often-held assumption that the intended HR practices will succeed. This assumption is risky for two reasons. First, HR processes are often neglected. The implementation of HR practices may fail because of a lack of communication, insufficient preparation, and resistance from managers and employees (Sikora & Ferris, 2014). Even if the intended practices are implemented and communicated to the employees, various deviations in practice by middle managers can produce a gap between intended and implemented practices (Piening, Baluch, & Ridder, 2014). Second, research indicates the perceptions of HR practices among employees differ as well (Bowen & Ostroff, 2004). In particular, when employees receive contradictory messages about their HR practices and these practices are not perceived as fair, employees neither experience consistency nor is consensus enabled by the HR system. As individual employees are subject to different experiences with the HR practices, this ambiguous situation can lead to confusion, disillusionment, and other negative reactions (Baluch, 2016). HR practices are more likely to take proper effect if employees are aware of the practices, accept them, and interpret them similarly as both useful for the organization and their own jobs.

While the aforementioned strategic perspective emphasizes the dominance of the strategic goals of an organization, the *Resource-Based View* highlights a different orientation. The Resource-Based View does not concentrate on external factors such as market position and competitors, but focuses instead on the question of which of the organization's resources are valuable enough to serve as a foundation of competitive advantage. These resources might be natural resources to which a competitor does not have access, but for the majority of organizations these resources are within a range of financial, structural, organizational, and human resources. They provide competitive advantage if they are of value, rare, non-imitable by the competitor, and are non-substitutable (Barney, 1991). While these resources build the foundation of competitive advantage, capabilities are still needed to deploy these resources in organizational processes. If the environment is turbulent, these capabilities are made up of dynamic processes that build, integrate, and reconfigure internal and external competencies in addressing the changing environment (Teece, Pisano, & Shuen, 1997). This resource-based and capabilities perspective has heavily influenced theoretical development in SHRM. Human resources are perfect candidates to be viewed as valuable, rare, non-imitable, and substitutable if they are scarce, firm-specific, and possess non-imitable knowledge (Shaw, Park, & Kim, 2013). The investment in people is one of the most promising means to achieving competitive advantage as knowledge can be built, integrated, coordinated, and adapted. Organizations consider that their mission, goals, products, and services have to attract highly motivated people. HR practices build on that orientation by carefully investing into training, work organization, and incentives that build value, rareness, and inimitability in the long run.

Both the strategic and resource-based approaches were developed in the domain of private sector organizations and the question arises whether these orientations are adequate tools for NPOs. Of course, NPOs are different; they often operate under social, religious, environmental, or political missions, have challenging tasks mostly related to people and the external operating environment, while facing scarce resources, multiple stakeholders, and institutional constraints. From a resource and strategic perspective, however, all of these circumstances have to be considered when deploying scarce resources to achieve defined goals. According to a resource-based and capabilities view, NPOs possess valuable resources as seen in the research about the specificity of the HR capital pool (Ridder, Baluch, & Piening, 2012). Such NPOs emphasize the unique characteristics of their intrinsically motivated and often highly committed workforce when investing in and developing their employees, as we discuss in the section on the conceptual model of HR architecture in NPOs.

Strategic Human Resource Management in Nonprofit Organizations

Our knowledge of the extent and use of SHRM in NPOs still remains scarce, with only a few empirical studies shedding light on this issue. With regard to overall strategic planning in NPOs, studies highlight the differences in the generation and implementation of strategies in NPOs. McHatton, Bradshaw, Gallagher and Reeves (2011) emphasize the importance of membership involvement and stakeholder consensus in their case study of strategy formulation in a nonprofit professional organization in education. Considering the implementation of strategy, Tucker and Parker (2013) investigate how NPOs use management control systems. Drawing on interviews conducted in Australian NPOs, they conclude that control systems in implementing strategies are similar to private organizations but for different reasons: "institutional pressures are instrumental in driving control processes in relation to nonprofit strategy" (Tucker & Parker, 2013, p. 101). These studies suggest that formulating organizational strategy in NPOs entails participatory and democratic processes of negotiation among diverse constituencies. At the same time, isomorphic tendencies in the uncertain environment lead NPOs to control and monitor their strategy to ensure it is properly enacted.

In research examining SHRM in NPOs, Guo, Brown, Ashcraft, Yoshioka, and Dong (2011) used survey data to investigate the organizational and contextual determinants of SHRM across a sample of 229 NPOs. The authors found that NPOs that are larger, technologically experienced, and that cooperated with independent contractors are more likely to apply SHRM. Smaller NPOs tend to introduce SHRM if they are affiliates of national organizations. Additional research confirms that using professional managers as well as internal or external consultants with HRM expertise promoted fit and flexibility in HR practices of NPOs (Akingbola, 2013b). Regarding the dimensions of both strategy-focused and flexibility-focused HRM, Akingbola's (2013b) case study of two NPOs points to evidence of both vertical and horizontal fit. HRM was aligned with strategy to achieve fit through practices such as strategic recruitment, employee involvement, managerial training, and performance management, yet few HR practices consistent with indicators of resource and coordination flexibility were implemented. Taking the wider context into account, Walk, Schinnenburg, and Handy's (2014) case study in a large German NPO sheds light on the dominant factors influencing SHRM. Based on interviews with HR managers and employees, they identified the overwhelming perception of environmental influences, especially the policy environment and dramatic changes in labor supply. Themes regarding the architecture of SHRM in NPOs underscore the dominance of the overall pressure exerted by the external environment. Walk et al. conclude: "Thus, the interaction of external changes on internal processes exacerbates the influence of external factors and hinders the development and implementation of comprehensive HR bundles" (p. 1016).

As mentioned above, we do not have a clear picture of SHRM in NPOs yet. The prior studies take place across different countries and are usually based on small samples within various NPOs, using a range of methods. The non-profit field would thus still benefit from theory building and empirical research on SHRM. In this vein, Akingbola (2013a) provides a model with a twofold purpose. The model is developed as a basis for further research. At the same time, it offers nonprofit managers a framework to plan and implement SHRM. The model is theoretically founded and its core essentials consider the specifics of what we know about NPOs. It contains the following three aggregates (Akingbola, 2013a):

- A social mission is the foundation of the goals of the NPO. These goals are mediated by the resource base of the NPO leading to the NPO strategy. This strategy is interrelated with principles of the NPO. These principles are defined as "the overarching values, beliefs and approach adopted by management and/or board of directors in the design of its NHRM system" (Akingbola, 2013a, p. 223).
- The resulting HR policies and practices are embedded in interactions and processes. Akingbola (2013a) delineates four main parts of this interaction. In line with the literature, HR policies and practices interact heavily with the competency and behavior of managers, organization characteristics, funders and government, and system-level characteristics, such as social legitimacy and commitment of the employees. System-level characteristics and contextual variables drive HR policies and practices.
- HR policies and practices result in attitudes and skills of the workforce of the NPO, which finally lead to nonprofit performance.

This model considers the research on NPOs at length and its dual character (guidance for research, framework for managers) has several implications. First, research indicates that advanced SHRM is more or less a domain of large organizations with professional HR staff or supported by consultants (Ulrich, 1997). The sparse research in NPOs seems to support this tendency (Akingbola, 2013b; Guo et al., 2011). Second, even large NPOs suffer from external pressures that influence the use of HR practices. The study by Walk et al. (2014) demonstrates how changes in legislation and dramatic developments in the labor market can erode strategic thinking in NPOs. Therefore, and third, managers confronted with these constraints and pressures may interpret SHRM as too distant from their reality. Finally, the research shows there is no single consensus regarding the definition of nonprofit performance (Ridder et al., 2012). Helmig, Ingerfurth, and Pinz (2014) demonstrated in their literature review that this dependent variable has different theoretical foundations, definitions, and measures. Their study revealed that although the mission of NPOs is at the core of strategic models, the development of the dependent variable "mission accomplishment," as a natural result of the strategic process, is often neglected in research.

Given these implications and the opportunities they bear for further research, we draw on an analytical framework of HRM that affords us a more nuanced view of SHRM. Instead of outlining a normative model, we present an approach that acknowledges the wide spectrum of (S)HRM in NPOs and its implications for the design and implementation of HR practices.

A Conceptual Model of HR Architectures in NPOs

In order to better understand HR practices in NPOs and what shapes these practices, we developed a conceptual model of HR architectures in prior work (Ridder et al., 2012; Ridder & McCandless, 2010). This model entails four steps:

1 Drawing on the aforementioned theoretical perspectives of strategic HRM and resource based HRM and in line with the state of the art in nonprofit research, we derived two dimensions as the basis of a typology of HRM:

    i   The first dimension is developed from *strategic HRM theory*. In essence, this theoretical view focuses on a strategic perspective in which the environment (markets, competitors) plays a dominant role. Accordingly, organization combines observation of the external environment anticipation of future opportunities and constraints with internal ures and processes (vertical fit). Adapting these structures and ses has to be aligned with the existing HR practices, considering e culture and climate of the organization (horizontal fit). Research s demonstrates that not only markets and competitors play an ng role regarding the strategic perspective, but this strategic is also driven by their values, mission, and the expectations, d goals of internal and external stakeholders, such as funders Beattie, Livingstone, & Munro, 2001; Ridder & McCandless,

2010). In contrast to private sector organizations, the need to maximize shareholder value is absent; instead NPOs must carefully identify the needs and demands of their stakeholders and align these expectations with the mission and values of the NPO. Strategic challenges arise when, for example, the core mission faces pressure from competition among NPOs, public, or private organizations, scarce resources and the pluralistic environment. Consequently, we expect a wide range of strategic responses to these challenges, resulting in considerable variety in the use of HR practices. We refer to this as an organization's *strategic orientation* (Ridder & McCandless, 2010).

ii The second dimension stems from the *Resource-Based View* (Penrose, [1959] 1980; Wernerfelt, 1984; Barney, 1991). This perspective is less concerned with markets and more with the identification of valuable resources within the organization as a basis for competitive advantage. As such, it serves as a fruitful approach given that nonprofit research suggests the importance of internal resources, e.g. employees of NPOs have a mission–driven attachment to their organization (Brown & Yoshioka, 2003; Kim & Lee, 2007). In contrast to for-profit organizations, the specific characteristics of employees in NPOs entail their acceptance of intrinsic and relational incentives in place of extrinsic rewards (Borzaga & Depedri, 2005). Given this valuable advantage, the resource orientation implies that NPOs can have a competitive advantage due to employees' intrinsic motives and capabilities. HR practices that emphasize employee engagement, empowerment, and well-being instead of rewards that are performance-based as in private organizations are thus the basis to manage the organization's challenges through autonomous and highly motivated employees. As a result, we refer to this as the *HR orientation*. Accordingly, HRM in NPOs is influenced by the guiding principle that the motivations and needs of employees have to be considered as the basis of HR practices (Ridder et al., 2012).

2 In Ridder and McCandless (2010) we maintain that the strategic and HR orientations are likely to reflect a broad variety of characteristics. To cap this variety, we envisioned each of the dimensions along a conti NPOs differ widely in their missions and goals as well as in th resources. As a consequence, the strategic and HR orientation from a low to a high value. Taking into account the variety which organizations adopt and implement a range of HR p dimensions are not understood to be mutually exclusive.

3 Juxtaposing these two dimensions with different charac continuum, we developed a typology of HR architectures. HR architectures as an overall internally consistent and coh structure, which is a multi-level construct that encomp such as HR principles, policies, programs, practices, and Boyles, 2007; Becker & Gerhart, 1996). The combi

dimensions revealed four quadrants (Ridder et al., 2012), which are depicted in Figure 5.1.

The ideal-type "Administrative HRM" is scored as the minimum value on both dimensions.[1] A low HR orientation entails that these practices are not specifically aligned to the needs and values of the employees (Conway & Monks, 2008; Cunningham, 2010a). Due to the low degree of strategic orientation, HR practices are often merely copied from the for-profit sector without a synergistic relationship to the existing HR practices or the organizational strategy (Akingbola, 2006; Cunningham, 2001). In contrast, "Motivational HRM" marks the minimum value along the strategic orientation and the maximum value of the HR orientation. These NPOs can be assumed to focus on the internal development of employees, promotion, and participation to elicit and maintain their commitment to the organizational values and mission (Benz, 2005; Borzaga & Depedri, 2005). Furthermore, "Strategic HRM" is scored high on the strategic and low on HR orientation. Due to a strong emphasis on strategic goals related to different external stakeholders combined with a low focus on the specific needs of the employees, investments in human capital are selective and focused on the allocation of rewards based on measurable output criteria (Brandl & Güttel, 2007; De Prins & Henderickx, 2007). Finally, "Values-based HRM" is scored as the maximum value on both dimensions and represents NPOs in which HRM is driven by the core values of the mission and by the employees' strengths (Frumkin & Andre-Clark, 2000). Investments in HR that support the acquisition, development, and retention of highly qualified and satisfied employees are not only seen as a means to achieve the organization's strategic objectives but also as a primary goal in and of itself (Ridder & McCandless, 2010).

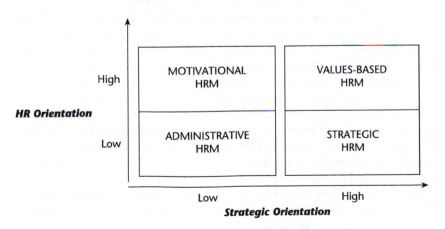

Figure 5.1 Types of HR architecture in nonprofit organizations

Source: Reprinted from Ridder et al. (2012). Copyright (2012), with permission from Elsevier.

4   Lastly, we propose that each of the types will have different HR architectures that, in turn, lead to variations in performance in NPOs (Ridder et al., 2012). HR practices are expected to impact organizational outcomes (e.g. service quality or productivity) through the mediating effect of employee outcomes (e.g. employee commitment and satisfaction) (Boselie, Dietz, & Boon, 2005; Dyer & Reeves, 1995; Paauwe, 2009). Depending on the strategic and HR orientations, the four types of HRM in NPOs are likely to display different performance outcomes.

Take, as an example, the negative effects on employees' attitudes and behaviors from a low HR orientation which is marked by short-term contracts and HR practices based on control rather than autonomy, thereby signaling a low level of support to employees (Allen, Shore, & Griffeth, 2003; Piening et al., 2014). In contrast, employees view HRM as supportive and fair when it is aligned with the organization's model of care, as exemplified in the values-based HR architecture (high HR orientation and high strategic orientation) (Eaton, 2000).

Empirical Evidence on HR Architecture in NPOs

To the best of our knowledge, two empirical studies have been conducted thus far on the basis of this model. In their multiple case study of NPOs providing health and social services in Germany, Ridder, Piening, and Baluch (2012) demonstrate that HR practices in *administrative HRM* signify a bureaucratic HR mode that addresses basic HR functions such as employment contracts, terms and conditions, and union–employer relations. Given the external demands these NPOs face, they adopt a cost-covering orientation that seeks to avoid negative HR outcomes. The study also reveals that in *motivational HRM*, the organizational mission is translated into humanistic principles about employees, leading to an emphasis in the HR mode on investing in employees as valuable individuals in and of themselves. The performance outcomes differ from administrative HRM, however, as these NPOs remain mission-driven, focusing on service users' needs (Ridder, Piening, & Baluch, 2012). In *strategic HRM*, the authors observe that HRM is aligned with strategy that is driven by market logics. HRM and organizational strategy are synergistic. Strategic HRM proactively seeks opportunities in the external environment. Long-term strategic development is generated in part by the employees themselves. The authors observe that multiple, often competing goals around HRM arise from varying strategic priorities that might be in tension. As a result, differences in strategic perspectives are found to result in various HR outcome goals.

Finally, Ridder, Piening and Baluch (2012) observe that NPOs with *values-based HRM* embrace both the market-related demands of their operating environment and the pressures stemming from organizational values. A values-based HR architecture thus combines the two poles of upholding strategic goals and employees' terms and conditions at the same time. In contrast to motivational and strategic HR architectures, values are clearly translated into strategic goals. As a result, positive employee outcomes are accomplished through balancing the mission with strategic imperatives to invest in the workforce. This balancing is achieved, for example, by viewing strategic outcomes as a vehicle to reinvest in developing and retaining employees.

Drawing on the typology by Ridder et al. (2012) as well, Walk et al. (2014) empirically examine the HRM types in their case study of HR managers and employees from a large German NPO. Identifying dominant themes within the quadrants, their interviews reveal the overwhelming perception that NPOs have to consider external pressures. By explicitly addressing these influences, the authors extend the original model. With regard to the typology, the following main themes emerged.

In *administrative HR*, the interviewees perceived three themes as critical: short-term employment contracts, cost-cutting strategies, and compensation. There is a striking difference between managers' and employees' perceptions of compensation levels as employees are dissatisfied while employers perceive this level as fair. Cost-cutting strategies are the answer to the dual problem of increasing tasks and shrinking budgets. Finally, short-term contracts are used as a means to reduce costs in anticipation of an uncertain future. In contrast, the main themes in *strategic HR* are the absence of strategic practices and professional development. Both time pressure and an uncertain future hinder any long-term strategic planning. Professional development is needed for managers as well as for workers (career planning, professional qualification). In *motivational HR*, working conditions, on-the-job-training, and appraisals are dominant themes on the agenda. Given the intrinsic motivation of employees in NPOs, good working conditions, especially the work climate, are seen as critical for employees. Although managers consider this need, it is at the same time contradicted by the decrease in public funding. On-the-job training is regarded as important in this orientation but conflicts with day-to-day routines and the lack of time. Although appraisal reviews are highly valued in the orientation, their extent and quality are below these expectations. Finally, in *values-based HR*, religious values and organizational identification are highlighted. Although these values play an important role in this orientation, they are weakened by external pressures.

To summarize, these few empirical studies using the model support our assumptions about the heterogeneity of HRM in NPOs. It could be argued that the empirical data in the study of Walk, Schinnenburg, and Handy (2014) centers on one large NPO in which the pressures facing its strategic orientation stem from the same environment. But even with this shared background, the spectrum of perceptions and reactions is impressive. NPOs do not respond automatically or similarly to decreasing budgets, increasing competition, and mounting tasks. Instead, their interpretation of the current situation and the anticipation of the future vary, leading to differences in strategic thinking and acting.

When the range of NPOs is broader, as demonstrated in the case study by Ridder, Piening, and Baluch (2012), these variations in organizational responses can be aggregated into clusters of strategic thinking. Of course, a dichotomy still occurs with NPOs sticking strictly to their HR orientation, and not surprisingly, with NPOs that believe that only a strategic orientation in line with for-profit practices will guarantee their survival. At the same time, a cluster emerges in which NPOs are configuring their HR practices by both adopting a proactive approach in dealing with external constraints to achieve quality in the competitive market, while attempting to respect their internal convictions in managing their employees. Rather than financial pressures undermining the role of HRM (Cunningham, 2010b), HRM is viewed as an integral part of the organizational strategy. Consequently, Ridder, Piening, and Baluch (2012) argue that this "third way" of configuring HRM represents a specific combination of these two orientations. They conclude that this third way may serve as a means for NPOs to strategically position themselves as distinct from the for-profit competitors who are moving into traditional areas of nonprofit service provision with lower costs (Chew, 2010).

Lessons Learned for the Practice of Managing Human Resources in NPOs

What are the lessons learned for HRM in NPOs? From the discussion above, it becomes evident that there are not any best practices that allow NPOs to move from strategy to HRM to outcomes, such as satisfied employees, low turnover, mission attainment, service quality, or other relevant nonprofit performance measures. The research suggests instead that there are different opportunities and pressures leading to various perceptions and responses. Therefore, NPOs first need a realistic diagnosis of the HR architecture within their organization. Second, this provides the basis for either professionalizing this architecture or, third, shifting to the desired HRM type. We will now discuss these lessons learned for the practice of managing human resources in greater depth.

1. Aligning HR Architecture with the Strategic Orientation of the NPO

Like all organizations, NPOs have to analyze their HR architecture and their relationship to the overall strategic orientation of the organization. Several proposals in the literature provide guidance on how to conduct this diagnosis (Arthur & Boyles, 2007; Becker & Huselid, 2006; Colbert, 2004; Lepak & Snell, 1999; 2002). Adapted from Arthur and Boyles (2007), a diagnosis can be based on the following:

- *HR principles* pertain to the choice about which policies and practices are in use in the organization. In NPOs, missions and values are of utmost importance and the organization must clarify what are the guiding principles for their HR architecture.
- *HR policies* are aligned with organizational goals or objectives (staffing, training, rewards, and job design). Organizations have to decide whether these practices are focused on performance, productivity, or other financial

variables. Particularly in NPOs these practices are the basis for individual commitment as well.

- *HR programs* entail the assessment of whether bundles of internally consistent HR programs and practices exist. The organization will also evaluate the relationship between these programs and the desired employee-related outcomes (e.g. satisfaction, retention).
- *HR climate:* The organization evaluates whether there is a climate in place that supports the employees in collectively perceiving and interpreting the HR principles, politics, programs, and practices as intended.

Assessing these levels and their coherence will reveal the type of HRM in the NPO. The next lesson learned concerns whether this HR architecture is adequate for achieving the organization's goals or has to be adapted.

2. Professionalizing the HR Architecture

Once a consistent set of principles, policies, programs, and practices exists, the question of the quality still remains. Gratton and Truss (2003) highlight that there is often a gap between rhetoric and reality, i.e. the practice of HRM. For example, even if the NPO has come to the conclusion that administrative HRM is an adequate type for the organization, this orientation can still be professionalized. A low orientation in administrative HRM will leave the tasks to managers with—in the view of the organization—more important responsibilities. HRM is seen as a bureaucratic sideline job with lower skills in this realm and a tendency toward bureaucratic routines, especially in rewards. In such cases, the organization can consider outsourcing its HR function to professionalize it, or if part of a large NPO, joining a shared services center that bundles all HR needs of the different branches of the organization.

The other extreme is also valuable; the organization might intend strategic HRM to match the goals of NPO. The HR department may have precisely outlined what programs and practices exist and have to be added in order to reach the desired goals, but the NPO may be neither willing nor capable of (financially) supporting the necessary programs and practices. This exemplifies a strategic HR rhetoric. Either way, the message is that not every NPO can transform its existing HRM into a different HR architecture. Yet, if equipped with an analysis of the existing type of HRM, NPOs can more precisely estimate which programs and practices fit the type and, in turn, how to professionalize the respective HR function.

3. Shifting the HR Architecture

Lessons one and two may reveal the organization needs to shift its HRM type (Lepak & Snell, 1999; 2002). Again, there are no best practices for achieving this shift. What we have gleaned from the outlined empirical investigations is that

NPOs are faced with the challenge of combining strategic orientations and HR orientations under difficult competitive environments. Although the values-based quadrant is not imbued with a normative connotation, this HR architecture represents such efforts of NPOs. The combination points the NPO toward two vital aspects. With regard to the *content* of HRM, the translation of values into strategic goals leads to balancing in the organization's HRM principles, programs, and practices. This desired balancing of values with strategic requirements is not an easy task, but an ongoing struggle especially in changing environments (Swanson, 2013).

The second aspect refers to the *process* of implementing new HR practices. As indicated in recent research, employees' perception and interpretation of HRM matter for employee-related and performance outcomes (Baluch, Salge, & Piening, 2013). Intended HR practices are often mistaken for the actual practices employees experience daily. Top managers might believe adequate programs and practices are in place, only to find these are implemented differently by middle managers and heterogeneously interpreted by employees. Such research underscores that professionally shifting the HR architecture entails carefully observing its implementation and continually monitoring its further development. Regarding employees' experience of implemented HRM in NPOs, research by Piening, Baluch, and Ridder (2014, p. 17) demonstrates "the visibility of HR practices, consistency of HRM messages, continuity of usage of HR practices, and fairness of HR practices as the relevant categories that characterize the way employees perceive the organization's HR practices."

In sum, these three lessons invite nonprofit managers to reflect on their practice of HRM. All of these efforts require practitioners to devote their attention to HR processes with regard to implementation and consider the perceptions and acceptance of managers and employees, since these aspects have consequences for the way HR practices are used and responded to in the NPO.

Discussion Questions

Think of a nonprofit organization you have recently encountered. This might be, for example, a charity, church, nonprofit nursing home, or hospital you volunteered at, a nonprofit advocacy organization you donated to or an NGO you heard about in the media. Consider the following three questions with regard to your chosen organization:

1   What is the NPO's strategic orientation? Address the ways in which nonprofit managers can ensure the organization's HRM is aligned with its strategy.
2   Discuss why the NPO might want to pursue administrative HRM. In which scenarios might strategic HRM or motivational HRM be more appropriate?
3   Debate whether values-based HRM is achievable, given the constraints that NPOs are operating under. How might the NPO shift its HRM to develop and implement a values-based HRM?

Note

1   This paragraph was reprinted from Ridder, Piening, and Baluch (2012) with permission of International Society for Third-Sector Research and Johns Hopkins University. *Voluntas: International Journal of Voluntary and Nonprofit Organizations* is the official journal of the International Society for Third-Sector Research.

References

Ahearne, M., Lam, S. K., & Kraus. F. (2014). Performance impact of middle managers' adaptive strategy implementation: The role of social capital. *Strategic Management Journal, 35*, 68–87.

Akingbola, K. (2006). Strategy and human resource management in nonprofit organizations: Evidence from Canada. *International Journal of Human Resource Management, 17*, 1707–1725.

Akingbola, K. (2013a). A model of strategic nonprofit human resource management. *Voluntas: International Journal of Voluntary and Nonprofit Organizations, 24*, 214–240.

Akingbola, K. (2013b). Contingency, fit and flexibility of HRM in nonprofit organizations. *Employee Relations, 35*, 479–494.

Allen, D. G., Shore, L. M., & Griffeth, R. W. (2003). The role of perceived organizational support and supportive human resource practices in the turnover process. *Journal of Management, 29*, 99–118.

Arthur, J. B. & Boyles, T. (2007). Validating the human resource system structure: A levels-based strategic HRM approach. *Human Resource Management Review, 17*, 77–92.

Baluch, A. M. (2016). Employee perceptions of HRM and well-being in nonprofit organizations: Unpacking the unintended. *The International Journal of Human Resource Management*. Available at: http://dx.doi.org/10.1080/09585192.2015.1136672

Baluch, A. M., Salge, T. O., & Piening, E. P. (2013). Untangling the relationship between HRM and hospital performance: The mediating role of attitudinal and behavioural HR outcomes. *The International Journal of Human Resource Management, 24*, 3038–3061.

Barney, J. B. (1991). Firm resources and sustained competitive advantage. *Journal of Management, 17*, 99–120.

Batt, R. & Banerjee, M. (2012). The scope and trajectory of strategic HR research: Evidence from American and British journals. *The International Journal of Human Resource Management, 23*, 1739–1762.

Becker, B. & Gerhart, B. (1996). The impact of human resource management on organizational performance: Progress and prospects. *Academy of Management Journal, 39*, 779–801.

Becker, B. E. & Huselid, M. A. (2006). Strategic human resources management: Where do we go from here? *Journal of Management, 32*, 898–925.

Benz, M. (2005). Not for the profit, but for the satisfaction? Evidence on worker well-being in non-profit firms. *Kyklos, 58*, 155–176.

Borzaga, C. & Depedri, S. (2005). Interpersonal relations and job satisfaction: Some empirical results in social and community care services. In B. Gui & R. Sugden (Eds.), *Economics and Social Interaction: Accounting for Interpersonal Relations* (pp. 132–153). Cambridge: Cambridge University Press.

Boselie, P., Dietz, G., & Boon, C. (2005). Commonalities and contradictions in HRM and performance research. *Human Resource Management Journal, 15*, 67–94.

Bowen, D. E. & Ostroff, C. (2004). Understanding HRM–firm performance linkages: The role of the "strength" of the HRM system. *Academy of Management Review, 29*, 203–221.

Boxall, P., Ang, S. H., & Bartram, T. (2011). Analysing the 'black box' of HRM: Uncovering HR goals, mediators, and outcomes in a standardized service environment. *Journal of Management Studies, 48*, 1504–1532.

Brandl, J. & Güttel, W. H. (2007). Organizational antecedents of pay-for-performance systems in nonprofit organizations. *Voluntas: International Journal of Voluntary and Nonprofit Organizations, 18*, 176–199.

Brown, W. A. & Yoshioka, C. F. (2003). Mission attachment and satisfaction as factors in employee retention. *Nonprofit Management & Leadership, 14*, 5–18.

Canales, I. J. (2015). Sources of selection in strategy making. *Journal of Management Studies, 52*, 1–31.

Chew, C. (2010). Strategic positioning and organizational adaptation in social enterprise subsidiaries of voluntary organizations: An examination of community interest companies with charitable origins. *Public Management Review, 12*, 609–634.

Colbert, B. A. (2004). The complex resource-based view: Implications for theory and practice in strategic human resource management. *Academy of Management Review, 29*, 341–358.

Conway, E. & Monks, K. (2008). HR practices and commitment to change: An employee level analysis. *Human Resource Management Journal, 18*, 72–89.

Cunningham, I. (2001) Sweet charity! Managing employee commitment in the UK voluntary sector. *Employee Relations, 23*, 226–240.

Cunningham, I. (2010a). Drawing from a bottomless well? Exploring the resilience of value-based psychological contracts in voluntary organizations. *The International Journal of Human Resource Management, 21*, 699–719.

Cunningham, I. (2010b). The HR function in purchaser–provider relationships: Insights from the UK voluntary sector. *Human Resource Management Journal, 20*, 189–205.

Dyer, L. & Reeves, T. (1995). Human resource strategies and firm performance: What do we know and where do we need to go? *International Journal of Human Resource Management, 6*, 656–70.

Eaton, S. C. (2000). Beyond 'unloving care': Linking human resource management and patient care quality in nursing homes. *International Journal of Human Resource Management, 11*, 591–616.

Frumkin, P. & Andre-Clark, A. (2000). When missions, markets, and politics collide: Values and strategy in the nonprofit human services. *Nonprofit and Voluntary Sector Quarterly, 29*, 141–163.

Gooderham, P., Parry, E., & Ringdal, K. (2008). The impact of bundles of strategic human resource management practices on the performance of European firms. *The International Journal of Human Resource Management, 19*, 2041–2056.

Gratton, L. & Truss, C. (2003). The three-dimensional people strategy: Putting human resources policies into action. *The Academy of Management Executive, 17*, 74–86.

Guo, C., Brown, W. A., Ashcraft, R. F., Yoshioka, C. F., & Dong, H. K. D. (2011). Strategic human resources management in nonprofit organizations. *Review of Public Personnel Administration, 31*, 248–269.

Helmig, B., Ingerfurth, S., & Pinz, A. (2014). Success and failure of nonprofit organizations: Theoretical foundations, empirical evidence, and future research. *Voluntas: International Journal of Voluntary and Nonprofit Organizations, 25*, 1509–1538.

Jiang, K., Lepak, D. P., Hu, J., & Baer, J. C. (2012). How does human resource management influence organizational outcomes? A meta-analytic investigation of mediating mechanisms. *Academy of Management Journal, 55*, 1264–1294.

Kehoe, R. R. & Wright, P. M. (2013). The impact of high performance human resource practices on employees' attitudes and behaviors. *Journal of Management, 39*, 366–391.

Kellock, H., Beattie, G. R. S., Livingstone, R., & Munro, P. (2001). Change, HRM and the voluntary sector. *Employee Relations, 23*, 240–256.

Kim, S. E. & Lee, J. W. (2007). Is mission attachment an effective management tool for employee retention? An empirical analysis of a nonprofit human services agency. *Review of Public Personnel Administration*, 27, 227–248.

Kramar, R. (2014). Beyond strategic human resource management: Is sustainable human resource management the next approach? *The International Journal of Human Resource Management*, 25, 1069–1089.

Kuvaas, B. (2008). An exploration of how the employee–organization relationship affects the linkage between perception of developmental human resource practices and employee outcomes. *Journal of Management Studies*, 45, 1–25.

Lepak, D. P. & Snell, S. A. (1999). The human resource architecture: Toward a theory of human capital allocation and development. *Academy of Management Review*, 24, 31–48.

Lepak, D. P. & Snell, S. A. (2002). Examining the human resource architecture: The relationships among human capital, employment, and human resource configurations. *Journal of Management*, 28, 517–543.

McHatton, P. A., Bradshaw, W., Gallagher, P. A., & Reeves, R. (2011). Results from a strategic planning process: Benefits for a nonprofit organization. *Nonprofit Management & Leadership*, 22, 233–249.

Mirabeau, L. & Maguire S. (2014). From autonomous strategic behavior to emergent strategy. *Strategic Management Journal*, 35, 1202–1229.

Paauwe, J. (2009). HRM and performance: Achievements, methodological issues and prospects. *Journal of Management Studies*, 46, 129–142.

Penrose, E. T. (1980 [1959]). *The theory of the growth of the firm*. Oxford: Oxford University Press.

Piening, E. P., Baluch, A. M., & Ridder, H.-G. (2014). Mind the intended–implemented gap: Understanding employees' perceptions of HRM. *Human Resource Management*, 53, 545–567.

Prins, P. de & Henderickx, E. (2007). HRM effectiveness in older people's and nursing homes: The search for best (quality) practices. *Nonprofit and Voluntary Sector Quarterly*, 87, 1–23.

Ridder, H.-G., Baluch, A. M., & Piening, E. P. (2012). The whole is more than the sum of its parts? How HRM is configured in nonprofit organizations and why it matters. *Human Resource Management Review*, 22, 1–14.

Ridder, H.-G. & McCandless, A. (2010). Influences on the architecture of human resource management in nonprofit organizations: An analytical framework. *Nonprofit and Voluntary Sector Quarterly*, 39, 124–141.

Ridder, H.-G., Piening, E. P., & Baluch, A. M. (2012). The third way reconfigured: How and why nonprofit organizations are shifting their human resource management. *Voluntas: International Journal of Voluntary and Nonprofit Organizations*, 23, 605–635.

Shaw, J. D., Park, T.-Y., & Kim, E. (2013). A resource-based perspective on human capital losses, HRM investments, and organizational performance. *Strategic Management Journal*, 34, 572–589.

Sikora, D. M. & Ferris, G. R. (2014). Strategic human resource practice implementation: The critical role of line management. *Human Resource Management Review*, 24, 271–281.

Swanson, L. A. (2013). A strategic engagement framework for nonprofits. *Nonprofit Management & Leadership*, 23, 303–323.

Teece, D. J., Pisano, G., & Shuen, A. (1997). Dynamic capabilities and strategic management. *Strategic Management Journal*, 18, 509–533.

Tucker, B. P. & Parker, L. D. (2013). Managerial control and strategy in nonprofit organizations: Doing the right things for the wrong reasons? *Nonprofit Management & Leadership*, 24, 87–107.

Ulrich, D. (1997). *Human resource champions: The next agenda for adding value and delivering results*. Boston: Harvard Business School Press.

Walk, M., Schinnenburg, H., & Handy, F. (2014). Missing in action: Strategic human resource management in German nonprofits. *Voluntas: International Journal of Voluntary and Nonprofit Organizations, 25*, 991–1021.

Wernerfelt, B. (1984). A resource-based view of the firm. *Strategic Management Journal, 5*, 171–180.

Wright, P. M. & McMahan, G. C. (1992). Theoretical perspectives for strategic human resource management. *Journal of Management, 18*, 295–320.

6

Recruitment and Selection for Nonprofit Organizations

Rikki Abzug

Introduction

As Millennials and all generations of workers interested in public service increasingly focus their job search efforts on the nonprofit sector as their arena for employment, they create an actual pool of human resources from which organizations may choose. As such, organizations of the nonprofit sector are increasingly (and often gratefully) challenged to upgrade their recruitment and selection processes to ensure fit. Strategic nonprofit recruitment and selection are so important because research continually highlights the relationship between employment practices (such as recruitment and selection) and both organizational performance and individual well-being in the nonprofit sector (Haley-Lock & Kruzich, 2008).

Indeed, nonprofit practitioners and academics alike care deeply about both nonprofit performance and the benefits to those who labor to fulfill the organizational mission. To those ends, recruitment and selection are studied as both independent variables correlated with organizational and individual sustainability/well-being, as well as dependent variables that, themselves, may be sustained and enhanced. In this chapter, we review the literature on nonprofit recruitment and selection as both independent and dependent variables in order to glean best practices for sustaining and enhancing recruitment and selection in the sector, and, through that, organizational and individual effectiveness.

The beginning of the chapter is also a good place to remind the reader of the importance and uniqueness of recruitment and selection to organizations of the nonprofit sector (Watson & Abzug, 2016). Haiven argued: "The axiom of recruiting the 'right' people making an organization and recruiting the 'wrong' ones breaking it has special significance in the voluntary and nonprofit sector for three reasons" (2004, p. 83). These reasons were that: (1) the relative scarcity of funding in the sector puts excessive pressure on managers to ensure hiring decisions do not lead to wasted resources; (2) choosing experienced people is essential to professionalism in the sector; and (3) the sector's relatively poor-paying and thankless jobs need to be supplemented by amicable work environments that can only be achieved through careful recruitment and selection processes. Just as Haiven painted unique recruitment and selection in the sector as a burden on nonprofit human resource professionals, Watson and Abzug (2016) highlighted the distinctiveness in a more positive way. Noting the primacy of mission focus in nonprofits, Watson and Abzug argued most staff are attracted to nonprofits because they are motivated by their organization's mission. Thus compared to their for-profit counterparts, "nonprofits have an extremely powerful advantage in all aspects of their human resource systems," and they regard human resources "as the central conduit through which organizations succeed" (pp. 599–600).

Thus, nonprofit recruitment and selection are unique on both the dependent and independent variable dimensions because, respectively, the nonprofit mission is a particularly effective recruitment and selection tool (see, also, Brown & Yoshioka, 2003), and because nonprofit staff who are effectively recruited and selected directly effectuate societally beneficial organizational performance. Of course, despite the uniqueness we often observe and, perhaps, more often, extol, there is also tremendous overlap in the philosophies and practices of recruitment and selection across the sectors. In this review, we recognize and draw inspiration from the latter (the overlap), but stay focused, where we can, on the former (the nonprofit novelty).

And yet, before we dive in, a caveat derived from the tension between overlap/novelty is in order. Our review of the literature is designed to unearth "best practices" revealed in the research, in the fully plural sense of the term. For every "best practice" identified in the literature review, there is likely to be a nonprofit organization impervious to its impacts. Although the individual studies reviewed may suggest a "one-size-fits-all" recruitment or selection solution, this chapter will not follow suit. Indeed, past research in the sector has made clear the pitfalls of "one-size-fits-all" nonprofit solutions (see Abzug, 1995; Carson, 2002; Miller-Millesen, 2003; Robinson, 2001) and we will advocate a configurational approach (Ridder et al., 2012; Toh et al., 2008; Watson & Abzug, 2010) to the suggestions garnered from the literature. Specifically, we remind the reader that because nonprofit organizations differ greatly by, at least, size, lifecycle, and subsector/industry, all suggested "best practices" must be reviewed in the context of such organizational variability. Indeed, just as recruiting personnel for museums differs greatly from recruiting personnel for animal welfare agencies, selecting staff for large national research universities differs greatly from selecting staff for small, local river keeper organizations. While not all of the reviewed literature will make explicit distinctions between organizations of different sizes, ages, subsectors, etc., as solutions are proffered, we will try to provide the context for making just such distinctions. Further, we note that much of the literature we review has explored nonprofit human resources in the United States, still, we will try to incorporate findings from international studies wherever possible.

The chapter will proceed as follows. We will begin with an overview of the research positing differential recruitment processes in the nonprofit sector. We will follow that with a review of the literature on predictions/antecedents of successful nonprofit recruitment and then selection. Finally, we will review the literature on the impact or consequences of recruitment and selection processes in the sector.

Recruitment and the Nonprofit Labor Force

From whence a nonprofit labor force? Before a nonprofit comes to select an employee, a potential employee may need to select the nonprofit sector. Foundational work in public service recruitment and selection provides a compelling (and nonprofit/public conflating) proposition. In 1990, Perry and Wise sought to identify a typology of motives associated with public service. In delineating the behavioral implications of such Public Service Motivation (PSM), they proposed a general attraction–selection framework. Interestingly, from our vantage point, they validated their framework using Rawls, Ullrich, and Nelson's (1975) findings that nonprofit entrants valued helpfulness, cheerfulness, and forgiveness more highly than for-profit job seekers. Perry and Wise (1990), thus, used Rawls et al.'s (1975) nonprofit finding to support their notion that Public Service Motivation would attract and select employees into public (and, apparently nonprofit) organizations. International research has also identified a related "voluntary sector ethos" (Cunningham, 2005; Nickson, Warhurst, Dutton, & Hurrell, 2008) based on an original "public sector ethos" (Hebson, Grimshaw, & Marchington, 2003). In the United States, local and industry-specific reports mostly confirm potential nonprofit employees are a breed apart. Hansen, Huggins, and Ban (2003, p. 2), surveying employee recruitment by nonprofit organizations in the Pittsburgh area, demonstrated that "[n]on-profit employees are primarily interested in jobs offering opportunities to do good or to help others; for-profit employees are more concerned with financial remuneration. But both groups give the highest ratings to interesting or challenging jobs." In 2013, LeRoux and Feeney, studying managers in the nonprofit sector, found the greater freedom over work functions and greater control over work schedules in the nonprofit sector were particular attractors. We might argue, then, that the wicked societal problems addressed by mission in the nonprofit sector, as opposed to, say, a more straightforward maximization of bottom line in the for-profit sector, would afford greater challenges and flexibility to service providers in the former sector.

More recent research sheds light on how a specifically nonprofit labor force is created. Nemenoff's (2013, p. 1) dissertation begins by suggesting an individual's interactions with a variety of nonprofit organizations over their lifecycle "may lead to a heightened awareness of nonprofit work, and help promote awareness of careers in the nonprofit sector." Nemenoff (2013, p. 14) develops a model of nonprofit career awareness, implicating the interplay of "parental and role model socialization to voluntary and philanthropic behavior" with "continued engagement through both volunteering and service-learning." However, her research with nonprofit practitioners ultimately found "a disconnect between having a desired occupation that involved helping people, and knowing that those types of careers, in other words paid employment, are found in the nonprofit sector" (Nemenoff, 2013, p. 115). Nemenoff's (2013, p. 121) identification of an "accidental career" in the nonprofit sector is consistent with past findings (see, for example, Lyons, 1992; Weaver & Herman, 1991), but, nonetheless, points to great potential returns on early nonprofit career education. Indeed, the earlier that potential practitioners learn there are organizations and careers in the nonprofit sector that would allow them to do good while doing well, the easier it will be for such organizations to have an attractive pool of potential employees. This view is supported by research by Tschirhart, Reed, Freeman, and Anker (2008), who, in surveying recent MBAs and MPAs, find that whether through self-selection or educational inculcation, students who are attracted to careers in the nonprofit sector originally, remain loyal. Rose's (2013) work on undergraduates points to earlier educational intervention, noting that the nonprofit sector is particularly attractive to students displaying commitment to public interest, compassion, and self-sacrifice.

So, for recruiting purposes then, there exists a manifest nonprofit labor force, and a latent nonprofit labor force. The manifest labor force may further provide clues about who comprises the potential labor force. Organizational actors charged with recruitment activities might be particularly interested in the characteristics of the nonprofit labor force as unearthed by decades of research (see Chapter 3 in this volume for a more extensive review). Indeed, much of what we assume about the nonprofit labor force (in the United States) can be traced back to the pioneering work of Preston (1989; 1990; 1994) and Odendahl and O'Neill (1994). As early as 1990, Preston determined the nonprofit labor market was dominated by white-collar occupations (specifically, service provision as opposed to goods manufacturing) and employees who were both female and well-educated. Comparing that 1989 picture with the nonprofit labor force in 2015, Gazley (2016) noted such similarities as the consistent 66% of the nonprofit workforce that is female, and that the sector is substantially more educated than the U.S. workforce at large.

Gazley (2016), following work by Salamon and Geller (2007) and Salamon, Sokolowski, and Geller (2012), notes that nonprofits have been fairly resilient in meeting workforce challenges, due in no small part to nonprofit demand demonstrating countercyclical tendencies to the U.S. economy. However, as Gazley (2016) notes, the great variability in the sector coupled with concerns about noncompetitive compensation practices (see Chapter 9 in this volume) has led to a perception (if not reality) of recruitment challenges in the sector. But, as the literature suggests, many of these challenges may be overcome by strategic human resource management.

Summing up the research findings on ways that recruiting differs in the nonprofit sector, we can point, on the supply side, to a pool of potential employees with a Public Service Motivation, who are hungry for the challenges and satisfaction of working to solve societal problems in interesting and relatively autonomous jobs. Nonprofit employers who can communicate and/or augment such working conditions are likely to appeal to a motivated potential workplace. We turn to a review of how nonprofit organizations find that success in recruiting.

Nonprofit Recruiting Best Practices: Findings on Antecedents

The Role of HR Specialists

First in 2004, and then again in 2010 and 2016, Watson and Abzug underscored the importance of strategic alignment of human resources with organization strategy. Recruitment, then, as well as all other human resource management activities, in best practice, would flow from the strategic (mission-driven) direction of the nonprofit. Watson and Abzug (2004; 2010; 2016) further suggest small or large nonprofit organizations can think strategically about putting "people first." They recommend working backwards from the goals of the recruitment program: "Is the organization trying to attract a large applicant pool? Is diversity of applications a major objective? Is promotion from within the desired outcome?" (Watson & Abzug, 2004, p. 642). Indeed, if an organization's strategic priorities include, for instance, demographically diversifying their staff to appeal to a broader constituent set, then promoting from within a relatively demographically homogeneous workforce might limit progress toward the strategic goal of diversification. Conversely, if staff development and retention are key to outstanding service provision, recruiting externally may engender, among extant staff, a climate of distrust or feelings of betrayal. Watson and Abzug (2016, p. 617) also note that "nonprofits would do well to strategically consider the staffing mix at start-up, at present, and for a future desired state." Watson and Abzug's emphasis on strategic approaches to recruitment and selection that begin with the desired end state begs the question of who is best to oversee such efforts.

One answer comes from the number of studies that have suggested that having human resource specialists on board can better focus recruitment efforts (Ban, Drahnak-Faller, & Towers, 2003; Haiven, 2004). Haiven's (2004) national comparative study of human resources in nonprofits in Britain versus Canada noted British nonprofits followed the protocol of best practices (job analysis conducted, job description drawn up, job posted and advertised internally and externally, applications submitted then culled, a short-list selected by hiring committee/panel, interviews with short-listed candidates conducted, candidates scored, best candidate selected), much more closely than their Canadian counterparts. Haiven attributes the Canadian nonprofits' propensity to resort to recruiting and selecting shortcuts to lack of trained human resources managers.

Haiven (2004) defined the human resource specialists as those who had taken course work or professional certification in the personnel field.

Only about a quarter of Ban et al.'s (2003) Pennsylvania nonprofits had a formal HR organizational structure and the others coped by relying on board members' expertise or the largesse of umbrella organizations. Yet, Ban et al. found most nonprofits (regardless of size or professionalization of the HR function) were relatively satisfied with their recruiting efforts, although hiring in technology and development posed difficulties, and use of the internet, at least at the turn of the Millennium, remained limited.

Whoever does the recruiting, both the prescriptive and the research literature have outlined two major pathways to attracting recruits in the nonprofit sector: internal (identified by Marsden (1994) as informal) approaches and external (Marsden's (1994) formal) approaches. The following lays out findings about each.

Internal/Informal Recruitment Approaches and the Role of Social Networks

In 1994, Marsden set out to use data from the National Organizations Survey to explore the methods used by U.S. establishments to publicize the availability of job opportunities to potential workers. He found that both for-profit and nonprofit organizations were more likely to use informal referrals for recruitment than were public sector organizations. Almost twenty years later, Eng, Liu, and Sekhon (2012) noted social networks are particularly important and effective in the recruitment of NPO staff. They argue the motivation to support social or charity activities is both a key indicator of successful organization integration and much more difficult to identify than basic business skills. As such, they found personal relationships can best identify/refer friends/colleagues with requisite motivation sets. Of course, another good way to ensure a candidate's motivation to support the mission is to hire from within. In 2004, Haiven discovered that every Canadian nonprofit (most with very informal human resource practices), in her study, gave preference to internal applicants. She noted Canadian nonprofits used internal hiring as a way to help staff advance their careers.

A year earlier, Ban et al. (2003) found most of their sample nonprofits, regardless of size, relied primarily on social network word-of-mouth and newspaper ads. The larger organizations in their sample were more likely to employ professional networks while the smaller organizations reported greater use of e-mail networks. The authors attributed reliance on word of mouth to the relative low cost, minimal need for technology, and local focus of these methods. They noted these methods resulted in great satisfaction with applicants identified. Still, following Werther and Berman (2001), they cautioned word-of-mouth and employee referral processes also represented a potential challenge to attracting a diverse pool of candidates and could also lead to the creation of potentially disruptive cliques (Ban et al., 2003).

Indeed, Watson and Abzug (2016, p. 602) specifically note that "recruiting by internal referral is so successful" because "individuals who know insiders are much more likely to understand what the organization is about and accurately assess whether or not they would like to work there." And yet, they, too, caution that "fit is not a synonym for homogeneity" (Watson & Abzug, 2016, p. 602), suggesting that the more "successful organizations tend to seek and engage diverse viewpoints." Organizations would need to undertake internal recruitment or encourage word-of-mouth referrals within the context of encouraging insiders to think broadly about their networks and creatively about staff promotion.

External/Formal Recruitment Approaches and the Role of Competition

On the cusp of internal and external approaches to recruitment sit social networks of the technological (as opposed to word-of-mouth) variety. While a generic organizational literature captures the growing role of social media in recruitment (Karl & Peluchette, 2013; Kluemper, 2013; Ollington, Gibb, & Harcourt, 2013; Roulin & Bangerter, 2013; Zide, Elman, & Shahani-Denning, 2014), there is a distinctly nonprofit flavor to this as well. Research on Millennials (roughly the children of the Baby Boomers born between 1984 and 2000) has noted how this hyperconnected generation connects specifically with nonprofit organizations through social media sites such as Facebook (McCorkindale, DiStaso, & Sisco, 2013).

Indeed, understanding the different external avenues to reach distinct groups of potential employees is particularly important in an environment of competition for resources between mission-driven organizations. Hall and Hall (1996) noted similarly situated social movement organizations may finely granulate different recruitment strategies such that one organization may seek maturity and perspective in their candidates while a competing organization may seek youth and zeal. Indeed, nonprofit organizations interested in appealing to the sensibilities of potential Millennial employees would want to hone their social media presence across the newest and hottest platforms, while nonprofits (perhaps even in the same subsector) who are interested in recruiting more seasoned/experienced employees may place their recruitment resources in more traditional media including trade journals and newspapers.

Other Antecedents of Successful Recruitment

Some of the studies of antecedents to successful recruitment in nonprofit organizations do not fall neatly into effectiveness of internal or external approaches. In a summary statement, Gazley (2016) has implicated competitive salaries, benefits, and advancement opportunities as key organizational factors supporting nonprofit staff recruitment. Yet, to the extent that nonprofits find it difficult to compete focusing on such extrinsic motivation factors, Gazley (2016) suggests that nonprofits take pains to also understand the intrinsic motivations of prospective employees. She counsels that nonprofits can achieve this latter objective "by engaging in the foundational activities of effective recruitment: job design, screening, and interviewing, where a purposeful discussion of employee goals can be achieved" (Gazley, 2016, p. 98). Indeed, Ban, Drahnak-Faller, and Towers (2003) pointed out that nonprofits have particular flexibility in their human resource strategy compared to public agencies constrained by civil service rules and regulations. This flexibility would characterize both recruitment and selection processes.

Reviewing the literature on recruitment, we see best practices emerging in internal/informal recruitment, external/formal recruitment, and studies that do not fit neatly into either of the former. We note how authors use the concepts of increased "fit" and lower costs in explaining the popularity of internal/ informal recruitment, even as they warn that precautions must to be taken to ensure personal networks can lead to diverse applicant pools. In the external/ formal recruitment literature, we also note a concern for attracting diverse applicant pools, as authors describe how various media (social and traditional) can be utilized to target different audiences. Finally, we return to the theme that nonprofit recruitment may be differentiated from recruitment in other sectors due to the relative advantage of using mission as an attractor compared with for-profit recruiting and the relative advantage of private sector flexibility compared with governmental recruiting.

Nonprofit Selection

There does not appear to be a huge scholarly empirical literature on selection in the nonprofit sector. Perhaps because the sector as a whole (exceptions abound, of course) seems to be perennially portrayed as under-staffed (see, for example, Lynn, 2003; Rehling, 2000; Silverman & Taliento, 2006), there may be a sense that selecting among multitudes of candidates is a nonprofit's fantasy. Then again, Ban et al.'s (2004) study of Pennsylvanian nonprofits noted that "focus group participants reported no shortage of good resumes to choose from, especially when the very top-level positions such as executive director became vacant" (p. 137). In reviewing the credentials of the applicants, Ban et al.'s Pennsylvanian nonprofits used a variety of selection methods—with some organizations consciously trying to hire locally. One of the few studies that appears in a search for "employee selection in nonprofits" makes the claim that the relatively lower wages of the sector may be causing *self*-selection for (at least) managers in nonprofits (Handy & Katz, 1998).

Nickson, Warhurst, Dutton, and Hurrell (2008), writing in the Scottish context, promulgate the related idea of a social process model of recruitment and selection to help make sense of the recruitment conundrum of lower wages in the sector (for global perspectives on nonprofit recruitment difficulties, see Barnard, Broach, & Wakefield, 2004, and Wilding, Collis, Lacey, & McCullough, 2003). They suggest the social process model of recruitment and selection—whereby selection is a two-way street where both the applicant and organization size up person/organization fit—is particularly appropriate for the voluntary sector. They suggest, following Herriot (1989), that selection is actually the beginning of a two-way relationship.

Other studies provide suggestions for future selection criteria in the sector. Bish and Becker (2015), for instance, suggest their findings of unique nonprofit manager capability requirements—an emphasis on personal knowledge and experience and a commitment to the nonprofit sector and organizational values—have implications for establishing selection criteria. Such a commitment to organizational values in the selection criteria might presuppose the adoption of the social process model as opposed to a more traditional (read: for-profit) selection focus solely on the "'product' or 'procedural' characteristics of selection (e.g., reliability, validity of selection tools)" (Derous & De Witte, 2001, p. 319).

Limited empirical studies are supplemented by theoretical or modeling exercises of nonprofit selection. For instance, Caers, DuBois, Jegers, De Gieter, De Cooman, and Pepermans (2009) use economic modeling to recommend "the importance of a strong commitment to the organization's mission and caution for both a strong self-interest and a strong devotion to the well-being of the clients" (p. 173), for the selection of nonprofit employees.

Bringing together Caers, DuBois, Jegers, De Gieter, De Cooman, and Pepermans' (2009) admonishments with Nickson, Warhurst, Dutton, and Hurrell's (2008) work in Scotland seems to point to the value of a negotiation or social process model in nonprofit selection. According to Derous and De Witte (2001, p. 319), such a model would include eight process characteristics that applicants could expect from nonprofits:

> (1) provision of general information on the job opening, (2) participation and control, (3) openness to assertiveness, (4) creation of transparency of testing, (5) provision of feedback, (6) guarantee of objectivity and standardization, (7) assurance of human treatment, and (8) respect for privacy and job relevance of information gathering.

The research seems to be pointing away from a for-profit reliance on testing of applicants in selection, and toward a more non-profit friendly, mutually getting-to-know you process.

The Impact of Nonprofit Recruitment and Selection

The success (or not) of nonprofit recruitment and selection can have profound organizational effectiveness and consequences for employee well-being. A meta-analysis of the large literature on individuals' fit at work (Kristof-Brown, Zimmerman, & Johnson, 2005) corroborated that person-organization fit strongly correlates with job satisfaction and organizational commitment. In the nonprofit sector, as Gazley (2016, p. 95) notes, "An organization's inability to find the right staff will make the jobs of other staff more challenging. An inability to find staff who reflect the demographic characteristics of clients will make it more difficult to serve particular client populations." Indeed, Kettlitz, Zbib, and Motwani (1997) found that poor selection practices, including not using weighted application blanks (WABs) in pre-employment screening, are correlated with nursing aides turnover. Although focused specifically on nursing aides in nursing homes, Kettlitz et al. (1997) linked higher turnover to applicants who left information about prior length of service, prior wage increases, and percent of general (non-nursing) coursework blank on their applications. They also implicated applicant unemployed status, finding the job through the newspaper, and finding the job through referral by a current employee as correlates to shorter tenure. Further, Kettlitz, Zbib, and Motwani's (1997) research supported the use of biographical information blanks (personal history data) to predict employee theft, as well as turnover.

Research by Taylor and McGraw (2006), coming out of the study of nonprofit sport organizations in Australia, found the strong emphasis placed on the recruitment and selection of paid staff (in comparison to that of volunteers): (1) was not correlated with further employee development or training; (2) reflected funding limitations on training and development coupled with the belief that recruiting and selecting for strong business and management skill and expertise would obviate the need for training; and (3) suggested these organizations believed employing the right people would pay off in the long run. These findings circle back to the idea that self-selection in/to organizations of the sector helps delineate what is both unique and potentially enviable in recruitment and selection in nonprofit organizations.

Indeed, the limited empirical data on the impact of (poor) recruitment and selection processes in the nonprofit sector seems to suggest that, given high costs associated with subsequent training as well as the liabilities inherent in making recruitment/selection mistakes, nonprofits are well advised to invest resources upfront to strategize these all-important core activities.

Lessons Learned

This review of a somewhat delimited empirical literature on recruitment and selection in nonprofit organizations has still unearthed some common themes: (1) recruitment in the sector, though vitally important given scarce human resources, is often comparatively informal; (2) such informality decreases as the human resource function professionalizes, yet, such informality is not always seen as problematic; (3) self-selection into the sector confirms a differentially-motivated labor force while also, often, substituting for more formal selection processes; and (4) recruitment and selection, especially in the nonprofit sector, have profound individual, organizational, and societal impacts.

In the end, then, the extant literature suggests that nonprofit recruitment and selection are of utmost strategic importance to the success of the nonprofit mission, yet may still be, too often, performed informally. Yet, formalizing strategic recruitment and selection need not entail hiring staffing experts, although that might be preferable where funding is plentiful. However, for most nonprofits with smaller staffing budgets, where every hire is crucial, strategic planning and implementation of recruitment and selection processes are still achievable with commitment from the governing team. Nonprofit managers, working backwards from thoughtfully delineated recruitment/selection goals, can economically adopt best practices, including the strategic use of informal networks and social media platforms coupled with a social process model of selection. Indeed, the individual, organizational, mission, and societal payoff from investing time, thought, and resources into the nonprofit recruitment and selection process will likely be tremendous.

Discussion Questions

1   Think back to when you (or a friend/family member) were recruited and selected to a nonprofit organization. To what extent did the organization follow the best practices reviewed in the chapter? What other best practices did the organization use?
2   In what ways would recruiting and selecting volunteers differ from the recruitment and selection of paid staff members at nonprofits?
3   What roles might the Board of Trustees play in the recruitment and selection of nonprofit staff?

Exercises

1   Look for nonprofit ads in the *Chronicle of Philanthropy* or on Idealist.org. Work with a group to determine what other recruitment avenues the organization might use to fill this position. Next, working in your group, put together a plan to make a selection among qualified candidates.
2   Consider a nonprofit organization with which you have worked or volunteered. Put yourself in the place of the Board of Trustees and write a strategic plan for future recruitment and employee selection.

References

Abzug, R. (1995). Different cities, different trustees: Geographic variation in the composition of the fundraising board. *New Directions for Philanthropic Fundraising*, *1995*(7), 31–48.

Ban, C., Drahnak-Faller, P., & Towers, M. (2003). Human resource challenges in human service and community development organizations recruitment and retention of professional staff. *Review of Public Personnel Administration*, *23*(2), 133–153.

Barnard, J., Broach, S., & Wakefield, V. (2004). *Social care: The growing crisis*. London: Social Care Employers Consortium.

Bish, A. & Becker, K. (2015). Exploring expectations of nonprofit management capabilities. *Nonprofit and Voluntary Sector Quarterly*, doi:0899764015583313.

Brown, W. A. & Yoshioka, C. F. (2003). Mission attachment and satisfaction as factors in employee retention. *Nonprofit Management & Leadership, 14*(1), 5–18.

Caers, R., DuBois, C., Jegers, M., De Gieter, S., De Cooman, R., & Pepermans, R. (2009). A micro-economic perspective on manager selection in nonprofit organizations. *European Journal of Operational Research, 192*(1), 173–197.

Carson, E. D. (2002). Public expectations and nonprofit sector realities: A growing divide with disastrous consequences. *Nonprofit and Voluntary Sector Quarterly, 31*(3), 429–436.

Cunningham, I. (2005). Struggling to care: Employee attitudes to work at the sharp end of service provision in the voluntary sector. Paper presented at the 23rd Annual Labour Process Conference, Glasgow, April.

Derous, E. & De Witte, K. (2001). Looking at selection from a social process perspective: Towards a social process model on personnel selection. *European Journal of Work and Organizational Psychology, 10*(3), 319–342.

Eng, T. Y., Liu, C. Y. G., & Sekhon, Y. K. (2012). The role of relationally embedded network ties in resource acquisition of British nonprofit organizations. *Nonprofit and Voluntary Sector Quarterly, 41*(6), 1092–1115.

Gazley, B. (2016). The nonprofit sector labor force. In R. C. Kearney & J. D. Coggburn (Eds.), *Public Human Resource Management: Problems and Prospects* (pp. 90–103). Thousand Oaks, CA: Sage.

Haiven, J. (2004). How do nonprofits recruit paid staff? In *Proceedings of the Atlantic Schools of Business Conference* (pp. 81–93). November 4-6, Halifax, NS.

Haley-Lock, A. & Kruzich, J. (2008). Serving workers in the human services: The roles of organizational ownership, chain affiliation, and professional leadership in frontline job benefits. *Nonprofit and Voluntary Sector Quarterly, 37*(3), 443–467.

Hall, L. M. & Hall, M. F. (1996). Big fights: Between poor people's social movement organizations. *Nonprofit and Voluntary Sector Quarterly, 25*(1), 53-72.

Handy, F. & Katz, E. (1998). The wage differential between nonprofit institutions and corporations: Getting more by paying less? *Journal of Comparative Economics, 26*(2), 246–261.

Hansen, S. B., Huggins, L., & Ban, C. (2003). Explaining employee recruitment and retention by non-profit organizations: A survey of Pittsburgh area university graduates. University of Pittsburgh: A Report to the Forbes Fund.

Hebson, G., Grimshaw, D. & Marchington, M. (2003). PPPs and the changing public sector ethos: Case study evidence from the health and local authority sectors. *Work, Employment and Society, 17*(3), 481–501.

Herriot, P. (1989). Selection as a social process. In M. Smith & I. T. Robertson (Eds.), *Advances in selection and assessment*. Chichester: John Wiley and Sons Ltd.

Karl, K. & Peluchette, J. (2013). Possibilities and pitfalls of using online social networking in human resources management. *Psychology for Business Success, 4*, 119–138.

Kettlitz G. R., Zbib I., & Motwani, J. (1997). Reducing nurse aide turnover through the use of weighted applications bland procedure. *Health Care Supervisors, 16*, 41–47.

Kluemper, D. H. (2013). Social network screening: Pitfalls, possibilities, and parallels in employment selection. In T. Bondarouk & M. Olivas-Lujan (Eds.), *Advanced series in management* (pp. 1–21). Bingley: Emerald Group Publishing Ltd.

Kristof-Brown, A. L., Zimmerman, R. D., & Johnson, E. C. (2005). Consequences of individuals' 'fit at work': A meta-analysis of person–job, person–organization, person–group, and person–supervisor fit. *Personnel Psychology, 58*(2), 281–342.

LeRoux, K. & Feeney, M. K. (2013). Factors attracting individuals to nonprofit management over public and private sector management. *Nonprofit Management & Leadership, 24*, 43–62.

Lynn, D. B. (2003). Symposium human resource management in nonprofit organizations. *Review of Public Personnel Administration, 23*(2), 91–96.

Lyons, M. (1992). *Managing large community organisations: The approaches of sixteen chief executive officers*. CACOM UTS.

Marsden, P. V. (1994). The hiring process: Recruitment methods. *American Behavioral Scientist, 37*(7), 979–991.

McCorkindale, T., DiStaso, M. W., & Sisco, H. F. (2013). How millennials are engaging and building relationships with organizations on Facebook. *The Journal of Social Media in Society, 2*(1).

Miller-Millesen, J. L. (2003). Understanding the behavior of nonprofit boards of directors: A theory-based approach. *Nonprofit and Voluntary Sector Quarterly, 32*(4), 521–547.

Nemenoff, E. K. (2013). You mean I can get paid to work here? The impact of happenstance, socialization, volunteering and service-learning on nonprofit career awareness. Doctoral dissertation, University of Missouri-Kansas City.

Nickson, D., Warhurst, C., Dutton, E., & Hurrell, S. (2008). A job to believe in: Recruitment in the Scottish voluntary sector. *Human Resource Management Journal, 18*(1), 20–35.

Odendahl, T. & O'Neill, M. (Eds.). (1994). *Women and power in the nonprofit Sector*. San Francisco: Jossey-Bass.

Ollington, N., Gibb, J., & Harcourt, M. (2013). Online social networks: An emergent recruiter tool for attracting and screening. *Personnel Review, 42*(3), 248–265.

Perry, J. L. & Wise, L. R. (1990). The motivational bases of public service. *Public Administration Review, 50*(3), 367–373.

Preston, A. E. (1989). The nonprofit worker in a for-profit world. *Journal of Labor Economics, 87*, 438–463.

Preston, A. E. (1990). Women in the white-collar nonprofit sector: The best option or the only option? *The Review of Economics and Statistics, 64*, 560–568.

Preston, A. E. (1994). Women in the nonprofit labor market. In T. Odendahl and M. O'Neill (Eds.), *Women and power in the nonprofit sector* (pp. 39–77). San Francisco: Jossey-Bass.

Rawls, J. R., Ullrich, R. A., & Nelson, Jr., O. T. (1975). A comparison of managers entering or reentering the profit and nonprofit sectors. *Academy of Management Journal, 18*, 612–623.

Rehling, L. (2000). Doing good while doing well: Service learning internships. *Business Communication Quarterly, 63*(77), 77.

Ridder, H. G., Baluch, A. M., & Piening, E. P. (2012). The whole is more than the sum of its parts? How HRM is configured in nonprofit organizations and why it matters. *Human Resource Management Review, 22*(1), 1–14.

Robinson, M. K. (2001). *Nonprofit boards that work: The end of one-size-fits-all governance* Chichester: John Wiley & Sons, Ltd.

Rose, R. P. (2013). Preferences for careers in public work examining the government–nonprofit divide among undergraduates through public service motivation. *The American Review of Public Administration, 43*(4), 416–437.

Roulin, N. & Bangerter, A. (2013). Social networking websites in personnel selection. *Journal of Personnel Psychology, 12*(3), 143–151.

Salamon, L. M. & Geller, S. L. (2007). *The nonprofit workforce crisis: Real or imagined?* Baltimore, MD: Johns Hopkins University Center for Civil Society Studies and Institute for Policy Studies.

Salamon, L. M., Sokolowski, S. W., & Geller, S. L. (2012). Holding the fort: Nonprofit employment during a decade of turmoil. *Nonprofit Employment Bulletin, 39*, 1–17.

Silverman, L. & Taliento, L. (2006). What business execs don't know–but should–about nonprofits. *Stanford Social Innovation Review, 11*(16).

Taylor, T. & McGraw, P. (2006). Exploring human resource management practices in nonprofit sport organisations. *Sport Management Review, 9*(3), 229–251.

Toh, S. M., Morgeson, F. P., & Campion, M. A. (2008). Human resource configurations: Investigating fit with the organizational context. *Journal of Applied Psychology, 93*(4), 864.

Tschirhart, M., Reed, K. K., Freeman, S. J., & Anker, A. L. (2008). Is the grass greener? Sector shifting and choice of sector by MPA and MBA graduates. *Nonprofit and Voluntary Sector Quarterly, 37*(4), 668–688.

Watson, M. R. & Abzug, R. (2004). Finding the ones you want, keeping the ones you find: Recruitment and retention in nonprofit organizations. In R. D. Herman & Associates (Eds.), *The Jossey-Bass handbook of nonprofit leadership and management* (2nd ed.; pp. 623–659). San Francisco: Jossey-Bass.

Watson, M. R. & Abzug, R. (2010). Recruitment and retention in nonprofit organizations. In R. D. Herman & Associates (Eds.), *The Jossey-Bass handbook of nonprofit leadership and management* (3rd ed.; pp. 669–708). San Francisco: Jossey-Bass.

Watson, M. R. & Abzug, R. (2016). Effective human resource management. In D. O. Renz & Associates (Eds.), *The Jossey-Bass handbook of nonprofit leadership and management* (4th ed.: pp. 597–638). San Francisco: Jossey-Bass.

Weaver, E. T. & Herman, R. D. (1991). Nonprofit executives' career paths: An explanatory study. Paper presented at Independent Sector 1991 Spring Research Forum, Cleveland, Ohio.

Werther, W. B. Jr. & Berman, E. M. (2001). *Third sector management: The art of managing nonprofit organizations*. Washington, DC: Georgetown University Press.

Wilding, K., Collis, B., Lacey, M., & McCullough, G. (2003). *Futureskills 2003: A skills foresight research report on the voluntary sector paid workforce*. London: VSNTO.

Zide, J., Elman, B., & Shahani-Denning, C. (2014). LinkedIn and recruitment: How profiles differ across occupations. *Employee Relations, 36*(5), 7.

Succession Planning and Management in Nonprofit Organizations

Yeonsoo Kim

It's always wise to look ahead, but difficult to look further than you can see.
(Winston Churchill)

To ensure the sustainability of the organization, nonprofits need to be serious about planning for the transition of key positions and leadership (Allison, 2002). Being ready with a strategic plan in place for an effective transition, whether due to an expected vacancy or the anticipated transition of a leader, can help organizations get ready for inevitable challenges of leadership transition.
(National Council of Nonprofits, n.d.)

Introduction

Since many nonprofits are typically small and heavily reliant on a deeply motivated staff, planning for sustained leadership is critical for nonprofit organizations (Adams, 2010). In recent years, nonprofit practitioners and scholars have pointed to challenges with leadership transition and succession planning for executives as critical for organizational success (Allison, 2002; Froelich, McKee, & Rathge, 2011; Stewart, 2016). Despite the projected retirement of many nonprofit executives in the coming decade, few nonprofits have created or implemented formal succession plans (Wolfred, 2008). Surveys have consistently demonstrated nonprofits are aware of their leadership development gaps, but have not identified strategies to address them (Tierney, 2006). Therefore, as a key human resource management (HRM) practice, nonprofits have a lot of work to do in building their HRM capacity associated with transitions and succession.

Many nonprofit organizations are relying on the practices and evidence developed for for-profit organizations for succession planning. However, a close examination suggests these strategies are ill suited to the nonprofit context due to key differences between the sectors (Froelich, McKee, & Rathge, 2011). Effective succession planning should be a system and program that address each organization's unique situation and help address future challenges. As Froelich et al. (2011) highlighted, nonprofit organizations are different from for-profit organizations in terms of end goals, reliance on volunteers, a complex relationship between the executive director and board of directors, and an increasingly complicated mix of revenue streams. Similar to other systems and programs of management, effective succession planning and management begins with understanding the core concepts of the practice, including definition and general models. Based on an accurate understanding, each nonprofit organization should then think about their particular context and figure out how to tailor succession planning and management practices to their organizations. With this, these nonprofits will be able to design an effective succession planning system and implement succession planning and management as a program. Therefore, this chapter has two primary goals. First, we provide general information about succession planning and management, including the definition and an overview of some common models of succession planning and management. Second, we provide information and best practices for nonprofit organizations to begin to create their own succession plans and manage the process effectively.

Definition of Succession Planning and Management

Succession planning is the process of identifying and developing new leaders to succeed current leaders (Kramer & Nayak, 2013). Succession planning is a means of identifying key positions in an organization, starting with supervisors and managers up to the highest positions in the organization (Carter, 1986). At its best, it is a proactive and systematic process to build a clear pipeline of leaders (creating strong bench strength) within an organization and to identify strong external candidates, so when transitions are necessary, the organization is ready to act. The potential of effective succession planning, as a system, lies in its ability to help organizations in developing and sustaining a leadership pipeline. This helps assure leadership continuity for key positions, fosters the engagement of the senior management team in a structured process to review talent over time (not simply in a reactive mode), facilitates the examination of diversity issues to guide leadership development, encourages a periodic re-examination of unit structures, processes, and systems, and finally aligns human resource management functions to support the leadership renewal process (Liebman et al., 1996).

In today's dynamic environment, especially in the nonprofit sector, traditional succession planning, which encourages organizational stability, needs continuous modification to remain useful in addressing various organizational challenges. An effective succession plan cannot simply be a list of future promotions. To remain effective, succession planning should serve as a means to regenerate a nonprofit's leadership and fulfill the goal of developing a strong leadership team (Froelich et al., 2011). The best means to realize the potential of succession planning lies in succession management, which moves planning into a more active approach to leadership and talent development (Rothwell, 2005). Succession management assumes a more dynamic organizational environment and career development of people within an organization. In contrast, succession planning focuses upon the slating process, which identifies individuals who are ready to lead or who have the potential to lead. For example, traditional succession planning would look to identify key actors who are ready now (or in six months) to take which position, with the assumption that the position and its requirements remain largely unchanged (Rothwell, 2005). The succession management process, on the other hand, asks the current leadership to create a strategy to develop future leadership, focusing on developing the needed and required future competencies and delivering an array of supporting development opportunities, with the assumption of changing organizational needs (Liebman et al., 1996). To be effective and competitive, succession planning and management must work in concert to produce desired outcomes for nonprofit organizations (Froelich et al., 2011; Rothwell, 2005). However, for nonprofits, especially those who struggle with resources for training and development, succession planning and management can be a challenge. We argue it is worth the investment and that nonprofits cannot ignore their future leadership needs.

A succession planning and management program is a deliberate and focused effort to maintain continuity of key positions, through both retention and development of future intellectual and knowledge capital, and to encourage the advancement for individuals (Rothwell, 2005). The need for succession planning and management is not confined to management or senior roles. Effective succession planning and management work to ensure critical backups and individual development across job categories—including key clerical, front-line, professional, technical, and production positions. The extension of succession planning and management beyond management ranks is even more important as organizations take active steps to build higher performance and create environments that involve their workers, as in many service areas including the nonprofit sector, these environments involve decentralized decision-making, empowered employees, diffused leadership throughout the workforce, and accumulated technical knowledge based on experience in the organization (Rothwell, 2005). These environments create a fertile ground to involve employees in thinking about the future.

A key goal of succession planning and management is the alignment of the organization's current talent with future talent needs: What do you have now and what will you need in the future? A second goal is enabling organizations to better address operational and strategic challenges by matching employees to the needs and actions of the nonprofit at the right time. When challenges arise for nonprofit organizations, succession planning and management should allow a nonprofit to evaluate how well their current workforce was able to weather these challenges and what was learned about the existing human capital stock and how it could be improved. In this sense, succession planning and management are important tools to allow organizational learning. Succession planning and management ensure that the institutional memory and collective experiences are preserved and synthesized to achieve continuous improvement in work outcomes. This can enable double loop learning, which helps to challenge underlying values and assumptions that may get in the way of organizational progress (Argyris, 1999; Senge, 1990). In other words, succession planning ensures continued development of leadership and talent through structured reflection and development and aids in the management of knowledge in the nonprofit organization over the long term (Froelich et al., 2011; Rothwell, 2005).

Succession Planning and Management and HR Processes: Distinguishing the Concepts

Although the term succession planning is used often, succession planning and management are often misunderstood and used interchangeably with related terms such as replacement planning, workforce planning, and talent management. Since the purpose and scope of those relevant terms are different and could lead to different strategies in terms of program implementation, we now clarify the differences between key concepts and terms related to succession planning and management.

Replacement Planning

Although replacement planning is often a compatible and overlapping activity, succession planning and management are distinct from replacement planning. Replacement planning is "the process of identifying short-term and long-term emergency backups to fill critical positions or to take the place of critical people" (Rothwell, 2011, p. 87). This planning focuses more on filling gaps based on extraordinary circumstances or temporary disruptions versus more sustained leadership development and succession. At its core, replacement planning is a strategy to manage organizational risk. In contrast, succession planning does not focus *per se* on identifying staffing backups within a department; it is a more comprehensive approach to examining needs at different levels of the organization. However, many people consider replacement planning as succession planning or as a part of succession planning. Unlike replacement planning, succession planning is a strategic effort and system of human resource management instead of a plan to address an episodic event. Having backups identified is a good first step, but it is not enough for the long term.

Workforce Planning

Unlike succession planning, which focuses on succession, transition, and development of key positions in an organization, workforce planning is a broader HRM practice tied to the planning and development of the workforce, a comprehensive approach to the entire workforce for an organization (Bechet, 2008). This type of planning is also known as human resource planning. Workforce planning involves matching the number and quality of people to the organization's strategic objectives. The goals of workforce planning and succession planning are the same. These processes plan for the right number and right type of people to meet the organization's needs over an extended time (Rothwell, 2011). However, workforce planning is different from succession planning in several aspects, including its focus on staffing jobs in current time, hiring forecasts and internal resources projection, and its budget-driven aspect (Pynes, 2013). Workforce planning also focuses on understanding labor market and trends that impact the clients, services, and funders, and developing individual and organization-wide strategies and changes that will impact job, internal activities, and costs (*Workforce Magazine*, 2012). While often associated with workforce planning, succession planning is an approach with the specific purpose of ensuring that selected (typically senior leaders of an organization) staff are trained, experienced, and ready for future leadership positions. Succession planning is often embedded within a larger framework of workforce planning and overall strategic human capital management (Pynes, 2013; Selden, 2009).

Talent Management

The recent interest in talent management has led to the growing popularity of the terms talent strategy, talent management and succession planning being used interchangeably to capture a larger approach to developing an organization's human capital (Kim et al., 2014). However, the differences between talent management and succession planning are distinct. Talent management moves beyond succession planning toward the larger goal of competing and developing talent. Generally, talent is a tool for managing the "best-in-class talent"—the upper 1–10 % of employees (Smart, 2005). Talent management involves a broad spectrum of HR activities, including identifying, developing, appraising, deploying, and retaining high performing and high potential employees (Collings & Scullion, 2007). It is the process of attracting, developing, and retaining the best people. This threefold-integrated focus distinguishes talent management from succession planning (Rothwell, 2011). Talent management and development are covered in Chapter 8 of this volume.

Talent management is comprised of many typical human resource management (HRM) practices, functions, and activities (Lewis & Heckman, 2006). In this way, talent management is similar to strategic human resource management. Talent management focuses on the most talented employees (commonly mentioned as high performing and high potentials). Therefore, talent management typically classifies employees into top, middle, and low performers. It then focuses on development activities for these top performers. Talent management also concentrates on mobility and flows of employees within an organization, which encompasses succession planning and human resource planning (Collings, 2014).

Lastly, talent management emphasizes the key positions within an organization in relation to the strategic goals of the organization. It is believed these positions and the employees currently holding them can allow an organization a competitive edge. The critical focus of talent management is not on talented employees *per se* but on key positions within the organization from a strategic perspective (Collings & Mellahi, 2009).

As mentioned earlier, the terms replacement planning, workforce planning, talent management, and succession planning are often used interchangeably due to some similarity in terms of strategic aspects and goals, but the differences between these terms should be clarified as distinct HR activities or programs aligned under an organization-wide HR strategy. But it is also important to understand that each of the HR activities and programs described should be designed and planned carefully to be aligned and integrated within the entire human resource management strategies and goals of an organization in order to be effective. It is worthwhile reviewing different models that provide various perspectives that can be adapted as a guide to developing effective succession planning and management.

Models of Succession Planning and Management

Succession planning and management are composed of processes and systems that must be adapted or specifically tailored to the unique needs and situations of organizations. For succession planning to be a valuable management capacity investment for a nonprofit, it is critical to consider what approach best suits the needs of the organization. While there has been a lot of research on this management process and the consultants working in this area, there are several different models and approaches that are most commonly used and may be best suited for nonprofits. Among them, the three models widely used for succession planning and management across the different sectors are: (1) the Leadership Pipeline Model; (2) the Acceleration Pool Model; and (3) the Seven-Pointed Star Model. The Leadership Pipeline Model by Charan et al. (2001), based on the work of Mahler, provides the basis to initiate a succession planning and management system in an organization. The Acceleration Pool Model by Byham et al. (2002) highlights the identification and development of a pool of candidates by providing a step-by-step process of implementation. The Seven-Pointed Star Model by Rothwell (2005) provides comprehensive procedures to develop a succession planning and management program. These three models provide different perspectives and approaches for succession planning and management that can be applied to nonprofit organizations with some tailoring and modification.

The Leadership Pipeline Model

The Leadership Pipeline Model (Charan et al., 2001) provides an approach to overall leadership development rather than a systematic guide to develop a

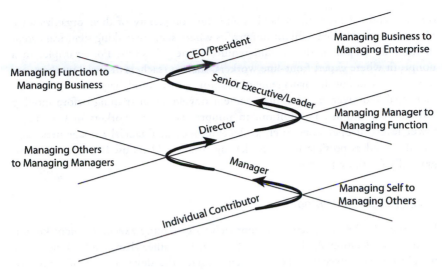

Figure 7.1   The Leadership Pipeline Model

Source: Adapted from Charan et al. (2001, p. 8).

succession planning and management program. This model formed the basis for modern succession planning (Mahler & Graines, 1983, p. ix). Charan et al. (2001) propose that in large decentralized organizations, career hierarchy can be represented by six career passages or pipeline turns (Figure 7.1). The pipeline is not a direct path and each bend represents a change in organizational hierarchy and complexity, requiring attention to the HR process and how the individual is managed at those different levels. At each level, a significant turn must be made to reach a different level of complexity and leadership. Making these turns involves large shifts in job requirements, new skills demands, and work values. If an organization is unable to identify and recruit candidates at the top, it is likely they will face difficulties at lower levels of leadership.

Based on this assumption, Charan et al. (2001) argue organization must fill the pipeline with high-performing people to ensure every leadership level has sufficient talent to draw from for current and future needs. In order to do so, they propose a five-step plan for succession planning. In the first step, the organization adjusts the Leadership Pipeline Model to the needs of their organization. In the second step, the organization translates standards for performance and potential that can be used to guide individuals in the positions and targeted for the positions. In the third step, the organization documents and communicates the standards set in the previous step. In the fourth step, organizations evaluate succession candidates using a combined potential-performance matrix. The matrix used employs a nine-box grid, which rates the potential of the candidate and their performance. In the final step, the plans and progress in terms of talent pipeline are seriously reviewed on a regular basis. The applicability of this model would vary for nonprofits based on the depth of their career ladders and the complexity of their organizations. However, it could be useful for nonprofits where staff are making significant steps in their development that would require some job shifts. For example, in a nonprofit where expert front-line workers, such as teachers or social workers, are moved into nonprofit management positions, this could help the workers be identified and given targeted management development training before moving into those positions. In addition, in nonprofits where workers may work in lower levels of operations, such as development or financial management, and are identified as possible future leadership, this could be used to develop them gradually for those positions.

Acceleration Pools Model

Byham et al. (2002) suggested an approach to grooming executive talent known as the "Acceleration Pools Model." This model, rather than handpicking a few people for each executive position, emphasizes the development of a pool of high-potential candidates for executive positions. Development of individual pool members is accelerated through stretch and taskforce assignments which serve as learning experiences. Other development opportunities can include: training, mentoring, coaching, special developmental activities such as university executive programs and action learning sessions, and high visibility assignments. The Acceleration Pools Model entails five phases (Byham et al., 2002). Figure 7.2 displays the phases of the Acceleration Pools Model and the sub-process involved in each phase.

The Seven-Pointed Star Model

Rothwell (2001; 2005) proposes use of the "Seven-Pointed Star Model" for systematic succession planning and management. The first step requires an organization's decision-makers to commit to the process of succession planning and management. Then, decision-makers must clarify and evaluate the work requirements and the competencies of the key leadership positions in the organization. This allows the organization to assure individuals targeted for advancement are doing so based on current rather than outdated or inaccurate work requirements. The third step requires a critical evaluation of individual job performance of targeted individuals before they can advance. At this stage, an inventory of talent is developed to clarify the availability of human assets. The fourth step requires a focus on competency needs of leadership positions in the future. This step attempts to overcome the current status quo understanding of the workforce needs in order to prepare the organization to cope with change. In the fifth step, individuals are assessed and matched to projected requirements and competencies.

The Seven-Pointed Star Model requires organizations to create a process to assess the individual potential of employees. This process is separate from past

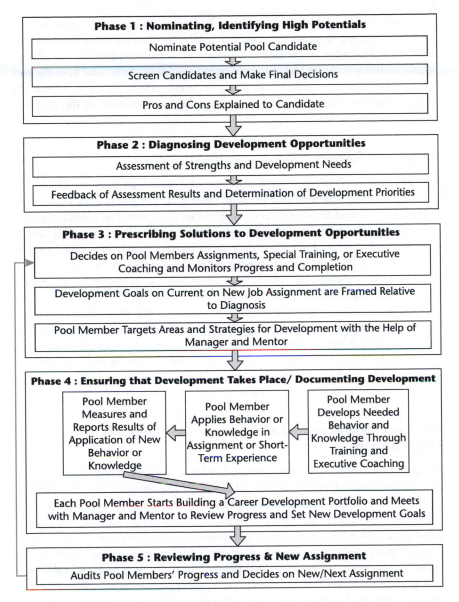

Phase 1 : Nominating, Identifying High Potentials

Nominate Potential Pool Candidate

Screen Candidates and Make Final Decisions

Pros and Cons Explained to Candidate

Phase 2 : Diagnosing Development Opportunities

Assessment of Strengths and Development Needs

Feedback of Assessment Results and Determination of Development Priorities

Phase 3 : Prescribing Solutions to Development Opportunities

Decides on Pool Members Assignments, Special Training, or Executive Coaching and Monitors Progress and Completion

Development Goals on Current on New Job Assignment are Framed Relative to Diagnosis

Pool Member Targets Areas and Strategies for Development with the Help of Manager and Mentor

Phase 4 : Ensuring that Development Takes Place/ Documenting Development

Pool Member Measures and Reports Results of Application of New Behavior or Knowledge

Pool Member Applies Behavior or Knowledge in Assignment or Short-Term Experience

Pool Member Develops Needed Behavior and Knowledge Through Training and Executive Coaching

Each Pool Member Starts Building a Career Development Portfolio and Meets with Manager and Mentor to Review Progress and Set New Development Goals

Phase 5 : Reviewing Progress & New Assignment

Audits Pool Members' Progress and Decides on New/Next Assignment

Figure 7.2 The Acceleration Pools Model

Source: Adapted in part from Byham et al. (2002, pp. 20–21).

and present employee performance appraisals. During the sixth step, organizations create an ongoing internal program for leadership development. In order to supplement leadership development, alternatives to traditional promotion-from-within methods must be examined to meet succession needs. The seventh and final step involves continual evaluation of effectiveness of the program. The results of the evaluation refine the program and maintain commitment to the program (Rothwell, 2001; 2005).

Lifecycles of Succession Planning and Management

Rothwell (2001; 2005) explained organizations cannot go from no succession planning to a fully implemented program overnight. For this reason, he suggests organizations should phase in succession planning. This phased-in approach guides organizations through a lifecycle of development to gradually phase in succession planning and management. Through each successive generation, organizations acquire skills and knowhow to increase their ability to reach the next level of implementation (Rothwell, 2005). He described the lifecycle of succession planning and management in five generations, summarized in Table 7.1.

The fifth and most sophisticated level of succession planning and management includes the creation of policies and procedures, and value statements to guide the program; competency models for key employees; assessment efforts; individual employee development plans; and skill inventories of talent pools inside and outside the organization. The plan then examines how organizations can implement systematic succession planning and management.

Succession Planning and Management in Nonprofit Organizations

A single approach to succession planning and management cannot be applied to all organizations and settings (Rothwell, 2005). While there are many similarities in succession planning and management across the business, government, and nonprofit sectors, there are some key differences to consider. As Rothwell (2005) highlights, non-profit entities do share some characteristics and practices with business and government. Therefore, effective succession planning and management for nonprofit organizations will follow a hybrid model of successful strategies in the private and public sectors. To be successful, succession planning and management need support and sponsorship from leaders, executives, and senior management of the organization.

In that respect, the nonprofit organization's succession planning is similar to the private sector. However, unlike the private sector, nonprofit organizations' succession planning needs to consider the involvement of dedicated leadership who have made their careers committed to the mission of the organization such as the founder(s), the board of directors, and significant contributors (Allison, 2002; Froelich et al., 2011). The support and sponsorship needs for succession

Table 7.1 Five generations of the succession planning and management lifecycle

Lifecycle of SP	Typical implementation plan	Major components
Generation 1	A simple replacement plan for CEO	• A simple replacement plan for CEO
Generation 2	A replacement plan for the CEO and his or her immediate reports	• Simple replacement plan for CEO and his or her immediate reports (the senior leaders, the senior executive team) • Involvement of senior managers
Generation 3	A succession planning and management program for middle managers and perhaps their key reports	• Succession planning and management program for middle managers • Drafts of policies and procedures for succession planning and management • Use of competency model • Value statement
Generation 4	A talent pool approach focused inside the organization	• Focusing on development of internal talent pools • Everyone in organization considered a possible successor for key position • Provide tool for career development for future • No-more organization chart • Use of competency model, performance appraisal, individual development plan, full-cycle multi-rater assessment, and other sophisticated methods for development
Generation 5	A proactive talent pool approach focused inside and outside	• Include external talent pool

Source: Adapted from Kim (2006, p. 26).

planning in a nonprofit organization are more complex than those for-profit corporations. In this way, succession planning and management for nonprofit organizations more resemble government entities (Rothwell, 2005). Indeed, one of the unique challenges of succession planning and management in the nonprofit sector is the nature of the relationship between the executive director and the board of directors (Froelich et al., 2011), especially given how nonprofit governance differs from for-profit governance (McFarlan, 1999).

In addition, the majority of nonprofits are small in terms of the number of employees. While larger nonprofits may have the capacity to invest in long-term strategic planning such as succession planning, it is hard for most small nonprofit organizations to prioritize succession planning. In smaller nonprofits, staffing and resources are already stretched thin and most organizations cannot support multiple managers for replacement planning. Due to the smaller size of these organizations and few dedicated resources for leadership development, succession planning for nonprofits focuses on the search outside the organization (Froelich et al., 2011; Santora, Caro, & Sarros, 2007). It is important to note that small nonprofit organizations are likely at more risk if they fail to plan for the future in terms of leadership and other needs because their margin for error is so tight. Nonprofits need to scale their succession planning based on their level of management capacity, but this planning and management cannot be ignored if nonprofits want to maintain their sustainability.

Current Status of Succession Planning in Nonprofits

Executive leadership is a component key factor in the success of nonprofit organizations (Bell, Moyers, & Wolford, 2006; Stewart, 2016). The size of the nonprofit sector has continued to grow in terms of the nature and complexity of these organizations (Salamon, Sokolowski, & Geller, 2012). Surveys have shown nonprofit organizations are aware of their leadership gaps, but struggle to address those gaps by strengthening the leadership bench. Froelich, McKee, and Rathge (2011) found that organizations struggle to replace long-serving leaders, but few proactive steps have been taken.

One of the largest obstacles to addressing the issue of succession is actually the failure of current leaders to make addressing the issue a priority. Often current leaders and boards of directors wait to plan for leadership development until a succession crisis is underway or imminent (Kramer & Nayak, 2013). At this point, these actions may be too late or at least less effective than they could have been. It is important to understand succession planning is not an episodic event triggered by a departure of key leader(s). Instead, successful succession planning is a practice—indeed it is management—that requires investment in building the pipeline of leaders for a nonprofit at all levels.

Nonprofit organizations often hobble their own leadership development efforts due to the unique resource challenges including limitations on allowable overhead, and restrictions on the use of donor and contract funds (Pynes, 2013). These restrictions leave few resources to invest in their people and infrastructure. Therefore, experts suggest different approaches for succession planning and management for nonprofit organizations. Several organizations provide guides and best practices for succession planning by nonprofits focusing on executive succession. Two prominent resources include a publication by CompassPoint, which outlines three different approaches to succession planning (Wolfred, 2008) and the Nonprofit Executive Succession-planning Toolkit by the Federal Reserve Bank of Kansas City (Federal Reserve Bank of Kansas City, 2009). The Federal Reserves' toolkit provides a detailed method for planning and implementation of succession planning. A third resource by the Bridgespan Group, Nonprofit

Leadership Development (Kramer & Nayak, 2013), provides a detailed step-by-step process for succession planning and management.

Considering Succession Planning in the Nonprofit Sector

CompassPoint Nonprofit Services and Transition Guides developed a guide outlining three approaches to succession planning and management. These three approaches speak to different resources levels, preparation, and lead time for nonprofits facing or planning for leadership transitions.

- *Emergency succession (or leadership) planning* ensures that key leadership and administrative functions, as well as agency services, continue uninterrupted. This is meant for organizations facing an unplanned or temporary but longer-term absence of a key leader.
- *Departure-defined succession planning* is recommended for organizations facing the announced departure of a long-term leader with two or more years of lead-time. This process involves identifying the agency's future goals and how the next leader should connect to those goals; determining the skill needs of a possible successor; and building the capacity of the remaining leadership team and systems to sustain the organization.
- *Strategic leader development* is recommended for organizations not facing the imminent departure of a leader but who want to prepare for future leadership needs. This practice engages the agency's strategic vision to identify the leadership and management skills needed to achieve those goals. It also involves recruiting and retaining talented individuals who currently have or have the potential to develop the needed skills (Wolfred, 2011).

Nonprofit Executive Succession Planning Toolkit of Federal Reserve Bank of Kansas City

The toolkit by the Federal Reserve Bank of Kansas City, which serves a seven-state region, was developed based on a district-wide assessment of nonprofit organizations. The toolkit includes information about succession planning and the roles of board members, executives, and key staff in succession planning, questions assessing readiness, an overview of the succession planning process, and templates and documents following the three approaches of succession planning suggested by CompassPoint. The toolkit also contains links to other online resources for use in the succession planning process.

Succession Planning Roles

Successful planning for nonprofit succession requires a collaborative effort between the incoming executive, key staff, and the governing board. Table 7.2 outlines the key roles of each member in planning for succession in general.

Table 7.2 The key roles of members in succession planning

Members	Roles in succession planning
Board Members	• Secure the organization's future by clarifying direction and ensuring strong leadership. A succession plan promotes the availability of a strong executive when needed. • Understand the complexity and responsibilities of the executive role. Select, support and evaluate the executive on a regular basis. • Leverage board contacts and expertise, especially during periods of leadership transition. • Play a lead role in working with the executive to develop and approve succession plans for various scenarios. • Appoint a board committee to address transitional issues in the event of an unexpected departure of the executive.
Executives	• Provide a process for regularly reviewing and stretching the board's effectiveness. • Ensure legacy and succession occur. Draft an emergency succession plan and submit to the board for approval. • Implement process to develop key staff members and promote a culture that encourages professional development. • Work with the board chair to schedule board meetings dedicated to the succession-planning process. • Evaluate their role in the organization, promote and encourage the executive succession-planning process. • Implement, upon board approval, and communicate the succession plan with affected staff.
Key Staff	• Support successful transition of new executive and provide program and organizational information as requested. • Continue to provide services to clients in absence of executive and during transition. • Ensure they are aware of the defined internal and external communication plan so they can address public inquiries.

Source: Adapted from the Federal Reserve Bank of Kansas City (2009).

Types of Succession Planning by the Federal Reserve Bank of Kansas City

The eight steps of *emergency succession planning* are:

1 Update the executive job description.
2 Define interim executive key responsibilities.
3 Define internal and external communication plan.
4 Process to appoint interim executive.
5 Cross-training plan for interim appointees.

6   Board oversight and support of interim executive, including an information system making critical information accessible to the board chair in the event of an emergency.
7   Process to transition and assimilate new executive.
8   Approval of Emergency Succession Plan.

(Federal Reserve Bank of Kansas City, 2009, p. 10)

The seven steps of a departure-defined succession planning are:

1   Prepare for a smooth departure of the existing executive, including events to recognize their service to the organization and assure they will support their successor if needed (Wolford, 2011).
2   Update job description and the performance priorities to prepare the organization for future success and sustainability.
3   Form a succession planning committee and clearly define their roles and responsibilities in the process.
4   Create a communication plan to articulate clear messages about the process and transition.
5   Conduct a sustainability audit by reviewing the factors most likely to impact sustainability of the organization.
6   Promote successful transition of new executive by creating goals for their first 90 days, identifying relevant professional development opportunities and resources, and setting up meetings and feedback mechanisms for relevant stakeholders.
7   Approval of the Departure–Defined Succession Plan is the final stage of the process and it simply asks decision-makers to formally approve of the actions and plans created.

(Federal Reserve Bank of Kansas City, 2009, p. 11)

The steps of *strategic leader development planning* involve an ongoing process for organizations who wish to plan for future talent needs but are not facing an immediate leadership transition. Implementation of the strategic leader development planning is accomplished through the following nine steps:

1   Draft and approve a strategic plan that encompasses goals for leadership and talent development needed to achieve identified strategies.
2   Implementation of an annual executive performance review including assessment and feedback about performance relative to the strategic objectives.
3   A process for annual self-assessment of the board's performance in key areas including: quality of financial oversight, legal compliance, understanding and assessment of programs, and feedback given to the executive.
4   Implementation of an annual staff evaluations system to ensure performance on job duties and skills.
5   Promotion of ability of senior management to work as a team.

6   Cultivation of relationships with stakeholders by staff, the board and executive.
7   Creation of a six-month financial reserve for operating costs.
8   Examination of financial management systems to assure they comply with industry standards.
9   Document and update operational manuals for administrative systems.

(Federal Reserve Bank of Kansas City, 2009, p. 11)

Nonprofit Leadership Development Toolkit by Bridgespan Group

Bridgespan's Nonprofit Leadership Development Toolkit proposes a succession planning tool they call Plan A (Kramer & Nayak, 2013). Plan A asks organizations to plan and create a vision for the organization's future leadership team, including an examination of the capabilities and roles needed to achieve particular strategies and the steps required to build that team. Plan A is a succession planning and management system that differs from a simple succession plan in that it is focused on comprehensively engaging the senior leadership and board in the process. Plan A involves the following five steps:

1   *Engage senior leaders*: The CEO and senior leadership team need to be on the same page about the importance of leadership development and succession planning. This group should design the process, including expectations and processes and ensure the organization moves forward with implementation. The CEO's role is critical here—the CEO needs to emphasize leadership development as a priority, set clear expectations with associated accountability, build (and develop) a senior leadership team, engage the board, and harness the power of the nonprofit's human resources (Kramer & Nayak, 2013, pp. 24–25).

2   *Map out a vision of the future leadership team*: This kind of structured development process requires thinking about what the future should look like. With this understanding and associated strategic discussion, the organization can assess the potential of current staff to become future leaders to meet emerging needs. Kramer and Nayak (2013, p. 53) suggest these procedures:

> Step 1: Define the critical leadership capacities needed to fulfill your organization's mission in the next three to five years.
> Step 2: Assess the potential of your staff (current and future leaders) to take on greater responsibility.
> Step 3: Create your Plan A for what leadership teams within the organization will look like in three years.

3   *Develop future leaders*: Future leaders need to be identified, with associated development needs, and a plan to address those needs. Leaders often develop on the job—nonprofits traditionally have been good about giving employees

a wealth of experience and opportunities to learn. However, a systematic process is needed. To do this effectively requires individualized attention to development needs, with this being a joint effort between leadership and employees, who should be deeply involved in crafting their individual development plans. The steps to develop future leaders include identifying "talent champions," considering the needs of the organization, and working with individuals to both design development plans and implement these plans (Kramer & Nayak, 2013, p. 85).

4   *Seek new talent to fill gaps (hiring externally to fill gaps)*: Internal promotions are not always going to fill position gaps, no matter how much attention a nonprofit places on succession planning. There will be times when future positions cannot be filled by current staff, so the organization should have strategic hiring and ongoing onboarding practices to integrate new leaders into the organization. The steps involved in doing this align with model HRM practices for effective recruitment and selection (Kramer & Nayak, 2013).

5   *Monitor and improve the process of developing leaders*: Like most processes, leadership development is not a one-time process—it needs to be viewed as iterative, with a focus on tracking performance and making adjustments along the way. Successful nonprofits gather data to track their progress and review what is working and what is not, with adjustments made to the leadership development process. The detailed steps include: (1) revisiting the objectives and actions that are being emphasized to make sure they are still appropriate; (2) building steps into the process to emphasize and ensure accountability; (3) assessing progress toward goals; and (4) identifying possible problems or roadblocks and making adjustments where necessary (Kramer & Nayak, 2013, p. 124).

Succession Planning and Management in Nonprofits: The Future

Experts and seasoned professionals in nonprofit organizations agree leadership change is inevitable for nonprofit organizations. As Froelich et al. (2011, p. 17) conclude: "The reality is that many current executive leaders will leave the workforce in the coming years; even if later rather than sooner, evidence suggests that nonprofit organizations are not well prepared for this important transition." Lack of preparation for this change is present even when the current leader is the founder. Founders, despite forming organizations that address important societal needs, often have a hard time imagining the future of the organization without them. However, at some point, the founder/leader should and will move on from the nonprofit. Changes in leadership are rarely easy or smooth and often present difficult challenges. Nevertheless, avoiding this inevitable change or pretending that it will not happen could put an organization's very survival in jeopardy. It is more important to face this dilemma and begin to think strategically to ensure the organization will keep its agility and sustain its success through the leadership transition.

As mentioned earlier, while there are many similarities in successful succession planning programs, but there is no single approach to succession planning and management which will work in all venues and organizations. Similar to the for-profit sector, for each nonprofit organization, the most important part of succession planning is to develop a realistic and effective succession planning with careful consideration of constraints and resources available. As Rothwell (2015) mentioned, organizations cannot jump from nothing to a state-of-art high succession planning in a short time. As a systematic strategic planning process, succession planning is a process that requires engagement of all aspects and people associated with the organization.

Efforts to streamline and increase the effectiveness of leadership transitions began as early as the 1960s. Succession planning and management started to gain attention from leaders of organizations in the 1980s. It went on to become a critical component of management in the 1990s. In the early years of succession planning, the vast majority of attention was on top management and executives. Currently organizations realize succession planning and management are not only about executives and senior leadership positions but also the broader work-force. To be effective and strategically contribute to the organization's vitality and sustainability, succession planning has evolved and broadened its scope to all key positions, including professional, technical, and administrative positions and the key knowledge needs of the organization. As Rothwell (2015) empha-sizes, an organization cannot jump into a state-of-art succession planning in a short time, it takes many years of collaborative efforts of leaders and members of an organizations to plan, design, and implement a succession planning and management program that fits into an organization. The unique challenges of the nonprofit sector have led to the underdevelopment of succession planning in nonprofit organizations so far. Many nonprofit organizations are still in the early stages of succession planning development such as focusing exclusively on executive succession. While the importance of effective succession planning for executives should not be ignored or belittled, nonprofits still need to prepare themselves to be more strategic and forward-thinking in terms of succession planning and succession management to ensure the continuity of the organization beyond current leaders.

As Froelich et al. (2011) pointed out, while nonprofit organizations often strongly prefer their next leaders to come from within or from similar organizations, the investment in leadership development activities in nonprofit organizations is not high. In addition, many nonprofits are still not prepared to implement succession planning as a strategic and systematic program rather than due to an event of the chief officer's transition. Furthermore, traditional leadership development and succession planning do not provide the flexibility needed for the rapidly changing environment facing organizations today (Gothard & Austin, 2013). The current literature calls for a fundamental shift from traditional replacement-succession planning toward a more comprehensive succession management approach to meet the demands of the organization (Gandossy & Verma, 2006). These call for additional research to better aid the ability of nonprofits to navigate management succession by expanding the focus beyond executive succession planning.

Discussion Questions

1 Examining the vignettes below (modified from Rothwell, 2015, pp. 3–4), how would you address these succession problems?

2 What aspects of the nonprofit sector would make these situations challenging?

Vignette 1: Your nonprofit organization serves vast rural areas of Nevada. In order to build bridges with decision-makers and other stakeholders in the rural areas of the state, senior management often travels together to disparate locations. As the director of human resources, you receive a call in the middle of the night informing you a car with several of your top staff members and the Board President was in a serious accident, leaving no survivors. You are shocked and upset at the loss of life but also dismayed at the damage this may present for your nonprofit organization. The next morning as you arrive at work, you turn to your office manager and pose the question, "What do we do? Do we even know who is in charge?"

Vignette 2: On the way to a meeting in Mexico, the CEO of a large environmental nonprofit organization is seized and held for ransom by a gang of criminals who engage in kidnapping for profit. They demand $1 million within 72 hours for her safe return. The other executives in the organization call a meeting to develop a plan on how best to resolve the situation for both the CEO and the organization.

Vignette 3: Veronica, the distribution management supervisor for the food bank, just called in sick after years without an absence. She handles all the distribution and scheduling of delivery, as well as overseeing volunteers for distribution. The manager of the department does not know how all the distribution systems function, absent this individual. In part, this is because Veronica is the only one who knows how all of the pieces fit together in terms of operations. The manager is sure that distributions will not go well because Veronica has no trained backup.

Vignette 4: Bill Well is preparing to retire as the Executive Director (ED) of Clean Water for Everyone. For years, Bill has been working with Yen Chen to take over as the next ED. Yen has held the post of executive vice president and chief operating officer, and his performance has been exemplary in those positions. Bill is convinced Yen will make an excellent ED. Not everyone is as convinced, which begins to make Bill nervous as he nears his retirement date. Several other executives and the board of directors have asked him privately if Yen is really able to take on this role, since he is rumored to have possible issues in his personal life and his relationship with some of the women in the nonprofit is problematic. They do not think he can overcome his personal issues to become an effective leader. Bill feels he owes the job to Yen and hates to involve himself in the personal lives of his employees. But he has started considering whether to initiate an executive search for a ED candidate from outside of the organization.

References

Adams, T. (2010). Sustaining great leadership: Succession planning for nonprofit organizations. 10 things every board member needs to know. Chicago: First Nonprofit Foundation.

Allison, M. (2002). Into the fire: Boards and executive transitions. *Nonprofit Management & Leadership, 12*(4), 341–351. http://dx.doi.org/10.1002/nml.12402

Argyris, C. (1999). *On organizational learning* (2nd ed.). Malden, MA: Blackwell Business.

Bechet, T. (2008). *Strategic staffing: A comprehensive system for effective workforce planning* (2nd ed.). New York: Amacom.

Bell, J., Moyers, R., & Wolfred, T. R. (2006). *Daring to lead 2006: A national study of nonprofit executive leadership*. New York: CompassPoint/Meyer Foundation.

Byham, W. C., Smith, A. B., & Paese, M. J. (2002). *Grow your own leaders: How to identify, develop, and retain leadership talent*. Upper Saddle River, NJ: Prentice Hall.

Carter, N. H. (1986). Guaranteeing management's future through succession planning, *Journal of Information System Management, 3*(3), 13–14.

Charan, R., Drotter, S. J., & Noel, J. L. (2001). *The leadership pipeline: How to build the leadership-powered company*. San Francisco: Jossey-Bass.

Collings, D. G. (2014). Integrating global mobility and global talent management: Exploring the challenges and strategic opportunities. *Journal of World Business, 49*(2), 253–261. doi: http://dx.doi.org/10.1016/j.jwb.2013.11.009.

Collings, D. G. & Mellahi, K. (2009). Strategic talent management: A review and research agenda. *Human Resource Management Review, 19*(4), 304–313. doi: 10.1016/j.hrmr.2009.04.001.

Collings, D. G., & Scullion, H. (2007). Resourcing international assignees. In C. Brewster, P. Sparrow, & M. Dickman (Eds.), *International human resource management: Comtemporary issues in Europe* (pp. 87–106). Basingstoke: Palgrave Macmillan.

Federal Reserve Bank of Kansas City. (2009). Nonprofit Executive Succession-Planning Toolkit. Kansas City, MO: Federal Reserve Bank of Kansas City.

Froelich, K., McKee, G., & Rathge, R. (2011). Succession planning in nonprofit organizations. *Nonprofit Management & Leadership, 22*: 3–20. doi:10.1002/nml.20037.

Gandossy, R. P. & Verma, N. (2006). Passing the torch of leadership. *Leader to Leader, 40*, 37–44.

Gothard, S. & Austin, M. J. (2013). Leadership succession planning: Implications for nonprofit human service organizations. *Administration in Social Work, 37*(3), 272–285. doi:10.1080/03643107.2012.684741.

Kim, Y., Williams, R., Rothwell, W. J., & Penaloza, P. (2014). A strategic model for technical talent management: A model based on a qualitative case study. *Performance Improvement Quarterly, 26*(4), 93–121.

Kramer, K. & Nayak, P. (2013). *Nonprofit leadership development: What's your "Plan A" for growing future leaders?* Boston, MA: The Bridgespan Group.

Leibman, M., Bruer, R. A., & Maki, B. R. (1996). Succession management: The next generation of succession planning. *HR, Human Resource Planning, 19*(3), 16. Available at: http://ezproxy.library.unlv.edu/login?url=http://search.proquest.com/docview/224585178?accountid=3611

Lewis, R. E. & Heckman, R. J. (2006). Talent management: A critical review. *Human Resource Management Review, 16*(2), 139–154. doi:10.1016/j.hrmr.2006.03.001.

Liebman, M., Bruer, R., & Maki, B. (1996). 'Succession management: the next generation of succession planning', *Human Resource Planning, 19*(3), 16-29.

Mahler, W. R. & Graines, F. (1983). *Succession planning in leading companies.* Midland Park, NJ: Mahler Publishing Company.

McFarlan, F. W. (November, 1999). *Working on nonprofit boards: Don't assume the shoe fits.* Boston: Harvard Business School Press.

National Council of Nonprofits. (n.d.). Succession planning for nonprofits. Available at: National Council of Nonprofits, Available at: www.councilofnonprofits.org/tools-resources/succession-planning-nonprofits

Pynes, J. E. (2013). *Human resource management for public and nonprofit organizations: A strategic approach* (4th ed.). San Francisco: Jossey-Bass.

Rothwell, W. J. (2001). *Effective succession planning: Ensuring leadership continuity and building talent from within* (2nd ed.). New York: Amacom.

Rothwell, W. J. (2005). *Effective succession planning: Ensuring leadership continuity and building talent from within* (3rd ed.). New York: Amacom.

Rothwell, W. J. (2011). Replacement planning: A starting point for succession planning and talent management. *International Journal of Training and Development, 15*, 87–99. doi: 10.1111/j.1468-2419.2010.00370.x.

Rothwell, W. J. (2015). *Effective succession planning: Ensuring leadership continuity and building talent from within* (5th ed.). New York: Amacom.

Salamon, L. M., Sokolowski, S. W., & Geller, S. L. (2012). Holding the fort: Nonprofit employment during a decade of turmoil. *Nonprofit Employment Bulletin, 39*, 1–17.

Santora, J. C., Caro, M. E., & Sarros, J. C. (2007). Succession in nonprofit organizations: An insider/outsider perspective. *SAM Advanced Management Journal, 72*(4), 26.

Selden, S. (2009). *Human capital.* Washington, DC: CQ Press.

Senge, P. M. (1990). The fifth discipline: The art and practice of the learning organization (1st ed.). New York: Doubleday.

Smart, B. D. (2005). *Topgrading: How leading companies win by hiring, coaching, and keeping the best players*(Rev. ed.). New York: Portfolio.

Stewart, A. J. (2016). Exploring nonprofit executive turnover. *Nonprofit Management & Leadership, 27*(1), 43–58.

Tierney, T. J. (2006). The leadership deficit. *Stanford Social Innovation Review, Summer,* 26–35.

Wolfred, T. (2008). *Building leaderful organization: Succession planning for nonprofit. Executive transition* Monograph Series, (6). Baltimore, MD: Johns Hopkins University Press.

Wolfred, T. (2011). Departure defined succession planning: The seven essential elements for a successful CEO Transition. *Compass Point.* Available at: www.compasspoint.org/sites/default/files/documents/Depature-Defined%20Sccession%20planning%20-%20final_0.pdf

Workforce Magazine. (2012, May). Is there a meaningful distinction between workforce planning and succession planning? Available at: www.workforce.com/2012/05/01/is-there-a-meaningful-distinction-between-workforce-planning-and-succession-planning

8

Talent Management

Heather L. Carpenter

Introduction

Talent management is defined as "systematically and strategically picking the best people and developing them to make them even more productive" (Rothwell, 2012, p. 33). Even though the nonprofit sector employs 10% of the US private workforce (Bureau of Labor Statistics, 2014), talent management is often overlooked as a viable option for organizational success. However, talent management cannot be ignored by nonprofit organizations. A recent article by the Bridgespan Group, "The Talent Development Deficit," shows that nonprofits continually struggle with developing their internal talent and as a result are dealing with the "Turnover Treadmill," which means nonprofits are losing their internal talent (Landles-Cobb, Kramer, & Smith Milway, 2015). There is not necessarily a talent deficit as previous studies have implied, but the problem lies with nonprofits not developing their internal talent and, as a result, people are leaving to find better opportunities where their skills are developed. This chapter discusses various talent manage-ment components and models to help nonprofits develop their internal talent. The chapter also provides resources and discusses barriers nonprofits face in implementing talent management strategies.

Talent management is a competency-based approach comprised of acquiring new talent, developing the talent you have, and retaining good talent. There are three stages of talent management, which include personnel control, people development, and talent multiplication (Cheese, Thomas, & Craig, 2007). Personnel control is focused on administering people, making sure they are doing the required tasks; whereas people development is about developing your people; and talent multiplication is about using employees' knowledge, skills, and abilities as a collective and collaborative force to achieve the overall strategy of the organization (Cheese et al., 2007). Most organizations tend to focus on personnel control and need to move toward talent multiplication. Lack of time and money are the main reasons why organizations get stuck in the personnel control mode, but they can make the move to talent multiplication by employing the following strategies:

- improving the degree of alignment between talent management activities and business strategies;
- achieving integration of all talent management activities;
- moving from adding value by managing talent efficiently and effectively to creating extraordinary value for the organization by multiplying talent;
- shifting responsibility for talent management from the HR function and getting the entire organization involved in multiplying talent (Cheese et al., 2007, p. 86).

This chapter describes the key components of talent management as well as strategies for managing talent effectively. Then it discusses talent management models that have been developed in the nonprofit and for-profit sectors; the resources available from infrastructure organizations to support talent in the nonprofit sector, as well as the barriers nonprofits face in integrating talent management strategies within their own organizations.

Components of Talent Management

Scholars have attempted to map the literature around talent management to identify common themes and components, yet there is little empirical research on the subject of talent management (Thunnisen, Boselie, & Frutieyer, 2013). They found talent management practices vary according to the organization's external environment and type of work, as well as the internal circumstances of an organization. Using the findings of Thunnisen et al. (2013), and Cheese et al. (2007), this chapter describes the components of talent management that can be used by nonprofit organizations, including identifying talent needs, developing competencies, recruiting talent, investing in talent through training and development, and retaining talent.

Identifying Talent Needs

The first common component of talent management is to identify an organization's talent needs, which is also known as workforce planning. In order to identify talent needs, the organization must conduct a gap analysis and determine what talent currently exists within the organization (Lavelle, 2007). Common strategic planning processes can be used, such as identifying the personnel strengths, weaknesses, opportunities, and threats, as well as tracking certain key workforce statistics (Cotton, 2007). Cotton (2007, p. 58) recommends tracking the following statistics:

- *General workforce measures.* These measures examine demographic patterns in the workforce and staffing trends.
- *Recruitment measures.* These indicators can be used to assess whether or not the agency is hiring the right people—those who are qualified to do the job and who are also a good fit for the organization.
- *Employee retention measures.* These indicators can be used to measure the success of retention efforts, assess the work environment, and assess employee morale.

The gap analysis and key workforce statistics should reveal talent gaps, areas where the organization needs additional talent as well as talent surpluses and shifting roles.

Developing Competencies

Once organizations have identified their talent needs, they should develop the competencies to meet their strategic goals. Competencies are defined as the knowledge, skills, abilities, and other characteristics (KSAOCs) that a position must include in order to achieve those strategic goals (Pynes, 2009). Competencies are often mapped to a proficiency level so employees know at which level to perform the competency. Competencies have been discussed for many years as being important in building a high performance team and a high performance organization (Rodriguez, Patel, Bright, Gregory, & Gowing, 2002). Although competencies are rarely discussed in the context of nonprofit sector employment, Carpenter and Qualls (2015) identified a set of ten core social change competencies, after an extensive review of scholarly and practitioner literature assessing the training needs and general competencies nonprofit managers should possess. The competencies can be used as a starting point for nonprofit organizations. These ten core competencies[1] include:

- Advocacy and Public Policy
- Communications, Marketing, and Public Relations
- Financial Management and Social Entrepreneurship
- Fundraising and Resource Development
- Grantmaking or Direct Service
- Human Resources Management and Volunteerism
- Information Management
- Leadership and Governance
- Legal and Regulatory
- Planning and Evaluation.

Nonprofits can then create sub-competencies specific to the strategic goals of the organization, departments, and positions within the organization. These sub-competencies may include components of emotional intelligence, or sub-components included in the ten core social change competencies. Emotional intelligence is defined as "the ability to monitor one's own and others' feelings and emotions, to discriminate among them and use this information to guide one's thinking and actions" (Salovey & Mayer, as cited by Tan, 2012, p. 10).

There are four quadrants of emotional intelligence as defined by Goleman (2005) (Self-awareness, Self-management, Social awareness, and Social skills). One or more of the quadrants could be an important sub-competency to an organization, department, or an individual position. The competencies and sub-competencies will help organizations develop their current talent as well as identify talent that will be needed in the future.

Recruiting Talent

Once the competencies and sub-competencies are identified, they are added into employee and volunteers' job descriptions. There are different philosophies, methodologies, and resources for creating and revising job descriptions, which will not be covered in this chapter. However, experts emphasize the importance of current job descriptions (Rothwell, 2012). Figure 8.1 presents the main components of job descriptions.

Another aspect of recruiting top talent is providing marketing to get the right individuals to apply for positions, offering competitive salaries to attract talent, and developing candidates once they are hired (Kim et al., 2014). Since most nonprofits lack a human resource manager (Guo et al., 2011), recruiting top talent is often a struggle. However, organizations that make efforts to recruit top talent have seen lower turnover rates.

Investing in Talent through Training and Development

As described above, effective talent management involves developing staff and volunteers from their first day on the job. This is a different way of thinking and operating for many organizations that are personnel control-focused. Training is defined as "the systematic approach to affecting individuals' knowledge, skills, and attitudes in order to improve individual, team, organizational effectiveness," and development is defined as "systematic effort affecting individuals' knowledge or skills for purposes of personal growth or future jobs and/or roles" (Aguinis & Kraiger, 2009, p. 452). Training and development help improve employee job satisfaction and retention (Lee & Bruvold, 2003). Organizations that are good at talent management develop their internal staff and volunteers on an ongoing basis.

Often training and development involve performance management. In performance management, organizations assess or review employees based on a set of standards that usually connects to job description or specific job components. A piece of performance management is employee evaluations. There are many different employee evaluation formats and methods that will not be discussed in this chapter. However, successful talent management involves using employee

Components of a Good Job Description	
Job Title:	
Department (if applicable):	
Status	Exempt/Non-Exempt or Full Time/Part Time
Salary Range	Add a range, low to high to allow flexibility in hiring and promotion.
Reports to/ Supervisory Responsibility	List the roles this individual will report to and supervise.
Information about the Organization	One to two paragraph overview of your organization.
Position Information	One to two paragraph summary of the position.
Responsibilities Mapped to Social Change Competencies	This section is where you will categorize each job responsibility within the core competencies needed for the role.
Qualifications	The levels of experience required for the position in the many different competencies the position requires.
Educational Requirements	The education level the position requires.
Work Environment	One to two paragraphs describing the culture of your organization, the space in which the individual will work, how many employees and volunteers they will be work with, etc.

Figure 8.1   Components of a good job description

Source: Carpenter & Qualls (2015). http://pj.news.chass.ncsu.edu/2015/08/03/creating-job-descriptions-that-work-for-you/

evaluations as opportunities for employee development and identifying talent who can be given greater responsibilities within the organization.

When employees understand the competencies where they need to improve, and have identified their development gap, then they can create a development plan for the future (Rothwell, 2012). In addition, when top talent are recognized for their accomplishments, they are more likely to stay with the organization (CEB, 2015). Cheese and colleagues explain, "High performing organizations have institutionalized methods for matching and moving the best internal and external talent to the most critical positions for which they are well-suited, ensuring sufficient organizational capability to face current and future challenges and opportunities" (2007, p. 144).

Talent Retention

The last component of talent management is talent retention. Talent retention involves rewarding employees for their work. Talent rewards, along with all the other components listed previously, will in return reduce employee turnover. It is estimated that it costs an organization 75–150% of an employee's annual salary to replace them (Krause, 2014). Many people are attracted to work in the nonprofit sector because of non-monetary factors (Word & Carpenter, 2013) and there are many resources and methods through which nonprofits can provide non-monetary benefits to their staff and volunteers. Intrinsically motivated staff and volunteers are rewarded simply by doing the work they enjoy doing, whereas extrinsically motivated staff and volunteers seek public recognition in the form of certificates of achievement and acknowledgment in front of their peers.

Even though there are many intrinsically motivated employees, a recent study shows the number one reason why employees left their jobs in the nonprofit sector was due to low compensation followed by lack of employee development (Landles-Cobb, Kramer, & Smith Milway, 2015). Therefore, extrinsic rewards such as compensation, benefits, work environment, the type of work performed, and employee development also influence talent retention. In conclusion, we have discussed the major components of talent management and how nonprofits can implement talent management components into their work. The next section will discuss talent management models and ways to incorporate many of the talent management components into effective talent management practices.

Talent Management Models

There is no one right way to manage talent. Kim et al. explain that talent differs by organization, "What an organization considers 'talent' depends on the nature of its work and is generally defined as those positions most integral to the success of the particular organization" (2014, p. 111). With that said, five models of talent development are discussed here. The five models covered are not exhaustive lists of what is available to nonprofit and philanthropic organizations, but different ways to approach talent management. The models are: (1) the Talent Development Platform (Carpenter & Qualls, 2015); (2) Strategic and Tactical Talent Management (Rothwell, 2012); (3) Technical Talent Management (Kim et al., 2014); (4) Leadership Development Process (Kramer & Nayak, 2013); and (5) Nonprofit Leadership Development (Bonner & Obergas, 2009).

The Talent Development Platform

The Talent Development Platform is a new model of managing talent management in the nonprofit sector (Carpenter & Qualls, 2015). Figure 8.2 shows the platform.

The Talent Development Platform addresses nonprofits' time management challenges by providing a practical guide to tying strategic goals to professional development.

The first part of the platform is where organizations take an organizational learning assessment to determine the learning culture, and if they are ready to

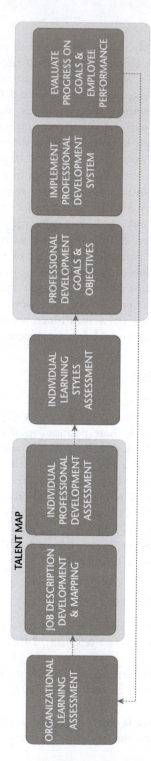

Figure 8.2 The Talent Development Platform

Source: Carpenter & Qualls (2015).

undertake the other steps in the platform. The next stage of the platform is to develop a talent map. The talent map is developed to support the organization's strategic goals and mission achievement. Through the talent mapping process, organizations write and revise their job descriptions, create competencies (using the ten core social change competencies developed by Carpenter and Qualls, and identify proficiency levels that fit with the created competencies. The process also involves developing organization, department, and position-based sub-competencies, and then assessing employees against the competencies and proficiency levels with the Individual Professional Development Assessment.

After the Talent Map has been developed, organizations administer the Learning Styles Assessment. Then, based on the results of the Individual Professional Development Assessment and Learning Styles assessments, organizations and individual employees develop professional development goals and objectives that enhance the organization's strategic goals. The professional development goals are tied to on-the-job learning, mentoring, and training. The next step is implementing the professional development activities in a year-long time frame. The Talent Development Platform provides a variety of resources including timelines, mentoring plans, budgets, and a return on investment calculator to help with talent retention. The last stage of the Talent Development Platform is evaluating professional development goals and employee performance. A year into the professional development implementation, employees retake the Individual Professional Development Assessment and evaluate the progress of the talent development implementation. The Talent Development Platform is a step forward for the nonprofit sector's understanding of talent management. It allows organizations to integrate talent management in their strategic planning process.

Strategic and Tactical Talent Management

The Strategic and Tactical Talent Management Model was developed by Rothwell (2012) for the corporate sector but can be used in the nonprofit sector as well. Rothwell explains the difference between strategic and tactical talent management as: "Strategic talent management is focused on integrating talent management efforts with the organization's strategic business plan. Tactical Talent Management is the process of driving talent management efforts into the daily thinking and actions of organizational leaders" (Rothwell, 2012, p. 6). Nonprofits struggle with thinking of talent on a daily basis, therefore the Strategic and Tactical Talent Management Model can help organizations shift their thinking and include talent in their daily mindset. The model involves 13 components or steps in identifying and developing top talent within an organization, as well as considering the talent needed for the future.

The first step of this model is to get input from all stakeholders in the organization; the second step is to consider all the ways work can be done; the third step is to formulate a talent management strategy and link it to business strategy;

the fourth step is to recruit and select the best people; the fifth step is to clarify work performance and the best people to do the work; the sixth step is to evaluate performance; the seventh step is to clarify future work to be performed and the people needed to perform that work; the eighth step is to identify people within the organization who have potential for promotion and help them develop/or identify their career goals; the ninth step is to close development gaps and build future competencies; the tenth step is to reward for talent; the eleventh step is to help senior employees to transfer knowledge to junior employees; the twelfth step is to plan for integrating talent management into daily work; the thirteenth and final step is to evaluate talent management results. The model is cyclical so once an organization gets through the 13 steps, they start the process again (Rothwell, 2012). Since nonprofits struggle with developing internal talent, retaining internal talent, and identifying the talent for the future (Landles-Cobb et al., 2015) the Strategic and Tactical Talent Management Model cyclical steps help organizations identify and develop talent planning, talent development, and talent retention strategies into overall organizational planning.

Technical Talent Management Model

The Technical Talent Management Model was developed by Rothwell and his colleagues (Kim et al., 2014) and is very similar to the Strategic and Tactical Talent Management Model developed by Rothwell (2012) but with only 11 steps. The Technical Talent Management Model is also focused on knowledge management, which means the information that an employee possesses to be able to perform his or her work (Cheese et al., 2007). The first step in the model is getting commitment for technical talent management; the second step is formulating a talent strategy; the third step is recruiting the best knowledge workers; the fourth step is clarifying the competencies needed to be performed by the knowledge workers; the fifth step is evaluating employee performance; the sixth step is clarifying future competencies needed and the career paths that knowledge workers can take to achieve the future competencies; the seventh step is identifying the future knowledge workers within the organization; the eighth step is preparing the future knowledge workers in the pipeline and addressing their talent gaps; the ninth step is rewarding and retaining the knowledge workers; the tenth step is helping the senior knowledge workers transfer information to employees in the pipeline; and the eleventh and last step is to evaluate the talent program (Kim et al., 2014). The Technical Talent Management Model is different from the model above because it can be used to tap into the knowledge of individual employees to help with mission achievement, rather than the strategic talent management practices.

Leadership Development Process

The Leadership Development Process was created by the Bridgespan Group (Kramer & Nayak, 2013) to help nonprofits with talent management and talent

Figure 8.3 Leadership Development Process

Source: Permission received from Kramer and Nayak (2013, p. 17).

development. They define leadership development as "identifying and developing those individuals who will lead the critical functions of your organization, and who, in partnership with other leaders, will be responsible for its overall health and impact" (Kramer & Nayak, 2013, p. 12). Their model is not inclusive of all employees within an organization but is meant to build what they call "future leaders." The first step involves engaging the senior leaders within the organization. The second step is understanding the future talent needs of the organization; the third step is developing future leaders; the fourth step is hiring externally to fill gaps, and the fifth step is monitoring and improving talent practices (Kramer & Nayak, 2013) (Figure 8.3).

The Leadership Development Process is important for nonprofit organizations because of the challenges they face in succession planning. The process allows organizations to identify future leaders in the organization and develop those leaders for future positions. Therefore, organizations hire less from outside the organization, which has been shown as more challenging and leads to higher turnover (Martin, 2014), and can focus on employee retention and supporting future leaders within the organization.

A Model for Nonprofit Leadership Development

Dewey and Kaye and the Looking Glass Institute created a model for leadership development after interviewing 38 nonprofit leaders around the United States (Bonner & Obergas, 2009). Their model involves eight steps. The first step is "identifying the challenges and strategies that will impact the organization of the next five years" (Bonner & Obergas, 2009, p. 3). The second step is creating a set of competencies that will be used to accelerate the organization forward. They identified key core competencies based on their research of the 38 nonprofit leaders. The competencies include: client focused; decision quality; delegation skills; ethics; integrity and trust; interpersonal skills; managing vision and mission; motivating others; presentation skills; priority setting; strategic agility. The third step is identifying "high potential" successors for each job. The fourth step involves using performance assessments to assess the individuals against the competencies the organizations have created. The next step involves identifying who will be ready to fulfill positions now and in 2–4 years and how each individual can contribute to the organization; the sixth step is creating a tailored development program for each individual within the organization so they can become ready for their new positions. The seventh step is measuring progress frequently and providing feedback to their employees on their performance. The last step is moving people to their new positions when they have achieved their development goals (Bonner & Obergas, 2009). The model for nonprofit leadership development is important for talent management within nonprofit organizations because it also helps organizations identify high potential successors. The model also combines nonprofit competencies, succession planning, and training and development.

In this section, five talent management models were described that nonprofits can use when implementing talent development strategies within their organizations. The next section discusses the efforts of infrastructure organizations in supporting and developing talent within the nonprofit and philanthropic sector.

Efforts to Support Talent within the Nonprofit and Philanthropic Sector

Various organizations (for the most part, foundations and infrastructure organizations—organizations that provide professional development to nonprofit organizations) have created programs to help develop and retain talent within the nonprofit sector. These initiatives include: the Talent Philanthropy Project; the Initiative for Nonprofit Talent and Leadership through the Independent Sector; the Nonprofit Talent and Leadership Toolkit for Emerging Practitioners in Philanthropy (EPIP); the Talent Development Initiative; the Nonprofit HR Talent Management Conference, and the American Express Nonprofit Leadership Academy.

The Talent Philanthropy Project

The Talent Philanthropy Project, started by Rusty Stahl, advocates for foundations to #fundthepeople, and more specifically talent philanthropy, which is defined as "intentional philanthropic investment in grantee and nonprofit talent in order to increase performance and impact" (Stahl, 2013, p. 40). The project is raising awareness of the major lack of funding for talent management efforts within the nonprofit sector. Stahl explains talent is different from capacity building and general operating support and there are specific strategies funders can employ to invest in the talent of their grantees. These strategies include:

1 Build talent within your grantmaking priorities and portfolio.
2 Build talent at all levels of the organization.
3 Don't look at grantee staff as overhead; see talent as integral to organizational success.
4 See talent investment leading to long-term impact.

5   Invest in teams and systems beyond the C-suite.
6   Advance values and offer living wages to grantees.
7   Make advancing diversity among grantees a top priority.
8   See that talent philanthropy benefits staff, constituents and the community as a whole.
9   View talent as integral at all levels of the organization.
10 Support talent within foundations as well (Stahl, 2013, pp. 41–42).

In more recent work, Stahl (2015) provides examples of funders who are investing in their grantees. These examples include the Community Memorial Foundation, providing a variety of support for talent philanthropy to their grantees including: technical assistant grants, professional coaching to executive directors, educational workshops on board leadership, leadership development for middle managers, and memberships to professional organizations. Another example is the Evelyn and Walter Hass Jr. Fund, which provides a consultant to grantees to implement talent development, and hosts convenings to share the talent development successes and challenges (Stahl, 2015). The Talent Philanthropy Project is one of the only initiatives that focuses on the funding side of talent management and it provides real case studies and solutions for funders to support talent within nonprofit organizations.

Initiative for Nonprofit Talent and Leadership

The Independent Sector with support from the American Express Foundation developed the Initiative for Nonprofit Talent and Leadership. Their theory of change states "valuing nonprofit talent and leadership through a focused investment of time, attention and resources is one of the most effective ways to catalyze transformational results for thriving communities" (Independent Sector, 2012, p. 3). The Independent Sector has a three-year plan of prioritizing leadership in the nonprofit sector, and states "leadership isn't about a person or position, it is an ongoing practice exercised at all levels" (2012, p. 3). The three-year plan involves:

1   Rallying individuals across the sector to champion leadership as a means to significantly increase the sector's impact in our community.
2   Identifying a critical mass of organizations who will demonstrate a commitment to best practices in leadership development.
3   Scaling a significantly increased number of sector leaders to engage annually in high-quality leadership development that equips them to deliver significant results.
4   Engaging public and private financial investments in philanthropic leadership development (2012, p. 4).

The Independent Sector also provides a leadership development program for 12 emerging leaders each year through the American Express NGEN fellowship, and their NGEN leadership award "honors one accomplished nonprofit or philanthropic leader age 40 or under who has already demonstrated significant impact in addressing society's critical needs" (Independent Sector, 2015, para. 1). The Initiative for Nonprofit Talent and Leadership is helpful for the sector because it is raising awareness of the importance of leadership development. The products the NGEN fellows create each year advance awareness of emerging leaders and the ever changing leadership demographics in the sector.

Nonprofit Talent and Leadership Toolkit from Emerging Practitioners in Philanthropy (EPIP)

The Emerging Practitioners in Philanthropy mission is to "develop emerging leaders committed to building a just, equitable, and sustainable society" (EPIP, 2015, para. 1). EPIP offers a variety of programs to support philanthropic leaders in their professional and personal lives. One of the programs is to invest in talent development and retention within the philanthropic sector. They developed the Nonprofit Talent and Leadership Development Toolkit focused on creating a talent culture within organizations, and it features case studies of foundations supporting talent development within nonprofit and philanthropic organizations. The toolkit focuses on three areas of talent:

1 renewing leaders for long-term service;
2 creating succession and transition talent;
3 reengaging proven leaders as interim directors.

EPIP has also created a series of competencies that emerging leaders can strive for and use to prepare for leadership within the nonprofit and philanthropic sector. The Nonprofit Leadership and Talent toolkit is helpful to advancing talent management practices within the sector because it provides solutions to help prevent burnout of senior leaders within organizations. The toolkit also helps organizations with succession planning efforts.

Talent Development Initiative

The Talent Development Initiative was started by Pathfinder Solutions in collaboration with the Colorado Nonprofit Association and the Louisiana Nonprofit Association in 2010. The goals of the multi-year initiative were to do the following:

1 Introduce people to ways their energies and abilities can make a difference and have a profound impact upon their own lives.
2 Bridge the gaps in the path to nonprofit leadership so that people from all backgrounds can become involved in creating effective, dynamic organizations.

3   Increase individual job satisfaction and lower employee turnover by providing quality training and professional development.
4   Create metrics focused on enhancing individual performance, organizational effectiveness, and community outcomes.
5   Improve the impact of organizations and strengthen sustainability (Pathfinder Solutions, 2016, para. 3).

During the Talent Initiative, Pathfinder Solutions worked with many foundations, nonprofit associations, college classes, and groups such as AmeriCorp across the United States and even in other countries. Two products were created as a result of the Initiative. First, the work became the research underpinnings for the book *Compassionate Careers: Making a Living by Making a Difference* (Pryor & Mitchell, 2015). Second, Pathfinder Solutions created a comprehensive talent assessment and an online workbook to accompany the book. In all, the Talent Initiative confirmed nonprofits are more sustainable when they prioritize talent management and leadership development (Pathfinder Solutions, 2016).

Nonprofit HR Talent Management Conference

The mission of Nonprofit HR is to "partner with the country's leading nonprofit organizations in consulting, talent acquisition, executive search and education, all with the objective of making the nonprofit workforce the best it can be" (Nonprofit HR, 2015, para. 1). Nonprofit HR provides talent-related resources for nonprofit organizations and workers. Its annual employment trends survey and national conferences report on the most pressing workforce issues in the nonprofit sector. In April 2016, it held the first ever Nonprofit Talent and Culture Summit and brought together all the leading experts in talent management. The convenings and research produced by Nonprofit HR show that talent management practices are gaining importance within the nonprofit sector and cannot be ignored by organizations.

The American Express Nonprofit Leadership Academy

The American Express Nonprofit Leadership Academy was "founded in 2008 in partnership with the Center for Creative Leadership, today the Leadership Academy includes five nonprofit partners, encompasses nine separate programs, spans four countries and impacts hundreds of high-potential emerging leaders annually" (American Express, 2015, para. 1). There are three main components to the American Express Leadership Academy:

1   targeting high potential emerging leaders for leadership development opportunities;
2   curriculum blending personal leadership skills with business skills;
3   an assessment-based approach with coaching and feedback throughout (2015, para. 1).

American Express has seen tremendous growth and success in the program since its inception and most recently partnered with the Presidio Institute in San Francisco to deliver online leadership development trainings to nonprofit organizations.

The efforts described above were created to help develop and retain talent within the nonprofit sector and continue to gain momentum each day. As more nonprofits receive funding for their people, take leadership development training, and implement succession planning best practices, they will reap the benefits of lower turnover and increased sustainability, as indicated by the research. With that said, there are still major barriers, which are listed below, that nonprofits must overcome to implement talent management strategies.

Barriers to Implementing Talent Management Strategies

Even with all the efforts by foundations and infrastructure organizations, nonprofits face many barriers to integrating talent management practices. Experts such as Dan Pallotta (2010) have written about the charity culture and the fact the nonprofit sector largely emerged out of volunteer-run organizations. As a result of this charity culture, donors and the general public still believe many nonprofit workers should not be paid at all or be paid minimal amounts. The no and low overhead culture is so prevalent that in 2013 infrastructure organizations such as Guidestar and the Charity Navigator had to write a letter to both donors and nonprofits to get them not to focus on overhead ratios so much (Overhead Myth, 2013). The letter is ironic because these same infrastructure organizations have been rating charities for many years based on low overhead percentages. While there are many barriers to successful talent management, this chapter focuses on the major barriers to each talent management component including barriers to: identifying talent needs, developing competencies, recruiting talent, supporting talent through training and development, and retaining talent.

Barriers to Identifying Talent Needs

The main barrier in identifying talent needs is lack of data about nonprofit employees and volunteers. Since most nonprofits are focused on employees and volunteers doing the work, few focus on the level at which employees and volunteers perform the work. A recent study of the professional development needs of Michigan nonprofits identified data-based decision-making as one of the most pressing professional development needs (Carpenter, Clarke, & Gregg, 2013). This professional development need translates into few nonprofits knowing how to track important workforce metrics including but not limited to such measures as their staff time, staff efforts, and turnover rates. Since this data is rarely tracked, nonprofits struggle with identifying where they have the largest talent needs.

Barriers to Developing Competencies

Competencies, defined as the knowledge, skills, abilities and other characteristics which one must have in order to perform the job duty (Pynes, 2009), is a popular term among human resource management (HRM) professionals and well known in the corporate sector. Since only a small percentage of nonprofits have paid human resources staff (Guo et al., 2011), few organizations use competencies. Since few nonprofits track their talent needs, they then face increased barriers in knowing which competencies their employees should possess, and as a result may have lower performing organizations with employees and volunteers not necessarily in the right position, given the competencies the employee or volunteer possesses.

Barriers to Recruiting Talent

In a recent nonprofit employment trends survey, 33% of respondents indicated they had challenges recruiting staff and 52% stated they did not have a formal recruitment strategy (Nonprofit HR, 2015). As stated above, since few nonprofits have designated HR staff (Guo et al., 2011), as a result, recruitment is often a last-minute, quick fill for an open position task. Therefore, another barrier is nonprofits having adequate staffing or a strategy for recruitment.

Commongood Careers conducted a study to determine the challenges in building and sustaining diverse organizations aimed at coming up with strategies and solutions for overcoming obstacles in recruitment, retention, and prioritizing diversity within nonprofit organizations. Out of the 1,638 current and former nonprofit employees who completed the survey, "9 out of 10 of respondents indicated their organizations value diversity and inclusiveness but 7 out 10 believe their employer does not do enough to create a diverse and inclusive work environment" (Schwartz, Weinberg, Hagenbuch, & Scott, 2011, p. 8). This lack of a diverse and inclusive environment is another barrier to recruiting the best and brightest talent.

Barriers to Training and Development

As stated above, once the best and brightest talent is hired, they must be developed from day one. Research shows that nonprofits only spend approximately 2% of their annual budgets on professional development (Carpenter, Clarke, & Gregg, 2013). Professional development support in nonprofits is often piecemeal. For example, staff members may receive funding to attend a conference but there is no effort to tie that professional development activity back to the individuals' jobs or the strategic goals of the organization. One talent support organization believes the barriers to implementing professional development include a lack of seeing talent development from within, absence of a competency model to assess talent, hoarding talent (e.g. worrying that good talent will leave the organization), lack of critical feedback, and limited professional development support for staff (Bonner & Obergas, 2009). Therefore, with small professional development resources as well as not seeing the talent they currently have, talent management efforts are stifled.

Barriers in Talent Retention

Studies show that many emerging leaders in the sector want professional development (Dobin & Tchume, 2011) and will leave the sector if they do not get the support they need. Younger leaders are not the only talent in need of development; senior leaders need to be developed too. The average cost to replace one employee is $13,996 (O'Connell & Kung, 2007). Small and large nonprofits are facing a crisis from burnt out staff, staff who leave for better-paying jobs, and staff who leave because they do not feel supported.

These barriers demonstrate that nonprofits have a long way to go in implementing proven talent management strategies and reaching the multiplication of talent. Nonprofits are not alone in their struggle to implement talent management strategies. So far this chapter has discussed the talent management components, models, resources for nonprofits to implement talent management strategies, and barriers to implementing these strategies; next, it will discuss what the future holds for nonprofits in regard to talent management.

What Does the Future Hold in Talent Management?

Experts believe the nonprofit sector cannot continue to operate under the charity mentality (Palotta, 2010; 2012). It is losing high quality talent to other sectors through the turnover treadmill (Landles-Cobb et al., 2015). Organizations need to be flexible enough to integrate talent management practices throughout the organization. Guo et al. (2011) found larger, more technology-savvy nonprofits, younger nonprofits, and ones that did not have a dedicated HR staff were able to integrate strategic HR practices (which includes talent management). The nonprofit of the future needs to be flexible enough to perform simple procedures such as tracking staff turnover and work on daily basis, and developing core competencies. Foundations need to provide more funding to nonprofits to support talent management efforts within individual organizations.

This chapter shows there are talent management components, talent management models, and infrastructure organizations and funders who are working to support talent within the nonprofit sector. However, there are still many barriers nonprofit organizations must overcome to implement a talent management multiplication strategy where talent is fully integrated within the mission of the organization. Talent management will remain a struggle for many nonprofit organizations until there are shifts in funding for talent management and people are seen as an integral part of mission achievement. In the future, we envision reduced staff and volunteer burnout, more time and money for professional development, as well as rewards and increased job satisfaction among nonprofit workers.

Discussion Questions

1   If you were an executive director of a nonprofit organization, which talent management model would you choose to implement and why?
2   What talent management resource(s) would be the most appealing to emerging leaders or established leaders and why?
3   The chapter discussed barriers to implementing talent management strategies within nonprofit organizations. What are they and how can nonprofits overcome these barriers?

Note

1   Full descriptions of the social change competencies can be found at: www.talent 4socialchange.com/wp-content/uploads/2015/02/Competency-Descriptions1.pdf

References

Aguinis, H. & Kraiger, K. (2009). Benefits of training and development for individuals and teams, organizations and society. Available at: www.annualreviews.org/doi/pdf/10.1146/annurev.psych.60.110707.163505 (accessed August 8, 2015).

American Express Foundation. (2015). American Express Leadership Academy. Available at: http://about.americanexpress.com/csr/nla.aspx (accessed August 6, 2015).

Bureau of Labor Statistics. (2014). US Nonprofit Workforce Statistics. Available at: http://beta.bls.gov/labs/blogs/2014/10/17/announcing-new-research-data-on-jobs-and-pay-in-the-nonprofit-sector/ (accessed August 6, 2015).

Bonner, L. & Obergas, J. (2009). *Nonprofit leadership development: A model for identifying and growing leaders within nonprofit organizations*. Pittsburgh, PA: Looking Glass Institute.

Carpenter, H., Clarke, A., & Gregg, R. (2013). *2013 Nonprofit needs assessment: A profile of Michigan's most urgent professional development needs*. Michigan: Grand Valley State University.

Carpenter, H. & Qualls, T. (2015). *The Talent Development Platform: Putting people first in social change organizations*. San Francisco: Jossey-Bass.

CEB. (2015). The career path is dead! Long live careers! *CHRO Quarterly Magazine*. Available at: https://www.cebglobal.com/exbd/human-resources/corporate-leadership-council/career-pathing/article/index.page? (accessed January 6, 2015).

Cheese, P., Thomas, R. J., & Craig, E. (2007). *The talent powered organization: Strategies for globalization, talent management and high performance* (Reprint ed.). London: Kogan Page.

Cotton, A. (2007). Seven steps to effective workplace planning. Available at: www.uquebec.ca/observgo/fichiers/92684_qqq.pdf (accessed August 6, 2015).

Dobin, D. & Tchume, T. (2011). Good in theory, problems in practice. Available at: https://d3n8a8pro7vhmx.cloudfront.net/ynpn/pages/302/attachments/original/1434746810/Good_in_Theory_Problem_in_Practice_FULL_REPORT.pdf?1434746810 (accessed August 6, 2015).

Emerging Practitioners in Philanthropy. (2015a). About EPIP. Available at: www.epip.org/about (accessed August 6, 2015).

Emerging Practitioners in Philanthropy. (2015b). Nonprofit talent and leadership development toolkit. Available at: www.epip.org/the_nonprofit_talent_and_leadership_development_tool_kit (accessed August 6, 2015).

Goleman, D. (2005). *Emotional intelligence: Why it can matter more than IQ* (10th anniversary ed.). New York: Bantam Books.

Guo, C., Brown, W. A., Ashcraft, R. F., Yoshioka, C. F., & Dong, H.-K. D. (2011). Strategic human resources management in nonprofit organizations. *Review of Public Personnel Administration, 31*(3), 248–269. http://doi.org/10.1177/0734371X11402878

Independent Sector. (2012). Initiative for nonprofit talent and leadership. Available at: www.independentsector.org/uploads/INTL/FinalStrategydocument.pdf (accessed August 6, 2015).

Independent Sector. (2015). NGEN. Available at: www.independentsector.org/ngen (accessed August 6, 2015).

Kim, Y., Williams, R., Rothwell, W. J., & Penaloza, P. (2014). A strategic model for technical talent management: A model based on a qualitative case study. *Performance Improvement Quarterly, 26*(4), 93–121. http://doi.org/10.1002/piq.21159

Kramer, K. & Nayak, P. (2013). Nonprofit leadership development: What's your plan A for growing future leaders? Available at: www.bridgespan.org/Publications-and-Tools/Career-Professional-Development/Develop-My-Staff/Plan-A-How-Successful-Nonprofits-Develop-Leaders.aspx#.Vco193iM-xI (accessed August 6, 2015).

Krause, J. (2014). Avoiding high turnover begins with making the right hire. Available at: www.linkedin.com/pulse/20140617141517-13362262-avoiding-high-turnover-begins-with-making-the-right-hire (accessed August 6, 2015).

Landles-Cobb, L., Kramer, K., & Smith Milway, K. (2015). The nonprofit leadership development deficit. *Stanford Social Innovation Review.* Available at: http://ssir.org/articles/entry/the_nonprofit_leadership_development_deficit (accessed November 8, 2015).

Lavelle, J. (2007). On workforce architecture, employment relationships and lifecycles: Expanding the purview of workforce planning & management. *Public Personnel Management, 36*(4), 371–385. http://doi.org/10.1177/009102600703600406

Lee, C. H. & Bruvold, N. T. (2003). Creating value for employees: investment in employee development. *The International Journal of Human Resource Management, 14*(6), 981–1000. http://doi.org/10.1080/0958519032000106173

Martin, J. (2014). For senior leaders, fit matters more than skill. *Harvard Business Review,* January 17, 2014.

Nonprofit HR. (2015a). 2015 Nonprofit employment practices survey. Available at: www.nonprofithr.com/wp-content/uploads/2015/02/2015-Nonprofit-Employment-Practices-Survey-Results-1.pdf (accessed August 6, 2015).

Nonprofit HR. (2015b). Homepage. Available at: www.nonprofithr.com (accessed August 6, 2015).

O'Connell, M. & Kung, M. C. (2007). The cost of employee turnover. *Industrial Management, 49*(1), 14–19.

Overhead Myth. (2013). Available at: http://overheadmyth.com (accessed August 6, 2015).

Palotta, D. (2010). *Uncharitable.* Lebanon, NH: Tufts University Press.

Palotta, D. (2012). *Charity case.* San Francisco: Jossey-Bass.

Pathfinder Solutions (2016). Talent development initiative goals. Available at: www.pathfindersolutions.org/cultivate/talent-development-initiative/ (accessed October 16, 2016).

Pynes, J. E. (2009). *Human resources management for public and nonprofit organizations: A strategic approach* (3rd ed.). San Francisco: Jossey-Bass.

Rodriguez, D., Patel, R., Bright, A., Gregory, D., & Gowing, M. K. (2002). Developing competency models to promote integrated human resource practices. *Human Resource Management, 41*(3), 309–324. http://doi.org/10.1002/hrm.10043

Rothwell, W. J. (2012). Talent management: Aligning your organisation with best practices in strategic and tactical talent management. *Training & Development*, *39*(2), 12–14.

Schwartz, R., Weinberg, J., Hagenbuch, D., & Scott, A. (2011). The voice of nonprofit talent: Perceptions of diversity in the workplace. Commongood Careers.

Salovey, P. & Mayer, J. D. (1990). Emotional intelligence. *Imagination, Cognition and Personality*, *9*, 185–211.

Stahl, R. (2013). Talent philanthropy: Investing in nonprofit people to advance nonprofit Performance. *The Foundation Review*, *5*(3). http://doi.org/10.9707/1944-5660.1169

Stahl, R. (2015). Talent investing: Raising and granting funds to develop social change leadership. In H. Carpenter & T. Qualls (Eds.), *The talent development platform: Putting people first in social change organizations* (pp. 485–510). San Francisco: Jossey-Bass.

Tan, C. (2012). *Search inside yourself: The unexpected path to achieving success, happiness (and world peace)*. New York: Harper One.

Thunnisen, M., Boselie, P., & Fruytier, B. (2013). A review of talent management: "infancy or adolescence?." *International Journal of Human Resource Management*, *24*(9), 1744–1761. http://doi.org/10.1080/09585192.2013.777543

Word, J. & Carpenter, H. (2013). The new public service? Applying the public service motivation model to nonprofit employees. *Public Personnel Management*, *42*(3), 315–336. http://doi.org/10.1177/0091026013495773

9

Compensation Practices in Nonprofit Organizations
Examining Practices Adopted by High Performing Nonprofits

Sally Coleman Selden

Introduction

Recruiting, retaining, and motivating employees in the nonprofit sector is critical to an organization's ability to accomplish its mission. A critical practice associated with recruiting, retaining, and motivating employees is compensation. Few studies have examined compensation practices comprehensively in nonprofits or in high-performing nonprofits (Hallock, 2002). Most compensation studies in the nonprofit sector focus on executive compensation or differences in compensation between the nonprofit, public, and private sectors (Barragato, 2002; Cortis, 2000; Garner & Harrison, 2013; Grasse, Davis, & Ihrke, 2014; Faulk et al., 2012; Nikolova, 2014; Oster, 1998; Roomkin & Weisbrod, 1999; Ruhm & Borkoski, 2003; Theuvsen, 2004). In order to design a compensation system that attracts, retains, and motivates high quality employees, nonprofit managers need an understanding of how other nonprofit organizations leverage different compensation strategies and which strategies are most effective.

The nonprofit sector, comprised of nearly 2 million nonprofit organizations, employs more than 10.7 million people and produces more than $1.9 trillion in revenue (Salamon, Sokolowski, & Geller, 2012). The Bureau of Labor Statistics estimated that in 2012, nonprofits accounted for 11.4 million jobs, which is 10.3% of the U.S. private-sector workforce. Between 2000 and 2010, employment in the nonprofit sector grew faster than the overall U.S. economy (Roeger, Blackwood, & Pettijohn, 2012). During the Great Recession, the sector continued to add jobs as the need for nonprofit services grew. McKeever (2015) estimated the nonprofit sector contributed about $905.9 billion to the U.S. economy in 2013, which is around 5.4% of the gross domestic product (GDP). In a 2015 survey of nonprofits, the most common retention challenge mentioned by 27% of nonprofits was competitive pay, which is consistent with the fact that many nonprofits operate within a limited salary budget (Nonprofit HR, 2015). Given the importance of the nonprofit sector to the U.S. economy and to the delivery of human services, there is a strong need to understand compensation and how to ensure effective compensation practices in nonprofits. As nonprofits grow and employ a more professional human capital stock, these organizations need to develop more capacity to manage these professionals to maintain them in their roles and direct them toward the accomplishment of organizational goals and nonprofit missions.

Although compensation has always been challenging for the nonprofit sector, the period since the Great Recession has resulted in a particularly constrained funding environment. While demand for services provided by nonprofits has increased, the competition for funding has grown. Although we know that individuals often do not elect to work in the nonprofit sector for high wages, research has demonstrated that compensation impacts employee satisfaction and performance (Selden & Sowa, 2014). Because nonprofits compete in a common labor market, they need to understand the larger environment in which they compete for labor and formulate strategic choices about compensation to help them leverage their human capital. The differences in compensation in the nonprofit sector reflect the competitive pressures they face in the labor market where shifts in the supply and demand impact the market rate.

Alliances have developed within and across states to develop and conduct compensation surveys, which provide guidance to nonprofits about setting wages. While useful for setting levels of compensation, these studies are much less likely to explore different compensation strategies that can be used to reward performance or loyalty; they are generally focused on occupational and market rates, which are discussed later in this chapter. Scholars and practitioners need to move beyond studying rates of compensation and compensation comparisons to think about how compensation connects to human capital acquisition and development, overall sustainability, and performance in nonprofit organizations. This chapter briefly reviews the regulatory context related to compensation, the literature examining compensation in the nonprofit sector, and presents results from an eight-state study of human service nonprofits, focusing on compensation strategies adopted by high performing nonprofits.

Regulations Influencing Compensation in Nonprofit Organizations

Before considering the larger strategic implications of compensation, nonprofit organizations must comply with legal requirements related to compensation, including the Fair Labor Standards Act (FLSA), administered by the Department of Labor's Wage and Hour Division, the Lilly Ledbetter Fair Pay Act of 2009, the Employee Retirement Income Security Act, and the Internal Revenue Service. Nonprofits must provide required benefits, including social security, unemployment insurance, and Workers' Compensation Insurance.[1] Information is readily available about assessing reasonableness of compensation as defined by the IRS and as applied to executive compensation in nonprofit organizations (e.g., Vogel & Quatt, 2015). Far less attention in the academic literature has been devoted to compensation across organizational ranks and the implications of changing federal regulations on nonprofits.

Nonprofits that are not exempt from the FLSA are grappling with how to address the sweeping set of new regulations implemented on December 1, 2016. According to the Department of Labor's frequently asked questions webpage (2016a),

> Generally, employees of enterprises that have an annual gross volume of sales made or business done of $500,000 or more are covered by the FLSA. In addition, employees of certain entities are covered by the FLSA regardless of the amount of gross volume of sales or business done. These entities include: hospitals; businesses providing medical or nursing care for residents; schools (whether operated for profit or not for profit); and public agencies.

The new regulation raises the minimum salary level that white-collar employees must be paid (from $23,660 to $47,476) in order for them to be classified as exempt from overtime pay, which is time and half of wages for hours worked in excess of 40 in any week. Moreover, the new regulation increases the minimum salary level for "highly compensated employees" from $100,000 to over $134,004 per year. The Department of Labor regulations exempt "highly compensated employees" if these employees' total annual compensation exceeds $134,004 and they "customarily and regularly perform at least one of the exempt duties or responsibilities of an executive, administrative, or professional employee" (National Council of Nonprofits, 2016).[2]

Nonprofits will be faced with determining whether to classify employees as exempt from overtime given the new salary test, which is one of three required conditions. The Department of Labor places the burden on the employer to demonstrate that an employee is exempt from the overtime provisions by requiring that an employee satisfy three tests. First, the salary basis test requires that the employee be paid a predetermined weekly or annual salary not adjusted, based on whether the person worked certain hours. In other words, they are paid a salary rather than being paid and tracked by the hour. Second, the duties test requires that the individual's primary job duties involve executive, administrative, and professional duties as defined by the Labor Department regulations. Third, the salary level test requires that an employee be paid at or above the minimum specified amount, defined as $47,476 per year (National Council of Nonprofits, 2016).

The minimum wage and overtime provisions of the FLSA generally apply to nonprofit organizations, which is not a change. The newly adopted regulations may result in nonprofits reclassifying employees who were exempt to nonexempt status if they are unable to meet the new salary threshold. Nonprofits are not permitted to utilize compensatory time for salaried employees instead of paying overtime. However, government agencies (including federal, state, and local government agencies) are permitted to use compensatory time rather than paying overtime (Department of Labor, 2016c). Nonprofits need to critically examine their compensation structures and the design of jobs to make sure that they are in compliance with these regulations, but also to ensure that they are designing compensation systems that will support the well-being of employees and the goals and sustainability of the nonprofit.

Summary of Compensation Research in Nonprofit Sector

In addition to ensuring that they are in compliance with federal and state regulations with their compensation practices, nonprofits also need to consider what is their overall approach to compensation and how that supports the goals and mission of their organizations. However, this remains a gap in the nonprofit research base. Although some research has examined executive compensation in the nonprofit arena, few studies have examined compensation for other employees in nonprofit organizations outside of the healthcare and education industries (Benson & Hornsby, 2002; Rhodes, Bechtle, & McNett, 2015). With a few notable exceptions (Frumkin & Keating, 2001; Hallock, 2002; Jobome, 2006; Oster, 1998), more research is needed on compensation as it relates to practices adopted for nonexecutive employees.

As stated, a few studies have sought to explain executive compensation in terms of levels and patterns, while others have examined the relationship between executive compensation and nonprofit performance (Barragato, 2002; Cortis, 2000; Garner & Harrison, 2013; Grasse, Davis, & Ihrke, 2014; Faulk et al., 2012; Nikolova, 2014; Oster, 1998; Roomkin & Weisbrod, 1999; Ruhm & Borkoski, 2003; Theuvsen, 2004). For example, Nikolova's (2014) panel study of executive compensation in human service nonprofits demonstrated that greater monitoring —reporting, auditing, or director observation—of nonprofit executive behavior was associated with lower compensation of the executive director. In a study linking compensation and performance, Garner and Harrison (2013) found that nonprofits that paid their executive director above average compensation had lower performance as measured by program service expenses. A year later, however, Grasse et al.'s (2014) study found a positive and significant relationship between performance and compensation. Rather than examining performance as the dependent variable, Grasse et al. (2014) included it as a predictor of executive compensation and found it to be correlated with executive compensation across different types of nonprofit. While these studies offer insights into the role and influence of executive pay, little research has explored compensation for nonexecutive employees. Therefore, in designing compensation systems, it is important to be clear about the strategic principles underlying those systems and how the design of these systems aligns with certain organizational characteristics.

The next two sections of this chapter address concepts that are directly applicable for understanding, establishing, and implementing compensation systems in nonprofit organizations.

Compensation Principles of Internal and External Equity

There are two compensation doctrines that apply to developing a sound, principled pay system for any type of organization and that warrant examination: internal and external equity. Historically, compensation focused on managing pay from an internal, organizational perspective. This approach focused on internal equity or consistency of pay, job evaluation, and satisfaction with pay (Dulebohn & Werling, 2007). To determine internal equity, an organization compares how jobs are compensated relative to their worth to ascertain the alignment between job responsibilities and pay. In theory, internal equity exists when employees in an organization perceive that they are being rewarded fairly according to the relative value of their jobs within an organization. While there are a number of different job classification/evaluation systems that can be employed to determine relative worth, they often fall within two broad categories: whole job and quantitative.

The quantitative approaches are more defensible but they are also much more time-consuming and complex to implement. Traditionally, this approach has focused on hiring people in entry-level positions and promoting employees within well-defined job families with specified pay levels. Fair-wage theory, which is consistent with Stacy Adams' equity theory, suggests that employees compare their wages to those of their colleagues to determine fairness (Burger & Walters, 2008). Employees who perceive that their wages are low are likely to reduce their effort and miss work. Levine (1991) noted that perceptions of pay inequality or pay compression may undermine relationships among employees and added that wage inequality can negatively impact teams, undermining cooperation among employees, and decreasing cohesiveness in teams. Organizations focused only on internal equity do not tend to focus on external equity or pay relative to similar jobs in the external market (external equity).

External equity, often referred to as market competitiveness, is the comparison of an organization's compensation for positions with similar positions in its identified market. To determine this, a nonprofit would build a competitive pay structure by conducting a market survey that would examine the pay levels of incumbents in similar positions in selected organizations (including other nonprofits and public or private organizations) in the identified labor market. Jobs are then benchmarked to establish market wages. The selection of benchmark jobs should include positions with a broad range of departments, pay grades, and work duties. The organization can establish starting wages based upon the market, but they can also examine current wages of employees, determining whether they are below, at, or above market wages. External equity is achieved when employees in an organization perceive that they are compensated fairly in relation to those who perform similar jobs in other organizations in the local market. For example, if a nonprofit human service organization employs licensed clinical social workers (LCSW) to provide casework services to their clients, this nonprofit should compare the pay rates of LCSWs in similar size nonprofits and in public organizations and make a decision about where to position the salaries of the employees in relation to those comparison groups.

It is sometimes difficult for organizations to maintain internal alignment and external competitiveness, which can result in salary compression, whereas newly hired employees may receive compensation nearly as large as their more senior colleagues (Toutkoushian, 1998). More challenging is salary inversion when compensation paid to newer employees is higher than the compensation of more senior employees. Using a different approach to equity, Hamann and Ren (2013) examined the impact of wage inequality on service quality and employee effort in nursing homes. They measured inequality using two internal measures: the 80th/20th percentiles salary ratio and the ratio of the salaries of Registered Nurses to Certified Nursing Assistants. The study showed that ownership—whether it was a nonprofit or a for-profit nursing home—moderated the relationship between wage inequality and service quality. Wage inequality negatively impacted service quality in the nonprofit nursing homes, which was the opposite of the impact of wage inequity in the for-profit sector. The study also showed that wage inequality in the nonprofit sector had a more significant impact or influence on employee discretionary action. They also found that wages in the nonprofit sector were more compressed than in the private sector.

Faulk et al. (2012) found that gender gaps in the nonprofit sector were lower than in the for-profit sector. Faulk et al. (2012, p. 1281), however, concluded that "instead of intentionally compensating women more equitably in the non-profit sector, relative gender pay equality appears to be a convenient consequence of men accepting lower pay in traditionally nonprofit and female jobs." But Hallock's (2002) study of nonprofit managers suggests that real pay disparity exists between men and women in the sector. His research revealed that women in the role of executive director earned approximately 20% less than men in the same role. Lewin's (2001) article highlighted a recent study by GuideStar, which also demonstrated a significant gap in pay between women and men executive directors both for large and smaller nonprofit organizations. Therefore, when designing their compensation systems, nonprofits need to clearly understand the underlying principles for effective compensation systems and settle upon clear principles that will determine pay rates and allow them to promote a sense of equity along multiple dimensions for their employees to the degree that they have the available resources.

Key Elements of Compensation Structure

Nonprofits, like other organizations, may establish a philosophy or set of goals and expectations that guide their compensation structure. The first element of the compensation system is establishing base pay rates, which may be guided by both internal and external equity, and establishing a salary structure. Once an organization determines how to establish base pay, the second element is to establish how to adjust compensation, which is most frequently done on an annual basis. Historically, organizations adjusted salaries by rewarding longevity by periodic step increases based upon years of service or adjusted for the changes in the cost of living by implementing across the board cost of living adjustments (COLA). Longevity and step adjustments signal that the organization values employees who remain with the organization, whereas COLA awards recognize that employees are impacted by changes in the cost of living.

Today, organizations tend to place more attention on linking pay adjustments to performance than on tenure either individually or collectively as a team as a bonus or added to the base salary, but the research on this topic in the nonprofit human services and smaller nonprofits is limited. Some studies have examined the application of pay for performance in the nonprofit sector (Brandl & Güttel, 2007; Chen, Ren, & Knoke, 2013; Jobome, 2006; Werner & Gemeinhardt, 1995). Because nonprofits have historically avoided paying bonuses even for executive directors, introducing performance-based pay in the sector has been controversial (Speckbacher, 2013). Speckbacher (2013) derived three "nonprofit characteristics" that he theorized would impact the use and effectiveness of incentive pay in nonprofits. The characteristics, which may vary across non-profits, include the challenge of developing an overall measure of performance, the difficulty of identifying factors that motivate nonprofit employees, and "the trust-based social character." Quatt Associates conduct an annual compensation survey of large nonprofits, including public broadcasting, museums, performing arts institutions, foundations, and others. In 2013, they found that of those large nonprofits providing an annual bonus to executive directors, the middle 50% of bonuses were, on average, between 11 and 36% of the executive director's annual salary (Quatt Associates, 2013).

Using a case study design, Brandl and Güttel (2007) explored why some nonprofits adopted pay for performance and others did not. At the time of their study, none of the nonprofits examined had fully implemented a pay-for-performance compensation system. However, their findings suggested that non-profits that perceived their environment to be more competitive were more likely to adopt pay for performance. Chen, Ren, and Knoke (2013) found that for-profit organizations were significantly more likely to employ bonuses or profit sharing and gain sharing than public and nonprofit organizations. This finding held whether the authors examined group or individual performance-based pay. When examining pay for skill systems, however, the differences between sectors were not significant (Chen, Ren, & Knoke, 2013). A recent study examining the impact of high performance work systems on job satisfaction and performance in human service nonprofits found employees who worked in nonprofits with performance-based compensation elements were more satisfied (Selden & Sowa, 2014). Johnson and Ng's (2015) study of Millennials found that young nonprofit workers are less likely to move from the nonprofit sector to the for-profit or government sector due to pay. On the other hand, they found that pay mattered to Millennial managers. Managers who were compensated more were significantly more likely to remain within the nonprofit sector (Johnson & Ng, 2015).

Studies have also examined the influence of organizational size on nonprofit compensation (Chen, Ren, & Knoke, 2013; Gray & Benson, 2003; Hallock, 2002). In general, executive compensation increases with the size of the organization, which may be an indirect reflection of organizational complexity (Gray & Benson, 2003). Thus, we might expect that larger human service nonprofits would adopt more sophisticated employment practices related to compensation than smaller nonprofit organizations with less complexity. Overall, the effect of organizational size has also been supported by the literature (Brown & Medoff, 1989). Chen, Ren, and Knoke (2013) found that larger organizations were more likely to adopt incentive, performance, and skills compensation systems. Therefore, when considering the compensation practices of a nonprofit, it is important to understand their size and complexity and how this may influence the systems and practices that are both available to them and that they have the capacity to implement.

This study adds to the emerging research on nonprofit compensation systems by exploring the compensation practices of human service nonprofit organizations and whether those practices differ between high performing nonprofits, between nonprofits led by men and women, and between nonprofits of different sizes.

Research Setting: Multi-State Study of Human Service Nonprofits

To examine compensation practices in nonprofit organizations, this chapter uses data collected by a multi-state study (Selden & Sowa, 2014). First, the study surveyed executive directors of human service nonprofits in eight states. Based upon the survey data collected, the second stage of the study focused on identifying a set of 16 high performing human service nonprofits and interviewing the executive director of each and the staff member responsible for human resources.[3]

The study surveyed executive directors of human service nonprofit organizations in eight states across the United States between May and July 2012. To account for possible regional variations, states were selected to encompass a representation of the major regions in the United States, with states from the Northeast, the South, the Midwest, and the West included in the sample. Nonprofits in the following eight states were surveyed: New Hampshire, Vermont, Michigan, Virginia, Idaho, Utah, New Mexico, and Wyoming. The sample was constructed through a search of GuideStar on the selected NTEE codes, with the sample restricted to organizations with budgets between $500,000 and $10,000,000.[4] Completed surveys were received from 344 of the 872 executive directors surveyed for a response rate of 39.5%. However, approximately 289 completed the majority of questions included in this analysis for an effective response rate of 33%. Although the original sample included nonprofits with reported revenues between $500,000 and $10,000,000, 21 of the nonprofits responding to the survey indicated that their current revenues were less than $500,000.

Since this study was interested in examining the differences in compensation strategies between high performing nonprofits, a performance score was calculated as an index of the following measures (Cronbach alpha = 0.85; mean = 3.88; std = 0.56):

How would you compare the organization's performance over the past 2 years to that of other nonprofit organizations in your local community of similar size or that provide similar services and programs? (response: 5 point Likert scale from a lot below average to a lot better than average):[5]

- Quality of services and programs
- Ability to raise money
- Ability to secure grants
- Ability to attract essential employees
- Ability to retain essential employees
- Satisfaction of customers or clients
- Relations between management and employees
- Relations among employees
- Relations with funders
- Relations with volunteers

To be considered a high performer, nonprofits had to score a 4.5 or above on this index (n = 42). Beyond performance, the focus of this study is the human resource management practices of these nonprofits. Of these 42, interviews were completed in 16 nonprofits representing each of the states.

Compensation Practices of Human Service Nonprofits

As shown in Table 9.1, on average, nonprofits were slightly more likely to examine internal equity than external equity (3.31, 3.18, respectively). Some 40% of organizations consulted wage and salary surveys to determine external equity (e.g., pay competitive to the market) to a great extent compared to 36.1% of nonprofits that examined internal equity. As shown in Table 9.2, almost 30% of the nonprofits surveyed considered both internal and external equity to a great extent when establishing wages, whereas only 11.8% of nonprofits considered neither internal nor external equity when establishing wages.[6]

Next, the analysis examined whether the patterns differed for nonprofits identified as high performing. High performing nonprofits were significantly

Table 9.1 Internal and external equity practices

Practice	N	Mean	Standard deviation
Consultation of wage and salary surveys to determine external equity (e.g., pay competitive to the market)	289	3.1765	1.18145
Internal evaluations to determine internal equity (e.g., pay levels are consistent across the organization)	284	3.3099	1.06458
Scale: 1 (not at all) to 5 (to very great extent)			

Table 9.2 Cross-tabulation of organizations exploring internal and external equity

			Consultation of wage and salary surveys to determine external equity (e.g., pay competitive to the market)			
			Little to none	To some extent	To a great extent	Total
Internal evaluations to determine internal equity (e.g., pay levels are consistent across the organization)	Little to none	Count	33	12	5	50
		% of Total	11.8	4.3	1.8	17.9
	To some extent	Count	23	54	24	101
		% of Total	8.2	19.3	8.6	36.1
	To a great extent	Count	14	32	83	129
		% of Total	5.0	11.4	29.6	46.1
Total		Count	70	98	112	280
		% of Total	25.0	35.0	40.0	100.0

more likely to engage in both practices (see Table 9.3). In total, 57.9% of high performing nonprofits consulted wage and salary surveys to determine external equity (e.g., pay competitive to the market) to a great extent and 61.1% of nonprofits examined internal equity to a great extent. High performing nonprofits were more likely to assess internal equity when compared to the entire sample of nonprofits, 61.9% and 46.1%, respectively. Similarly, high performing nonprofits were more likely to assess external equity when compared to the entire sample of nonprofits, 57.0% and 40.0%, respectively.

One executive director of a high performing nonprofit observed that she participates in nonprofit wage surveys so she can have access to the data to help establish wages. She recognizes the need to think systematically about the

Table 9.3 Difference of means tests for internal and external equity consideration: High performing nonprofits

		N	Mean	Std. Deviation	T test
Consultation of wage and salary surveys to determine external equity (e.g., pay competitive to the market)		247	3.09	1.14	2.80
	HP	42	3.64	1.30	p=.005
Internal evaluations to determine internal equity (e.g., pay levels are consistent across the organization)		242	3.23	1.06	3.02
	HP	42	3.76	.96	p=.00

Scale: 1 (not at all) to 5 (to very great extent)

compensation in her organization and compare it with outside organizations to promote a stable and competitive workforce.

> The first time I ever did one of these ... probably eight years ago ... part of that I was (like) you know ... this is the person's level of responsibility ... it should follow this way because if I need somebody else to take that job, I want it to be appealing, and so on. When it got to the surveys and I realized I'm going to have to pay someone who has a Master's level in Social Work ... to keep them, I'm going to have to pay them more competitively. I have more competition in the area than I have for a receptionist. I can find another receptionist. It's going to be harder to find that person ... But I also can look and say the hospital pays their Social Workers this ... schools pay this ... other non-profits pay this. Where do I want to fall? I want to fall somewhere in the middle of that so that when someone leaves me, we're still competitive. They're only going to make a few thousand more and I say that they're not going to get a $15,000 jump because we pay so pathetically. That's where I don't want to be. I want to be (kind of) in the middle and that's a discussion with the Executive Committee.

As shown in Table 9.4, almost half (47.6%) of the high performing nonprofits (HPN) used both internal and external equity studies when setting salaries, compared to 29.6% of the total sample of nonprofits. This helps the nonprofits to be more strategic in relation to particular positions in their organization. For example, one executive director observed:

> We, probably, focus more on internal equity than external equity because being a non-profit, it's difficult for us to compete with the marketplace. Over the years we've tended to raise particular job groups up when we were

Table 9.4 Cross-tabulation of organizations exploring internal and external equity for high performing nonprofits

| | | | Consultation of wage and salary surveys to determine external equity (e.g., pay competitive to the market) | | | |
			Little to none	To some extent	To a great extent	Total
Internal evaluations to determine internal equity (e.g., pay levels are consistent across the organization)	Little to none	Count	3	0	0	3
		% of Total	7.1	0	0	7.1
	To some extent	Count	4	5	4	13
		% of Total	9.5	11.9	9.5	31.0
	To a great extent	Count	2	4	20	26
		% of Total	4.8	9.5	47.6	61.9
		Total	9	9	24	42
		% of Total	21.4	21.4	57.1	100.0

struggling with recruitment, [such as with nurses]. It was . . . very difficult to recruit nurses when we can't afford to pay what they can make out in the hospitals and more acute nursing care settings. So we would decide this year we're going to increase the nursing wages. Then, maybe, a few years later it was the social workers or the case workers that we hadn't looked at in a while. So we tended to do targeted job position increases but we set (kind of) pay ranges for the different positions, again, in terms of how we value those jobs within the company.

As illustrated by this data, good compensation strategies maintain a balance between internal equity and external equity or competitiveness.

In addition to balancing internal and external equity when establishing wages, nonprofits may employ other compensation strategies. As shown in Table 9.5, the most often used compensation strategy is to tie pay increases to knowledge, skills, or competencies (2.85), followed by high performance (2.76). However, over 34% of nonprofits in the sample did not or did in a very limited way connect pay increases to knowledge, skills, or competencies. Similarly, 39.2% of nonprofits did not increase or did so only to a little extent increase compensation related to high performance. Even fewer nonprofits connected compensation and group or team awards with any regularity; 78.2% responded not at all or to a limited extent. Because nonprofits have been less likely to connect compensation and performance, this study examined whether or not nonprofits used nonfinancial rewards to recognize high performers. Over 55% of nonprofits did not use

Table 9.5 Compensation strategies adopted by nonprofits

	N	Mean	Std. Deviation
Increased compensation for high performers	283	2.76	1.16
Pay increases tied to group or team performance	284	1.81	.95
Pay increases tied to knowledge, skills, or competencies	283	2.85	1.13
Significant nonfinancial rewards for performance (e.g., parking, extra days off, gift certificates)	283	2.45	1.18
Pay increases tied to tenure or seniority	284	2.25	1.11
Scale: 1 (not at all) to 5 (to very great extent)			

nonfinancial rewards as an incentive for high performers or did so in limited ways. Finally, the study explored the extent to which nonprofits used traditional methods of compensation, which are tied to tenure and seniority. Some 59% of the nonprofit executive directors shared that they did not or did only to a limited extent link compensation and seniority. Therefore, based on the data in this study, nonprofits have room to grow the current package of compensation strategies used and need to think critically about the tools available to use compensation strategically to reward and motivate their employees.

As shown in Table 9.6, when compared to other nonprofits, high performing nonprofits (HPN) were significantly more likely to connect compensation to knowledge, skills, or competencies (2.73, 3.56 for HPN) and to high performance

Table 9.6 Difference of means tests: High performing nonprofits

		N	Mean	Std. Deviation	T test
Increased compensation for high performers		241	2.68	1.11	2.32
	HP	42	3.19	1.33	p =.02
Pay increases tied to group or team performance		242	1.78	.91	1.71
	HP	42	2.05	1.15	p =.09
Pay increases tied to knowledge, skills, or competencies		242	2.73	1.05	3.82
	HP	41	3.56	1.32	p =.00
Significant nonfinancial rewards for performance (e.g., parking, extra days off, gift certificates)		241	2.39	1.14	2.59
	HP	42	2.81	1.37	p =.03

Table 9.6 Difference of means tests: High performing nonprofits *(continued)*

	N	Mean	Std. Deviation	T test
Pay increases tied to tenure or seniority				
	242	2.21	1.09	1.31
HP	42	2.45	1.17	p =.19

Scale: 1 (not at all) to 5 (to very great extent)

(2.68, 3.19 for HPN). High performing nonprofits were also significantly more likely to use nonfinancial rewards to recognize high performing employees (2.39, 2.81 for HPN). Their patterns of using seniority-based pay and group performance rewards did not vary.

Interviews with executive directors of the high performing nonprofit organizations hinted that across the board small raises were often used rather than merit or performance-based pay. One director noted that he had supported giving smaller across-the-board increases but planned to return to the merit pay system. This decision was driven, in part, because managers had not been consistent with providing performance reviews and, in part, because there were concerns about the budget. Every decision about compensation requires larger discussions about where these nonprofits are going to find the funding, so they are not decisions made lightly. Another organization shared that rather than a percentage, they award $1,000 per year and periodically adjust salaries based upon market rates. This same nonprofit had a policy that limits the executive director's salary to no more than 30% of the lowest paid person in the organization. In general, high performing nonprofits are more likely to link compensation to high performance and to leverage nonfinancial rewards to recognize performance.

Previous studies have explored differences in pay for women and men executive directors, demonstrating that male executive directors are paid, on average, higher than female executive directors (Faulk et al., 2012; Hallock, 2002; Lewin, 2001). This study, however, focuses on whether adoption of different compensation system differs depending upon whether the executive is male or female. In this sample, 71% of the human service organizations had a female executive director. As shown in Table 9.7, patterns of adoption of compensation strategies did not differ significantly between nonprofits led by women and men.

Previous studies have examined the relationship between organizational size and compensation systems. As illustrated in Table 9.8, this study examined whether organizational size was associated with different adoption patterns. Only two of the seven compensation practices were significantly related to size: examination of market rates and increased compensation for high performance. Larger nonprofits were significantly more likely to consider market competitiveness or external equity. Similarly, larger nonprofits were more likely to leverage compensation to recognize high performance.

Table 9.7 Difference of means tests: Male and female executive directors

		N	Mean	Std. Deviation	T test
Consultation of wage and salary surveys to determine external equity (e.g., pay competitive to the market)	Male	68	3.24	1.17	.74
	Female	166	3.11	1.20	p =.46
Internal evaluations to determine internal equity (e.g., pay levels are consistent across the organization)	Male	69	3.39	1.02	.86
	Female	166	3.11	1.20	p =.39
Increased compensation for high performers	Male	69	2.90	1.20	1.11
	Female	167	2.71	1.16	p =.27
Pay increases tied to group or team performance	Male	69	3.39	1.02	1.11
	Female	168	3.26	1.07	p =.27
Pay increases tied to knowledge, skills, or competencies	Male	69	2.90	1.20	.25
	Female	167	2.71	1.16	p =.80
Significant nonfinancial rewards for performance (e.g., parking, extra days off, gift certificates)	Male	69	2.26	1.07	1.50
	Female	167	2.52	1.23	p =.13
Pay increases tied to tenure or seniority	Male	69	2.90	1.16	1.14
	Female	167	2.86	1.14	p =.26

Scale: 1 (not at all) to 5 (to very great extent)

Conclusion

The data presented in this chapter demonstrated that the adoption of compensation practices varied across the studied nonprofit organizations. Interviews with executive directors of 16 high performing nonprofits revealed that they were reflective and strategic in their thinking about rewards, often mentioning the need to align pay with the market and to develop benefits packages that could make employment more attractive. High performing nonprofits leveraged both compensation and nonmonetary rewards to recognize employees for high performance and to demonstrate how much the organization values their contributions. One executive director reflected:

> I think there are certain things we do here, like, we have a staff picnic every year, we have staff appreciation in June and for the last number of years, if we have had a good fiscal year, and we know in June, we've given out staff bonuses. Then, the other fun thing we do, is our board authorizes $3,000.00 to be utilized through various gift cards. You come to this thing, or if you are on duty, your name is put into the hat, and the top two people get $300.00, and it goes down from there. We are doing stuff and then we do some fun team building things together and you know, crazy stupid kind of stuff and it gets back to that old [XXX] family.

Table 9.8 ANOVA: Size and use of compensation systems

		N	Mean	Std Dev	F test
Consultation of wage and salary surveys to determine external equity (e.g., pay competitive to the market)	Between $100,000 and $500,000	21	2.62	1.02	7.30
	Between $500,001 and $1.5 million	103	2.90	1.16	p =.00
	Between $1.51 million and $5 million	76	3.32	1.17	
	Above $5 million	36	3.78	1.10	
Internal evaluations to determine internal equity (e.g., pay levels are consistent across the organization)	Between $100,000 and $500,000	21	2.95	0.97	1.86
	Between $500,001 and $1.5 million	105	3.20	1.10	p =.14
	Between $1.51 million and $5 million	77	3.45	1.05	
	Above $5 million	36	3.44	0.94	
Increased compensation for high performers	Between $100,000 and $500,000	21	2.67	0.97	3.41
	Between $500,001 and $1.5 million	105	2.54	1.10	p =.02
	Between $1.51 million and $5 million	76	2.97	1.20	
	Above $5 million	36	3.14	1.31	
Pay increases tied to group or team performance	Between $100,000 and $500,000	21	1.90	0.94	p =.96
	Between $500,001 and $1.5 million	105	1.72	0.90	.41
	Between $1.51 million and $5 million	77	1.81	1.00	
	Above $5 million	36	2.03	1.06	
Pay increases tied to knowledge, skills, or competencies	Between $100,000 and $500,000	21	2.86	1.11	1.75
	Between $500,001 and $1.5 million	105	2.77	1.06	P =.16
	Between $1.51 million and $5 million	76	3.12	1.22	
	Above $5 million	36	2.69	1.19	

(continued)

Table 9.8 ANOVA: size and use of compensation systems *(continued)*

		N	Mean	Std Dev	F test
Significant nonfinancial rewards for performance (e.g., parking, extra days off, gift certificates)	Between $100,000 and $500,000	21	2.38	1.07	p=.18
	Between $500,001 and $1.5 million	105	2.41	1.25	.91
	Between $1.51 million and $5 million	76	2.53	1.18	
	Above $5 million	36	2.42	1.11	
Pay increases tied to tenure or seniority	Between $100,000 and $500,000	21	2.00	1.14	.47
	Between $500,001 and $1.5 million	105	2.26	1.09	p=.78
	Between $1.51 million and $5 million	77	2.30	1.16	
	Above $5 million	36	2.14	1.25	

Scale: 1 (not at all) to 5 (to very great extent)

Another executive director noted that she had explained to her staff:

> We weren't able to give you a raise but this is a way we can say thank you. I know it would be so much better if I could give you a dollar an hour more but I can't. But, here's something at the end of the year the Board can do. And, sometimes, it looks like $200 but sometimes it's been $1000 and I've heard staff say, wow, I got to buy that recliner I've always wanted ... or I got to buy ... or I was able to pay for my ... pay off some of my student loan ... I'm not somebody who considers the financial management as strongly as I consider caring for [XXX]. So my first inclination is to be (like) ... give it to her. I care so I want her to be here. And my second thing ... that I don't act on the first one before I consider is ... how does that affect the organization? It's slowly becoming where they are equal.

As compensation is often restricted in many nonprofits and budget growth is typically constrained, nonprofit executive directors were required to think creatively about compensation and recognition, employing many different strategies and focusing on more than money. One interviewee posited:

> No amount of money is going to keep an unhappy person in play but the truth is, if they are otherwise happy, feel valued, feel like they are making decisions, feel critical to the team, feel that the team is succeeding—it's 'fun' to be on a Superbowl team and you're getting paid well ... retention and performance will not be a concern.

Theuvsen (2004) would agree that nonprofits are not likely to attract employees who primarily seek extrinsic rewards and seek income maximization. In an empirical study, Leete (2000) found that nonprofit employees were not primarily motivated by financial rewards. Because the dominant type of employees attracted to and working in the nonprofit sector historically has not been focused on contingent rewards, this may account for the limited use of performance pay in this study of human service nonprofits (Beyer & Nutzinger, 1993; Rawls et al., 1975). However, as more people are seeking to serve the public and give back through nonprofit organizations as their primary career venue, well-designed, supportive compensation systems that support these nonprofit professionals cannot be ignored by nonprofits and are worth the necessary capacity investment.

Brandl and Güttel (2007) found differences between groups of nonprofits that had not adopted pay for performance and those that were beginning to adopt pay for performance. For nonprofits that had not adopted a pay for performance system, Brandl and Güttel observed that the nonprofits emphasized the incompatibility of monetary incentives with their culture and the potential negative impact of awarding monetary rewards for employees performing similar tasks and holding similar positions. They further reflected that nonprofits who had not adopted pay for performance perceived that the "NPO's mission, objectives, activities, and values form the core stimulation for intrinsic motivation. The intrinsic motivation is activated by the organization's 'spirit' (which is also called "NPO-bonus" due to its immaterial character)" (Brandl & Güttel, 2007, p. 187). In contrast, nonprofits who adopted pay for performance sought to attract high performing employees, which they perceived would improve the nonprofit's competitiveness and ability to acquire needed funds. Because these nonprofits sought employees with a high performance orientation, they believed this value needed to be reflected in monetary rewards. This study's findings reinforce the linkage suggested by Brandl and Güttel (2007). High performing nonprofit organizations were more likely to increase compensation for high performers, link pay to team performance, and tie pay to knowledge, skills, and competencies. Moreover, these nonprofits were also more likely to use nonmonetary incentives to reward high performance.

The most often employed compensation system in the total sample and for high performing organizations was pay increases tied to knowledge, skills, or competencies. Chen, Ren, and Knoke's (2013) research found no significant differences between nonprofit, government and for-profit organizations in their adoption of pay for skills. They reasoned that this finding "might mean that, with the development of technology, training for skills is as important within for-profit organizations as it is outside the for-profit sector" (Chen et al., 2013, p. 301). Their work might suggest insight into why this was the most often adopted practice. This compensation practice is premised upon the assumption that new knowledge, skills, and competencies contribute to the nonprofit's ability to execute its mission and reach its goals. As employees gain new capabilities, they become more flexible resources for the organizations. Managers can more easily shift employees to different areas as needs and conditions change. Paying employees for new capabilities encourages them to change behaviors and to advance the nonprofit's goals. Nonprofit managers and executive directors would be well served to examine their compensation systems and practices and consider how well these practices are supporting the goals of the organization.

Figure 9.1 presents a framework for nonprofits to use to organize their approach to compensation strategies. A nonprofit's compensation philosophy and objectives should align its mission and goals and then, in turn, should influence decisions related to base pay, internal and external equity, nonmonetary recognition and rewards, and pay adjustments. Possible compensation objectives include:

- Providing a fair wage
- Providing wages that keep pace with the cost of living
- Providing incentives for employees to remain with the organization
- Rewarding high performance at the individual and/or group level
- Aligning employee goals to organizational goals
- Being competitive with other nonprofits
- Recruiting top talent to the organization
- Providing special recognition to employees
- Ensuring gender equity
- Building team bonds

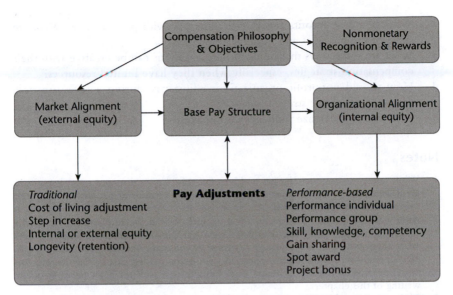

Figure 9.1   Strategic Compensation Model to guide nonprofit decision-making

- Making employees feel valued
- Sharing prosperity
- Addressing generation-specific reward preferences.

For example, based upon Johnson and Ng's (2015) recent studies, nonprofits may want to consider their objectives as it relates to generational need, expectations, and reward preferences.

Because nonprofit budgets are typically limited, executive directors and their leadership team will need to make difficult decisions about how to allocate resources. Nonprofits should consider how they will balance benefits and compensation. By implementing a strategic compensation and recognition philosophy that is consistent with their mission, nonprofits will be better able to inculcate a culture that includes their philosophy and guides resource allocation. Whether to devote resources to attracting the best candidates or to retaining existing employees will continue to be a critical question for nonprofits to address. At the same time, a strategic approach will encourage nonprofit leaders to be intentional about the creative ways in which they can recognize employee performance and can make employees feel that they are valued by the organization.

Discussion Questions

1   For those of you currently employed in the nonprofit sector, locate a salary survey and see where your position falls in relation to that salary survey. What do the results tell you about what compensation principles are held by your organization?

2   Why should nonprofits consider aligning pay with performance? What are some of the positives and negatives of this?
3   What are some ways that nonprofit organizations can be creative with their compensation strategies, especially when they have limited resources?
4   How should nonprofit organizations adjust pay during a recession or a period of economic stress?
5   How does budget size influence compensation?

Notes

1   While compensation includes pay and benefits, this chapter does not cover benefits in great detail due to space constraints. For further discussion of benefits in nonprofit organizations, see Pynes (2013).
2   After a federal judge's decision in Texas against delayed the implementation of the Obama administration's new overtime rule regarding the Fair Labor Standard Act's salary threshold. The judge placed a temporary injunction against the overtime rule, placing employers in the United States in legal limbo (Miller, 2017). The decision has been appealed to the 5th Circuit Court, but the case had not been heard as of the writing of this chapter.
3   The author would like to thank the Society for Human Resource Management (SHRM) Foundation for the grant that supported this research.
4   The National Taxonomy of Exempt Entities (NTEE) is a classification system for tax-exempt organizations that was developed by both practitioners and scholars. The NTEE codes were designed to create a common language for reporting on organizational purpose and are used by the IRS on the 990 form and by the National Center for Charitable Statistics to classify organizations (Lampkin, Romeo, & Finnin, 2001). The NTEE codes used in the sampling strategy for this study were the following: E32 E40 E42 I70 I71 I72 I73 K30 K31 K34 K35 K36 O20 O21 O22 023 030 031P20 P21 P22 P24 P26P P27 P28 P29 P30 P40 P42 P43 P44 P45 P46 P60 P61 P62 P70 P72 P73 P74 P75 P80 P81 P82 P83 P84 P85 P86 P87.
5   This study used the approach employed by Dess and Robinson (1984) modified for the nonprofit sector.
6   The measures used to assess compensation were drawn from the following sources: Datta et al. (2005); Jensen et al. (2011); Messersmith and Wales (2011); WorldatWork and Towers Watson (2010).

References

Barragato, C. A. (2002). Linking for-profit and nonprofit executive compensation: Salary composition and incentive structures in the U.S. hospital industry. *Voluntas: International Journal of Voluntary and Nonprofit Organizations, 13*(3), 301–311.
Beyer, H. & Nutzinger, H. G. (1993). Hierarchy or co-operation: Labor–management relations in church institutions. *Voluntas: International Journal of Voluntary and Nonprofit Organizations, 4*(1), 55–72.
Benson, P. G. & Hornsby, J. S. (2002). The view from the top: The controversies over executive pay. In G. R. Ferris, M. R. Buckley, & D. B. Fedor (eds.), *Human resource management: Perspectives, context, functions, and outcomes.* Englewood Cliffs, NJ: Prentice Hall.
BLS Commissioner. (2016). Announcing new research data on jobs and pay in the nonprofit sector. Bureau of Labor Statistics, February 17, 2016. Available at: http://beta.bls.gov/labs/blogs/2014/10/17/announcing-new-research-data-on-jobs-and-pay-in-the-nonprofit-sector/

Brandl, J. & Güttel, W. H. (2007). Organizational antecedents of pay-for-performance systems in nonprofit organizations. *International Journal of Voluntary and Nonprofit Organizations, 18*(2), 176–199.

Brown, C. & Medoff, J. (1989). The employer size-wage effect. *Journal of Political Economy, 97*(5), 1027–1059.

Burger, J. & Walters, S. (2008). Testing fair wage theory. *Journal of Labor Research, 29*(4), 318–332.

Carroll, T., Hughes, P., & Luksetich, W. (2005). Managers of nonprofit organizations are rewarded for performance. *Nonprofit Management & Leadership, 16*(1), 19–41.

Chen, X., Ren, T., & Knoke, D. (2013). Do nonprofits treat their employees differently? Incentive pay and health benefits. *Nonprofit Management & Leadership, 24*(3), 285–306.

Cortis, N. (2000). Gender, pay equity, and human service work: A New South Wales case study. *Australian Journal of Political Science, 35*(1), 49–62.

Datta, D. K., Gutherie, J. P., & Wright, P. M. (2005). HRM and labor productivity: Does industry matter? *Academy of Management Journal, 48*(1), 135–145.

Department of Labor. (2016a). Frequently asked questions. Available at: www.dol.gov/whd/overtime/final2016/faq.htm#G1 (accessed July 31, 2016).

Department of Labor. (2016b). Guidance for non-profit organizations on paying overtime under the Fair Labor Standards Act. Available at: www.dol.gov/whd/overtime/final2016/nonprofit-guidance.pdf (accessed July 31, 2016).

Department of Labor. (2016c). Questions and answers from the overtime webinar for the non-profit sector. Available at: www.dol.gov/whd/overtime/final2016/webinarfaq_np.htm (accessed July 31, 2016).

Dess, G. G. & Robinson, R. B. (1984). Of objective measures: Measuring organizational performance in the absence of objective measures: The case of the privately-held firm and conglomerate business unit. *Strategic Management Journal, 50*(3), 265–273.

Dulebohn, J. H. & Werling, S. E. (2007). Compensation research past, present and future. *Human Resource Management Review, 17*(2), 191–207.

Faulk, L., Edwards, L. H., Lewis, G., & McGinnis, J. (2012). An analysis of gender pay disparity in the nonprofit sector: An outcome of labor motivation or gendered jobs. *Nonprofit and Voluntary Sector Quarterly, 42*(6), 1268–1287.

Frumkin, P. & Keating, E. K. (2001). The price of doing good: Executive compensation in nonprofit organizations. *Policy and Society, 29*(3), 269–282.

Garner, J. L. & Harrison, T. D. (2013). Boards, executive excess compensation, and shared power: Evidence from nonprofit firms. *The Financial Review, 48*, 617–643.

Grasse, N., Davis, T., & Ihrke, D. (2014). Understanding the compensation of nonprofit executive directors: Examining the influence of performance and organizational characteristics. *Nonprofit Management & Leadership, 24*(3), 377–398.

Gray, S. R. & Benson, P. G. (2003). Determinants of executive compensation in small business development centers. *Nonprofit Management & Leadership, 13*(3), 213–227.

Hallock, K. (2002). The gender pay and employment gaps for top managers in U.S. nonprofits. Cornell University. Available at: http://digitalcommons.ilr.cornell.edu/cgi/viewcontent.cgi?article=1092&context=workingpapers

Hamann, D. J. & Ren, T. (2013). Wage inequality and performance in nonprofit and for-profit organizations. *Nonprofit Management & Leadership, 24*(2), 207–228.

Jensen, J. M., Pankaj, C. P., & Messersmith, J. G. (2011). High-performance work systems and job control: Consequences for anxiety, role overload, and turnover intentions. *Journal of Management,* Advance On-line publication, doi: 10.1177/0149206311419663.

Jobome, G. O. (2006). Management pay, governance, and performance: The case of large UK nonprofits. *Financial Accountability and Management, 22*(4), 331–358.

Johnson, J. M. & Ng, E. S. (2015). Money talks or millennials walk: The effect of compensation on nonprofit millennial works sector-switching intentions. *Review of Public Personnel Administration*, 1–23. Published online before print June 1, 2015, doi: 10.1177/0734371X15587980.

Lampkin, L., Romeo, S., & Finnin, E. (2001). Introducing the nonprofit program classification system: The taxonomy we've been waiting for. *Nonprofit And Voluntary Sector Quarterly*, 30(4), 781–793.

Leete, L. (2000). Wage inequity and employee motivation in nonprofit and for-profit organizations. *Journal of Economic Behavior and Organization*, 43(4), 423–446.

Levine, D. (1991). Cohesiveness, productivity, and wage dispersion. *Journal of Economic Behavior and Organization*, 15(2), 237–255.

Lewin, T. (2001, June 2). Women profit less than men in the nonprofit world, too. *New York Times*. Available at: www.nytimes.com/2001/06/02/national/02PAY.html

McKeever, B. O. (2015). The nonprofit sector in brief 2015. Urban Institute. Available at: www.urban.org/sites/default/files/alfresco/publication-pdfs/2000497-The-Nonprofit-Sector-in-Brief-2015-Public-Charities-Giving-and-Volunteering.pdf

Messersmith, J. G. & Wales, W. J. (2011). Entrepreneurial orientation and performance in yong firms: The role of human resource management. *International Small Business Journal*, 31(2), 115–136.

Miller, S. 2017. What's next for employers under the FLSA overtime rule. Available at: www.shrm.org/ResourcesAndTools/hr-topics/compensation/Pages/FLSA-overtime-rule-forecast.aspx (accessed July 31, 2016).

National Council of Nonprofits. (2016). Available at: www.councilofnonprofits.org/trends-policy-issues/overtime-regulations-and-the-impact-nonprofits

Nikolova, M. (2014). Principals and agents: An investigation of executive compensation in human service nonprofits. *Voluntas: International Journal of Voluntary and Nonprofit Organizations*, 25, 679–706.

Nonprofit HR. (2015). 2015 nonprofit employment practices survey results. Available at: www.nonprofithr.com/wp-content/uploads/2015/02/2015-Nonprofit-Employment-Practices-Survey-Results-1.pdf

Oster, S. M. (1998). Executive compensation in the nonprofit sector. *Nonprofit Management & Leadership*, 8(3), 207–221.

Pynes, J. E. (2013). *Human resource management for public and nonprofit organizations: A strategic approach* (4th ed.). San Francisco, CA: Jossey-Bass.

Quatt Associates. (2013). *2013 not-for-profit compensation survey*. Washington, DC: Quatt Associates.

Rawls, J. R., Ullrich, R., & Nelson, O. T. (1975). A comparison of managers entering or reentering the profit and nonprofit sectors. *Academy of Management Journal*, 18(3), 616–623.

Rhodes, C. A., Bechtle, M., & McNett, M. (2015). An incentive pay plan for advanced practice registered nurses: Impact on provider and organizational outcomes. *Nursing Economics*, 33(3), 125-131.

Roeger, K. L., Blackwood, A. S., & Pettijohn, L. (2012). *The nonprofit almanac 2012*. The Urban Institute.

Roomkin, M. J. & Weisbrod, B. A. (1999). Managerial compensation and incentives in for-profit and nonprofit hospitals. *Journal of Law, Economics, and Organization*, 15(3), 750–781.

Ruhm, C. J. & Borkoski, C. (2003). Compensation in the nonprofit sector. *Journal of Human Resources*, 38(4), 992–1021.

Salamon, L. M., Sokolowski, S. W., & Geller, S. L. (2012). Holding the fort: Nonprofit employment during a decade of turmoil. *Nonprofit Employment Bulletin, 39*, Johns Hopkins University. January 2012. Available at: www.thenonprofitpartnership.org/files/ned_national_2012.pdf

Scheitle, C. P. (2009). Leadership compensation in Christian nonprofits. *Sociology of Religion*, 70(4), 384–408.

Selden, S. C. & Sowa, J. E. (2014). High performance work systems in nonprofit organizations: Surfacing better practices to improve nonprofit HRM capacity. Final Report for the Society for Human Resource Management Foundation. Available at: www.shrm.org/about/foundation/research/Documents/FinalReportSelden%20Sowa.pdf

Speckbacher, G. (2013). The use of incentives in nonprofit organizations. *Small Business Economics, 41*(2), 379–399.

Theuvsen, L. (2004). Doing better while doing good: Motivational aspects of pay-for-performance effectiveness in nonprofit organizations. *Voluntas: International Journal of Voluntary and Nonprofit Organizations, 15*(2), 117–136.

Toutkoushian, R. K. (1998). Using regression analysis to determine if faculty salaries are overly compressed. *Research in Higher Education, 39*(1), 87–100.

Vogel, B. H. & Quatt, C. W. (2015). *Nonprofit executive compensation.* Washington, DC: Boardsource.

Werner, S. & Gemeinhardt, G. (1995). Nonprofit organizations: What factors determine pay levels? *Compensation and Benefits Review, 27,* 53–60.

WorldatWork & Towers Watson. (2010). Creating a sustainable rewards and talent management model. Available at: www.worldatwork.org/waw/adimLink?id=42295&nonav=yes

10

Labor Relations in Nonprofit Organizations

Joan E. Pynes

Due to an inability to reach a contract agreement, The Atlanta Symphony Orchestra (ASO) was locked out by its management. Other recent labor management contract disputes in the arts could be found with the Indianapolis Symphony Orchestra, Minnesota Orchestra and the Metropolitan Opera. Employees of New York's Museum of Modern Art (MoMA) protested at its "Party in the Garden" gala with protest signs reading "MoMA, don't cut our health care," "Modern art, ancient wages," "Average MoMA senior staff salary: $349,00 Average MoMA employee salary: $49,000: MoMA staff deserves a fair contract."

(Brooks, 2015; Cooper, 2014a, 2014b; Eddings, 2014;
Maloney, 2014; Pousner, 2014)

Doctors working at the student health clinics on University California (UC) campuses of Berkeley, Davis, San Francisco, Santa Cruz and Merced participated in a rolling strike accusing UC of unfair labor practices.

(Gordon, 2015)

Unite Here is the union that represents food service workers at the National Museum of the American Indian and the National Museum of American History.

(Fletcher, 2013)

Centro de los Derechos del Migrante (CDM) is a nonprofit that has recovered more than $5 million in stolen wages from migrant workers. Many employment and labor laws are regularly violated impacting the low wage and often immigrant labor force.

(Erickson, Jr, 2015)

Introduction

These are examples of current activities of employees working for nonprofit organizations and attempts to have some influence over their work life. In the first two examples, the employees were locked out of work or went on strike. During the recession, nonprofits faced significant economic pressures; a number merged with other nonprofits and some closed, due to significant reductions in public funding, a loss of donations, fees for services, subscriptions and memberships resulted in stagnant wages. In addition to no pay increases, in many cases employees were tasked with contributing more of their salaries toward their fringe benefits. Once the economy improved and organizations' revenues increased, employees were looking to regain what they lost during the recession and unions became more assertive. The third example is one where employees working for a for-profit firm contracted to provide services to a large nonprofit organization joined a union to raise their wages and improve their benefits. The last example indicates a newer strategy by nonprofit organizations to assist non-unionized employees and make sure they are not being exploited.

According to the U.S. Bureau of labor Statistics, in 2014, the unionized private workforce was 7.4 million workers, which is 6.6% of the private sector workforce (U.S. Bureau of Labor Statistics, 2015). There has been a consistent decrease in the number of employees belonging to unions.

Despite the overall downward trend in union membership, an increasing number of professional and service industry employees have joined unions. Professional union members account for 54% of union members in March 2015 (Department of Professional Employees, AFL-CIO, 2015a, p. 6). Professional employees such as medical doctors, social workers, graduate students, lawyers, musicians, and nurses, are examples of some professional/occupational groups that have unionized in nonprofit organizations (Department of Professional Employees, AFL-CIO, 2014a, 2015a). There has also been an increase in the number of technical workers and paraprofessional workers such as nursing assistants, laboratory technicians, and other service workers joining unions. This chapter discusses the legal environment of labor relations, threats to union organizing activities, the ambivalence of support of unions and collective bargaining, why workers join unions, and changes in social policy.

The Legal Environment

Labor-management relations in the nonprofit sector have been covered under the National Labor Relations Act of 1935 (NLRA) since 1976. The NLRA permits employees to organize and join unions. Under this law, employers must bargain in good faith with employee unions and could be cited for unfair labor practices if they attempt to interfere with the establishment of unions. The NLRA established the National Labor Relations Board (NLRB) as the administrative agency responsible for enforcing the provisions of the act. Similar to a for-profit organization, the board would have jurisdiction over a nonprofit employer if the organization was sufficiently involved in the flow of money or goods across state lines and a labor dispute would interrupt that flow of commerce. The board established a jurisdictional standard of $250,000 annual revenue for all social service agencies other than those for which there is another specific standard application for the type of activity in which the organization is engaged (Feldacker, 1999; NLRB, 2015). Most small nonprofits may not meet the NLRB's jurisdictional standards.

The NLRB holds jurisdiction over nonprofit service organizations that provide services to or for an exempt governmental agency supported by state or federal funds (Feldacker, 1999). These agencies are covered by the Act, even though they are government funded, as long as they retain independence in labor-management matters, such as establishing the wages, hours, and working conditions of their employees. The sole standard for taking jurisdiction is whether the contractor has "sufficient control over the employment conditions of its employees to enable it to bargain with a labor organization as its representative." The board looks closely at the nature of the relationship between the government institution and the contractor.[1]

Changes in the Landscape: Threats to Unions

Unions promote the "interests" of employees often expressed as salaries and benefits. We often forget that unions are responsible for the 40-hour work week, facilitating the provision of employer-provided health, retirement, education, employee training and development, and other benefits. Unions also help guarantee or protect the "rights" of employees in regard to how they are treated and how rules are administered.

Management officials often oppose unions because they are perceived as raising costs and restricting management discretion. The recession of 2007–2009 led to increased attacks against unions. In many service-related industries, as well as the public and the nonprofit sectors, the biggest expense is typically the cost of labor. Data from 2014 indicates the median weekly earnings of full-time wage and salary workers belonging to a union was $970 per week compared to $763 for workers not in a union (U.S. Bureau of Labor Statistics, 2015, Table 41 Median weekly earning of full-time wage and salary workers by union affiliation and selected characteristics 2015). The unionization of employees is perceived to inflate wages and benefits and create administrative inefficiencies. As a result, the collective bargaining rights of employees have come under attack in a number of states.

"Right to Work" laws have been passed by 28 states (National Conference of State Legislatures, 2017). These laws prohibit individuals from being forced to join or pay dues to a labor union nor are they required to join a union to acquire or retain employment. States may also outlaw various forms of union security provisions. The "Right to Work" states are: Alabama, Arizona, Arkansas, Florida, Georgia, Idaho, Indiana, Iowa, Kansas, Louisiana, Michigan, Mississippi,

Nebraska, Nevada, North Carolina, North Dakota, Oklahoma, South Carolina, South Dakota, Tennessee, Texas, Utah, Virginia, Wisconsin, and Wyoming. In the nonprofit and private sectors, Section 14(b) of the LMRA permits states to outlaw various forms of union security provisions:

> Nothing in this Act shall be construed as authorizing the execution or application of agreements requiring membership in a labor organization as a condition of employment in any State or Territory in which such execution or application is prohibited by State or Territorial law.

This provision means an employer can reject a union's demands for the recognition of union security arrangements illegal under state law. Union security regulations address the degree to which unions can require or mandate the payment of dues to support activities related to collective bargaining. Most collective bargaining contracts contain some kind of union security provision. Employers typically deduct the payments from the employees' pay and give them to the union. This reduces the administrative costs unions have in collecting the funds and also ensures payment from employees who might prefer to be free riders. This is a way to reduce the financial resources of unions and ultimately their strength when opposing management.

Originally, most "Right-to-Work" states were found in southern or Sunbelt states, but the three most recent states to pass legislation, Michigan, Indiana, and Wisconsin, are Midwestern states with long traditions in collective bargaining. Missouri almost became the 26th state to have enacted "Right-to-Work" legislation. Most of the Republican legislature voted to pass the Bill but 24 Republicans broke rank and voted against making Missouri a "Right-to-Work" state citing support for unions by their constituents who may be socially conservative but who belong to unions. The Republicans who broke rank based it on the following: Unions can attract employers because they provide a trained workforce that corporate leaders need to do business; There are plenty of nonunionized employers that individuals who are opposed to unions can work for; and that debates over "Right-to-Work" legislation distract from other issues that need attention, such as taxes, education, and infrastructure (DePillis, 2015). The split opinion in regard to the value of unions and collective bargaining in the Republicans that dominated state legislature appears to reflect the mixed views the general public holds in regard to unions and collective bargaining.

Mixed Views on Unions and Collective Bargaining

Despite the decrease in the number of workers who belong to labor unions and attempts to weaken them, a Pew Research Center poll conducted in 2015 found the public has mixed views on union membership. Some 52% of the respondents believe the drop in union representation has negatively impacted working people compared with 40% who say it has been mostly good. When asked whether certain occupational workers should be able to join unions, respondents had different responses. Some 82% supported manufacturing and factory workers' right to join unions, 74% public transportation workers, 72% police and firefighters, 71% public school teachers, 68% supermarket and retail sales workers and 62% fast-food workers (Pew Research Center, 2015). There were differences among Democrat and Republican respondents in their opinions about allowing workers to unionize. Among Democrats, the support ranged from 77% for fast-food workers, 86% public school teachers, 83% supermarkets and retail sales workers, 88% public transportation, 83% police and fire and 92% manufacturing and factory workers.

Republicans supported the right of employees to form unions but the percentages were lower: 71% said factory and manufacturing workers should be able to unionize, 59% said police and firefighters, 58% public transportation workers, 52% supermarkets and retail sales workers and 54% public school teachers. Among Republicans and respondents identified as Republican leaning, the younger respondents (18–31 years of age) and those with a high school education had more favorable views of unions than older respondents and those with a college degree and higher income.

Differences existed in union support across ages; of those 18–29 years of age, 55% were in favor of unions and 29% not in favor, and among those older, the results were mixed. For respondents between the ages of 30–49, 46% held a favorable view of unions compared to 40% with an unfavorable view. Of those between the ages of 50–64, the percentages were 46% favorable and 43% unfavorable, and for respondents aged 65 and older, 46% held a favorable view of unions compared to 42% with an unfavorable view.

Sixty percent of Blacks surveyed had a favorable view, 49% for Hispanics and 45% for Whites (Pew Research Center, 2015). While the survey was not specifically addressing occupations in the nonprofit sector (teachers, retail/service and transportation workers can be found in both sectors). Many nonprofit occupations are often under-paid and often deal with vulnerable populations in difficult circumstances. Women tend to be concentrated in community, social service, healthcare, and healthcare support and technical occupations, and provide support to individuals, families, and communities. In 2013, 20.7% of social workers, 20% of counselors and 21.4% of other community and social service workers were union members (Department of Professional Employees, AFL-CIO: 2014b, p. 3).

A recent survey of Michigan residents supported passing a law entitled "the Safe Patient Care Act," establishing minimum staffing levels of registered nurses in Michigan hospitals. The law, if passed, would require hospitals to have staffing plans for each unit that follows minimum nurse-to-patient ratios based on professional standards (Michigan Nurses Association, 2015; Anonymous 2015). In 2030, it is projected that 20.3% of the population will be 65 years and older as compared to 13.7% in 2012 (Ortman, Velkoff, & Hogan, 2014). As the U.S. population continues to age, there will be an increase in the need for community, social service, healthcare, and healthcare support occupations.

Projected Occupational Growth—Much Is in the Nonprofit Sector

Some of the fastest projected occupations between 2012 and 2022 are in the health and personal care service sector (U.S. Bureau of Labor Statistics, Employment Projections, 2013a). Additional data show the projections of employment by major occupational group industry 2012–2022. Many of those occupations have a large presence in the nonprofit sector. Occupations in the life, physical and social sciences; community and social service occupations; education, training and library occupations; healthcare practitioners and technical occupations; healthcare support occupations, food preparation and serving-related occupations; personal care and service occupations; and office and administrative support occupations all have a large presence in nonprofit organizations (U.S. Bureau of Labor Statistics, Employment Projections, 2013b).

These professions/occupations often work for nonprofits that are partially or fully dependent upon some government funding. A breakdown of public charities shows that Human Service nonprofits are 35.5% of public charities, followed by Education, 17.1%; Health, 13%; Public and Social Benefit, 11.6%; Arts, culture and humanities, 9.9%; Religion-related, 6.1%; Environmental and animals, 4.5%; and International and foreign affairs, 2.1% (McKeever, Brice, & Pettijohn, 2014). In 2012, the combination of government contracts and grants comprised nearly one-third (32.2%) of nonprofit revenue (McKeever, Brice, & Pettijohn, 2014).

Despite the nation's economic recovery, a survey conducted by the Nonprofit Finance Fund found the largest nonprofit subsectors are still facing challenges. The top challenges are financial sustainability, staff retention, a lack of unrestricted revenue, reductions in government funding, meeting the demand for services, having fewer employees than needed, the inability to develop cash reserves, and lacking a reliable cash flow (Nonprofit Finance Fund, 2015). Many of the findings are consistent with previous research conducted by the Urban Institute. An Urban Institute study on nonprofits that receive government contracts and grants found some problems for nonprofit recipients. Often payments did not cover the full cost of contracted services, the application and reporting processes were complicated and time-consuming; government funders made changes to the contracts or grants during the execution, and there were late payments. Other problems include limits on program administration or overhead costs; and sometimes the contracts and grants required cost sharing (Pettijohn, Boris, & Farrell, 2014).

Another characteristic of nonprofits is that there are typically more women employees than men working in nonprofits (Preston & Sacks, 2010). One theory suggests that because of the mission of nonprofits and the intrinsic nature of much of the work, women are more likely to donate their labor. Another reason may be that many of the services provided by nonprofits consist of what is considered to be women's work. Tasks consisting of caring, negotiating, empathizing, smoothing troubled relationships, and working behind the scenes to enable cooperation, and sometimes referred to as emotional labor can be found in nonprofit organizations (England, Budig, & Folbe, 2002; Guy & Newman, 2004; Guy, Newman, & Mastracci, 2008; Mastracci, Guy, & Newman, 2012).

Many individuals view unionization as a mechanism to defend professional autonomy, improve working conditions, and maintain or improve economic security. Employees who feel vulnerable are more likely to join unions. Given the uncertainty of government funding and often the lack of respect for emotional labor and care work, it is possible that social and community service employees will follow the lead of nurses and healthcare employees and choose to join unions.

In fact, early research on labor unions in social service agencies provides evidence that unions have expanded the scope of bargaining to include such issues as agency-level policymaking, agency missions, standards of service, coverage for malpractice and professional liability insurance, legal representation of workers, workload issues, the provision of in-service training, financial assistance for licensing examinations, and remuneration for enhanced education (Hush, 1969; Karger, 1988; Pynes, 1996; Tambor, 1973, 1988a, 1988b). These issues continue today and as information and communication technologies (ICT) keep employees tethered to their workplaces when not physically at work through smartphones and tablets, email and groupware, topics such as what is considered overtime and the workday have become part of the standards of service and working conditions.

Worker Interests

Today, the most active union-organizing activity among nonprofit subsectors is in healthcare. The Service Employees International Union (SEIU) has a unit, SEIU Healthcare, that specializes in unionizing employees working in healthcare organizations. It represents doctors and nurses, home care, and nursing home workers, lab techs, environmental service workers, and dietary aides. Its members can be found working in hospitals, health centers, nursing homes, in-home care and in the community (SEIU Healthcare; www.seiu.org/seiuhealthcare/). CIO, AFSCME also organizes healthcare workers. The National Union of Hospital and Health Care Employees mission can be found at www.nuhhce.org/Mission. Priorities in its mission include protecting all its workers, promoting and safeguarding the economic interests of its members and families, and protecting and advancing the technical status of its members in all types of healthcare institutions.

Market-based healthcare reforms are having a negative impact on the work environment of registered nurses. These reforms, aimed at cost savings, means they have been replaced with less qualified and less expensive personnel, such as licensed practical nurses and technicians. Reforms have also meant an increase in patient-staffing ratios. Many nurses believe some of the reforms threaten the quality of patient care. Many nurses are now seeking union membership as a means to gain greater control over patient care. Under collective bargaining, professionals are able to demand the standards of their profession be respected and enforced. Often the decision to vote for unionization is done under the threat of losing control over their professional work environment (www. uannurse.org). Registered nurses (RNs) in a hospital in Michigan agreed to a lower percentage pay increase in favor of the hospital hiring 25 additional nurses so that patient care could be delivered in a more effective manner (Department of Professional Employees, AFL-CIO, 2015b).

It is not just hospitals and other healthcare nonprofits that are reacting to market-based reforms. There has been an increase in alternative employee work arrangements, an increase in part-time work and the use of a contingency workforce. Nonprofits are also contracting out services once provided by employees working directly for nonprofits. An important National Labor Relations Board (NLRB) decision in regard to contract and temporary workers was made in August 2015. In a 3-2 ruling, the NLRB revised its "joint employer" standard for determining when one company shares responsibility for employees hired by another. The ruling will make it easier for unions to negotiate wages and benefits for contingent workers. The majority on the Board stated the NLRB has not kept pace with an evolving workplace in which increasing numbers of U.S. workers are employed through temporary staffing agencies, or when organizations misclassify their employees as independent contractors to avoid paying taxes, overtime, and benefits. This change may have an impact on contracting out services, hiring independent contractors, or using a contingent workforce. It is too soon to tell (DePillis, 2015; Trottman, 2015).

Confronted with an increase in the demand for services, increased competition, reductions in funding, and general economic instability, this has in some cases resulted in mergers among nonprofits providing similar services or organizational restructuring. Union contracts have called for employers to notify employees of impending layoffs and to offer voluntary leaves of absences to employees before reducing their hours. Unions have sought to expand the scope of bargaining to include standards of service, and professional judgment.

Union contracts with nonprofit agencies recognize that new issues have emerged and that labor-management understanding and cooperation are important. Labor market and workplace changes have increased insecurity and undermined the belief that wages are competitive and jobs are secure. There has been a decrease in employee benefits, an increase in the use of a temporary workforce, and reduced or lost pensions. These changes, along with sometimes arbitrary or unfair management, often lead employees to unionize when they feel threatened. Employees have also joined unions to defend their professional autonomy and improve working conditions. While unions are still concerned with "bread and butter" issues such as wages, hours, and working conditions, new topics have emerged.

Newer employee benefits include mental health and substance abuse benefits, childcare benefits, employee individual development plans, incentive awards, and alternative work schedules. Workplace safety precautions have also become part of the collective bargaining agreement. These precautions include: guidelines covering the use of video display terminals (VDTs), protective clothing, violence protection programs, and indoor air quality (Department of Professional Employees AFL-CIO, 2014a, 2015a, 2015b; SEIU, 2015; National Nurses United, 2015; UFCWIU, 2015).

Worker Rights

In addition to bargaining for the interests of employees, unions help guarantee or protect the "rights" of employees in regard to how they are treated and how rules are administered. When a union believes that management has violated the terms of a labor contract and files a grievance, a neutral third party is asked to resolve the disagreement that could not be settled by the union and management. This is referred to as grievance arbitration. A hearing is held and the arbitrator renders a decision based on the merits of the case. The decision tends to be final and legally binding on both parties.

Grievance arbitration is expressly authorized by statute in the nonprofit and for-profit sectors. The NLRA/LMRA requires that all contracts contain a grievance resolution procedure. It is believed that grievance arbitration is necessary to protect employees from unfair, discriminatory, unsafe, and arbitrary treatment by employers.

Why Protect Employees?

One argument is that protection "pays for itself" through increased productivity. Research has demonstrated that employees develop a psychological contract which is the unwritten expectations employees and employers have about the nature of their work relationship. Tangible items such as wages, benefits, employee productivity and attendance and intangible items such as loyalty, fair treatment, and job security exist. In times of pay freezes, workforce downsizing, the elimination of or increased cost of employer-provided benefits, employees need to feel that they have some control and perceived rights in the organization (Kehoe & Wright, 2013; Ko & Hur, 2014; Pierce, Kostova, & Dirks, 2001). The second argument is that there is an ethical imperative to treat employees fairly. Many believe that employees are entitled to or ought to be entitled to fair treatment, respect, and safe working conditions. Research indicates that higher levels of organizational justice are related to job satisfaction, trust in management, greater productivity, and lower turnover intentions (Choi, 2011; Greenberg, 1996; Rubin, 2011).

Social Policy: Beyond Members' Bread-and-Butter Issues

Labor unions have not always been thought of in the best of light. There are many reasons for this. A number of labor unions have had a history of discrimination against women, racial and ethnic minorities, and Lesbian, Gay, Bisexual and Transgendered (LGBT) workers. They have been reluctant to welcome new members into their unions. There have been union leaders found guilty of corruption and stealing from the union and its members for their personal gain. Unions have been associated with organized crime and have been criticized for being reluctant to change and adapt to new technologies and flexible work rules (Bielski Boris, 2010; Crain, 1995; Jacobs & Peters, 2003; Kelly & Lubitow, 2015; Leymon, 2011; Riccucci, 1990; Zullo, 2012).

While that is accurate, some progressive unions have been at the forefront of social policy issues (Craver, 2011; Clawson & Clawson, 1999; Fletcher & Gapasin, 2011). Craver (2011) notes that many of the social movements of the 1960s utilized union tactics and civil rights organizations like the NAACP often worked closely with sympathetic unions leaders to oppose segregation policies (p. 9). Liberal trade union leaders protested with anti-war groups to end the involvement of the United States in the Vietnam War (DeBenedetti & Chatfield, 1990, cited in Craver, 2011). In other locations, unions also provided support to rent strikers. Joint Council 13 of the Teamsters Union in St. Louis, MO, helped low cost housing residents form the Civil Alliance for Housing to protest rent increases that the tenants could not afford. The Southern Christian Leadership Conference, the Black Coalition, CORE, Action, the Zulu 1200s, the Black Liberators, and African American politicians, churches, fraternities, and sororities, along with white organizations, supported the strike including church groups, the *St. Louis Post Dispatch*, the National Tenants Organization and the New Democratic Party. Members were from a broad coalition of religious, civic and business organizations (Corr, 1991, pp. 155, 166).

In an effort to remain viable, many unions shifted their focus to public policy concerns that went beyond the wages and benefit self-interests of their membership. They began to focus on workforce diversity and the promotion of equal job opportunities, equal access to the allocation of benefits such as training and career-enhancing opportunities, commitment to workforce productivity, the need for affordable and safe daycare, maternal and family leave benefits, an increased ability to work flexible hours, the elimination of sexual harassment and discrimination in the workplace, and eliminating the exploitation of immigrant workers (Brown & Peters-Hamlin, 1989; Craver, 2011; Milkman, 2012; Pynes, 1996).

Due to changes in family structures and society, some union contracts included flexible benefit programs that include coverage for childcare, eldercare, and domestic partners. Public sector unions were at the forefront of advocating for comparable worth for job positions typically occupied by women and developing upward-mobility training programs for lower-skilled members. Some union contract provisions included newborn care leave, family care leave, dependent care reimbursement accounts, professional family care resources, referral services, adoption assistance, flexible work hours and on-site child care to dependent care financial assistance (Cowlee, 1993; Watts, 1983; York, 1993).

Unions have also been significant in advancing education and training opportunities. Going back to the 1950s, unions have negotiated career advancement opportunities in the industrial and craft sectors. More than 40 years ago, there were training and education programs in the healthcare sector in New York City and across New York State and efforts have continued to expand across the country (Klingel & Lipsky, 2010). Recognizing the limited ability of low-wage workers in the healthcare industry to move into higher-paying occupations due to the lack of education and training credentials, unions and management have developed multi-employer joint labor-management healthcare training programs (Klingel & Lipsky, 2010). According to Klingel and Lipsky, the joint labor-management multi-employer training partnership and fund model is different from other models of workforce training because it relies on the cooperation of labor and management and different employers within a region as its main organizing principle. Education is linked to employment opportunities through a labor-management partnership. Employers benefit by linking training investments to the retention and development of incumbent employees. The multi-employer approach combines employer investments with those of other employers to fund programs that would be cost-prohibitive or might not attract enough participants at a single location or employer. Training needs can be targeted to the needs within a specific geographic area and the strategic human resource needs of an employer.

Union members benefit because they are provided with educational opportunities ranging from obtaining a GED to college preparation courses, college and university degree programs, continuing education and certification programs, and other skill training programs. This often leads to higher-paying positions. Partnering with unions and their members assisted in identifying obstacles to participating in career advancements. As a result, classes began to be provided on-site and at non-traditional hours for the convenience of the employee students who had alternative working hours. Improved morale and retention have been an outgrowth of the joint multi-employer programs. Nonprofits and foundations have often been criticized for not investing in the training and development of nonprofit employees and for funding infrastructure and technology improvements (Bridgespan Group, 2011; Dorfman, 2015). As executives and managers retire, and greater accountability from funders becomes the rule, nonprofits and unions can partner to develop new training programs for internal talent and develop longer-term objectives to address impending changes.

Most of the national unions have revised their platforms to emphasize issues dealing with the growing inequality and instability, such as wage stagnation, employment insecurity, and the increasing economic inequality between workers and owners. Unions are attempting to address issues such as corporate responsibility, democracy in the workplace, and worker rights. Unions have begun to emphasize the need for greater racial, gender, and class equality and improving the political and economic status of workers and their communities. However, employer responsibility, democracy in the workplace and worker rights, healthcare, and providing wages at levels where families can support their families need to be addressed. These are issues that affect a broader population beyond union members. Unions have attempted to address these issues by forming coalitions with local and national nonprofit community groups and advocacy groups. Under *Issues* on its website, the AFL-CIO (www.aflcio.org/Issues) notes the importance of affordable healthcare, retirement security, quality education for our children, job safety, and civil and workplace rights as being essential for all working people.

Some of the groups allied with the AFL-CIO include: American Rights at Work; American Center for Labor Solidarity (Solidarity Center); Alliance for Retired Americans; American Center for International Labor Solidarity (Solidarity Center); Community Services Network; International Labor Communications Association; Jobs with Justice; Labor Heritage Foundation; Lawyers Coordinating Committee; National Day Laborer Organizing Network; National Domestic Workers Alliance; National Guestworker Alliance; United Students Against Sweatshops; Working America; and Working for America Institute. Similar issues and allied organizations can be found on most of the national labor union websites.

In a report entitled "Broken laws, unprotected workers: Violations of employment and labor laws in America's cities," Bernhardt et al. (2009) found employment and labor laws are regularly violated, impacting low wage workers in large cities. There were minimum wage violations, overtime violations, off the clock violations, meal break violations, pay stub and illegal deductions, illegal employer retaliation, and workers' compensation violations. Violations varied by occupation, childcare workers had high minimum wage and overtime violation rates, women were more likely than men to experience minimum wage violations, and foreign-born workers were twice as likely as U.S.-born employees to have minimum wage violations. Foreign-born Latino workers had the highest minimum wage violations, African-American workers had violation rates triple that of their white counterparts (2009, pp. 2–5).

Recommendations from the study include the need to strengthen government enforcement of employment and labor laws. Partnerships with immigrant worker centers, unions, service providers, legal advocates and responsible employers need to be encouraged and facilitated. Social media has been used to provide access to information about employers who violate labor and employment laws. The states, local governments, and the U.S. Department of Labor have been slow to respond to wage theft and misclassification violations. There has been some movement by public authorities, and wage theft prevention acts have been proposed and passed in some local governments and states, but nonprofits were first in calling attention to the issues (Leffert, Goodman, Zaimes, & Newman, 2015; National Consumers League, 2015).

Rachel Micah-Jones created a nonprofit agency, Centro de los Derechos del Migrante (CDM), to assist employees who have been taken advantage of by unethical employers. The group recovered more than $5 million in stolen wages. CDM developed Contratadors, a system called the "Yelp" for migrant workers because it allows workers to tell their stories and draw attention to abuses.

Employers and their recruiters are evaluated anonymously. It allows workers to share their experiences. It also informs workers of common job-market hazards and how to seek help. Visitors to the website can listen to audio and explore comic-book style illustrations. They can also print out informational posters to post around their job sites (Ericson, Jr., 2015, p. 30).

This is important because while many workers feel insecure, the immigrant, low-waged, and less-educated are the most vulnerable and are often in industries that are the hardest to unionize. Fine (2006) notes that it is difficult for labor unions to win union-organizing drives, so *worker centers* have evolved providing services like CDM. They are community-based organizations that target occupations such as daycare or home health/domestic service where workers are employed in decentralized locations. Some worker centers are based on ethnic or national identities, while others have a geographic or neighborhood focus. Some target workers who are not covered by labor law like street vendors or taxi drivers (Fine, 2006; Milkman, 2012, p. 54). They sometimes have different names and provide different services. Their activities often involve organizing workers at the grassroots level. These grassroots efforts provide assistance to workers experiencing labor law violations or campaign against workplace injustices. Some worker center nonprofits offer social and education services, and engage in policy and legislative advocacy to improve labor law enforcement. Some focus on a medial outreach approach to expose employer abuses to the public through direct appeals to consumers. Many of the worker centers are aligned with community development agencies and churches to provide workshops on worker rights and some provide job training, English language lessons, or social services. In some cases they have volunteers, professional staff or attorneys who file legal claims to remedy labor law violations. For a comprehensive review of worker centers and how they advocate for workers, their origination, their differences, the other types of nonprofits and religious institutions they often collaborate with and examples of the services they provide, see Fine (2006). Even where nonprofits may not have unionized workforces, other nonprofits have stepped in to advocate for and in some cases partner with unions in providing worker protections and defending employee rights.

Conclusion

There has been a change in the social contract between workers and employers. As noted by Baines (2010, p. 10), the nonprofit services sector has been affected by neoliberal and pro-market restructuring and alternative forms of service delivery. It is not just public agencies that have been affected by the new public management approach to redesign agencies to operate more like the private sector with an emphasis on cost-effectiveness. Market mechanisms have been integrated to the nonprofit sector as well. Competition, reducing costs, and greater productivity have become more important. As a result, organizations often are restructured and jobs are lost. Retained employees are often expected to do more with less. Wage and salary increases tend to be infrequent and benefits are often reduced. There has been an increase in alternative work arrangements such as part-time work, project-based work or temporary work; strategies often used to decrease costs. On the positive side there has been recent recognition that American workers are falling behind. A number of the candidates running for President of the United States have called attention to the decline in the middle class. There have also been statewide and citywide successes in raising the minimum wage to be above the federal minimum wage. Unions have mobilized workers and joined with other nonprofit advocacy groups to call attention to low wages, and a number of health and safety and other workplace issues.

In the Spring 2015 edition of the *Nonprofit Quarterly*, an article written by Jon Pratt and Ruth McCambridge offers seven practices for nonprofits to adopt. They suggest: (1) nonprofit employees be paid a livable wage; (2) the ethnic and racial diversity in its leadership and staff should be reviewed; (3) leaders should advance the organization's mission and the people they serve; (4) Board members should be recruited who represent the organization's constituents; (5) each organization should assess its own equality footprint to examine whether it has an effect on the equality of conditions; (6) organizations should assess their diversity both in leadership and other parts of the organization; and (7) executive compensation should be proportionate (Pratt & McCambridge, 2015, pp. 1, 20, 21).

Providing an environment free from discrimination, offering healthcare and other benefits, providing training and career opportunities to staff, and offering wages and salaries where workers can support their families should exist. If not, we may see an increase in the unionization of nonprofit organizations. For nonprofit organizations that are not yet unionized, it is important to have a progressive human resources management system in place that respects employees. Often, whether workers join unions depends on their perceptions of the work environment and their desire to participate in or influence employment conditions.

Discussion Questions

The Department for Professional Employees (DPE)
http://dpeaflcio.org/

The Department for Professional Employees (DPE) is a coalition of 22 national unions affiliated with the AFL-CIO which represents highly skilled professional and technical workers. DPE unions include professionals in healthcare and education; science, engineering and technology; journalism, entertainment and the arts; public administration; and law enforcement.

1   Go to the DPE website and look under public policy. What are the issues that the DPE is concerned about?
2   Identify and explain the two issues that are most important to you and why.

3   Explain why you think or do not think professional employees should belong to a union. Provide specific examples.

American Postal Workers Union (APWU)

Go to the APWU link www.apwu.org/news/deptdiv-news-article/social-movement-unionism-much-needed-new-model. Read about *Social Justice Unionism*.

1   Explain what you think about the need for social justice unionism. What are the issues that are most important to you?
2   How can unions, other nonprofits, individuals, and the community benefit from social justice unionism?

The Semi-Annual Labor Activity in Health Care Report

The *Semi-Annual Labor Activity in Health Care Report* prepared by the American Society for Healthcare Human Resources Administration (ASHHRA) found the issues important in healthcare organizing to include pay, staffing levels, benefits, having input in decisions, job security, leadership "interpersonal skills," leadership " management practices," quality of patient care, workload/distribution of work, safety/security/ and situational staffing coverage. The National Nurses Union filed a grievance against the James A. Haley Veterans' Hospital in Tampa which it said is 100 registered nurses short of the minimum staffing levels mandated by the Department of Veterans Affairs. The understaffing of hospital staff is a criticism in healthcare organizations in the nonprofit, for-profit and public sectors.

1   Assume you are a member of the collective bargaining team for a healthcare union. What would be the contract terms/language you would seek to place in the contract for the following issues?

   i   staffing levels
   ii   quality of patient care
   iii   workload distribution

2   Do you believe the above contract issues are interrelated? Do you believe that employees should have some influence on them? Explain your reasoning with specific examples or data.

Note

1. This has been covered previously (Pynes, 1997, 2004, 2009, 2013; Pynes & Lombardi, 2012).

References

AFUCLO Committee on the Evolution of Work. (1985). *The changing situation of workers and their unions*, AFUCLO, Washington, DC.

American Society for Healthcare Human Resources Administration and IRI Consultants. (2009). *Semi-Annual Labor Activity in Health Care Report*. Available: Detroit, MI: IRI Consultants. Available at: www.iriconsultants.com

Anonymous. (2015). Michigan voters want more nurses on job, poll says. Available at: http://publicnewsservice.org. October 16, 2015.

Baines, D. (2010). Neoliberal restructuring, participation and social unionism in the nonprofit social services. *Nonprofit and Voluntary Sector Quarterly*, *39*(1), 10–28.

Bernhardt, A., Milkman, R., Theodore, N., Heckathorn, D., Auer, M., DeFilippis, J. et al. (2009). Broken laws, unprotected workers: Violations of employment and labor laws in America's cities. Available at: http://nelp.3cdn.net/1797b93dd1ccdf9e7d_sdm6bc50n.pdf

Bielski Boris, M. (2010). Fighting for equal treatment. How the UAW won domestic partnership benefits and discrimination protection for lesbian, gay and bisexual members. *Labor Studies Journal*, *35*(2), 157–180.

Bridgespan Group. (2011). Building leadership capacity: Reframing the succession challenge. Bridgespan. Available at: www.bridgespan.org.

Brooks, K. (2015). Why MoMA protestors are demanding better treatment, in 11 brilliant posters. *The Huffington Post*, 6/4/2015. Available at: www.huffingtonpost.com/2015/06/04/moma-protest-posters_n_7513648.html

Brown, B. B. & Peters-Hamlin, K. (1989). AT&T family leave union agreement: A harbinger of change in corporate America? *Employment Relations Today*, *16*: 205–209.

Choi, S. (2011). Organizational justice and employee work attitudes: The Federal case. *The American Review of Public Administration*, *41*(2), 185–204.

Clawson, D. & Clawson, M. A. (1999). What happened to the US labor movement? Union decline and renewal. *Annual Review of Sociology*, *25*, 95–119.

Cooper, M. (2014a, July 29). Labor struggles at Metropolitan Opera have a past. *The New York Times*. Available at: www.nytimes.com/2014/07/30/arts/music/labor-struggles-at-metropolitan-opera-have-a-past.html?_r=0

Cooper, M. (2014b, July 31). In final hours, Metropolitan Opera extends contract deadlines for unions. *The New York Times*. Available at: www.nytimes.com/2014/08/01/arts/music/met-opera-unions-agree-to-federal-mediator-as-deadline-looms.html

Corr, A. (1991). *No trespassing!: Squatting, rent strikes, and land struggles worldwide*. Cambridge, MA: South End Press.

Cowlee, S. (1993). Family policy: A union approach. In D. S. Cobble (Ed.), *Women and unions: Forging a partnership* (pp. 115–128). Ithaca, NY: ILR Press.

Crain, M. (1995). Women, labor unions, and hostile work environments sexual harassment: The untold story. *Texas Journal of Women and the Law*, *4*, 15–88.

Craver, C. B. (2011). Impact of labor unions on worker rights and on other social movements. *ABA Journal of Labor and Employment Law*, *26*. Available at: http://papers.ssrn.com/sol3/papers.cfm?abstract_id=1871952

DeBenedetti, C. & Chatfield, C. (1990). *An American ordeal: The antiwar movement of the Vietnam era*. Syracuse, NY: Syracuse University Press.

Department of Professional Employees, AFL-CIO. (2014a). *The future of work and workers in professional and technical occupations*. Washington, DC: DPE-AFL-CIO. Available at: http://dpeaflcio.org/issue-fact-sheets/future-work-workers-professional-technical-occupations/

Department of Professional Employees, AFL-CIO. (2014b). *Social service workers: An occupational overview*. Available at: http://dpeaflcio.org/programs-publications/issue-fact-sheets/socail-service-workers-an-occupational-overview/

Department of Professional Employees, AFL-CIO. (2015a). *The professional and technical work force: Fact sheet 2015*. Available at: http://dpeaflcio.org/issue-fact-sheets/the-professional-and-technical-workforce/

Department of Professional Employees, AFL-CIO. (2015b). *The benefits of collective bargaining for professionals*. Available at: http://dpeaflcio.org/wp-content/uploads/Benefits-of-Collective-Bargaining-2015.pdf

DePillis, L. (2015a, May 20). The conservative case against picking on unions. A block of GOP legislators kept a right-to-work law form willing a veto-proof majority in the state. Here's why. *The Washington Post*. Available at: www.washingtonpost.com/blogs/wonkblog/wp/2015/05/20/the-conservative-case-against-picking-on-unions-courtesy-of-missouri-republicans/

DePillis, L. (2015b, August 27). In landmark case, labor board lets more workers bargain with their employer's employer. *The Washington Post*. Available at: www.washingtonpost.com/news/wonkblog/wp/2015/08/27/labor-board-moves-to-make-businesses-accountable-for-their-subcontractors/

Dorfman, A. (2015). Why don't foundations build capacity in fundraising? National Committee for Responsive Philanthropy. Available at: http://blog.ncrp.org/2015/09/foundations-build-fundraising-capacity.html.

Eddings, B. (2014, May 5). The broken circle: What we've learned from the Minnesota Orchestra debacle. *The Minnesota Post*. Available at: www.minnpost.com/community-voices/2014/05/broken-circle-what-weve-learned-minnesota-orchestra-debacle

England, P., Budig, M., & Folbe, N. (2002). Wages of virtue: The relative pay of care work. *Social Problems, 49*(4), 455–473.

Erickson, E. Jr. (2015). A 'Yelp' for migrant workers. *The Chronicle of Philanthropy, 27*(9), 29–31.

Feldacker, B. (1999). *Labor guide to labor law* (4th ed.). Englewood Cliffs, NJ: Prentice Hall.

Fine, J. (2006). *Worker centers: Organizing communities at the edge of the dream*. Ithaca, NY: ILR.

Fletcher, Jr, B. & Gapasin, F. (2011). A need for social justice unionism. *Social Policy, 41*(1), 16–26.

Fletcher, M. A. (2013). Some low-wage federal contract workers form union. *The Washington Post*. Retrieved December 17, 2015. https://www.washingtonpost.com/business/economy/2013/12/16/f5a4348c-6672-11e3-8b5b-a77187b716a3_story.html?utm_term=.83b285f2266a

Gordon, D. (2014, July 11). 4 of the most powerful health care unions. *Becker's Hospital Review*. Available at: www.beckershospitalreview.com/workforce-labor-management/5-of-the-most-powerful-national-healthcare-unions.html

Gordon, L. (2015, April 9). Doctors at UC student health clinics start strike. *LA Times*. Available at: www.latimes.com/local/education/la-me-ln-uc-strike-20150409-story.html

Greenberg, J. (1996). *The quest for justice on the job: Essays and experiment*. Thousand Oaks, CA: Sage.

Guy, M. E. & Newman, M. A. (2004). Women's jobs men's jobs: Sex segregation and emotional labor. *Public Administration Review, 64*(3), 289–298.

Guy, M. E., Newman, M. A., & Mastracci, S. H. (2008). *Emotional labor: Putting the service in public service*. Armonk, NY: M. E. Sharpe.

Hush, H. (1969). Collective bargaining in voluntary agencies. *Social Casework, 50*, 210–213.

Jacobs, J. B. & Peters, E. (2003). Labor racketeering: The mafia and the unions. *Crime and Justice, 30*, 229–282.

Karger, H. J. (Ed.). (1988). *Social workers and labor unions*. New York: Greenwood Press.

Kehoe, R. R. & Wright, P. M. (2013). The impact of high performance human resources practices on employees' attitudes and practices. *Journal of Management, 39*(2), 366–391.

Kelly, M. & Lubitow, A. (2015). Ride at work: Organizing at the intersection of the labor and LGBT movements. *Labor Studies Journal, 39*(4), 257–277.

Klinger, S. & Lipsky, D. B. (2010). *Joint labor-management training programs for healthcare worker advancement and retention.* Ithaca, NY: Cornell University, ILR School, Scheinman Institute on Conflict Resolution. Available at: Digital Commons @ILR.http://digitlabecommons.ilr.corness.edu/reports

Ko, J. & Hur, S. U. (2014). The impacts of employee benefits, procedural justice, and managerial trustworthiness on work attitudes: Integrated understanding based on social exchange theory. *Public Administration Review, 74*(2), 176–187.

Leffert, K. A., Goodman, M. E., Zaimes, J., & Newman, A. L. (2015). Recent developments in state "wage theft" prevention statutes. Mayer Brown LLP. Available at: www.lexology.com/library/detail.aspx?g=8bb64839-5d54-49ef-87d5-164b9bf0d095 (accessed October 25, 2015).

Leymon, A. S. (2011). Unions and social inclusiveness: A comparison of changes in union member attitudes. *Labor Studies Journal, 36*(3), 388–404.

Maloney, J. (2014, August 20). Metropolitan Opera contracts give unions a voice in decisions. *The Wall Street Journal.* Available at: www.wsj.com/articles/metropolitan-opera-reaches-deal-with-stagehands-1408526766

Mastracci, S. H., Guy, M. E., & Newman, M. A. (2012). *Emotional Labor and Crisis Response: Working on the Razor's Edge.* Armonk, NY: M. E. Sharpe.

McKeever, B. S. & Pettijohn, S. L. (2014). *The nonprofit sector in brief 2014. Public charities, giving and volunteering.* Washington, DC: The Urban Institute. Available at: www.urban.org/research/publication/nonprofit-sector-brief-public-charities-giving-and-volunteering-2014

Michigan Nurses Association. (2015). MI voters: Lack of limits on nurses' workloads is hurting patient care in hospitals. Available at: www.misaferhospitals.org/uploads/7/7/1/1/7711851/rn_workload_poll_press_release.pdf (accessed October 23, 2015).

Milkman, R. (2012). Immigrants and the road to power. *Dissent, 59*(3), 52–47.

National Conference of State Legislatures. (2015). Right to work resources. Available at: www.ncsl.org/research/labor-and-employment/right-to-work-laws-and-bills.aspx (accessed May 12, 2015).

National Consumers League. (2015). Workers' rights. Available at: www.natlconsumersleague.org/worker-rights/148-wage-theft/532-wage-theft-laws-protecting-workers (accessed October 25, 2015).

National Conference of State Legislatures. (2017). Right-to Work Resources. Available at: www.ncsl.org/research/labor-and-employment/right-to-work-laws-and-bills.aspx (accessed March 5, 2017).

National Labor Relations Board Jurisdictional Standards. (2015). Available at: www.nlrb.gov/rights-we-protect/jurisdictional-standards (accessed May 3, 2015).

National Nurses United. (2015). Retrieved www.nationalnursesunited.org/

Nonprofit Finance Fund. (2015). *The state of the sector: 2015.* Available at: http://nonprofitfinancefund.org/state-of-the-sector-surveys

Ortman, J. M., Velkoff, V. A., & Hogan, H. (2014). An aging nation: The older population in the United States, current population reports, P25-1140. U.S. Census Bureau, Washington, DC.

Pettijohn, S. L., Boris, E. T., & Farrell, M. R. (2014). *National study of nonprofit government contracts and grants: 2013: State profiles.* Washington, DC: The Urban Institute. Available at: www.urban.org

Pew Research Center. (2015, April 27). Mixed views of impact of long-term decline in unions Membership: Public says workers in many sectors should be able to unionize. Available at: www.people-press.org/2015/04/27/mixed-views-of-impact-of-long-term-decline-in-union-membership/

Pierce, J. L., Kostova, T., & Dirks, K. T. (2001). Toward a theory of psychological ownership in organizations. *The Academy of Management Review, 26*(2), 298–310.

Pousner, H. (2014, September 10). Locked out ASO musicians receiving chorus of support nationally, locally. *Atlanta Journal Courier.* Available at: http://artsculture.blog.

ajc.com/2014/09/10/locked-out-aso-musicians-receiving-chorus-support-nationally-locally/

Pratt, J. & McCambridge, R. (2015). Not adding to the problem: Seven ways your nonprofit can avoid mirroring practices that perpetuate inequality. *The Nonprofit Quarterly, 22*(1), 18–22.

Preston, A. & Sacks, D. W. (2010). Nonprofit wages: Theory and evidence. In D. R. Young & B. Seaman (Eds.), *Handbook of research on nonprofit economics and management* (pp. 106–119). Cheltenham, UK: Edward Elgar.

Pynes, J. E. (1996). The two faces of unions. *Journal of Collective Negotiations in the Public Sector, 25*(1), 31–40.

Pynes, J. E. (1997). *Human resources management for public and nonprofit organizations*. San Francisco: Jossey-Bass.

Pynes, J. E. (2004). *Human resources management for public and nonprofit organizations: A strategic approach* (2nd ed.). San Francisco: Jossey-Bass.

Pynes, J. E. (2009). *Human resources management for public and nonprofit organizations: A strategic approach* (3rd ed.). San Francisco: Jossey-Bass.

Pynes, J. E. (2013). *Human resources management for public and nonprofit organizations: A strategic approach* (4th ed.). San Francisco: Jossey-Bass, Inc.

Pynes, J. E. and Lombardi, D. L. (2012). *Human Resources Management for Health Care Organizations: A Strategic Approach*. San Francisco: Jossey-Bass, Inc.

Riccucci, N. (1990). *Women, minorities and unions in the public sector*. Santa Barbara, CA: Praeger.

Rubin, E. V. (2011). Exploring the link between procedural fairness and union membership. *Review of Public Personnel Administration, 31*(2).

Service Employees International Union (SEIU). (2015). Retrieved from www.seiu.org/

Tambor, M. (1973). Unions and voluntary agencies. *Social Work, 18*, 41–47.

Tambor, M. (1988a). Collective bargaining in the social services. In P. R. Keys & L. H. Ginsberg (Eds.), *New management in human services* (pp. 81–101). Silver Springs, MD: National Association of Social Workers, Inc.

Tambor, M. (1988b). Social service unions in the workplace. In H. J. Karger (Ed.), *Social workers and labor unions*. New York: Greenwood Press.

Trottman, M. (2015, August 27). Ruling clears way for unions. Fast-food, construction to feel effects of labor board decision on temp and contract workers. *The Wall Street Journal*. Available at: www.wsj.com/articles/labor-board-ruling-puts-more-companies-on-the-hook-for-temporary-workers-1440704018

United Food and Commercial Workers International Union (UFCWIU). (2015). Retrieved www.ufcw.org/

U.S. Bureau of Labor Statistics. (2013a). Employment Projections Fastest projected job occupations between 2012—projected 2022. Available at: www.bls.gov/emp/ep_table_103.htm (accessed May 12, 2015).

U.S. Bureau of Labor Statistics. (2013b). Employment Projections. Projections of employment by major occupational group industry 2012- projected 2022. Available at: www.bls.gov/emp/ep_table_101.htm (accessed May 12, 2015).

U.S. Bureau of Labor Statistics. (2015, January 23). Union members summary. Available at: www.bls.gov/news.release/union2.nr0.htm (accessed May 12, 2015).

Watts, G. (1983). Training and retraining workers will be an important challenge for unions in the 21st century. *Personnel Administrator, 28*, 82–84.

Western, B. & Rosenfeld, J. (2011). Unions, norms, and the rise in U.S. wage inequality. *American Sociological Review, 76*(4), 513–537.

York, C. (1993). Bargaining for work and family benefits. In D. S. Cobble (Ed.), *Women and unions: Forging a partnership* (pp. 129–147). Ithaca, NY: ILR Press.

Zullo, R. (2012). The evolving demographics of the union movement. *Labor Studies Journal, 37*(2), 145–162.

11

Engagement, Satisfaction, and Nonprofit Organizations

Kunle Akingbola

Introduction

There are many things an archetypal nonprofit is supposed to represent, actualize, and advocate as an organization. In addition to their basic characteristics such as providers of public goods, harbinger of the values of society, protector of social justice, channel for addressing the problems and opportunities not addressed by the government and for-profit organizations (Quarter, Mook, & Richmond, 2003; Salamon & Anheier, 1998) and many more highlighted characteristics in this book, nonprofits are also expected to be a progressive type of organization for employees. Irrespective of the size and type of nonprofit, the progressive orientation is assumed to play out in the human resources (HR) policy and practices of the organization (Akingbola, 2013). To achieve this orientation, a number of behavioral antecedents are imperative. The behavior of employees and volunteers is the essential ingredient that nonprofit organizations must facilitate and influence to achieve this orientation. In this chapter, we explore two of the behavioral antecedents: engagement and satisfaction.

The chapter starts with a background of the concept of engagement and satisfaction. This is followed by a discussion of the varied definitions of engagement from the perspective of management practitioners and the academic literature. Next, the chapter offers a review of the existing research on engagement and briefly discusses the link between engagement and satisfaction. It ends with an examination of research on engagement in nonprofits and what this portends for human resource management in the sector.

What Is Engagement?

Similar to many recent concepts in human resource management and organizational behavior, employee engagement is a relatively new concept that draws upon and combines many existing concepts (Wefald & Downey, 2009a). Beyond the relative newness of the concept, employee engagement has gained significant currency among management practitioners to the extent that research is playing catch-up to provide empirical evidence to explain its meaning, dimension, contributory antecedents, and its impact on employees and the organization (Macey & Schneider, 2008). Hence, it is logical to start with an overview of the definition and determinants of employee engagement offered by management practitioners.

Management Practitioners

For management consultants, engagement appears to be all about discretionary effort. Towers Perrin defines engagement as the "employees' willingness and ability to help their company succeed, largely by providing discretionary effort on a sustainable basis" (Towers Perrin, 2003a). Their second report explained that engagement could be seen as "the extent to which employees put discretionary effort into their work, in the form of extra time, brainpower, and energy" (Towers Perrin, 2003b, p. 3). In a literature review for the Conference Board, Gibbons (2006) defines employee engagement as the connection an employee has to their job, organization, manager, or co-workers, a connection that should lead to the application of additional discretionary effort in their work. The discretionary effort narrative has been further simplified in recent reports by consultants, emphasizing the discretionary effort of employees to go beyond their job expectations (Towers Watson, 2014). The Towers Watson report noted that there are three measurable elements that are essential to sustainable engagement:

- traditional engagement—employees' willingness to expend discretionary effort on their job;
- enablement—having the tools, resources, and support (typically through direct-line supervisors) to do their job effectively;
- energy—having a work environment that actively supports physical, emotional, and interpersonal well-being (Towers Watson, 2014, p. 3).

The definitions offered by management practitioners appear to emphasize the connection of the employee to the job, the work environment, and the organization. They suggest that employees rely on this connection to determine their level of engagement.

Determinants of Employee Engagement

The management practitioner literature has also been quick to highlight the important factors or drivers of employee engagement in organizations. The Towers

Perrin (2003b) report identified the following as key drivers of employee engagement: challenging work; senior management's sincere interest in employees' well-being; employees have appropriate decision-making authority, customer satisfaction, employees work well in teams; employees have resources needed to perform jobs in a high-quality way; employees have appropriate decision-making input; career opportunities; company's reputation as a good employer.

Over time, the number of drivers has since been extended to include more dimensions, especially the role of managers and the learning environment. The two examples below from the management practitioner literature incorporated these additional drivers. Key drivers of engagement are (Schmidt, 2009):

- Leadership and management
- Learning and development and career growth
- Rewards and recognition
- Work environment, encompassing teamwork and relationships with coworkers.

Lowe (2012) proposed a list of top 10 work environment drivers of engagement, rank-ordered by their net influence on engagement scores. This includes perceptions of trust in the organization, the opportunity to improve one's work, the perception of the value of one's work by the organization, clear goals, commitment of senior leadership, team connections, and work-life balance, and sufficient resources and supervisor assistance to do the work.

The definitions and the large body of survey reports on the construct by management practitioners have contributed significantly to the application of employee engagement in management practices. In particular, the work by management consultants has not only fostered the understanding of the basic premise of employee engagement, it has encouraged managers to seek how they can use engagement to enhance employee and organizational outcomes. However, many of the available management practitioner literature have linked engagement to outcomes which are yet to be validated by research. As a result, although empirical research on engagement has also increased significantly in recent years, there appears to be a gap between management consultants and academic scholars.

Research

For all its popularity with management consultants, employee engagement is rooted firmly in empirical research. The original coining of the concept has been traced to the work of Kahn (1990) in which he introduced the concept of personal engagement. Kahn defines personal engagement as "the simultaneous employment and expression of a person's 'preferred self' in task behaviors that promote connections to work and to others, personal presence (physical, cognitive, and emotional), and active, full role performances" (p. 700). In this initial perspective on the concept, engagement is about how much of the physical, cognitive, and emotional energy or resources individuals are willing to draw upon from their personal selves in order to perform in their work roles.

A subsequent work that operationalized the concept of engagement with empirical measures defines it "as a positive, fulfilling, work-related state of mind that is characterized by vigor, dedication, and absorption" (Schaufeli, Salanova, Gonzalez-Roma, & Bakker, 2002, p. 74). They noted that engagement involves an ongoing and persistent state of mind that shows a disposition towards relentless effort, a high level of energy, and a drive for the job role. It also includes affective behavior such as enthusiasm, attachment to the job and the ability to overlook difficulties in the work role. In this definition, engagement includes presence of mind and an unencumbered focus on the job.

Saks (2006) introduced a multidimensional approach to the definition and conceptualization of engagement. He defines employee engagement as "a distinct and unique construct consisting of cognitive, emotional, and behavioral components . . . associated with individual role performance" (p. 602). He emphasized that there is a difference between job engagement and organization engagement. The importance of the organizational dimension was clear in a subsequent definition that described employee engagement as "an individual employee's cognitive, emotional and behavioral state directed toward desired organizational outcomes" (Shuck & Wollard, 2010, p. 103). This suggests that employees who are engaged will demonstrate attentiveness and mental absorption in their work and at the same time, they will have a high level of emotional connection to the organization (Kahn, 1990; Saks, 2006). Recently, it has been suggested engagement can manifest at an organizational level through social processes that facilitate shared perception and a degree of homogeneity in terms of characteristics and values of employees (Barrick, Thurgood, Smith, & Courtright, 2015). This conceptualization raises important questions especially for nonprofit organizations where value congruence and the relationship between employees and the organization are part of the fundamental characteristics of the sector. This perspective is discussed further later in the chapter. It also reinforces the position of theorists who have suggested that engagement includes legacy organizational behavior concepts such as job satisfaction.

What Is Job Satisfaction?

Job satisfaction is one of the legacy constructs that preceded and is incorporated in employee engagement. It refers to "a pleasurable or positive emotional state resulting from the appraisal of one's job or job experience" (Locke, 1976, p. 1300). Job satisfaction explains whether an employee likes or dislikes their job, people they interact with at work, and the work environment. We perceive and express job satisfaction through our feelings, behaviors, and the connections we establish and attach to our job and all the components of the job. Thus, research has shown that job satisfaction manifests through the cognitive, emotional, and affective responses to the characteristics and dimensions of the job (Judge & Ilies, 2004; Rich, Lepine, & Crawford, 2010).

Since the idea of job satisfaction has been around for a long time, there is abundant research on factors that could contribute to whether employees experience job satisfaction or not. Similarly, research has also provided valuable insight on the impact of job satisfaction for the employee and the organization. The summary below outlines some of the factors that have been identified as determinants of job satisfaction (Melnik, Petrella, & Richez-Battesti, 2013).

Determinants of Job Satisfaction

- Individual characteristics (gender, family responsibilities)
- Relationships with supervisors
- Working conditions
- Job characteristics (autonomy, stress, intrinsic interest of the job)
- Relationships with board of directors
- Working environment (trust, perceived ethical climate, and equity).

In terms of impact, research has linked job satisfaction to the following outcomes for employees and the organization (Gould-Williams, 2003; Lum, Kervin, Clark, Reid, & Sirola, 1998; Wall, Clegg, & Jackson, 1978).

Impacts of job satisfaction are:

- Reduced turnover
- Reduced absenteeism
- Increased employee performance
- Improved employee wellness and life expectancy.

Similar to most micro organizational concepts, there is an element of reciprocity and interdependence in the process of job satisfaction. When an organization facilitates employees' job satisfaction through working conditions, HR practices and the overall organizational climate (Hellriegel & Slocum, 1974; Schneider & Snyder, 1975), the organization creates an enabling condition for the employees to repay the organization through increased commitment and organizational citizenship behavior. As discussed below, due to their organizational character-istics, nonprofits are especially likely to be expected to foster employee commit-ment through their HR policies and practices. Job satisfaction in nonprofits is related to the individuals' perceptions of the work environment, the mission, and values of the nonprofits (Melnik, Petrella, & Richez-Battesti, 2013). The notion of reciprocity is central to the theories that have been used to explain employee engagement.

Employee Engagement: Conceptualization and Research

As noted above, the interest in employee engagement among management practitioners and scholars has increased significantly in recent years. This spike in interest has brought about a considerable body of application, theoretical and empirical work on engagement. For nonprofits, the interest is to be expected. The centrality of human capital and the emphasis on non-financial intrinsic reward (Akingbola, 2006; Borzaga & Tortia, 2006) signal the need to research engagement in order to understand employees, volunteers, and their relationship with the job and nonprofit organizations. Beyond the definition, there appears to be a broad pattern discernible in many of the published works. Drawing from the literature (Macey & Schneider, 2008; Shuck, 2011), this chapter provides an overview of the explanation and research on employee engagement organized into two themes: (1) engagement and organizational outcomes; and (2) theoretical approaches in employee engagement.

Engagement and Organizational Outcomes

Management Practitioners

Management consultants and managers have been particularly concerned about the need to explain the impact of employee engagement on organizational outcomes (Wefald & Downey, 2009b). The numerous reports have suggested there is a relationship between employee engagement and organizational outcomes at employee, team, and organizational levels. For example, at the *employee level*, a meta-analysis of dozens of different studies by the Gallup organization indicated that a positive employee engagement environment is consistently associated with decreased employee turnover and higher employee productivity (Harter, Schmidt, & Keyes, 2003). For *teams*, a study of a case organization found teams that are highly engaged achieved better business sales results than less engaged teams with a difference of $2.1 million dollars in total sales (Vance, 2006).

It is perhaps at the *organizational level* that most of the practitioner studies have tried to highlight the impacts of employee engagement. In addition to the findings of the meta-analysis above, which also included positive association between employee engagement and increased customer satisfaction, the findings from the study by Towers Perrin (2003a) pointed out the positive relationship between employee engagement and organizational outcomes such as product quality, better cost control, and financial performance. The findings on financial performance were consistent in the Watson Wyatt Worldwide (2007) study which also indicated the link between the nature of management communication practices and employee engagement. The communication finding suggests employee engagement was associated with better organizational communication practices. In their survey on employee engagement in nonprofit organizations, Accenture suggested that the correlation between engagement and organizational performance could explain why retention is a significant challenge in nonprofits (Accenture, 2014). They found that 25% of engaged employees—those with the highest measured levels of engagement—were "likely" or "extremely likely" in the next year to be actively pursuing other job opportunities.

Research

The benefits of employee engagement for the employee and the organization have also been central in the discourse among scholars. This has specifically been prominent in many subsequent definitions of the concept. For example, Shuck and Wollard (2010) proposed that employee engagement involves "an individual employee's cognitive, emotional, and behavioral state directed toward desired organizational outcomes"(p. 15). Similarly, Robinson, Perryman, and Hayday (2004) define engagement as "a positive attitude held by the employee towards the organization and its values. An engaged employee is aware of the business context, works with colleagues to improve performance within the job for the benefit of the organization" (p. 2). From this standpoint, employee engagement is explained not only in terms of driving the relationship between the employee and the work role but also how this relationship contributes to organizational outcomes. This perspective is increasingly dominating the discourse among scholars who research engagement. However, as discussed below, the limited research on engagement in nonprofit organizations is basically at the onset phase and is yet to discuss the organizational outcomes angle of engagement. Moreover, one should expect this line of research to be limited because of the multidimensional indicators of performance of nonprofit organizations.

For the *employees*, research has found a relationship between engagement and many individual employee outcomes. First, engagement has been linked to the enhanced quality of experience at work (Kahn, 1992). When employees are engaged, the individuals are likely to derive better experience from their work life than others who are not engaged. Second, research has also showed that employee engagement could help to mitigate burnout (Maslach, Schaufeli, & Leiter, 2001). The link to burnout was one of the early findings that demonstrated how engagement is inversely associated with a negative psychological outcome of the job for the individual employee. Third, engagement encourages employees to invest the self more in the work they deem and find challenging (Leiter & Bakker, 2010). Engaged employees know and are better able to put in effort and skills because the work is independently challenging to them. Fourth, engaged employees are better placed to access positive emotions (Yalabik, Popaitoon, Chowne, & Rayton, 2013), attitudes and behavior that are desirable to them (Bakker & Schaufeli, 2008). The research on the impact of engagement on employees continues to highlight the different dimensions of how engagement enhances critical individual outcomes that could contribute to organizational performance.

At the *organizational level*, the research interest in the outcomes of employee engagement mirrors similar efforts in the management practitioner literature. Thus, it is no surprise that the consequences of employee engagement have become a dominant research focus for academic scholars. The specific consequences of employee engagement for the organization that have been suggested in empirical research include profit, customer satisfaction, productivity, and employee turnover (Bakker & Schaufeli, 2008; Harter, Schmidt, & Hayes, 2002). A brief overview of the key findings is discussed below.

- *Engagement and profit.* Based on the findings from a meta-analysis, Harter et al. (2002) suggested that there is relationship between business unit profit and employee engagement. Luthans and Peterson (2002) also linked employee engagement to profitability. Their findings suggested that the manager self-efficacy scores have a positive relationship with employee engagement depending on how managers rate employee effectiveness and employees rate their manager's level of effectiveness positively.
- *Engagement and customer outcomes.* A study by Salanova, Agut, and Peiro (2005) finds that employee engagement mediates the relationship between organizational resources and service climate. The study showed that engagement contributes to service climate—how employees relate to customers—which is associated with customer loyalty.
- *Engagement and turnover.* The relationship between employee engagement and employees' turnover intention has been suggested in the findings of several studies (Saks, 2006; Shuck & Wollard, 2010; Shuck, Reio, & Rocco, 2011). Specifically, the findings from Saks (2006) indicated that job and organization engagement are associated with turnover intention. Both types of engagement mediated the relationships between antecedents such as job characteristics, perceived organizational support and the intention to turnover. Since research has suggested that turnover intention is a better predictor of actual turnover than job satisfaction (Steel & Ovalle, 1984), employee engagement is associated with turnover.

Beyond the specific examples highlighted in the brief overview, research has also suggested that employee engagement is associated with other organizational outcomes such as workplace accidents, organizational commitment and organization citizenship behavior (Rich et al., 2010; Shuck & Wollard, 2010). Furthermore, it has been suggested that employee engagement could play a role in organizational change (Reissner & Pagan, 2013). The continuously growing body of research has reiterated how the deployment of cognitive, emotional, and behavioral energy by employees could have an impact for the outcomes of the organization. Although the nonprofit context would add unique and additional dimensions to the research on engagement, the concept is yet to elicit significant inquiry among nonprofit management scholars. The summary of research presented below highlights the beginning of empirical work on engagement in nonprofit organizations.

Theoretical Approaches in Employee Engagement

To examine the theoretical approaches used to conceptualize employee engagement, it is necessary to briefly explain how the construct is related to well-known concepts, some of which have been compared to engagement in the literature. The debate on how engagement is similar or different from other well-known constructs such as motivation, commitment, and job satisfaction has led to the suggestion that engagement is basically a broader multidimensional construct that incorporates related concepts to explain the connection employees have to their job and their organization (Macey & Schneider, 2008; Salanova, Agut, & Peiro, 2005). Due to their close link to employee engagement and the context of nonprofits, we should highlight commitment and job satisfaction. An overview of the theoretical approaches of employee engagement is presented after this overview.

Commitment and Employee Engagement

Commitment signifies the deep relationship between an employee and the organization. Employees show commitment to the organization when they deploy behaviors that are consistent with attachment, bonding, and belongingness (Mowday, Porter, & Steers, 1982). It has been suggested that the conceptualization of organizational commitment has three components: affective; continuance; and normative commitment (Meyer & Allen,1991). Affective commitment is characterized by an "emotional attachment to, identification with, and involvement in the organization" (Meyer, Stanley, Herscovitch, & Topolnytsky, 2002, p. 21) while continuance commitment is based on the calculation of the cost of losing membership which influences the decision of the employee to remain with the organization (Meyer & Allen, 1991). Normative commitment has to do with the sense of obligation to the organization (Meyer & Allen, 1991). The obligation could develop from a sense of duty to repay the organization for the investment in the employee.

Although there is a consensus that commitment is not the same as employee engagement, the literature has consistently explained that commitment is embedded in employee engagement (Shuck & Wollard, 2010; Wefald & Downey, 2009a). Commitment is conceptualized as a general attitude or psychological state which is imbued in the level of engagement of the employee to the job performance (Saks, 2006). Moreover, in management practice and research, commitment has been linked as an antecedent to various organizational outcomes including employee engagement (Macey & Schneider, 2008). The three forms of commitment were found to be related to employee and organizational outcomes (Meyer, Stanley, Herscovitch, & Topolnytsky, 2002). The research indicated that commitment could be an antecedent of work engagement (Shuck et al., 2011) or an outcome that is mediated by job and organization engagement (Saks, 2006). The findings suggest that when employees have organizational commitment, they are likely to be engaged. The questions addressed in the findings are particularly relevant in nonprofit organizations and are evidenced in the research reviewed below.

Job Satisfaction and Employee Engagement

Similar to commitment, research has examined the relationship between job satisfaction and employee engagement. Again, the literature suggests that job satisfaction is related to work engagement (Saks, 2006). The findings indicated that job and organization engagement mediated the relationships between the antecedents and job satisfaction. While other studies have indicated that job satisfaction is an antecedent of employee engagement (Shuck & Wollard, 2010; Wefald & Downey, 2009), Simpson (2009) suggested that job satisfaction is a major predictor of employee engagement. This finding gives weight to the importance of job satisfaction in employee engagement. From a slightly different lens, Rich et al. (2010) suggested that the indirect relationships through engagement between the antecedents and the outcomes that they examined were also similar with job satisfaction as a mediator. Their finding seems to indicate that job satisfaction could have a similar indirect mediating relationship between antecedents and outcomes. The different findings suggest three key points about the relationship between job satisfaction and engagement. First, job satisfaction is associated with employee engagement. This could mean employees who have job satisfaction are more likely to be engaged than others. Second, the findings also appear to suggest that the relationship between antecedents and job satisfaction could depend on employee engagement as a mediating factor. Third, the literature has indicated that employee engagement appears not to predict job satisfaction, which suggests the relationship between the two constructs may not be vice versa.

Theoretical Approaches

Research on employee engagement has evolved alongside the examination of the theoretical explanation of the construct. Scholars have offered theories to elucidate the theoretical background and how engagement is related to relevant organizational behavior concepts. The chapter highlights five theoretical approaches that explain the state of employee engagement: (1) Kahn's (1990) need-satisfying approach; (2) Maslach et al.'s (2001) burnout-antithesis approach; (3) Harter et al.'s (2002) satisfaction-engagement approach; (4) Saks's (2006) multidimensional approach; and (5) Barrick, Thurgood, Smith, and Courtright's (2015) collective engagement approach. Shuck (2011) provides a detailed overview of four of the five approaches.

Kahn's (1990) Need-Satisfying Approach

In the original conceptualization of engagement, Kahn (1990) explained that in order to be engaged, employees have to fully apply the personal self in terms of the physical, cognitive, and emotional energy in the performance of their work roles. In contrast, employees are disengaged when there is disconnection of the personal self from work roles (Kahn, 1990). To determine whether to be engaged or disengaged, Kahn (1990) suggested that employees unconsciously asked themselves three questions: (1) How meaningful is it for me to bring myself into this performance?; (2) How safe is it to do so?; and (3) How available am I to do so? (p. 703). The presence of these three conditions—*meaningfulness, safety,* and *availability*—influence employees' engagement, and their absence conversely causes employees to be disengaged.

Meaningfulness is explained as the perception of the individual about the value, relevance, and importance of the work role in relation to the physical, cognitive, and energy invested by the individual (Kahn, 1990). Safety has to do with the perception of support and comfort to freely invest the self within a social system "without fear of negative consequences to self-image, status or career" (Kahn, 1990, p. 708). For psychological availability, the individual has self-perception and self-consciousness of adequate physical, emotional, and psychological resources required to complete the work role. Although Kahn's (1990) framework is the foundation of employee engagement, the approach was not widely used in empirical research until recently (Shuck, 2011).

Maslach et al.'s (2001) Burnout-Antithesis Approach

The burnout-antithesis approach was the second perspective that emerged after the original conceptualization of employee engagement (Shuck, 2011). The core idea of this approach is that employee engagement is the positive antithesis of burnout (Maslach et al., 2001). In other words, engagement is the positive and direct opposite of burnout. Maslach et al. (2001) noted that two trends emerged in burnout research at the time: (1) the link between burnout and human services professions in which employees interact directly with people such as healthcare and education was extended to include all professions; (2) burnout research has shifted towards its opposite, job engagement. The shift suggested that burnout research was extending its focus to the positive role of workers' well-being in engagement rather than focusing only on the negative domain (Maslach et al., 2001). This shift was supported by positive psychology which emphasizes positive characteristics and human strengths (Seligman & Csikszentmihalyi, 2000). Positive psychology has been found to be relevant in examining supported social enterprises in the nonprofit sector (Akingbola, Phaetthayanan, & Brown, 2015).

Maslach et al. (2001) explained that burnout is a negation of engagement in that, "what was once important, meaningful, and challenging work became unpleasant, unfulfilling, and meaningless" (p. 416). For example, their findings suggest that a lack of support from supervisors is a particularly important factor linked to burnout (Maslach et al., 2001). The framework was operationalized and extended with empirical measures (Schaufeli, Salanova, Gonzalez-Roma, & Bakker, 2002). The latter conceptualization also added affective behavior such as enthusiasm, attachment to the job, and the ability to overlook difficulties in work role to the meaning of engagement. Schaufeli, Bakker, and Salanova (2002) drew on relevant burnout research to extend the measures and to develop the Utrecht Work Engagement Scale (UWES), a popular measure of engagement (Shuck, 2011).

Harter et al.'s (2002) Satisfaction-Engagement Approach

Harter et al.'s (2002) satisfaction-engagement approach is based on a meta-analysis of the Gallup Organization data. As discussed above, the findings linked employee engagement to business unit profit. Also, the researchers used a positive psychology framework to emphasize that satisfaction, involvement, and enthusiasm are the core components of employee engagement. Luthans and Peterson (2002) extended Harter et al.'s (2002) research to link employee engagement to profitability. Their findings on the relationship between manager self-efficacy and employee engagement contributed to the theories of engagement reviewed in this section (Kahn, 1990; Maslach et al., 2001). The body of research that used Harter et al.'s (2002) approach has been updated over the years (Shuck, 2011).

Saks's (2006) Multidimensional Approach

As discussed above, Saks (2006) drew on social exchange theory (Blau, 1964) to specifically differentiate between job engagement and organizational engagement. He extended Kahn's (1990) model and Schaufeli et al.'s (2002) model of engagement by introducing a multidimensional approach to engagement. Job engagement is characterized by the degree to which the individual employees exert or invest the self in their work role (Rich et al., 2010; Saks, 2006), while organization engagement could be conceptualized as the greater investment of the self for higher job performance in response to organizational factors or decisions (Saks, 2006).

He explained that the antecedents and consequences of job and organizational engagement are different in a number of ways. In other words, the psychological prerequisites that must be at play for job and organizational engagement to exist and the outcomes of the two types of engagement are not necessarily the same.

Social exchange theory highlights the norm of reciprocity of action between parties, which are not set in any contractual framework to define the nature of the payback obligation (Blau, 1964; Gould-Williams & Davies, 2005). In relation to engagement, Saks (2006) suggested the more economic and socioemotional resources employees receive from the organization, the more obliged they feel to repay the organization by bringing more of the self into their work role. In effect, the cognitive, emotional, and physical energy employees bring to their work roles is dependent on the level of resources and support the organization provides to employees (Saks, 2006). In other words, engagement flows from employees' perception of organizational support and commitment. The findings of Saks (2006) suggest that employee engagement is associated with perceived organizational support and mediates the relationship between the antecedents and outcomes such as job satisfaction and organizational commitment.

Barrick et al.'s (2015) Collective Organizational Approach

The collective organizational approach is a new approach that has recently been proposed in the research literature. Barrick et al. (2015) suggest that engagement can manifest at an organizational level through social processes that facilitate shared perception and a degree of homogeneity in terms of characteristics and values of employees. They specifically noted that Kahn's (1990) conceptualization of engagement is a more complete description of the construct and extended the framework by integrating engagement theory with the resource management model. Barrick et al. (2015) define collective organizational engagement as "the shared perceptions of organizational members that members of the organization are, as a whole, physically, cognitively, and emotionally invested in their work" (p. 113). The collective organizational engagement is different from the aggregated individual-level engagement conceptualized by Saks (2006). The shared perception of engagement that is central to collective organizational engagement is developed and maintained in part through the various affective and social processes in the organization (Barrick et al., 2015; Hofmann & Morgeson, 1999) and the attraction–selection–attrition processes (Barrick et al., 2015; Schneider, 1987). The latter could lead to employees with similar characteristics and values which could contribute to engagement (Barrick et al., 2015).

The organizational engagement conceptualization implies that employees invest their whole selves collectively in their work roles. In effect, the collective organizational engagement is an organizational capability (Barrick et al., 2015). The antecedents of this engagement are therefore the resources of the organization. Barrick et al. (2015) proceeded to test the relationship between three organizational resources as antecedents: motivating work design; human resource management practices; and CEO transformational leadership. The findings suggest that collective organizational engagement has a mediating relationship between these organizational resources and performance.

The theoretical approaches in employee engagement illustrate the evolving theorization and application of the concept. Although the evolution and discourse of engagement have followed different but interrelated theoretical pathways (Shuck, 2011; Shuck et al., 2011), there is a sustained overriding assumption in research and management practice, engagement is a recipe for positive organizational outcomes. However, there remains a need to better understand different elements and operationalization of the concept including the contextual dimension, process, and organizational factors that contribute to, or that result from, engagement (Macey & Schneider, 2008; Rich et al., 2010; Truss, Shantz, Soane, Alfes, & Delbridge, 2013).

Engagement and Nonprofit Organizations

One area in which the research on engagement is playing catch-up with the understanding of the context of the organization is the nonprofit sector. Although a few studies have included nonprofit employees in their samples, including Kahn's (1990) original work and Schaufeli, Bakker and Salanova (2002), the focus of existing research in the nonprofit context has been tangential at best. This appears to be the case in both the practitioner literature and scholarly research. Again, management practitioners seem to have shown early interest in the dimension of employee engagement in nonprofit organizations long before the very recent and limited research by academics.

Management Practitioners

In a comparison of engagement level across different industries, the Towers Perrin (2003b) study found that employee engagement is substantially higher in the nonprofit sector than in every other sector they examined. The report noted that the higher level of engagement should be expected in nonprofits because employees are attracted to the sector due to the mission of the organization and not based on the compensation (Towers Perrin, 2003b). They contended that the findings on the nonprofit sector could be an indication that an organization cannot buy engagement with compensation.

The consulting firm, Accenture, has focused specifically on how to increase employee engagement in nonprofit organizations (Accenture, 2014). The Accenture report found that nonprofit employees are likely to evaluate the importance of their work based on their perceived connection between their job and the mission of the organization. They suggested that it is more common for nonprofit employees who are disengaged to choose not to quit because they strongly identify with the mission of the organization (Accenture, 2014). This could point to the importance of the context of nonprofits in explaining engagement in the sector.

Research

Empirical research on employee engagement that is specifically focused on nonprofit organizations is very rare. To date, Selander (2015) is one of only two of such empirical research. Selander applied the job demand-resources (JD-R) model to examine work engagement in a survey of Finnish third-sector employees. The JD-R model is an upshot of the Maslach et al. (2001) burnout-antithesis approach discussed above. Selander emphasized the importance of nonprofit contextual factors and characteristics of employees such as public employees' ideological orientation and funding in relation to work engagement. The findings indicate that nonprofit employees reported higher work engagement than other employees in similar work engagement studies (Selander, 2015). Also, the study found a relationship between work engagement and value congruence as well public service motivation. However, the focus on work engagement is limiting.

As noted by Rich et al. (2010), Kahn's (1990) conceptualization represents a more comprehensive and holistic view of engagement.

In another recent research, Akingbola and van den Berg (2016) draw on Kahn's (1990) theory of job engagement and Saks's (2006) multidimensional approach to examine the relationship between antecedents and consequences of engagement in nonprofit organizations. We emphasized that the unique characteristics of the nonprofit context and the behavioral orientation of their employees underlie the research. The study collected data from a sample of nonprofits in Ontario, Canada. The findings suggest that the consequences of job and organization engagement are the behavioral outcomes—job satisfaction, commitment, organization citizenship behavior—that nonprofits consider as critical to their organization and the employees emphasize. Perhaps the strongest evidence of the impact of engagement is the finding that nonprofit employees are more likely to experience these consequences and less likely to have intention to quit even if antecedents such as job characteristics and value congruence are less likely. Consistent with the literature, the findings also suggest that value congruence is a major determinant in the relationship between nonprofit employees and their jobs as well as with the organization. On antecedents of engagement, our findings provide evidence that while the characteristics of nonprofit jobs predicted job engagement, rewards and recognition appear to be of less importance to the employees. The research presents one of the first findings that result from empirically validated measures of engagement in nonprofits.

Conclusion

The issue of employee engagement is fundamental in nonprofits at the individual, organizational, and community levels. It is therefore imperative for nonprofit managers, employees, and board members to understand the concept and how it could impact the outcomes of the organization. This chapter provides an overview of employee engagement from the literature by management practitioners and in research. It highlights engagement as an umbrella construct that incorporates other well-known concepts such as organizational commitment and job satisfaction. The chapter also offers a detailed insight into the evolution and the theoretical approaches that showcase the state of employee engagement. Although research on employee engagement in nonprofits is limited, the available evidence points to the importance of understanding the context of the sector in relation to engagement. The findings from the research and management practitioner literature emphasize the need for human resource management in nonprofit organizations to pay particular attention to employee engagement.

Discussion Questions

1   You have been hired as a consultant to a small nonprofit organization. The board of directors has invited you to explain why the organization should

be concerned about employee engagement. What are the major points you will highlight in your presentation?

2   Jane has told you that she is satisfied with her job. However, she is not sure whether she is truly engaged. She wants you to explain the difference between the two concepts.

3   To be engaged involves the use of the physical, cognitive, and emotional energy in the performance of an individual's work role. Drawing on your experience, describe examples of when you showed you were engaged or disengaged.

4   Employee engagement impacts individual and organizational outcomes. Discuss some of the specific ways engagement could impact employee, volunteer, and organizational outcomes in nonprofit organizations.

5   In a recent management team meeting, a manager explained that employee engagement is the latest buzz word that is not supported by research. You offered to present a summary of the research on employee engagement at the next meeting. In bullet form, outline the key points and the research you will include in your presentation.

References

Accenture. (2014). Accenture – Increasing Employee Engagement in the Nonprofit Sector Available at: www.accenture.com/SiteCollectionDocuments/PDF/Accenture-Increased-Employee-Engagement-Online-View.pdf (accessed May, 2014).

Akingbola, K. (2006). Strategy and human resource management in nonprofit organizations: Evidence from Canada. *International Journal of Human Resource Management*, 17(10), 1707–1725.

Akingbola, K. (2013). Contingency, fit and flexibility of HRM in nonprofit organizations. *Employee Relations*, 35(5), 479–494.

Akingbola, K., Phaetthayanan, S., & Brown, J. (2015). A-way courier express: social enterprise and positive psychology. *Nonprofit Management & Leadership*, 26(2), 20–37.

Akingbola, K. & van den Berg, H. (2016). Antecedents, consequences and the context of employee engagement in nonprofit organizations. *Review of Public Personnel Administration* (In press).

Bakker, A. B. & Schaufeli, W. B. (2008). Positive organizational behavior: Engaged employees in flourishing organizations. *Journal of Organizational Behavior*, 29, 147–154.

Barrick, M. R., Thurgood, G. R., Smith, T. A., & Courtright, S. H. (2015). Collective organizational engagement: Linking motivational antecedents, strategic implementation, and firm performance. *Academy of Management Journal*, 58(1), 111–135.

Blau, P. (1964). *Exchange and power in social life.* New York: Wiley.

Borzaga, C. & Tortia, E. (2006). Worker motivation, job satisfaction and loyalty in public and nonprofit social services. *Nonprofit and Voluntary Sector Quarterly*, 35(2), 225–248.

Caldwell, M. (2011). Employee engagement: and the transformation of the health care industry. Towers Watson. Available at: www.towerswatson.com/en-US/Insights/IC-Types/Ad-hoc-Point-of-View/Perspectives/2011/Employee-Engagement-and-the-Transformation-of-the-Health-Care-Industry (accessed March 1, 2015).

Gibbons, J. (2006). Employee engagement a review of current research and its implications. *The Conference Board, Inc.*, 1–18. November, 2006. Available at: www.conference-board.org/publications/publicationdetail.cfm?publicationid=1238&centerId=1 (accessed March 1, 2014).

Gould-Williams, J. (2003). The importance of HR practice and workplace trust in achieving superior performance: A study of public-sector organizations. *International Journal of Human Resource Management, 14,* 1, 28–54.

Gould-Williams, J. & Davies, F. (2005). Using social exchange theory to predict the effects of HRM practice on employee outcomes. *Public Management Review, 7*(1), 1–24.

Harter, J. K., Schmidt, F. L., & Hayes, T. L. (2002). Business-unit-level relationship between employee satisfaction, employee engagement, and business outcomes: A meta-analysis. *Journal of Applied Psychology, 87,* 268–279.

Harter, J. K., Schmidt, F. L., & Keyes, C. L. M. (2003). Well-being in the workplace and its relationship to business outcomes: A review of the Gallup studies. In C. Keyes & J. Haidt (Eds.), *Flourishing: Positive psychology and the life well lived* (pp. 205–224). Washington, DC: American Psychological Association.

Hellriegel, D. & Slocum (Jr.) J. W. (1974). Organizational climate: Measures, research and contingencies. *Academy of Management Journal, 17*(2), 255–280.

Hofmann, D. A. & Morgeson, F. P. (1999). Safety-related behavior as a social exchange: The role of perceived organizational support and leader-member exchange. *Journal of Applied Psychology, 84,* 286–296.

Judge, T. A. & Ilies, R. (2004). Affect and job satisfaction: A study of their relationship at work and at home. *Journal of Applied Psychology, 89,* 661–673.

Kahn, W. A. (1990). Psychological conditions of personal engagement and disengagement at work. *Academy of Management Journal, 33,* 692–724.

Kahn, W. A. (1992). To be fully there: Psychological presence at work. *Human Relations, 45,* 321–349.

Leiter, M. P. & Bakker, A. B. (2010). Work Engagement: Introduction. In A. B. Bakker & M. P. Leiter (Eds.), *Work engagement: A handbook of essential theory and research* (pp. 1–9). Hove: Psychology Press.

Locke, E. A. (1976). The nature and causes of job satisfaction. In M. D. Dunnette (Ed.), *Handbook of industrial and organizational psychology* (pp. 1297–1349). Chicago: Rand McNally.

Lowe, G. (2012). How employee engagement matters for hospital performance. *Healthcare Quarterly, 15*(2), 29–39.

Lum, L., Kervin, J., Clark, K., Reid, F., & Sirola, W. (1998). Explaining nursing turnover intent: Job satisfaction, pay satisfaction, or organizational commitment? *Journal of Organizational Behavior, 19,* 3, 305–320.

Luthans, F. & Peterson, S. J. (2002). Employee engagement and manager self-efficacy: Implications for managerial effectiveness and development. *Journal of Management Development, 21,* 376–387. doi:10.1108/02621710210426864

Macey, W. & Schneider, B. (2008). The meaning of employee engagement. *Industrial & Organizational Psychology, 1,* 3–30.

Maslach, C., Schaufeli, W., & Leiter, M. (2001). Job burnout. *Annual Review of Psychology, 52,* 397–422.

Melnik, E., Petrella, F., & Richez-Battesti, N. (2013) Does the professionalism of management practices in nonprofits and for-profits affect job satisfaction? *The International Journal of Human Resource Management, 24*(6), 1300–1321.

Meyer, J. P. & Allen, N. J. (1991). A three-component conceptualization of organizational commitment. *Human Resource Management Review, 1*(1), 61–89.

Meyer, J. P., Stanley, D. J., Herscovitch, L., & Topolnytsky, L. (2002). Affective, continuance, and normative commitment to the organization: A meta-analysis of antecedents, correlates, and consequences. *Journal of Vocational Behavior, 61*(1), 20–52.

Mowday, R. T., Porter, L. W., & Steers, R. M. (1982). *Employee–organization linkages: The psychology of commitment, absenteeism and turnover.* London: Academic Press.

Quarter, J., Mook, L., & Richmond, B. J. (2003). *What counts: Social accounting for non-profits and cooperatives.* Upper Saddle River, NJ: Prentice-Hall.

Reissner, S. & Pagan, V. (2013). Generating employee engagement in a public–private partnership: Management communication activities and employee experiences. *The International Journal of Human Resource Management*, *24*(14), 2741–2759.

Rich, B. L., Lepine, J. A., & Crawford, E. R. (2010). Job engagement: Antecedents and effects on job performance. *Academy of Management Journal*, *53*, 617–635.

Robinson, D., Perryman, S., & Hayday, S. (2004). *The drivers of employee engagement*. Brighton: Institute for Employment Studies

Saks, A. M. (2006). Antecedents and consequences of employee engagement. *Journal of Managerial Psychology*, *21*, 600–619.

Salamon, L. & Anheier, H. (1998). Social origins of civil society: Explaining the nonprofit sector cross nationally. *Voluntas*, *3*, 213–248.

Salanova, M., Agut, S., & Peiro, J. M. (2005). Linking organizational resources and work engagement to employee performance and customer loyalty: The mediation of service climate. *Journal of Applied Psychology*, *90*, 1217–1227.

Schaufeli, W. B. & Bakker, A. B. (2003). UWES–Utrecht Work Engagement Scale: Test manual (Unpublished manuscript). Department of Psychology, Utrecht University, Utrecht, The Netherlands.

Schaufeli, W., Bakker, A., & Salanova, M. (2006). The measurement of work engagement with a short questionnaire: A cross-national study. *Educational and Psychological Measurement*, *66*(4), 701–716.

Schaufeli, W. B., Salanova, M., Gonzalez-Roma, V., & Bakker, A. B. (2002). The measurement of engagement and burnout: A two sample confirmatory factor analytic approach. *Journal of Happiness Studies*, *3*, 71–92.

Schmidt, F. (2009). Employee engagement: A review of the literature. Unpublished report prepared for the Office of the Chief Human Resources Officer, Treasury Board of Canada Secretariat.

Schneider, B. (1987). The people make the place. *Personnel Psychology*, *40*, 437–453.

Schneider, B. & Snyder, R.A. (1975). Some relationship between job satisfaction and organizational climate. *Journal of Applied Psychology*, *60*(3), 318–328.

Selander, K. (2015). Work engagement in the third sector. *Voluntas: International Journal of Voluntary and Nonprofit Organizations*, *26*(4), 1391–1411.

Seligman, M. E. P. & Csikszentmihalyi, M. (2000). Positive psychology: An introduction. *American Psychologist*, *55*(1), 5–14.

Shuck, B. (2011). Four emerging perspectives of employee engagement: an integrative literature review. *Human Resource Development Review*, *10*(3), 304–328.

Shuck, M. B., Reio Jr, T. G., & Rocco, T. S. (2011). Employee engagement: An examination of antecedent and outcome variables. *Human Resource Development International*, *14*, 427–445.

Shuck, B., & Wollard, K. (2010). Employee engagement & HRD: A seminal review of the foundations. *Human Resource Development Review*, *9*, 89–110.

Simpson, M. R. (2009). Predictors of work engagement among medical-surgical registered nurses. *Western Journal of Nursing Research*, *31*(1), 44–65.

Steel, R. P. & Ovalle, N. K. (1984). A review of the meta-analysis of research on the relationship between behavioral intentions and employee turnover. *Journal of Applied Psychology*, *69*, 673–686.

Towers Perrin. (2003a). Winning strategies for a global workforce, attracting, retaining and engaging employees for competitive advantage. Towers Perrin Global Workforce Study.

Towers Perrin. (2003b). The 2003 Towers Perrin talent report: U.S. report. Understanding what drives employee engagement. Stamford, CT.

Towers Watson. (2014). The 2014 Global Workforce Study: Driving engagement through a consumer-like experience, August 2014. Available at: www.towerswatson.com/

en-CA/Insights/IC-Types/Survey-Research-Results/2014/08/the-2014-global-workforce-study (accessed February 15, 2015).

Truss, C., Shantz, A., Soane, E., Alfes, K., & Delbridge, R. (2013). Employee engagement, organisational performance and individual well-being: Exploring the evidence, developing the theory. *International Journal of Human Resource Management, 24*(14), 2657–2669.

Vance, R. J. (2006). Employee engagement and commitment: A guide to understanding, measuring and increasing engagement in your organization. *A SHRM Foundation White Paper*. Arlington, VA: Society for Human Resource Management Foundation.

Wall, T. D., Clegg, C. W., & Jackson, P. R. (1978). An evaluation of job characteristics model. *Journal of Occupational Psychology, 51*, 183–196.

Watson Wyatt Worldwide. (2007). *Secrets of top performers: How companies with highly effective employee communication differentiate themselves: 2007/2008 communication ROI study*. Washington, DC: Author.

Wefald, A. & Downey, R. (2009a). Job engagement in organizations: Fad, fashion or folderol? *Journal of Organizational Behavior, 30*, 141–145.

Wefald, A. J. & Downey, R. G. (2009b). The construct dimensionality of engagement and its relationship with satisfaction. *Journal of Psychology: Interdisciplinary and Applied, 143*, 91–112.

Yalabik, Z. Y., Popaitoon, P., Chowne, J. A., & Rayton, B. A. (2013). Work engagement as a mediator between employee attitudes and outcomes. *International Journal of Human Resource Management, 24*, 2799–2823.

12

Volunteer Management

It All Depends

Jeffrey L. Brudney and Hayley K. Sink

Introduction

According to the U.S. Bureau of Labor Statistics, in the year ending in September 2015, 62.6 million Americans volunteered at least one time for an organization. In 2014, the U.S. Corporation for National and Community Service reported a total of 7.9 billion hours of volunteer service worth an estimated $184 billion. This "volunteer energy" (Brudney & Meijs, 2009) is critical in meeting the needs of our communities through service in public and nonprofit organizations. Managing this enormous repository of volunteer labor effectively is an essential skill for nonprofit leaders and managers.

The great majority of literature surrounding volunteer resource management presents a "universal" approach for the management of volunteer programs. Universal volunteer management holds that a single set of managerial principles works well, or at least well enough, to achieve results that meet organizational goals and fulfill volunteer needs. However, others argue that no one "best" way to manage volunteers works in every situation (for example, Meijs & Ten Hoorn, 2008; Paull, 2002). In this chapter we first review the universal approach to elaborate the fundamental elements of volunteer program management. Although the field does not question its general validity, we advise that to achieve best results the application of the universal model should be contingent on the varying circumstances facing the manager or administrator of volunteers. The key to volunteer management is to recognize these contingencies and adapt the precepts of the universal model accordingly.

We begin this chapter by presenting the various interpretations of the universal approach offered by scholars and practitioners. We then turn to the conditions and circumstances that influence how the various aspects of the universal approach can and should be applied. We ask, under what circumstances does the coordinator or administrator of the volunteer program (hereinafter, the "volunteer coordinator" or "volunteer administrator") need to tighten or loosen the universal model of volunteer administration to adapt to these contingencies? We pose and answer this question with the analogy of the "ratchet" tool or mechanism, as we propose that volunteer management should emulate the flexibility, subtlety, and adaptability of a ratchet or socket wrench to mechanical tasks. We show that application of the universal model depends on such factors as: intervals of volunteering, client population served, organization lifecycle, organization size, volunteer proximity, organization type, organizational scrutiny, as well as various human elements. We explain how these contingencies affect volunteer program administration and conclude with implications and best practices for volunteer administrators given particular situations.

In this chapter we show that successful volunteer management entails three major competencies:

1 Successful volunteer administration hinges on knowledge of the fundamental building blocks or "tool kit" provided by the universal approach to volunteer management.
2 Volunteer administrators must be able to adapt the universal approach to volunteer program management according to the requirements of the various conditions or contingencies that confront them in practice.
3 Finally, and more specifically, volunteer administrators must develop skills in recognizing when the principles of the universal approach should be applied more strictly or tightly to meet the needs of the organization for productive volunteer labor, or more flexibly or loosely to meet the needs and aspirations of volunteers as participants in public and nonprofit organizations.

A Universal Approach to Volunteer Management

The concept of volunteer management remains relatively new, with the first widely recognized model of volunteer administration developed by Harriet Naylor in 1967. Since Naylor and others inaugurated the field in the late 1960s and early 1970s, the academic and practitioner literature has typically treated volunteer management according to a "one-size-fits-all" or "universalistic" approach (Brudney & Meijs, 2014). The universal approach recognizes both the value of volunteers to organizational mission achievement and the importance of volunteer leadership to successful citizen involvement in nonprofit and public organizations. This literature conceives that volunteer management necessitates a volunteer administrator in place (paid or unpaid) who works to assure that volunteers provide reliable and critical human resources toward organizational goal achievement, and at the same time, feel that their contribution to the organization is valued. As we describe below, the prevailing models of volunteer management recommend similar components or requisites for the volunteer program (Safrit & Schmiesing, 2012). Although the literature certainly reveals nuance and adaptability, it does not usually consider systematically how variations confronting the volunteer administrator—for example, different organizational missions, policy areas, volunteer characteristics, economic sectors, and many other possible contingencies—may affect the volunteer management task.

Instead, and to its credit, much like a tool kit, the universal approach provides fundamental elements for overall implementation and operation of a volunteer program. Understanding the elements of the universal approach to volunteer management is essential both in its own right and because the model provides the foundation to the conditional approach discussed later in this chapter. The following models introduced by leading scholars and practitioners exemplify the universal approach to volunteer management as we have come to know it over the last half-century.

Harriet Naylor (1967): The Beginnings of Volunteer Administration

Naylor (1967) authored the first known treatment that conceptualized volunteer management as a professional field of study and practice. Naylor focused on leadership of volunteers who worked alongside paid staff to achieve a common organizational mission. Naylor provided many of the central principles of the universal approach, including:

- Keeping a record of all volunteer jobs and volunteer skills.
- Focusing on recruitment and selection of volunteers.
- Careful placement of the volunteer with a paid staff person.
- Training for both the volunteer and the paid supervisor.
- Guidelines for volunteer evaluation and grievance procedures.
- Opportunities for volunteer mobility and advancement within the volunteer program.

Naylor was concerned that

> [t]here are far too many ex-volunteers, able and conscientious people who have withdrawn from being personally involved, because of negative feelings about volunteer work. Some feel they were not appreciated, some feel that they were not making an important contribution, some that they cannot manage responsibilities that conflict with other interests and obligations.

She offered her model to address the situation (1967, p. 9).

Milton Boyce (1971): The ISOTURE Model

According to Safrit and Schmiesing (2012), the ISOTURE model developed by Boyce (1971) has been used in the development of most, if not all, of the (universal) volunteer management models that have followed. Boyce drew on contributions to the field of adult education to develop the model known by the acronym ISOTURE, which entails the following processes:

- **Identification.** To assure the recruitment of volunteers with the correct skills and abilities.
- **Selection.** To encourage potential volunteers toward the opportunity to impact the organization mission by filling a specific role that is believed to be a best fit.
- **Orientation.** To make volunteers aware of organizational expectations surrounding their involvement.
- **Training.** To increase the volunteer's knowledge, skills, and abilities to perform in organizational positions.
- **Utilization.** To provide volunteers with jobs that will allow them to utilize knowledge, skills, and abilities to the fullest within the position.
- **Recognition.** To acknowledge and reward volunteer efforts.
- **Evaluation.** To offer feedback and assess volunteer performance.

Jeffrey Brudney (1990): Volunteer Programs in the Public Sector

In a 1990 study Brudney extended earlier universalistic models by recognizing the importance of volunteers to the mission of public sector agencies, in addition to nonprofit organizations. Brudney highlighted the centrality of the volunteer administrator or manager to provide leadership in a volatile public sector. The manager should inform paid staff and volunteers of their respective roles in the agency; role clarification should aid the organization in alleviating potential conflict that could arise with paid staff apprehensive that volunteers may replace them, and volunteers equally concerned about their acceptance by the organization. Brudney emphasized that government agencies should evaluate volunteer programs from a cost-benefit perspective. He concluded that volunteers can add value to an organization by furthering its mission and services, and enhancing its impact—especially in the public sector where funding is typically limited. Brudney (1990) suggests the following as requisites for the volunteer program:

- The volunteer program must have a designated leader or manager.
- The organization must identify and establish positions for volunteers, i.e. job descriptions for volunteers.
- The volunteer manager must have employee buy-in to increase the effectiveness of the volunteer program and promote its legitimacy.
- The agency must develop an organizational structure for the volunteer program and link this structure to its operations.

Brudney's (1990) model also supports important aspects of the volunteer program described in the other models described above, such as recruitment, screening and interviewing applicants for defined volunteer positions; carefully placing volunteers; educating and training volunteers and employees for their respective work roles; evaluating volunteers to avoid poor performance that could hinder the effectiveness of the organization; and recognizing volunteers for their effort and performance.

Susan Ellis (2010): Volunteer Programs from the Top Down

Susan Ellis (2010) presents a widely accepted overview of best practices of the universalistic approach to volunteer management. Focusing on the roles of organization executives in creating successful volunteer programs as noted by her book title *From the Top Down*, Ellis urges these officials to recognize that volunteer personnel are valuable human resources, and to structure the volunteer program so that they can make a difference. Like Brudney (1990), Ellis (2010) proposes that the volunteer program have a mission, vision, goals, and objectives, as well as a formal place in the organizational structure or hierarchy. She recommends paid staff understand the roles of volunteers so they do not feel threatened, but also utilize volunteers to maximize impact for the organization. Ellis was one of the first to recognize that volunteer programs have costs and are not "free" to host organizations and observed that resources must be allocated to support program expenses, such as paid leadership, office supplies, travel, insurance, training, etc. Ellis also estimates a monetary value for the time donated by volunteers to the organization to calculate a return on investment. Table 12.1 summarizes the universal approach to volunteer management as outlined by Ellis (2010).

Table 12.1 Ellis' major elements of volunteer management

Major element	Best practices
Planning and Resource Allocation	Vibrant mission
	Define need of organization
	Establish volunteer program leadership
	Employee supervisory training
	Budgeting
	Cost-benefit analysis of the program
	Risk management
	Succession planning
Designing Volunteer Work	Be specific in written job descriptions
	Create a variety of job descriptions
	Involve volunteers at all levels
	Design innovative jobs
	Give consideration to individuals or groups, ongoing or episodic, one time and off-site
Recruitment and Public Relations	Market the volunteer program
	Be active in the community with recruitment
	Make volunteers advocators through empowerment

Major element	Best practices
Screening and Selection	Not all volunteer candidates are a fit All volunteers should have the same screening process Perform background checks, health assessments Keep hiring policies, nondiscrimination policies, and others the same for paid and nonpaid staff
Orientation and Training	Assure volunteers receive job-specific training Have continuing education opportunities Conference attendance for administrators and leaders
Volunteer-Employee Relations	All employees trained on volunteer engagement Motivate staff Define staff role as volunteer supervisor
Supervising and Partnering with Volunteers	Create a culture where staff value and assist volunteers Volunteers should expect to connect with paid staff Include volunteers on the organization chart
Coordination	Being sure all staff are aware of this complexity Each department should have a liaison to the volunteer manager Communication is critical in coordination
Recordkeeping and Reporting	Outcomes over outputs Mention volunteer impact in all department reports Data collection is key to funding opportunities Cost-benefit is important to the donor
Evaluation	Measurable goals and objective Have volunteers give organizational feedback
Recognition	Day-to-day recognition is highly valued End-of-year recognition is standard Tangible, ongoing recognition is key and as simple as thanking the volunteers
Volunteer Input	Develop ways for volunteers to give input Allow them to help build community collaboration Encourage volunteers to become involved on a committee
Volunteers as Supporters	Give marketing materials for volunteers to distribute Write to funders, legislators, media, etc. Organize one-time volunteer opportunities to attract new volunteers

Source: Ellis (2010).

Cracks in the Bedrock of the Universal Model

The universal model is the most widely accepted and utilized model of volunteer administration. Despite the common reference to elements and "best practices" of this model, however, contemporary research tends to dispute its general application, and has begun to identify important contingencies requiring adaptation of the universal model (for a full discussion see Brudney & Meijs, 2014). As Meijs and Ten Hoorn (2008, p. 29) summarize, "volunteering, volunteers and the way they are organized and managed differs from context to context."

Studer and von Schnurbein (2013) offer the most prominent example. Based on an extensive, theoretical qualitative analysis of the voluminous research in the field (N = 386 publications), found that

> volunteer coordination ... is concerned with gaining, orienting, retaining, and organizing volunteers in a formal organization to provide a public good ...successful volunteer coordination demands that the organizational settings are not only carefully assessed and aligned to the needs of volunteers but also to those of the organization and society at large.
>
> *(p. 406)*

Their analysis yields three primary clusters that influence effective volunteer administration: (1) volunteer coordination practices and human resource management influences; (2) volunteer coordination attitudes and social processes; and (3) organizational features affecting volunteers and volunteer coordination. The authors found that volunteer management practice varied according to these three sets of factors.

Contingency Approaches

The literature advances several contingency approaches. For example, Rochester (1999) elaborates four models of volunteer administration: service delivery, support role, member/activist, and co-worker. The service delivery model implies that volunteers are recruited based on knowledge, skills, and abilities. In the service delivery model, volunteers are supervised in a hierarchical structure. The support role focuses on how the volunteers can supplement paid staff in the organization; oversight in the support role ranges from collaborative-participatory to hierarchical. The service delivery and the support role models of volunteer management resemble a part-time employment approach. Conversely, the member/activist model illustrates a volunteer program where all roles within the organization are held by volunteers who support a shared cause, with no paid staff present to provide oversight. The co-worker approach encompasses a fluid relationship between the volunteer and the paid staff member. Volunteers identify their purpose or goals in the organization, as well as their desire to learn new skills. The member/activist model, with exclusively volunteer participation, and the co-worker model with volunteers often considered counterparts to paid-staff, are examples of participatory volunteer management. Rochester's (1999) approach illustrates the range of appropriate volunteer administration models that would align with the types of organization hosting the volunteers.

Meijs and Ten Hoorn (2008) propose a different contingency approach. They argue that the universal approach to volunteer management reflects too narrow a

Table 12.2 Management adjustment to contingencies in volunteer programs

Type of organization	Organizational members	
	Volunteers only	*Paid staff and volunteers*
Mutual Support	Membership Management	Program Management
Service Delivery	Program Management	Program Management
Campaigning	Membership Management or Program Management with Membership Management for Decision-making	Program Management with Membership Management for Decision-making

Source: Adapted from Meijs and Ten Hoorn (2008, p. 41).

view of the volunteer administrator's job and fails to appreciate the contingencies affecting volunteer management. These authors present a contingency approach to volunteer management, focusing on three types of organization: service delivery, campaigning, and mutual support (compare Handy, 1988). Service delivery organizations tend to use volunteers as if they were part-time, paid staff. By contrast, campaigning organizations are unique as they seek numerous supporters as volunteers but also exclude many individuals who do not share the same ideological or issue preference. Given the strong emotions that are aroused in campaigning organizations, tensions tend to arise between volunteers and paid staff (Meijs & Ten Hoorn, 2008). Mutual support organizations form as a result of a common cause. Although they often have scarce resources, they are fueled by the affiliation and membership of volunteers with the organization. For mutual support organizations, the volunteer management task is reduced to a coordinator role that organizes the efforts of members to support a shared goal but lacks the hierarchical structure or authority among members to enforce task assignments (Meijs & Ten Hoorn, 2008). Table 12.2 identifies the mutual support, service delivery, and campaigning models.

In her contingency approach, Rehnborg (2009) presents two dimensions that affect volunteer management. The first is the volunteer's connection to service, and the second is the volunteer's time commitment to service. Connection to service considers whether the volunteer is motivated by the mission of the organization, i.e., affiliation focused, or by the need to acquire a skill or fulfill a requirement, i.e., skills focused. A volunteer's time commitment considers whether the volunteer's contributed time to the organization is episodic or ongoing. Crossing the categories of connection to service and time for service, Rehnborg (2009) derives four contingencies that require different models of volunteer management (for a complete discussion see Rehnborg, 2009).

The universal model of volunteer management offers a valuable toolkit volunteer administrators must know and master. Although this approach normally appears without qualification in the literature, based on the research on contingencies of volunteer management and our own observation, we suggest that like any set of tools, it must be applied flexibly to meet the requirements of the situation at hand confronting the volunteer administrator. We introduce a new approach to accommodate these contingencies in the "Ratchet Model" below.

Confronting Contingency: The Ratchet Model of Volunteer Management

The critical challenge of volunteer management consists of meeting the needs of host organizations for productive labor, while at the same time meeting the needs of the volunteer for a satisfying experience. To address this challenge, volunteer administrators need to adapt the principles of the universal approach to the situations confronting them. Although contemporary research suggests that no single approach works effectively in all management situations, contingency views propose that certain techniques are more (or less) effective given the various circumstances or contingencies at hand. Existing universal models of volunteer administration can serve as a toolbox and useful reference for volunteer managers, but we encourage them to recognize conditions affecting their organizations and "loosen" or "tighten" their management of the volunteers accordingly to accommodate the situation. We refer to this approach as the "ratchet model" of volunteer management.

In our view, the universal model should be applied most strictly when certain conditions are met in public and nonprofit organizations. First, when volunteer work assignments are analogous to those of paid employees, the volunteer role can be seen as a part-time position without pay. In this instance, organization leaders may even name or describe the positions occupied by volunteers with this designation as, for example, "volunteer" secretary or "volunteer" intake specialist, to indicate that the only practical difference in the job to be performed by the volunteer is the compensation category (paid versus unpaid). Second, when the volunteer program is subsumed under the hierarchical authority structure of the organization (as specified, for example, in the formal organization chart or structure), the volunteer occupies a position, albeit unpaid, within the normal ranks of the organization and is expected to carry it out as a part-time employee (again, the only practical difference is the compensation category). Under these circumstances, a strict interpretation of the universal approach can be utilized to manage the volunteer program effectively. In these situations the volunteer is effectively a part-time employee, and the needs of the organization for productive labor are predominant. Strict adaptations of the universal model toward employment work well when volunteer positions are incorporated in the hierarchical structure of the organization, and volunteer positions are conceptualized as part-time jobs.

In other situations, though, the needs of the volunteers become paramount. In volunteering their time, citizens bring not only labor to an organization but also their motivations and aspirations as participants. From this participant standpoint, volunteers seek, for example, personal growth and development, a sense of solidarity and belonging, friendships and networks, job experimentation and experience, an opportunity to pursue a desired vision or goals, or a feeling of self-confidence or mastery. These aspirations cannot be met solely through performing specific part-time "jobs" as in the employment model. Instead, the volunteers must be viewed from the participant perspective as citizens motivated to achieve their own goals through helping the organization. Thus, the volunteer administrator cannot, and should not, apply the universal model so strictly that the volunteer experience resembles part-time paid employment that "anyone" could fill but must leaven or loosen volunteer involvement so that the volunteer also feels like a valued and unique participant.

Yet, the administrator must not reduce volunteer involvement to focus exclusively on the needs of volunteer participants either, lest the organization be distracted from pursuing its own goals—which require the employment (productive labor) of volunteers as well. To us, recognizing the poles of the universal approach toward the employment perspective on the one end and the participation perspective on the other, and tightening the balance between them toward the employment model when necessary or loosening it toward participation as required by organizational circumstances (contingencies), constitute the essence of volunteer management.

Some evidence for this perspective emanates from statistical trends and commentary. According to the Bureau of Labor Statistics (2015) the number of volunteers and time spent volunteering in the United States has declined over the past decade; the rate of volunteering stood at 26.7% in 2006 and by 2015 had dropped to 24.9%. Volunteer retention continues to falter according to Yanay and Yanay (2008) due to failure in volunteer management to meet the needs, desires, motivations, and experiences sought by volunteers as participants. Similarly, Brudney and Meijs (2009) maintain that the decline in volunteers results, at least in part, from the continued application of universal volunteer management toward the traditional workplace model that conceives of the volunteer as a part-time employee. Brudney and Meijs (2009) are concerned that this application of the universal model is not always well-suited to the circumstances confronting volunteer managers. Because volunteers are a valuable human resource to nonprofit organizations, accounting for an estimated 65% of total philanthropic resources (Salamon & Sokolowski, 2001), volunteer administrators must strive to ensure that volunteers are fulfilled in their work for host organizations. If volunteers are not fulfilled, they may show a lack of concern for their work, or even discontinue their service to the organization. Thus, adapting the universal model of volunteer management to embrace the needs of volunteers, for participation, as well as the organization, for employment, is a priority.

Brudney and Meijs (2009) have introduced a "regenerative approach" to volunteer management, which encompasses the asset-based community development model (Kretzmann & McKnight, 1993). Regenerative volunteer management is centered on meeting the needs of the community, the volunteer, and the organization, and it encourages managers to give volunteers a stake in the organization. The regenerative model emphasizes the importance of a cultural shift in the perception of contemporary volunteering with a focus on renewable, long-term, and life-time valued volunteer involvement. This model of volunteer management allows for a more comprehensive approach to volunteer recruitment by suggesting that organizations offer volunteers a variety of job and role options, the ability to discuss and advocate for a preferred volunteer work assignment, and the opportunity to fulfill their own needs and meet organizational demands at the same time (Brudney & Meijs, 2009).

The universal model of volunteer management does not vary according to circumstances, such as the size of the organization, clientele served, volunteer location, volunteer and employee needs etc., details of the application of the model are not relevant, or at least not addressed, for varying circumstances. By contrast, the goal of the contingency approach is to adapt the administration and management of volunteers to the important conditions or circumstances facing the organization and its volunteer program.

A New Approach to Volunteer Management: The Ratchet Model

The ratchet model proposes that volunteer management varies between two poles: On one extreme rests the "employment model" that conceives of volunteers as quasi-employees, i.e., a relatively strict or tight application of the universal principles discussed above. The emphasis centers on the needs of the organization to generate productive labor from volunteers. At the other extreme lies the "participation model." Here the ratchet must be loosened to meet the needs of the volunteer, for example, for fulfilling and stimulating involvement, personal exploration and growth, skill development and networking, or a sense of solidarity and belonging. Using the ratchet model requires the volunteer administrator to adjust the balance or tension between these two extremes to accommodate the circumstances at hand. The critical questions are:

1   What are the conditions or contingencies that necessitate adjusting the ratchet?
2   In what direction—tightening to focus on organizational needs versus loosening to respond to volunteer priorities—should the volunteer administrator adjust the ratchet to meet the critical contingencies confronting the volunteer program?

We refer to our approach to volunteer management as the "ratchet model." The analogy draws attention to balancing or adjusting the tension between tightening versus loosening volunteer administration to accommodate both organizational and volunteer needs, and applying finesse or a light touch rather than force or a heavy hand to the task of volunteer management. As every mechanic learns, the ratchet mechanism or tool locks onto a hexagonal screw or nut, such as the spark plugs on an automobile engine or the lug nuts that secure the wheels. The ratchet can access places that lie obscure or are difficult to locate and fix; these places correspond to the contingencies facing the volunteer program that need addressing. The ratchet device is designed so that the force needed by the operator to move or maneuver the screw or nut is greatly reduced. As with volunteer management, it takes just a supple twist of the wrist, i.e., a deft managerial intervention, to move the screw or nut to either tighten it (toward employment) or loosen it (toward participation) according to the tension (balance) required.

Analogous to the management craft, the ratchet device places the emphasis on finesse rather than power. It does most, though not all, of the work: The ratchet responds subtly and immediately to the wishes of the operator. As in management, the ratchet provides feedback to the operator as he or she tightens or loosens the tension. The role of the volunteer manager is to adjust the tension between strict or tight application of the universal model toward employment or a more relaxed or loose application toward participation.

Table 12.3 shows the ratchet model as it relates to the employment and participation models of volunteer management. The full turning of the ratchet

Table 12.3 The ratchet model of volunteer program management

"Loosen" ← ⬤ → "Tighten"

Volunteer management element	Participation model	Employment model
Recruitment and public relations	Undifferentiated calls for "help"	Based on organizational tasks to be completed
Screening and selection of volunteers	Minimal	Based on organizational tasks to be completed
Orientation of volunteers	Minimal, brief	Longer, more detailed
Training for volunteers	Minimal	Specific to the job
Structure of volunteer program	Flat, less hierarchical	Detailed, more hierarchical
Job descriptions for volunteers	General (provide "help")	Specific (perform tasks)
Record-keeping and reporting	Minimal	Greater
Evaluation of volunteers	Informal, if any	Formal
Recognition of volunteers	Minimal ("thank you")	Specific to the job or longevity

to either extreme will not benefit the volunteer program or the organization. A program based solely on the employment model will likely encounter a volunteer deficit leading to hasty recruitment, volunteer retention problems, and an organization that has to enlist more paid employees. Conversely, if the program is fixed solely on the participation model, the volunteers would likely not have the direction or the ability to achieve the desired goals or results sought by the organization—or their own individual goals.

Applying the Ratchet Model

The volunteer manager must adjust the organization's volunteer program to achieve a balance between the employment and participation models of volunteer management. The challenge to the administrator is to adjust the balance based on the contingencies confronting the volunteer program. The volunteer administrator must determine how tightly or loosely the volunteer program should be adjusted toward the employment or participation models. The important questions are: What are the crucial contingencies according to which the volunteer manager should adjust the program? What are best practices for how these contingencies should be addressed? Although volunteer management begins with the universal model, depending on the contingencies volunteer administrators will need to loosen elements of management toward the participation model or tighten them toward the employment model. We focus on the following major elements as primary contingencies: intervals of volunteering, client population, organizational lifecycle, organization size, volunteer proximity, organization type, organizational scrutiny, as well as human elements. Table 12.4 summarizes these contingencies and their implications for volunteer management.

- *Intervals of volunteering:* Many organizations sponsor events that are short-term or episodic, such as 5K runs and fundraising galas. For such episodic volunteering the organization does not require elaborate structure or procedures that link the volunteer permanently to the organization. This contingency suggests that the organization "loosen" the scope of volunteer management toward the participation model. A fun experience in short-term episodic volunteering may assist recruitment, but the trappings of the employment model are wasted and likely counter-productive. Though episodic events may require significant planning and preparation, as well as many volunteers, recruiting and placing ongoing volunteers in quasi-employment roles are not required. Instead, the organization need only provide modest orientation or training that will allow the volunteer to be successful in completing mundane tasks, such as greeting attendees and distributing snacks, as opposed to in-depth instruction. By contrast, regular, ongoing volunteer involvement necessitates a tightening of volunteer management toward the employment model. As opposed to episodic participants, these volunteers will continue to be connected to the organization, so that the organization needs to

Table 12.4 Management adjustment to contingencies in volunteer programs

Contingency	Description	The Participation Model is best suited to the following contingencies	The Employment Model is best suited to the following contingencies
		Management adjustment	
Intervals of volunteering	Episodic vs. Ongoing	Episodic	Ongoing
Client population	Vulnerable vs. Non-Vulnerable	Non-Vulnerable	Vulnerable
Organizational lifecycle	New vs. Established	New	Established
Volunteer proximity	Virtual vs. Traditional	Traditional	Virtual
Organization size	Larger vs. Smaller	Smaller	Larger
Organization type	Public vs. Nonprofit	Nonprofit	Public
Organizational scrutiny	Normal Operations vs. Scrutiny	Normal Operations	Scrutiny
Human elements	Morale	Lower morale	Higher morale
	Employee Complaints	Few complaints	Many complaints
	Cohesiveness	Low cohesiveness	High cohesiveness

exercise greater oversight and monitoring through the standard elements of the employment model.

- *Client population:* Organizations that deal with vulnerable populations, such as children, the elderly, and medical patients, require more provisions for protecting these clients. Additionally, stronger precautions must be in place by the organization to attend to risk management and liability. The organization will be held accountable for protecting the rights and well-being of vulnerable clients. Thus, in an organization that deals with vulnerable populations volunteer management should be "tightened" to invoke the employment model. In organizations that serve non-vulnerable populations as primary clientele, such as patrons of museums and cultural arts programming or participants in adult recreation leagues, volunteer management can be loosened toward the participation model.
- *Organizational lifecycle:* New organizations typically have fewer staff, both paid employees and unpaid volunteers. The organization, as well as the volunteer program, must remain fluid and supple to grow and mature. The demands of organizational survival require personnel to be flexible and adaptive. This contingency would suggest relaxing the volunteer program toward the participation model of volunteer involvement to respond to the pressures of survival and growth and to maintain flexibility. By contrast, more established organizations generally have more personnel and

standardized procedures, as well as a need for clarification and classification of work roles. Thus, a nudge toward the employment model is called for and appropriate.

- *Organization size:* Often accompanying organization longevity is organization growth. Larger, more structured organizations with multiple divisions, departments, and other subunits require increased coordination and control. The volunteer program must be part of this structure and explicitly linked to organization operations. Thus, the volunteer program must move toward the employment model. Although volunteer participation is valued, larger organizations tend to divide the work to be done more finely than smaller organizations. To maintain not only accountability, but also work flows and coordination, paid staff and volunteers alike must understand who is responsible for which tasks. The employment model establishes these relationships.

- *Volunteer proximity:* Increasing virtual or online volunteering off-site is becoming an alternative, or at least a complement, to traditional on-site or in-person volunteering. Cravens and Ellis (2014) suggest if a successful volunteer program is in place, the organization should be able to implement virtual volunteering relatively easily to increase organizational capacity. In volunteer programs with virtual volunteers assisting at a distance in the absence of direct organizational supervision, the employment model is advisable to provide oversight and control. An organization with substantial online, virtual volunteering requires classic features of the employment model, especially careful recruitment, screening, follow-up, and evaluation, to ensure accountable performance. Without personal oversight and supervision, volunteer administrators must rely on such procedures.

- *Organization type:* Government agencies have comparatively more rules, procedures, and regulations than nonprofit organizations. Because public funding and accountability are at stake, governments tend to be more formal and insist on more clearances and sign-offs and a clearer chain of hierarchy, command, and coordination than nonprofits. In addition, they tend to be older and larger. All of these factors suggest that volunteer managers in public organizations will need to lean strongly toward the employment model of volunteer administration.

- *Organizational scrutiny:* When things go wrong in any organization, the response of most leaders is to seize the reins of authority. Responsible leaders want to show that they are aware and in charge, the problems have been resolved, and lapses will not recur. The easiest, most convincing way to regain the confidence of the public and other stakeholders is to demonstrate, and publicize, the adoption of standards, rules, and procedures to address and surmount the problematic issue, and even to invite further scrutiny to establish accountability. Following the lead of organizational officials to tighten things up, in such situations the volunteer manager will need to turn the ratchet toward the employment model.

- *Human elements:* Human elements, including morale among volunteers, attitudes of paid staff toward the volunteer program, and overall cohesiveness and understanding of volunteer versus paid staff roles, present critical contingencies to the volunteer program that ebb and flow over an organization's life cycle. Based on the ratchet model, we advise that if volunteer morale is low, the volunteer manager will want to loosen the program toward the participation model to engage citizens more fully. By contrast, if paid staff are suspicious or unsatisfied about volunteer involvement, the volunteer manager would need to tighten the program toward the employment model to shore up organizational achievement. Finally, if cohesiveness or collaboration does not take hold between volunteers and paid staff, savvy volunteer managers will want to investigate and assess the underlying issues and adjust management toward either the participation model or the employment model based on their experience in the job and observation in the organization.

We have summarized some of the major contingencies likely to confront the volunteer administrator. Part of the job consists as well in identifying other contingencies that require an adjustment in the balance between the employment and the participation models. We suggest as other contingencies meriting further consideration by the volunteer administrator: whether or not paid employees have a union; whether volunteers constitute a relatively small versus large personnel component of the organization; whether or not the organization enlists youth volunteers; whether or not the organization is competing with other agencies for the services of volunteers.

Conclusion

In this chapter we have presented a new approach to volunteer administration and management that applies the universal model to contingencies volunteer administrators are likely to confront on the job, and provides direction for adjusting the volunteer program accordingly. We label this approach the ratchet model. We use this name because the ratchet tool offers analogies to management with respect to tightening or loosening organizational control over work processes and behavior, and relying more on finesse than force to accomplish desired organizational ends or goals. With respect to volunteer management, tightening the ratchet refers to adjusting the volunteer program to resemble more closely part-time paid work or employment to meet the goals of the organization. By contrast, loosening the ratchet means adjusting the program toward a more flexible, open participation style that helps volunteers meet their own needs, for example, for stimulation, interesting work, solidarity, networking, self-expression, or career exploration. The ratchet model encourages the volunteer administrator to achieve a balance between the two poles of employment versus participation in managing the volunteer program based on the key contingencies confronted.

The ratchet model entails four steps. Volunteer administrators should:

1　Begin by learning the elements of the universal approach.
2　Be aware and sensitive to the contingencies in the workplace that would suggest that the balance between the employment model and the participation model must be adjusted.
3　Know how to change their volunteer management style to adapt to the contingencies identified, and be comfortable making these changes.
4　Follow up by monitoring the volunteer program to evaluate whether the adaptations made are appropriate to fit the situation, and implement new adaptations should they prove necessary.

This chapter elaborates a framework for the volunteer administrator to use for successful adaptation of the volunteer program to various circumstances or contingencies. Two models of volunteer management—the Preparation Engagement and Perpetuation (PEP) model (Safrit, Schmiesing, Gliem, & Gliem, 2005) and the volunteer administrator guidelines of the Council for Certification in Volunteer Administration (2015)—likewise acknowledge that contingencies exist that may impact volunteer program administration.

The authors of the PEP model (Safrit, Schmiesing, Gliem, & Gliem, 2005) assert that theirs is the first empirical model of volunteer management. The model is based on findings from a study of volunteer administrators and experts in the field and highlights three categories: personal preparation, volunteer engagement, and program perpetuation. Across the three categories, the PEP model for volunteer administration derives seven "domain topic areas" (pp. 21–22): professional development, volunteer selection and recruitment, volunteer orientation and training, volunteer recognition, program maintenance, resource development, and program advocacy. The researchers maintain that the PEP model addresses the primary topics identified since the inauguration of the volunteer administration field (Safrit et al., 2005). Similarly, the Council for Certification in Volunteer Administration (2015) recognizes that the position of the volunteer administrator is multifaceted. CCVA (2015) alludes to the influence of contingencies on the effective performance of the job, which encompasses several different roles: strategic architect, articulate ambassador, relationship builder, talent cultivator, data manager, champion of quality, and passionate leader. The many roles of the volunteer administrator signify the importance of adapting management to the contingencies confronted in the volunteer program.

To make these adaptations, we recommend that both new and experienced volunteer administrators strive to seek a balance between the needs of the organization for productive work, as captured in the employment model, and the needs of volunteers for meeting their own aspirations, as articulated in the participation model. In our view, understanding these poles and creating an effective balance form the essence of the volunteer administration task.

Discussion Questions

1   What are the contingencies that you think would impact the volunteer administrator's job?
2   As a normal way of doing business (the "default option") on an everyday basis, how should the volunteer administrator go about doing his or her job?
3   What skills would be most useful to you in recognizing important contingencies in the workplace or among volunteers so that you would know when to tighten, or loosen, administration of the volunteer program?

References

Boyce, M. (1971). *A systematic approach to leadership development.* Washington, DC: USDA, Extension Service (ERIC document reproduction service no. ED 065-763).

Brudney, J. L. (1990). *Fostering volunteer programs in the public sector.* San Francisco, CA: Jossey-Bass.

Brudney, J. L. & Meijs, L. C. P. M. (2009). It ain't natural: Toward a new (natural) resource conceptualization for volunteer management. *Nonprofit and Voluntary Sector Quarterly, 38*(4), 564–581.

Brudney, J. L. & Meijs, L. C. P. M. (2014). Models of volunteer management: Professional volunteer program management in social work. *Human Service Organizations Management, Leadership & Governance, 38*(3), 297–309.

Bureau of Labor Statistics. (2015). *Volunteering in the United States, 2015.* Available at: www.bls.gov/news.release/volun.nr0.htm (accessed March 9, 2016).

Carroll, M. & Harris, M. (1999). Voluntary action in a campaigning context: An exploratory study of Greenpeace. *Voluntary Action, 2*(1), 9–18.

Corporation for National & Community Service. (2015). *The state of volunteering in America, 2015.* Available at: www.volunteeringinamerica.gov/infographic.cfm (accessed March 9, 2016).

Council for Certification in Volunteer Administration. (2015). *CCVA body of knowledge and competency framework.* Available at: http://cvacert.org/wp-content/uploads/2015/09/2015-CVA-Competency-Framework-FINAL-2015-Sep-03.pdf (accessed October 15, 2015).

Cravens, J. & Ellis, S. J. (2014). *The last virtual volunteering guidebook: Fully integrating online service into volunteering.* Philadelphia, PA: Energize, Inc.

Ellis, S. J. (2010). *From the top down: The executive role in successful volunteer involvement.* Philadelphia, PA: Energize, Inc.

Handy, C. (1988). *Understanding voluntary organizations: How to make them function effectively.* London: Penguin Books.

Kretzmann, J. P. & McKnight, J. L. (1993). *Building communities from the inside out: A path toward finding and mobilizing a community's assets.* (3rd ed.). Chicago: ACTA.

Meijs, L. C. P. M. & Ten Hoorn, E. M. (2008). No "one best" volunteer management and organizing: Two fundamentally different approaches. In M. Liao-Troth (Ed.), *Challenges in volunteer management* (pp. 25–90). Charlotte, NC: Information Age Publishing, Inc.

Naylor, N. H. (1967). *Volunteers today: Finding, training, and working with them.* New York, NY: Dryden Association Press.

Paull, M. (2002). Reframing volunteer management: A view from the West. *Australian Journal on Volunteering, 7,* 21–27.

Rehnborg, S. J. (2009). *Strategic volunteer engagement: A guide for nonprofit and public sector leaders.* Austin, TX: University of Texas, RGK Center for Philanthropy and Community

Service. Available at: www.volunteeralive.org/docs/Strategic%20Volunteer%20 Engagement.pdf

Rochester, C. (1999). One size does not fit all: Four models of involving volunteers in voluntary organizations. *Voluntary Action, 1*(2), 47–59.

Safrit, R. D. & Schmiesing, R. J. (2012). Volunteer models and management. In T. D. Connors (Ed.), *The volunteer management handbook* (2nd ed.; pp. 3–30). Hoboken, NJ: John Wiley and Sons, Inc.

Safrit, R. D., Schmiesing, R. J., Gliem, J. A., & Gliem, R. R. (2005). Core competencies for volunteer administration: An empirical model bridging theory with professional practice. *Journal of Volunteer Administration, 23*(3), 5–15.

Salamon, L. M. & Sokolowski, W. (2001). *Volunteering in cross-national perspective: Evidence from 24 countries* (Working Papers of the Johns Hopkins Comparative Nonprofit Sector Project No. 40). Baltimore, MD: The Johns Hopkins Center for Civil Society Studies.

Studer, S. & von Schnurbien, G. (2013). Organization factors affecting volunteers: A literature review on volunteer coordination. *Voluntas, 24*(2), 403–440.

Yanay, G. V. & Yanay, N. (2008). The decline of motivation? From commitment to dropping out of volunteering. *Nonprofit Management & Leadership, 19*(1), 65–78.

13

Training and Development in Nonprofit Organizations

Toby Egan

Across sectors, training and development (T&D) is a vital individual and career concern, as well as an important dimension in the life of organizations.

> Workforce learning has become a fundamental need for organizations that face a quick-changing world growing more complicated by the day ... For many decades, employee training has been viewed as an effective way to maintain and develop organization members' work capacity.
>
> *(Chang, Huang, & Kuo, 2013, pp. 25–26)*

Introduction

As varied organizations have identified employee and managerial training and development needs, multiple approaches to learning at and about work emerged, with T&D situated in the broader contexts of human resource development and organizational learning.

Employee and managerial T&D is viewed as an essential ingredient to improved nonprofit organizational effectiveness and performance outcomes (Hodgkinson & Nelson, 2001; Riddoch, 2009). Over the past three decades, T&D-related practitioners and scholars have increasingly come to see training from a "systems view"—important from individual, group/team, organizational, community, and sectoral perspectives (Jacobs, 1989). While nonprofit leaders and employees require training on a variety of topics and have continuous learning needs, it has become progressively clear that nonprofit training and development is firmly situated within the context of a larger organizational learning culture and system (Ebrahim, 2005; Egan, Yang, & Bartlett, 2004; McHargue, 2003).

T&D-related theory, practice, and research overall, and then with a focus on the nonprofit sector, are examined in this chapter. Over time, T&D professionals have utilized and shared related concepts and practices across sectors in a variety of professional roles. In many cases, the underlying T&D assumptions and practices share more similarities than differences; however, the nonprofit sector has distinct characteristics that can require unique T&D approaches. In addition, organization size plays an important role in determining the appropriate T&D strategy, and this dimension is particularly salient in the context of nonprofit organizations. This chapter is organized in the following way: exploring a brief history of T&D; defining and situating T&D in the larger context of organizational learning; examining related theories and professional practices; contrasting nonprofit training from other sectors; and elaborating on challenges faced by different sized nonprofits.

A Brief History of Work-related Training and Development

As organizations across sectors continue to develop an understanding of the significance of workplace learning, appreciation of the importance of T&D has also grown. The oldest form of work-related training in most parts of the world is the apprenticeship system (Tracey, 1974). Apprenticeship, usually a one-on-one training approach organized around a specific set of skills and related acquisition, was common among scribes in early Egypt and during the Middle Ages, but began to decline during the 1500–1600s (Snell, 1996). Further declines in apprenticeship practices occurred during the industrial revolution. Large-scale training, both on-the-job and in "classroom training," emerged during the latter part of the 19th and continued throughout the 20th centuries as cities, industries, organizations, and military forces all expanded—requiring new approaches to work-related learning and development (Swanson & Holton, 2001). Apprenticeships, though less prevalent, remain a part of workforce training worldwide, with about 450,000 apprenticeships annually in the United States (U.S. Department of Labor, 2015). As described in more detail below, other methods to facilitate workplace learning have evolved over the past 50 years on a larger scale.

In the United States, one of the earliest charities involved in large-scale training was the American Red Cross. Under founder Clara Barton, the Red Cross developed training programs that were first aimed at facilitating wartime medical field services and later at public health and wellness programs (Pryor, 1987). Dooley (2001) led, and later wrote about his efforts to form the World War II era Training Within Industry (TWI) programs in the United States. These wartime efforts involved the vocational training of tens of millions of U.S. citizens in factories and related efforts to support the United States from "the home front." These newly trained workers revolutionized understanding in the United States regarding T&D. These efforts involved the development of T&D programs on a previously unfathomable scale, with systematic instruction to thousands of trainees on a daily basis. The scope and scale required of paid and volunteer human resources required by World War II production needs provided a natural laboratory born out of necessity and brought forth more opportunities to design, test, and refine T&D than ever before.

Social scientist Elton Mayo (1933) and colleagues conducted the Hawthorne Studies exploring the role of working conditions and stimuli, other than financial compensation, on worker productivity. Later research would support the hypothesis that T&D positively influenced employee productivity (Bartlett, 2001). Frederick Herzberg, Kurt Lewin, Abraham Maslow, David McClelland, and Max Weber each contributed research that influenced thinking about T&D practices through related fields of study such as industrial-organizational psychology, organizational behavior, human resource management, and human resource development.

At this time a rich interplay between practice and academia began to emerge that stimulated the professionalization of T&D. Several T&D-related professional associations formed in the first half of the 20th century. One of the oldest, identified professional human resources associations, the Chartered Institute of Personnel Development (CIPD), opened in 1913 and was originally named the Welfare Workers' Association of England. The post-TWI of the 1940s war effort brought about the formation of several key HR-related developments in the United States, including the establishment of the American Society for Training and Development, now known as the Association for Talent Development or ATD, in 1944 (Koppes, 2006); the Society for Human Resource Management (SHRM) in 1948; and Cornell University's early industrial and labor relations higher education program in 1945. Soon after, the academic fields of industrial organizational psychology, industrial relations, industrial education, and vocational education emerged, with more recent advent of human resource development, organization development, and T&D specific academic programs.

As the 20th century progressed, so did training and human resources efforts in a great diversity of other national contexts. Workplace complexities, increased use of technology, and evolving organizational strategies led to greater appreciation in all sectors for the employee as a key asset. The work of U.S. economists Becker (1962) and Harbison and Myers (1964) advanced the importance of human capital and human resource development for individual, organizational, community, and even national impact.

As human capital was better understood as a key aspect of organizational success, T&D took center stage as a core element of human resource development (HRD) practice. Environmental complexity intensified in the 1980s with the emergence of new technologies and steady growth of global organizations, and continues unabated today. These complexities mandated agility by employees and more adaptive management. As a result, in the for-profit arena, investment by business and industry in T&D steadily increased over the last 30 years. ATD estimated that large U.S. companies spent $164 billion overall in 2013, approximately $1200 per employee, on training. As T&D practices evolved, related job roles became better defined and some aspects of professionalization and formalized training have emerged. Those working in T&D and related areas of workplace learning have a variety of titles including: Chief Learning Officer, Vice-President of Training, Instructional Designer, Leadership Development Professional, Technical Trainer, Training Coordinator, Learning Program Manager, Training Evaluator, Performance Improvement Specialist, and many more. In the U.S. context, organizations commonly create their own titles for training related roles. Although training related licensure and governmental oversight have been required of psychologists, social workers, public school teachers, medical doctors, and lawyers, T&D remains a professional role that is rarely government certified or licensed.

According to Hall (1994), while religious and charitable organizations are thousands of years old and have their own formalized apprenticeships and training systems to provide for their distinctive organizational needs, it took until the 1970s for the concept of a unified "nonprofit sector" to emerge as a discrete and widely recognized concept and institution in the U.S. (and even later in many other parts of the world). Approximately 90% of all nonprofit and nongovernmental organizations (NGOs) have emerged worldwide in the last 60 years (Hall, 2010). With the formation of over 1.5 million U.S. nonprofits today (NCCS, 2015), and uncounted numbers of NGOs worldwide, a recent acceleration of training and academic programs emphasizing the nonprofit sector has emerged (Mirabella, 2007).

While specific statistics regarding workplace training in the nonprofit sector appear not to be aggregated, nonprofits make up approximately 10% of the U.S. workforce, or approximately 12.5 million employees (U.S. Department of Labor, 2016). Along with sector-specific knowledge, nonprofit managers and employees require many of the same types of abilities and skills as the U.S. workforce overall. Without the benefit of statistics similar to ATD's study of for-profit training, we cannot accurately estimate U.S. nonprofit investment in training overall. While there is no evidence that U.S. nonprofits do not spend comparable amounts per worker to for-profit companies, even one half of the T&D investment made by large U.S. corporations per worker by U.S. nonprofits would likely top $7.5 billion. Whether nonprofits spend similar amounts of money on employees has not been adequately assessed; however, the overhead constraints experienced by many nonprofits, particularly smaller organizations, and the frequent emphasis on lowering administrative spending means investment in T&D may be neither a permanent, nor renewable line item in annual budgets.

Framing Training and Development

What immediately comes to mind regarding the definition of training and development is likely based on one's experience. While one may have an intuitive understanding of training and development, a closer look demonstrates a variety of viewpoints regarding the definition. In a recent set of interviews, 25 nonprofit leaders described training and development in a variety of ways—from classroom groups facilitated by a trainer to online videos, on-the-job learning, and self-directed employee learning (Egan & Adkere, 2015). Definitional and conceptual literature began to strongly emerge in the 1960s and then expanded over the past 50 years (Egan, 2016), with the following serving as representative definitions of T&D from a number of leading scholars and practitioners:

- a human capital investment that raises the worker's productivity (Becker, 1962);
- a process that provides conditions in which individuals gain knowledge, skills or ability (King, 1964);
- a maintenance subsystem, intended to improve organizational efficiency by increasing routinization and predictability of behavior (Katz & Kahn, 1978);
- learning provided by employers to employees related to their present jobs (Nadler & Nadler, 1989);
- the teaching of specific knowledge and skills required on the individual's present job. The term development refers to the growth of the individual and preparations for higher-level jobs (Kirkpatrick, 1993);
- a process of systematically developing work-related knowledge and expertise in people for the purpose of improving performance (Swanson & Holton, 2001);
- a planned effort by a company to facilitate employees' learning of job-related competencies. These competencies include knowledge, skills, or behaviors that are critical for successful job performance (Noe, 2010).

In Somasunduram and Egan's (2004) review of T&D definitions, four overarching aims of T&D were identified: (1) to develop or acquire knowledge; (2) to cultivate or gain skills; (3) to improve performance/productivity; and (4) to improve organizational efficiency/effectiveness. While definitions of T&D in the literature may be aimed at breadth, evidence suggests that organizations customize their definitions to fit their needs, assumptions, situations, and context. For instance, Somasunduram and Egan observed extant definitions of T&D often did not describe classrooms, trainers, curriculum, technology, or modalities of how training happens in a manner similar to nonprofit leaders (Egan & Adkere, 2015). This is likely because of the challenges in framing the variety of approaches to T&D. Many contextual issues are challenging to situate within a single T&D definition, including organization-specific and customized goals, resources, and approaches taken by training professionals, and the variety of individual learning styles and preferences. The evolution of technology, distance learning, tutoring/coaching, and other learning modalities has led organizations and individuals to try varied T&D-related approaches.

At times, the goal of T&D may be intended to advance awareness or growth with anticipated, but less tangible workplace outcomes (Deming, 1986). Based on a thorough exploration of definitions, and for the purposes of this discussion, T&D is defined as: *Work-related learning experiences aimed at knowledge and skill advancement for the purposes of improving awareness, expertise, performance and organizational impact.*

It is also important to note that most T&D definitions assume trainees to be employees, managers, and executives (or even consultants and contract workers). Unlike for-profit and governmental sectors, some nonprofit organizations rely heavily on volunteers. In many cases, volunteer workers in nonprofit organizations require training to increase volunteer retention and effectiveness (Hager & Brudney, 2011). While executive and board-related training could also be included, particularly given its importance to nonprofit organizations, it is not addressed extensively in the extant literature on T&D. Although scholars of nonprofit governance emphasize the importance of systematic board orientation, training, and evaluation (Brown, 2007), the literature on both corporate governance and nonprofit governance is largely decoupled from that focused on T&D. Though this is certainly an area for future reflection and research, this chapter centers on nonprofit manager and employee training.

Situating Training and Development in Organizations

Because of the aforementioned lack of professionalization of the T&D field and related roles in a single sector or industry, T&D is situated and interpreted within many organizational contexts and under a variety of organizational monikers including: human capital management, organization management, people management, talent management, personnel management, human resources, or manpower management. Depending on organization size, these names most often refer to human resources functions that serve as an umbrella over T&D. Basically, for-profit, public and nonprofit organizations can, and do, assemble endless combinations of human resources related functions together and label them almost any way they desire within their organization; therefore, the underlying assumptions of these organizational units or divisions reflect different types of considerations strongly influenced by the organizational context and history. At the same time, collective efforts have been made to consider T&D more holistically and systematically.

Perhaps the most comprehensive framing of organization-based learning is human resource development (HRD), which scaffolds learning at individual, group, and organization levels (Werner & DeSimone, 2012) in modalities including: career development, executive and other types of coaching and individualized learning (individual level); T&D, action learning (an approach where ideas are tested and put to work, examined, refined, and put back in use in a cycle oriented toward learning), and team building (group level); and organizational learning and organization development (organization level). HRD has also been framed in contexts larger than the organization level, including such domains as workforce development, community development, state/provincial, and national development (McLean & McLean, 2001). In part, HRD emerged simultaneously with the incorporation of systems theory (von Bertalynffy, 1968; described in more depth below) and the learning organization (Argyris & Schön, 1974) perspectives, as both serve as a critique and as a complement to T&D. Systems theory analyzes a phenomenon as a whole—not as the sum of essential parts. The key is the interrelationships between parts in order to better understand how an organization is structured, its inputs, functioning, and outcomes. It requires changes in points of view from holism to reductionism. Systems theory can be found in a variety of contexts including science, nature, economics, and organizations. The learning organization concept uses a systems perspective to consider learning across an organization. In this context, T&D is viewed as one part of the system. Systems can be found in nature, in science, in society, in an economic context, and within information systems. A distinctive characteristic of systems theory is that it developed simultaneously across various disciplines, with scholars working from a systems theory perspective building on the knowledge and concepts developed within other disciplines.

HRD viewpoints serve as a critique in that systems and learning organization perspectives demonstrated the work of trainers and trainees were insufficient if not well aligned with the larger organizational and stakeholder systems. At the same time, the systems perspective inherent in HRD incorporated T&D as an essential ingredient to organizational effectiveness. In effect, HRD introduced a systemic, strategic approach that shifted training as the central approach to workplace learning to one of a set of important tools to be utilized in the deployment of a learning organization strategy. The implications for this repositioning of T&D were strongly influenced by McLagan's study of for-profit HR, but with implications (and evidence of adoption) for nonprofit and governmental organizations as well (Kim, 2012).

With the incorporation of systems theory (described in more detail below) into social science scholarship and organizational HR and learning organization functions, the growth of HR and T&D related professional roles naturally led to the formation and growth of related professional associations, specified academic programs, and policymaking. Based on her study of HR practices in a number of large organizations, McLagan (1989) developed the HR Wheel (Figure 13.1). This model represents the larger organizational Human Resources System divided into three major subsets: (1) Human Resource Management (HRM); (2) Human Resource Development (HRD); and (3) Human Resources Information Systems (HRIS). Based on McLagan's study, T&D is situated within HRD and is interrelated with two other HRD areas—Organization Development (OD) and Career Development (CD).

McLagan's findings not only differentiated HR functions more clearly than before, they also provided key insights into managerial and employee development strategies and functions and their interrelationships within HRD. McLagan's study ran parallel to the emerging popularity of Peter Senge's (1990) work on learning organizations. As organizations in all three sectors began to experience increased dynamism and rapid change, Senge emphasized learning as key for organizational resilience and success. He also viewed systems-oriented, or holistic, approaches to learning as central to the survival and advancement of every organization. Senge adherents (along with predecessors like Argyris and Schön, 1980) elevated the importance of learning to boardroom and managerial levels that, until then, had not regularly occurred. This rising learning organization tide

229

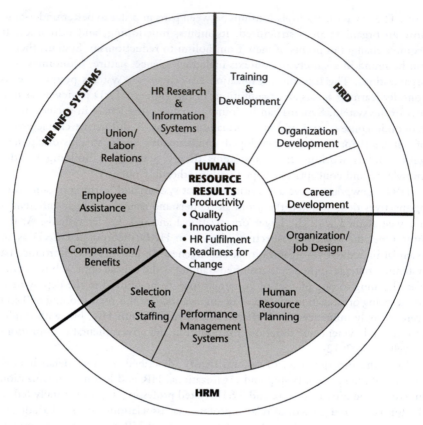

Figure 13.1   Human Resource Wheel

Source: Reprinted with permission of the Association for Talent Development.

reinvigorated the importance of T&D, while pointing to the care needed to reflect on the interrelationships between T&D and other HR functions. While the HR Wheel helps T&D professionals to situate their work with other of considerations, it is also important that T&D and HR professionals explore and synthesize a 'systems view' with other parts of their organizations as well—from operations and finance-to-customer service and marketing. Though foundational to conceiving a cohesive framing for HRD, this framing was largely agnostic with regard to sector or assumed a universality of applications across sectors. This has implications and imposes challenges for applying these frames to nonprofit contexts and for nonprofit leaders.

Nonprofit Challenges

There are several challenges and opportunities when considering nonprofit training and development. A key starting point is the size of the nonprofit organization engaging managers and employees in training. This nonprofit challenge is an overlapping issue for small businesses in the for-profit sector and for local government in townships and small municipalities. According to the U.S. Department of Labor (2015) businesses are considered "small" when employees number fewer than 500. While most medium-to-large sized businesses do not invest in more than a handful of training and development specialists, budgetary constraints and greater income volatility among many comparably small nonprofits make maintaining an internal training function quite challenging (Millesen & Bies, 2005). Following a more specific overview of T&D in the nonprofit sector and related theories and models, the differences in nonprofit size on T&D policies and training implementation are examined further.

Training and Development in Nonprofit Contexts

Over the past 40 years, learning and development has emerged as a central feature for organizational success. Nonprofit organizations have been included in ongoing discussions regarding the importance and impact of learning and learning systems in relation to practices in the sector (Millesen & Bies, 2005). In its broadest forms, T&D may occur in a variety of organizational contexts—for-profit, governmental and nonprofit—and may involve a variety of modalities (e.g., in-person training courses, online courses, group or individually oriented training programs, etc.). The emergence of learning technologies and systems-level approaches to learning have added richness and complexity to the exploration of T&D in nonprofit contexts.

While training-related professional associations (such as ATD) clearly emphasize for-profit contexts, members come from all sectors because of the commonalities of training efforts. In general, T&D emphasizes change or improvement in trainee knowledge, skills, and attitudes—with workplace-related training most often aimed toward specific tasks or jobs. The cumulative effect of training and other learning and performance improvement activities over time supports the long-term advancement of employees or managers, allowing both for impact in the near term and for future work responsibilities (Swanson & Holton, 2001). A common initial T&D experience comes in tandem with an employee's entrance into a new organization with employee orientation and introduction to key knowledge and skills being the inaugural experience into the new work setting. New employee orientation often consists of interactions and series of exchanges with those in the organization who have beneficial information and perspectives regarding what is required in the new role (Egan, 2016). In larger organizations, a T&D staff member and hiring supervisor work together to design and implement the orientation process. Related skills and technical training are often tailored in ways that best fit the employee's new role. Following integration into a work role, T&D-related activities often focus more on developmental aspects—utilizing managerial coaching, mentoring, developmental teams, workshops, and professional conferences (Millesen & Bies, 2005). Those in managerial and supervisory roles may be provided specific management training, seminars, academic courses, or professional association-sponsored programs.

Nonprofit Training and Development Literature

Although each context has unique characteristics, the framing of T&D in non-profits is often highly influenced by for-profit literature. A relatively early article on nonprofit training by Levinson (1987) highlighted the breadth of nonprofits and their unique training needs—including fundraising board relations, proposal writing, and volunteers—along with a number of topics important to organizations in any sector; financial management, leadership development, human resources administration, management techniques, communication, risk management, change management, and legal issues. Overall, the available literature on nonprofit T&D is very limited.

Much of the cross-sector training discussions focus on the intersections between for-profit and nonprofit training approaches—with the preponderance of literature pointing to the transferability of for-profit approaches to nonprofit practices. Paton, Mordaunt, and Cronforth (2007) contextualize nonprofit managerial training in the UK by pointing out governmental stimulus toward the use of for-profit training approaches in nonprofit contexts. Many nonprofit leaders perceive that a business oriented approach to training and the application of private sector business practices to be a priority (Milway & Saxton, 2011). The presence of for-profit leaders on nonprofit boards and cross-sector exchange between T&D professionals and managers make for natural comparisons, knowledge transfer and duplication in nonprofit contexts. Additionally, Peter Drucker (2006) and other management scholars have often emphasized the similarities between for-profits and nonprofits.

According to Chang et al. (2013), there are three major trends in nonprofit training-related research: (1) the aforementioned emphasis on utilization of business training paradigms in nonprofit contexts; (2) an emphasis on training volunteers and nonprofit academic programs; and (3) patchy, inconsistent, and asystematic training approaches. Chang et al. emphasize nonprofit training in the United Kingdom as a key example of how even government promoted nonprofit "enterprise culture" through the formation of policies encouraging nonprofit adaption of for-profit training practices. As previously identified, scholars such as Drucker (2006) and the common practice of utilizing for-profit leaders on nonprofit executive boards (Meehan & Jonker, 2015) led to a push to adapt for-profit training practices in nonprofits. Chang et al. also identified the preponderance of nonprofit training literature to emphasize the training of volunteers (e.g., Eisner, Grimm, Maynard, & Washburn, 2009; Gesthuizen & Scheepers, 2012) and formal academic programs (e.g., Dolan, 2002; Paton et al., 2007). Finally, nonprofit training practices are often described as asystematic (Chang et al., 2013) and are assembled in a sporadic fashion often emphasizing brief, non-sequential training events (Paton et al., 2007). As part of their investigation, Chang et al. were interested in practices used by nonprofits and the extent to which adaptation of practices from business and industry are applied. It was determined that nonprofit size and other key factors led nonprofits to emphasize on-the-job training more than the systematized training approaches often found in large for-profit organizations.

The T&D motivation for every organization relates to the need to recruit, retain, maintain, and advance talented employees who have key competencies that will align toward organizational success (Poell & van Woerkom, 2011). According to Chang et al. (2013), "employee training has been used as an important means to maintain organizational effectiveness" (p. 27). Egan et al. (2004) determined organizational cultures that support learning are associated with increased employee motivation, satisfaction and retention. Even in economically challenging times, U.S. organizations have invested substantially in T&D (ATD, 2014). On average, employees of organizations participating in the ATD learning survey received 31.5 hours of formal T&D annually. These numbers have increased over time and, although from the private sector, reflect a growth trend consistent in nonprofits as well (Chang et al., 2013). T&D-related data collection is usually focused on corporate investments in formal learning— defined as structured learning activities normally designed, implemented, and sponsored by employers—versus informal learning that is most often instigated and advanced by employees/managers individually. Learning and development occurs across sectors. Additionally, T&D involving volunteers—as trainees and trainers—is most common in nonprofit contexts. The relatively small amount of nonprofit T&D literature and research available will hopefully make it an attractive topic in an emerging nonprofit scholar and practitioner population.

Training Theories

Whether one is cognizant of the underlying influence of training theories in an overt way, or if such influences are the unnamed or underlying 'theories-in-use' (Argyris, 2000), assumptions about what T&D is for and how it works are important considerations. Similar to the aforementioned similarities and differences in T&D definitions, underlying theories of T&D elaborate and position key concepts such as training design and delivery assumptions, key outcomes, mechanisms underlying training transfer, and the ways in which trainers and trainees construct meaning and use power and influence. According to Noe (2010), while there are a number of training and development-related theories, there are a few highlighted more often. As emphasized by Lewin's (1945) oft-repeated statement "nothing is so practical as good theory" (p. 169), "it is important to examine these theories not only from a scholarly perspective, but from a practical perspective as well. Training and development and learning theories should have clear implications for practice" (Egan, 2009, p. 130).

Action Learning

Well aligned with the important intersection between theory and application, action learning theory emphasizes the core idea action and learning are firmly intertwined. The founder of action learning (Revans, 1980, 1983) regularly underscored that there cannot be action without learning, nor learning without action. As a theory and model associated with workplace training, action learning is viewed from a process perspective that includes: (1) focus problem or issue; (2) action learning team or group; (3) questioning and reflective listening process; (4) action to address the problem or issue; (5) focus on learning throughout; and (6) action learning coach/facilitator (Marquardt, 2004).

Revan's representative expression of action learning's underlying theory is $P + Q = L$—where P is programmed knowledge, Q is thoughtful questioning and L is learning.

Action learning-oriented training and development often blends existing or prepared learning materials (P) with a large amount of time for questioning and reflective listening (Q). Learning exchange is important because the action learning process (L) requires a commitment by participants to learn from each other in a manner aimed at accepting one another's points of view and offering constructive feedback and critiques (Zuber-Skerritt, 1996). Effective T&D facilitators utilizing action research emphasize participation and the expertise and experiences of trainees. It is most common for action learning trainers to support action-oriented learning through facilitated interaction between participants and invite experts and new information into the learning environment—rather than primarily engaging in PowerPoint presentations, or 'platform' training performances. The challenge of the action learning approach is that it may be very difficult to apply when highly technical or complex—requiring related subject-matter expertise from members, more time, or both. Conversely, the strength of this approach is that the participatory orientation to learning increases trainee buy-in and can lead to context/organization relevant outcomes and innovations. Revans and others have provided narratives and anecdotal support for the use of action learning in nonprofit organizations, the majority of action learning literature outside of the for-profit sector focuses on K-12 education.

Andragogy

Often juxtaposed in relationship to pedagogy, *andragogy* is defined as a learning approach aimed at adults and effective approaches to adult learning—which are considered to be unique as compared to pedagogy (Knowles, Holton, & Swanson, 1998). Like action learning theory, the theoretical viewpoint underlying andragogy is a humanist approach (Cooper & Henschke, 2007). However, unlike action learning theory, andragogy is often used to emphasize a more individually oriented approach to each training participant. While focusing on adult learning, andragogy does not identify a desired age for participation, rather it emphasizes behaviors associated with the capacity to be self-directed learners (Knowles, 1980). Additionally, andragogy-oriented training focuses on trainee-centered experiences oriented toward practice, collaboration, and problem solving as central to adult learning.

While this adult-learner-centered theoretical approach has grown considerably over the past 30 years, trainers not utilizing this approach may take a more uniform or top-down approach to trainees. The strength of andragogy is the importance it places on individually driven learning and independent motivation. In particular, the focus on adults' intrinsic learning needs and opportunities to support their learning styles and interests is a distinguishing element. Concurrently, a critique of andragogy is its focus on individuals in a manner that could position organizational or community needs secondarily, be more challenging when dealing with highly technical areas, or may eliminate or minimize trainer input and support. A focus on individualized adult learning can help develop individual approaches to dynamic work environments that make them more resilient and able to find their own learning approaches that adjust to collective needs. Zsiga's (2008) exploration of nonprofit leaders engaged in self-directed learning is one of very few studies exploring andragogy in nonprofit contexts.

Critical Action Research

Sharing several similar components to action learning, critical action research is a learning-training theory rooted in the critical philosophical tradition called critical theory (Carr & Kemmis, 1986) wherein the close examination of power dynamics and emancipatory interests are centered. Critical action research is most relevant when trainers have a strong interest in understanding trainees' specific contexts. Rather than emphasize individual learning goals, common to many training theories, this approach focuses on social and/or organizational problems— particularly inequity. Such an approach is not only helpful within organizations, it can be very beneficial to both understanding organizational intersections with communities and supporting organizational insight regarding how to have the best aligned impact.

Outcomes from critical action research can include resource sharing, policy change, organizational mission re-alignment, and empowering persons struggling with the imposition of social, physical, and/or financial obstacles. Facilitating critical action research, participants are asked to form learning groups that elaborate on inequities and social problems and, eventually, to determine their collective commitment to taking action toward change (Carson, 1990). In many cases, these adult learning focused groups become a team of change agents interested in altering the power dynamics or power relationships (Stringer, 2007). Dealing with resistance to change and attempts to ignore the recommendations and proactive behaviors of the critical action research are common.

In an effort to clarify the steps taken in critical action research in work and community contexts, Zuber-Skerritt (1996) presented the CRASP acronym:

(1) critical collaborative enquiry that is also self-critical and; (2) reflective framing learners as co-researchers and reflective practitioners aimed toward (3) accountability in making group outcomes and results public; (4) self-evaluating practice and engaged in (5) participatory problem solving and continuous professional development. As with action learning, participants' learning process is active and rooted in the experiences of each participant. Those critiquing this approach have indicated that trainers/facilitators of this type of learning must be careful to not be seen as coercive.

Additionally, while critical action research activities may lead to change, some worry the upheaval involved in the change process may lead to a different set of problems with similarly negative impacts. Conversely, "although organizations may not be interested, or may resist critical action, the breaking down of unnecessary or prohibitive power structures is beneficial in a variety of contexts: from corporate to NGO or other development related efforts" (Egan, 2009 p. 134). Critical action research can make great strides in development of greater awareness of organizational and community diversity, the formation of more just working environments, and commitments to redressing policies and decisions that perpetuate unfairness or that are implemented inequitably.

Facilitation Theory

Facilitation theory situates the trainer in a position to form and maintain a learning context in which trainees are able to explore new ideas. Training undergirded by facilitation theory supports trainees sharing their individual reactions in a nonthreatening environment. Facilitation theory is informed by psychologist Carl Rogers' one-on-one counseling approach called *client-centered therapy* (CCT). Rogers' (1970) CCT concepts of *unconditional positive regard* and *empathic understanding* are central for trainers enacting facilitation theory based training. As with Rogers' one-on-one approach with clients, training facilitators convey attitudes that are non-judgmental and are listening oriented. Time is built into such training for in-depth, trainee generated discussion that gives trainees the opportunity to discuss reactions, disclose feelings, and elaborate on their ideas and experiences. As with CCT, Kahn (1999) suggested the facilitator/trainer is unable to be entirely nondirective as her/his ideas will influence the direction of participants. Another major critique of training framed by facilitation theory is the dependence on learners to establish their own interests making the training sessions seem to some as lacking direction, clear objectives, and structure.

At the same time, recent developments in emerging fields such as positive psychology (Sheldon & King, 2001) and an infusion of appreciative inquiry practices in organization development (Bushe & Kassam, 2005; Cooperrider & Whitney, 1999) clearly support the foundations of facilitation theory. Those supporting this approach indicate a greater likelihood for productive learning outcomes and that, similar to andragogy, adults are ultimately made more responsible for (and perhaps are even enlightened to) the formation of their own learning and learning outcomes. Finally, such a facilitative approach can benefit multicultural contexts and diverse learning environments by formulating a way for all participants to voice their experiences and expand their sense of self-direction and influence through the openness and empathy of the facilitator. While literature directly connecting facilitation theory to nonprofits is uncommon, facilitative approaches to nonprofits, undoubtedly aligned with facilitation theory, can be found in case study narratives (Cooperrider & Whitney, 1999) and examination of leadership practices (Yukl, 1999).

Individual Learning Styles

The general concept underlying learning style theory is that individuals vary in the ways they learn. These different ways of learning can be called styles, types, or modes. Kolb (1976) and others popularized the theory of individualized learning styles in the 1970s. Since then, the concept of learning styles has been embraced by many teachers and trainers. The most common recommendation from those who favor the use of learning style theory is to assess each learner's style in the process of forming classroom methods and customizing the manner in which training is led. A more holistic approach, not involving individualized assessment, is to design training content and processes in a manner that reflects careful consideration and incorporation of each style.

Although several frameworks have emerged from a generalized theory of learning styles, Kolb's (1984) experiential learning cycle has been one of the most enduring. His four-part construct includes two areas of exchange—perception and processing. Within these there are both active (experimentation and doing) and reflective (observing and examining) processing along with abstract (discernment and thinking) and concrete (experience and feeling) perception. In Kolb's view, these types of perceptions and processing interacted with more or less dominant patterns for each individual. These patterns of preferences were assembled into four categories called learning styles, including:

- *Activist Accommodating*—A dynamic, intuitive learner oriented toward doing and feeling; a person with this preference is said to value experiences intrinsically.
- *Reflective/Diverging*—An imaginative learner oriented toward feeling and watching; a person who emphasizes reflection and reviewing as central to learning.
- *Theorist/Assimilating*—An analytical-theoretical learner oriented toward thinking and watching; a person who is comfortable extracting ideas and making inferences from experiences, including experiences.
- *Pragmatist/Converging*—A common-sense practical learner oriented toward thinking and doing; a person who enjoys thorough thinking and engaged planning.

By assessing, planning, and developing training and curricular designs that accommodate each of these learning styles, trainers are said to be better able to apply the most appropriate learning approaches and trainees to approach their own learning in a manner that creates the best likelihood for learning and performance. While there is a large body of evidence supporting that individuals express preferences for how information is conveyed and internalized, there is little empirical support for the application of learning style based approaches in training. As new research taking advantage of brain scans and biotechnological assessment become more widespread and accessible to researchers, the validity of the learning styles frameworks will be more clearly determined (Sousa, 2011). Until then, many teachers and trainees continue to identify with Kolb's and others' learning style inventories and related concepts. At the same time, it is important to note that Kolb and others have emphasized that the most important element regarding learning styles is that individuals take time to reflect regarding their own strengths and weaknesses. While inventories of all kinds, and awareness of learning styles, have emerged as a common aspect of T&D across sectors, there is a dearth of literature related to learning styles in nonprofit contexts.

Systems Theory

As described above, systems theory has been incorporated into our understanding of organizational learning and T&D. Most often credited to biologist von Bertalanffy (1969), systems theory was also adapted to the social sciences. Systems theory takes a transdisciplinary approach to examining the abstract, broad configurations of phenomena. This theory often situates a system as containing four aspects: (1) the elements, variables, or parts within a system; (2) attributes, properties, and/or qualities of a system and its objects; (3) the interrelationships between objects within a system; and (4) the environment in which the system is situated (von Bertalynffy, 1969). Brought together, these four aspects comprise a set of elements that impact one another within the context of the surrounding environment from which a unique set of interactions occurs.

Systems theory takes the notion of "the whole being the sum of its parts" and adds interaction, context and/or environment to describe the very unique way the parts interact within the whole. Systems theory transcends disciplines and applied fields of practice, including chemical and biological sciences (autopoietic elements; Maturana & Varela, 1975); natural sciences (equifinality, organic elements and homeostasis; Hannan & Freeman, 1977); information technology (cybernetic elements; Beer, 1985); and sociology and psychology (cognitive elements; Clark, 1993). Within organization and human resource development sciences, Senge (1990), Swanson (2001) and others incorporated the fundamental systems-interactive paradigm of organizational analysis (inputs→ throughputs→ outputs) to explicate the manner in which learning exchanges occur naturally and organizational structures and processes (like T&D) can be shaped with the intention of impacting employee learning and performance.

The interactive perspective determines whether a system is open (receives and exchanges information), closed (neither receives nor exchanges information) or some subset (open-in, receiving information; or open out, sending information). Generally, social scientists interested in human organizations focus on the relevance of open systems to things like effective learning, communication, responsiveness, and even survival. In organizational contexts, systems perspectives are helpful in pointing out interdependencies, chains of influence, the need for balance/homeostasis, and the importance of adapting to change. A good example of T&D situated within a system is the HR Wheel. While we can frame T&D as an independent activity, we benefit from thinking about the ways it is situated both within and between the development of the organization and the individual as well as how it is situated in relation to HRM. T&D efforts are more likely to have greater impact and to support ongoing organizational change when contextualized within the HRD, HRM and HRIS interdependencies. Systems theory has been identified as a relevant theory for nonprofit organizations both generally (Toepler & Anheier, 2004) and as central to exploring nonprofits as "learning organizations" (Gill, 2009).

Ideally theoretical perspectives serve to inform T&D practice in a manner whereby scholars and practitioners exchange perspectives, and work to identify and adapt theories (and/or theories-in-use). The interchange that can serve T&D best is the formation of a virtuous exchange between T&D practitioners and scholars engaged in praxis (or an ongoing cycle of action-and-reflection). While there is no doubt that T&D-related theory has impacted T&D practice, it is often difficult to see or surface T&D action rooted in underlying theoretical traditions or viewpoints. In many cases, theories and models interact to influence practice. T&D models for the development and implementation of training often interact with or are the byproducts of T&D related theories.

Developing Training: The ADDIE Approach

One of the most enduring models within workplace learning, the ADDIE (Assessment, Design, Develop, Implement, and Evaluate) approach to developing T&D content and deploying T&D programs has been utilized for decades. The largest, most concentrated, training efforts in the 20th century were facilitated in national military organizations that were the result of U.S. Training within Industry (TWI) programs (Dooley, 2001). According to Swanson and Holton (2001), the first in-depth work on approaches to creating T&D programs began with the U.S. military's Instructional System Design models and were further advanced through TWI and as business and industry determined the importance of T&D for organization success. These large-scale training efforts fostered the establishment and evolution of the five-step—Assessment, Design, Develop, Implement, and Evaluate—ADDIE model. ADDIE frames a systematic process for the establishment of "training needs, the design and development of training programs and materials, implementation of the program, and the evaluation of the effectiveness of training" (Allen, 2006, p. 431).

Although ADDIE emerged from the abovementioned large-scale training efforts, the originator of the approach has yet to be identified (Molenda, 2003). Nonetheless, ADDIE is the most commonly utilized approach to the creation of T&D programs today. According to Allen (2006), "there are more than 100 different variations of the ADDIE model; however, almost all of them reflect the generic 'ADDIE' process" (p. 430) including, but not limited to, the U.S. Air Force manual (U.S. Department of the Air Force, 2001). The earliest goals associated with this process were to maximize educational efficiency and effectiveness of training by aligning instruction to job descriptions and tasks that ensured trainees acquired the requisite knowledge and skills to execute a majority of job-related tasks. Training content emphasized the most critical areas central to the performance of the job.

When utilized effectively, ADDIE prescribes a set of procedures and decision points addressing how best to teach the knowledge, skills, and attitudes required to execute each job related task selected for instruction (Table 13.1). Each step in the proper application of ADDIE demands ongoing evaluation in relation to the job requirements assure that design and development decisions are made with supporting inputs regarding the performance requirements of the job. An instructional designer or trainer will carefully follow each step.

The ADDIE system is a five stage process. The first step in the ADDIE process is Analysis during which the learning needs are identified. This stage also identifies existing knowledge, goals, objectives, and audience needs. During the Analysis phase of ADDIE, the learning environment, content delivery options, and timeline for the project are also examined. If training is specific to the job, job task may also be examined and job performance standards either established or evaluated. The second phase of the ADDIE process is the Design phase; this involves a systematic process of clarifying and elaborating learning objectives. During this stage, detailed outlines, storyboards and/or prototypes are often developed along with look and feel of content. If tests are part of the training process they are also developed at this stage. The third stage of the ADDIE is Development during which content and learning materials are produced. This includes development of learning activities and instruction delivery and management plans. The fourth phase of ADDIE is Implementation. During the Implementation phase plans are put into place and delivered to the trainee group. The final phase of ADDIE is Evaluation. The Evaluation consists of both formative and summative evaluations to provide opportunities for feedback from participants and to revise materials and processes.

The conceptual steps of systematic T&D formation outlined by ADDIE have endured years of utilization and scrutiny—making it one of the most enduring T&D frameworks. Revision and adaptation have contributed to the resilience of ADDIE and to many interrelated variations. Key critiques of ADDIE include its complexity, resource demands to execute well, and the need to adjust the process to fit some variants in jobs or tasks. "When properly implemented, ADDIE has a proven record of creating training that results in learners acquiring specified

Table 13.1 ADDIE Training Model: Steps, tasks and deliverables

	SAMPLE TASKS	SAMPLE DELIVERABLES
Analysis	Performance analysis Training needs assessment Job analysis Task analysis Performance measure determination Analysis of related training Determine instructional setting	Learner profile Needs/problem statement Training task analysis report Learning space assessment Elaboration report of training in context of larger curriculum
Design	Write objectives Structure and sequence training Select methods Plan evaluation overall Develop tests/performance measures Determine content sequence Determine content Structure Innovate with related examples/activities	Goals and objectives Content outline Design plan Testing/Formal evaluation plan Possible activities/active learning approaches outlined
Development	Develop training materials Develop relevant training activities Develop approaches to assess learner knowledge	Lesson plans Training materials Training activities Evaluation instruments
Implementation	Conduct training Conduct learner based activities Test ongoing learner knowledge development	Learner outcomes Learner perceptions of content relevance Learner overall feedback Evaluation data
Evaluation	Collect more evaluation data Analyze and report the results	Evaluation report Revised curriculum and program

Source: Adapted from Toby Egan (2009).

expertise, [and] a foundation for performance" (Allen, 2006, p. 440). In addition to the demands models like ADDIE can make on T&D professionals and their organizations, the size of nonprofit organizations also impacts policies and strategies for delivering T&D. Without a dedicated T&D staff, nonprofit organizations must rely on external entities for T&D support. Although limited, a small amount of literature examines the use of ADDIE in nonprofit contexts (Chang et al., 2013).

How Nonprofit Organization Size Impacts Training and Development

There are a number of ways in which to frame and differentiate nonprofit organizations, including financial resources, board involvement, mission, scope, volunteers, and stakeholders (Urban Institute, 2015). Comparing differently sized organizations can be used as proxy for other organizational features such as general resources and capacity (Schmidt & Zimmerman, 1991). Approaches by different sized nonprofits to training is useful to understanding similarities and differences and drawing inferences regarding their T&D-related strategies. Like many nonprofit efforts, T&D is often deployed based on capacity and resource-based challenges and opportunities. In order to compare different sized organizations, a database of nonprofits in the central United States containing 2013 IRS Form 990 documents along with additional specific information regarding nonprofit organization size. Lists from five large metropolitan areas in the central U.S. nonprofit data were combined and then divided into seven size categories—Micro (<10 employees); Mini (10–50 employees); Smaller (50–250); Small (250–500); Medium (500–1000); Large (1000–5000); Extra Large (5000+). Organizations were selected at random from each of these categories until 33 organizations (N = 231) in each of the seven categories responded. A total of 469 organizations (just under a 50% response rate) were contacted in order to receive 231 responses.

Nonprofit organizations were asked to report several areas related to their use of T&D: (1) their training policies; (2) the types of T&D activities in which they engage; (3) training modalities most commonly used; and (4) the distribution of types of training used. Table 13.2 outlines responses for organizations in each of the seven size categories regarding training policy. The data present a clear relationship between nonprofit size and the level of established training policy with larger organizations being far more likely to have a written training policy. Within this sample, smaller organizations are likely to be less structured and systematic regarding their training policies. Based on this sample, it is logical to conclude that size matters in terms of T&D-related policy and structure. One key reason for this is that smaller organizations have fewer people to train and are unlikely to have the resources to dedicate a full-time person focused on T&D and related learning programs.

One question that emerges from this difference in underlying training policy structure is the types of T&D activities these organizations support: internal or

Table 13.2 Training policy: Level of formality

	<10	10–50	50–250	250–500	500–1000	1000–5000	5000+	# Responding
Written Training Policy (%)	5	15	33	45	63	65	78	
Informal Training Policy (%)	38	44	40	40	26	23	15	
None, need-based approach (%)	37	30	22	11	8	10	6	
No system at all (%)	20	11	5	4	3	2	1	
# Responding	33	33	33	33	33	33	33	231

Table 13.3 Training deployment: Internal versus external

	<10	10–50	50–250	250–500	500–1000	1000–5000	5000+
External Courses (%)	36	47	66	72	70	74	78
Internal Courses (%)	22	41	69	82	85	88	89
External Consultants/ Advisors (%)	22	25	37	40	42	41	58
Internal Mentors/ Apprenticeships (%)	54	49	34	33	35	39	40
Job Rotation (%)	19	26	31	40	42	44	52
# of Organizations Responding	33	33	33	33	33	33	33

external (Table 13.3). Overall, larger organizations were more likely to offer T&D developed and delivered by T&D-related staff internal to the organization and externally delivered courses developed and delivered by T&D-related staff external to the organization. Additionally, larger nonprofits were more likely to contract with T&D-related consultants and advisors. The smallest organizations in this study were most likely to offer internal mentors—with half the organizations with between 5 and 50 employees supporting internal mentoring and apprenticeships. Given that smaller organizations are likely to depend on many employees serving generalist roles, it was perhaps not surprising that larger organizations provided more job rotation as part of their employee T&D than smaller organizations.

Toby Egan

Table 13.4 Training delivery: In-person versus online

	<10	10–50	50–250	250–500	500–1000	1000–5000	5000+
In-Person Training Delivery (%)	45	48	51	55	53	54	48
Online Training Delivery (%)	40	32	31	24	23	19	20
Combined Training (both Online & In-person Delivery) (%)	15	20	18	21	24	27	32
# of Organizations Responding	33	33	33	33	33	33	33

Persistent advances in online T&D have led to expanded employee participation in all sectors. When it comes to in-person T&D (delivered face-to-face by a T&D professional), there appears to be few differences across organizations of different sizes. What does appear to be different is that employees in smaller organizations do more 'stand-alone' online training, while employees in larger organizations are offered more T&D programs that combine online and in-person delivery (Table 13.4). It is, again, likely that the fewer T&D resources available to smaller organizations make offering online training, without additional support, a less resource intensive option.

For the purposes of understanding the types of training offered, organizations were divided into two groups (Smaller = 5–500 employees; Larger = 500 or more employees) to determine the training topics they emphasize (Table 13.5). In general, smaller and larger organizations were similar in the amount of T&D offered across various types. Smaller organizations, focused slightly more on job specific and basic skills training while larger organizations focused more on compliance, employee orientation, and customer service.

Given the broad array of nonprofit organizations and their sizes, approaches to T&D are clearly influenced by the number of employees. The smallest of nonprofits were more likely to rely on individualized and apprenticeship/ mentoring approaches as the best option, while the largest nonprofits were more likely to have a combination of internal T&D staff dedicated and contracted external T&D support. Without far greater numbers of reports from nonprofit organizations, we cannot know if the above trends are generalizable; however, these study results are largely consistent with suggestions from the limited available literature on this topic. Organizational size considerations are essential in the development of the best aligned T&D strategies.

By considering T&D in the context of organizational size, we gain some insights regarding important similarities and differences across nonprofits. Although too small a sample to generalize, the data collected across these 231

Table 13.5 Training topics emphasized

	Smaller 5–500 employees (%)	Larger 500 or more employees (%)
Job Specific	16	13
Managerial/Supervisory	10	12
Work Processes	12	10
IT & Technology	12	11
Other (including grant writing)	11	9
Compliance	5	9
Basic Skills	11	7
Communication	6	8
Fundraising/Sales	6	7
Employee Orientation	5	7
Customer Service	4	6
Training Volunteers	3	2
Executive Leadership	2	5
Executive Board Training	1	<1

nonprofit organizations suggest, when it comes to T&D, organizational size matters in terms of training policy, deployment, modes of delivery, and training topic. T&D is a resource-intensive, and therefore a resource dependent, activity. Smaller organizations, most often, require managers and employees to be generalists in a number of areas, including T&D, while larger nonprofits often support T&D specialists with the ability to set T&D policy and deliver ongoing employee and managerial training more consistently.

Conclusion

T&D is a foundational need for nonprofit organizations as the development of the nonprofit sector is inextricably tied to the effectiveness of its managers and employees. The systematic examination of nonprofit T&D is at a very early stage. While we are just beginning to map the history and future of nonprofit T&D, it has been strongly influenced by past T&D-related events and current T&D trends across sectors. T&D theory, practice and research are beginning to emerge more strongly in the nonprofit context. Across sectors many of the underlying T&D assumptions and practices share more similarities than differences. At the same time, the nonprofit sector has distinct characteristics requiring sector-specific T&D approaches. In addition, the framing of T&D within a broader learning system and the varieties of nonprofit organizations in terms of size, plays an important role in determining the T&D strategy to be used. The relatively early history of the nonprofit sector, and even more recent focus on related organizational learning and T&D, create opportunities for further cross-sector integration of related T&D applications. There is ample opportunity for further consideration and application of nonprofit specific T&D practices and content in the contexts of HRM and HRD.

Discussion Questions

1   To gain a better understanding of your learning style go online to www.personal.psu.edu/bxb11/LSI/LSI.htm
2   What does your learning style suggest about the types of training/learning methods you should use? How is your style different from your classmates?
3   What are some of the challenges to training and employee development in the nonprofit sector? What are some ways organizations can deal with those challenges?
4   What was the last training you attended as part of work? In what ways was it effective? In what ways could it have been improved?
5   McLagan's model (Figure 13.1) suggests HR has many interrelated parts. What theory(ies) support the idea that T&D is interdependent? What are some examples where T&D can be made most effective through integration with other parts of Hr and/or the organization?

References

Allen, W. C. (2006). Overview and evolution of ADDIE training system. *Advances in Developing Human Resources, 8*, 430–41.

Argyris, C. (2000). *Flawed advice and the management trap: How managers can know when they're getting good advice and when they're not.* Oxford, England: Oxford University Press.

Argyris, C. & Schön, D. (1992). *Theory in practice: Increasing professional effectiveness.* San Francisco: Jossey-Bass.

ATD. (2014). State of the industry report. Alexandria, VA: ATD.

Bartlett, K. R. (2001). The relationship between training and organizational commitment: A study in the health care field. *Human Resource Development Quarterly, 12*, 333–352.

Becker, G. S. (1962). Investment in human capital: A theoretical analysis. *Journal of Political Economy, 70*, 9–49.

Beer, S. (1985). *Diagnosing the system for organizations.* New York: John Wiley.

Bertalynfy, L. von. (1968). *General systems theory.* New York: George Braziller.

Brown, W. A. (2007). Board development practices and competent board members: Implications for performance. *Nonprofit Management & Leadership, 17*, 301–317.

Bushe, G. & Kassam, A. (2005). When is appreciative inquiry transformational? A meta-case analysis. *Journal of Applied Behavioral Science, 41*, 161–81.

Carr, W. and Kemmis, S. (1986). *Becoming critical: Education, knowledge and action research.* London: Falmer Press.

Carson, T. (1990). What kind of knowing is critical action research? *Theory into Practice, 24*, 167–173.

Chang, W. W., Huang, Y. C., & Kuo, Y. (2015). Design of employee training in Taiwanese nonprofits. *Nonprofit and Voluntary Sector Quarterly, 44*, 25–46.

Clark, A. (1993). *Associative engines* Boston: MIT Press.

Cooper, M. & Henschke, J. (2007). Expanding our thinking about andragogy: A continuing research study. In K. King & V. Wang (Eds.), *Comparative adult education around the globe* pp. 151–194. Hangzhou, PRC: Zhejiang Univ. Press.

Cooperrider, D. L. & Whitney, D. (1999). *A Positive Revolution in Change: Appreciative Inquiry.* Taos, NM: Corporation for Positive Change.

Deming, W. E. (1986). *Out of the crisis.* Cambridge, Massachusetts: MIT Press.

Dolan, D. A. (2002). Training needs of administrators in the nonprofit sector: What are they and how should we address them? *Nonprofit Management & Leadership, 12,* 277–292.

Dooley, C. R. (2001). The training within industry report 1940–1945. *Advances in Developing Human Resources, 3,* 127–289.

Drucker, P. (2006). *The practice of management.* New York: Harper.

Ebrahim, A. (2005). Accountability myopia: Losing sight of organization learning. *Nonprofit and Voluntary Sector Quarterly, 34,* 56–87.

Egan, T. (2016). *Revisiting training and development definitions.* School of Public Policy: University of Maryland.

Egan, T. M. (2009). Training and development in our ever present globalization context: A theory-to-practice perspective, In K. P. King & V. C. X. Wang (Eds.), *Fundamentals of Human Performance and Training*, pp. 127–151. New York: Information Age.

Egan, T. & Adkere, M. (2015). *US nonprofit training and development strategies: A qualitative inquiry.* Do Good Institute: University of Maryland.

Egan, T., Yang, B., & Bartlett, K. R. (2004). The effects of organizational learning culture and job satisfaction on motivation to transfer learning and turnover intention. *Human Resource Development Quarterly, 15,* 279–301.

Eisner, D., Grimm, R. T., Maynard, S., & Washburn, S. (2009). The new volunteer workforce. *Stanford Social Innovation Review, 7,* 32–37.

Gesthuizen M. & Scheepers P. (2012). Educational differences in volunteering in cross-national perspective: Individual and contextual explanations. *Nonprofit and Voluntary Sector Quarterly, 41*(1), 58–81

Hager, M. A. & Brudney, J. L. (2011). Problems recruiting volunteers: Nature versus nurture. *Nonprofit Management & Leadership, 22,* 137–157.

Hall, P. D. (2010). Historical perspectives on nonprofit organizations. In R. D. Herman (Ed.), *The Jossey-Bass Handbook of Nonprofit Leadership and Management,* pp. 3–43. San Francisco: Jossey Bass.

Hannan, M. T. & Freeman, J. (1977). The population ecology of organizations. *American Journal of Sociology, 82*(5), 929–964.

Harbison, F. & Myers, C. A. (1964). *Education, manpower, and economic growth: Strategies of human resource development.* New York: McGraw-Hill.

Hodgkinson, V. & Nelson, K. (2001). Major issues facing America's nonprofit sector. *The Nonprofit Review, 1,* 113–118.

Jacobs, R. L. (1989). Systems theory applied to human resource development. In D. B. Gradous (Ed.), *Systems theory applied to human resource development,* pp. 27–60. Alexandria, VA: American Society for Training and Development.

Kahn, E. (1999). A critique of non-directivity in the person-centered approach. *Journal of Humanistic Psychology, 39,* 94–110.

Keefe, J. R. (2009). Stalin and the drive to industrialize the Soviet Union. *Inquiries Journal, 1,* 2–4.

Kim, N. (2012). Toward the use of human resource development for societal develop-ment issues, challenges, and opportunities. *Advances in Developing Human Resources, 14,* 345–354

Knowles, M. S. (1980). *The modern practice of adult education: From pedagogy to andragogy.* Englewood Cliffs: Prentice Hall.

Knowles, M. S., Holton, E. F., & Swanson, R. A. (1998). *The adult learner: The definitive classic in adult education and human resource development.* Houston: Gulf Publishing.

Kolb, D. A. (1984). *Experiential learning: Experience as the source of learning and development.* Englewood Cliffs, NJ: Prentice Hall.

Kolb, D. A. (1976). *The learning style inventory.* Boston: McBer.

Koppes, L. L. (2006). Historical perspectives in industrial and organizational psychology. Hillsdale, NJ: Lawrence Erlbaum Associates.

Lewin, K. (1945). The research center for group dynamics at Massachusetts Institute of Technology. *Sociometrics, 8,* 128–135.

Paton, R., Mordaunt, J., & Cornforth, C. (2007). Beyond nonprofit management education: Leadership development in a time of blurred boundaries and distributed learning. *Nonprofit & Voluntary Sector Quarterly, 36,* 148–162.

Pryor, E. B. (1987). *Clara Barton: Professional angel.* Philadelphia: University of Pennsylvania Press.

Marquardt, M. J. (2004). *Optimizing the Power of Action Learning.* Palo Alto: Davies-Black Press.

Maturana, H. R. & Varela, F. J. (1975). Autopoietic systems: A characterization of the living organization. Biological Computer Lab Report 9.4, University of Illinois, Urbana.

Mayo, E. (1933). *The human problems of an industrial civilization.* Cambridge, MA: Harvard.

McHargue, S. (2003). Learning for performance in nonprofit organizations. *Advances in Developing Human Resources, 5,* 196–204.

McLagan, P. (1989). *Models for HRD practice.* Alexandria, VA: American Society for Training and Development.

McLean, G. N. & McLean, L. D. (2001). If we can't define HRD in one country, how can we define it in an international context? *Human Resource Development International, 4,* 313–326.

Meehan, B. & Jonker, K. S. (2015). How to be a better nonprofit board member. Stanford Insights. Available at: www.gsb.stanford.edu/insights/how-be-better-nonprofit-board-member

Millesen, J. & Bies, A. L. (2005). Nonprofit "capacity-building orientation": The role of learning in building nonprofit performance. Pittsburgh, Pennsylvania: Forbes Funds.

Milway, K. & Saxton, A. (2011). The challenge of organizational learning. *Stanford Social Innovation Review, 9,* 44–49.

Mirabella, R. (2007). University-based educational programs in nonprofit management and philanthropic studies: A 10-year review and projections of future trends. *Nonprofit and Voluntary Sector Quarterly, 36,* 11–27.

Molenda, M. (2003). In Search of the elusive ADDIE model. *Performance Improvement. 42*(5), 34–36.

NCCS. (2015). US nonprofit organizations (2015). Available at: www.urban.org/sites/default/files/publication/72536/2000497-The-Nonprofit-Sector-in-Brief-2015-Public-Charities-Giving-and-Volunteering.pdf

Poell, R. F. & Van Woerkom, M. (2011). *Supporting learning in the workplace: Towards evidence based practice.* Dordrecht: Springer.

Revans, R. W. (1980). *Action learning.* Blond & Briggs, London.

Revans, R. W. (1983). Action learning: The forces of achievement or getting it done. *Management Decision, 21,* 44–54.

Riddoch, V. (2009). Staff training is key for third sector. *Regeneration and Renewal,* 19: www.regen.net/

Rogers, C. R. (1970). *Carl Rogers on encounter groups.* New York: Harper & Row.

Senge, P. M. (1990). *The fifth discipline: The art and practice of the learning organization.* New York: Doubleday.

Sheldon, K. M. & King, L. K. (2001). Why positive psychology is necessary. *American Psychologist*, *56*, 216–217.

Snell, K. D. M. (1996). The apprenticeship system in British history: The fragmentation of a cultural institution. *History of Education*, *25*, 303–322.

Somasunduram, U. V. & Egan, T. (2004). Training and development: An examination of definitions and dependent variables. *Proceedings of the Academy of Human Resource Development*, 850–857.

Stringer, E. (2007). *Action research in education*. Upper Saddle River, NJ: Prentice Hall.

Swanson, R. A. (2001). Human resource development and its underlying theory. *Human Resource Development International*, *4*, 299–312.

Swanson, R. A. & Holton, E. F. III. (2001). *Foundations of human resource development*. San Francisco, CA: Berrett-Koehler Publishers.

Tracey, W. R. (1974). *Designing training and development*. New York NY: AMCOM.

United States Department of the Air Force, (2001). Instructional system design. AF manual 36–2234.

United States Department of Labor. (2015). Apprenticeship Report: Office of Apprenticeship. https://www.dol.gov/featured/apprenticeship/2015

United States Department of Labor. (2016). Report: Office of Apprenticeship. https://www.dol.gov/featured/apprenticeship/2016

Werner, J. M. & DeSimone, R. L. (2012). *Human resource development*. Mason, OH: South-Western.

Zsiga, P. L. (2008). Self-directed learning in directors of a US nonprofit organization. *International Journal of Self-Directed Learning*, *5*(2), 35–49.

Zuber-Skerritt, O. (1996). *Action research for change and development*. Aldershot: Gower.

14

Making Nonprofits More Effective

Performance Management and Performance Appraisals

Marlene Walk and Troy Kennedy

Introduction

Human resources are regarded as the most critical asset contributing to the success and mission achievement of nonprofit organizations. Nonprofit organizations are increasingly confronted with pressures to become more competitive, thus, knowledge concerning how to effectively and efficiently manage human resources is vital. The implementation of performance management systems is regarded as a valuable way to demonstrate the continuous performance of employees to the organizations' stakeholders (Akingbola, 2015). Performance management also helps employees to identify their roles and responsibilities in mission achievement (Pynes, 2013). As such, performance management in nonprofit organizations is of both individual and organizational importance.

In this chapter, we follow Akingbola's (2015) definition of performance management as encompassing "all the activities, systems and processes that are deployed to enable and support employees to contribute the maximum of their knowledge, skills and abilities to the organization" (p. 164). Performance management is characterized as a continuous process that identifies, measures, and develops individual and team performance aiming to align performance with the strategic objectives of the organization (Aguinis, 2009a). Performance appraisals are regarded as a key component of any performance management system (Akingbola, 2015; Selden & Sowa, 2011).

Performance management and performance appraisals have long been regarded as key for effective strategic human resource management (SHRM) in the for-profit sector (Devanna, Fombrun, & Tichy, 1984) and have been widely researched in for-profit contexts (Cawley, Keeping, & Levy, 1998; Fletcher & Perry, 2002; Levy & Williams, 2004). As part of SHRM, performance management attempts to increase the fit between human resource (HR) practices to enhance individual performance with the objective of maximizing organizational outcomes (Den Hartog, Boselie, & Paauwe, 2004). Well-designed performance management systems have been found to positively affect employees, managers, and organizations (Aguinis, 2009a; Thomas & Bretz Jr, 1994). For instance, performance management systems help employees to comprehend how their behaviors affect the results required of their work, boost their self-esteem, and identify their strengths and mitigate their weaknesses. Performance management systems enable managers to learn about their subordinates, to develop their subordinates' performance awareness, and to better differentiate between good and poor performers. Through the introduction of performance management systems, organizations emphasize greater goal clarity, enable organizational change, and increase employee commitment and engagement (Aguinis, 2009a; Thomas & Bretz Jr, 1994).

Performance appraisals, now a key element of performance management, have, over time, evolved from being an annually reoccurring administrative requirement where individuals' strengths and weaknesses are discussed (Aguinis, Joo, & Gottfredson, 2011) and their past performance is documented (Lee, 2006) to a more strategic function within performance management (Den Hartog et al., 2004). Consequently, performance appraisals are now conceptualized as a process "including establishment of performance standards, appraisal related behaviors of raters within the performance appraisal period, determination of performance rating, and communication of the rating to the ratee" (Erdogan, 2003, p. 556). As such, performance appraisals today fulfill a broader, more holistic, function that is tightly integrated into the organizational strategy in form of performance management systems.

The mere existence of performance management systems might not be sufficient to increase organizational performance. To ensure a positive effect of performance management systems on organizational performance, the rating systems used should be reliable and valid to effectively discriminate between certain levels of performance (Twomey & Feuerbach Twomey, 1992). Moreover, scholars recommend a communicative process between managers and their employees (Den Hartog et al., 2004). It is important that the communication with the employee focuses on the organization's strategic objectives and the employee's contributions to achieve these while also being fair (Erdogan, 2003). Having bilateral processes in place facilitates the evaluation of employees, but also gives them a voice in the process (Erdogan, 2003; Roberts, 2003). Participative performance management systems that—by design—offer opportunities for regular feedback and ensure employee ownership in the evaluation of their performance, are more effective in attaining improved organizational performance (Roberts, 2003).

When implementing and evaluating performance management systems, scholars caution to pay attention to differences of employees' experience with performance management practices, how these practices are enacted by managers, and the initial intention when instituted by organizational leadership (Nishii &

Wright, 2008). For instance, Farndale and Kelliher (2013) find that employees are willing to reciprocate benefits through increased organizational commitment if they perceive performance appraisals to be enacted fairly by their managers. As such, organizational performance is only likely to increase when employees' perceptions and evaluation of performance management practices are acknowledged (Nishii, Lepak, & Schneider, 2008). Similarly, in another study employees' satisfaction with performance appraisals was found to contribute to organizational commitment and to reduce employees' intentions to leave the organization (Kuvaas, 2008).

Similar to the for-profit context, a variety of functions of performance management systems in nonprofit organizations have been identified, such as the translation of organizational goals to individual activities, evaluation of employee engagement, legal mitigation, job design, and career planning (Akingbola, 2015) as well as strategic decision-making on employee promotion, development and training, compensation, and retention or separation (Pynes, 2013). Despite the known merits of performance management systems, including appraisals (Aguinis, 2009b; Den Hartog et al., 2004), the extent of which these systems are implemented in nonprofit organizations varies widely (Pynes, 2013), both domestically (Selden & Sowa, 2011) and internationally (Walk, Schinnenburg, & Handy, 2014).

Given the specific set up of nonprofit organizations, tools for performance management from the for-profit sector might not be easily applicable to nonprofit organizations (Speckbacher, 2003). For instance, employees in nonprofit organizations tend to be highly intrinsically motivated and identify with the mission of the organization. As such, their preference structure differs from those of for-profit employees, who tend to be characterized as extrinsically motivated. From an organizational perspective, nonprofit organizations cannot easily reward employee performance with financial incentives such as salary raises or bonus payments, given their organizational characteristics (e.g., the non-distribution constraint) (Devaro & Brookshire, 2007; Speckbacher, 2003). Therefore, our objective is to summarize context-specific research on performance management and performance appraisals in nonprofit organizations and, based on this summary, to propose a comprehensive model of performance management and performance appraisals for the nonprofit context.

Methods

We searched the academic literature to identify studies for our review. In particular, we searched Google Scholar and EBSCOhost databases using terms such as performance & management, performance & appraisals, performance & evaluation, employee & evaluation, employee & performance, employee & appraisal followed by the classifier nonprofit organizations/nonprofits. We also manually searched four journals (*Nonprofit Management & Leadership, Voluntas: International Journal of Voluntary and Nonprofit Organizations, Nonprofit Voluntary*

Sector Quarterly, and *Human Service Organizations: Management, Leadership & Governance* [formerly *Administration in Social Work*]) that we knew had published research on performance management and appraisals. Our search of the literature yielded 108 articles. This survey of the literature does not include unpublished papers (e.g., dissertations and conference papers) or books, but focuses on articles published in journals and, thus, is not exhaustive.

As nonprofit organizations are pressured to become more efficient and effective, our search resulted in a compilation of articles on a variety of performance-related topics such as organizational performance, performance measurement, performance accountability, financial performance, board performance, network performance and pay for performance. Given our focus on organizational procedures that enable employee performance (Akingbola, 2015), we discarded articles that did not specifically focus on performance appraisals and performance management. The final number of articles that form the basis for this review is 22. An overview of all included papers can be found in Table 14.1.

As we were interested in a comprehensive overview of the past research on performance management and performance appraisals in the nonprofit context, we engaged in an inductive coding process whereby codes emerged as we went through the articles. We modified categories when new articles were added. We decided on our final coding scheme after having coded six articles.

Findings

In a first step, we identified four distinct clusters of studies when sorting the review articles. The first set focuses on performance appraisals as a stand-alone technique. Notably, three of four studies falling into this category were also the oldest studies in our sample (Millar, 1990; Pecora & Hunter, 1988; Potter & Smith, 2009; Wiehe, 1981). The second set of articles looked at performance management as a strategic tool to assess employee performance (Becker, Antuar, & Everett, 2011; Curran, 2002; Davenport & Gardiner, 2007; Helmig, Michalski, & Lauper, 2008; Selden & Sowa, 2011). These authors conceptualize performance appraisals as part of a broader performance management system. In the third set of articles, performance appraisals are integrated into human resource management strategies such as strategic human resource management or high performance work systems (Guo, Brown, Ashcraft, Yoshioka, & Dong, 2011; Ridder, McCandless Baluch, & Piening, 2012; Ridder, Piening, & McCandless Baluch, 2012; Robineau, Ohana, & Swaton, 2015; Rodwell & Teo, 2004, 2008; Selden & Sowa, 2015; Walk et al., 2014). In the final fourth set, neither performance appraisals nor performance management is the main focus of the respective studies, but aspects pertaining to either are discussed in relationship to other organizational constructs (Beem, 2001; Deckop & Cirka, 2000; Ebrahim, 2005; Packard, 2010; Rivas, 1984).

A clear trend emerges when looking at the first three clusters of articles. As three of the oldest articles in this review are forming the first category followed

Table 14.1 Article review sample

Authors	Year	Journal name	Category	Methods
Wiehe	1980	Administration in Social Work	Technique	Quantitative
Pecora, Hunter	1988	Administration in Social Work	Technique	Conceptual
Millar	1990	Administration in Social Work	Technique	Conceptual
Potter, Smith	2009	International Journal Management in Education	Technique	Qualitative
Curran	2002	Journal for Nonprofit Management	Strategic tool	Conceptual
Davenport, Gardiner	2007	Total Quality Management	Strategic tool	Qualitative
Helmig, Michalski, Lauper	2008	German Journal of Research in Human Resource Management	Strategic tool	Mixed Methods
Becker, Antuar, Everett	2011	Nonprofit Management and Leadership	Strategic tool	Mixed Methods
Selden, Sowa	2011	Public Personnel Management	Strategic tool	Mixed Methods
Rodwell, Teo	2004	Public Management Review	Human resource strategy	Quantitative
Rodwell, Teo	2008	International Journal of Human Resource Management	Human resource strategy	Quantitative

Author(s)	Year	Journal	Category	Method
Guo, Brown, Ashcraft, Yoshioka, Dong	2011	Review of Public Personnel Administration	Human resource strategy	Quantitative
Ridder, McCandless Baluch, Piening	2012	Voluntas	Human resource strategy	Conceptual
Ridder, Piening, McCandless Baluch	2012	Human Resource Management Review	Human resource strategy	Qualitative
Walk, Schinnenburg, Handy	2014	Voluntas	Human resource strategy	Qualitative
Selden, Sowa	2015	Human Service Organizations: Management, Leadership & Governance	Human resource strategy	Mixed Methods
Robineau, Ohana, Swaton	2015	The Journal of Applied Business Research	Human resource strategy	Qualitative
Rivas	1984	Administration in Social Work	Miscellaneous	Conceptual
Deckop, Cirka	2000	Nonprofit and Voluntary Sector Quarterly	Miscellaneous	Quantitative
Beem	2001	International Journal of Nonprofit and Voluntary Sector Marketing	Miscellaneous	Quantitative
Ebrahim	2005	Nonprofit and Voluntary Sector Quarterly	Miscellaneous	Conceptual
Packard	2010	Nonprofit and Voluntary Sector Quarterly	Miscellaneous	Quantitative

by newer studies in the next two categories, we can assume that, over time, performance appraisals were integrated into more holistic systems of either performance management or human resource management (Potter and Smith (2009) is an exception). This trend might be related to the increase of scholarly attention to effective practices in nonprofit organizations and the importance of bundling individual practices (Ridder, Piening, et al., 2012), conceptualizing performance appraisals as one tool among a larger set of practices that—when well aligned—contribute to the strategic goals of the organization. Corresponding to this trend, we noticed the conceptualization of performance appraisals was evolving overtime. Whereas earlier works defined "employee performance as an annual event" (Wiehe, 1981, p. 1), recent studies applied a more comprehensive view defining performance appraisals as "a formal and systematic process for reviewing performance and providing oral and written feedback to staff about performance at least annually" (Selden & Sowa, 2011, p. 253). These findings are well-aligned with trends in the for-profit context (Den Hartog et al., 2004).

As a second step, we engaged in an inductive analysis of the 22 articles. We particularly looked for patterns across clusters and identified six distinct categories: Purpose of performance appraisals, design and implementation of performance management and performance appraisals, integration into the organizational context, personal characteristics and manager/employee interactions, individual perceptions, and individual and organizational outcomes. Based on these categories, we developed a model of performance management in nonprofit organizations. As shown in Figure 14.1, some of these categories operate at the individual level, some at the organizational level, and one (outcomes) on both levels. We discuss the individual parts of the model and the relationship between the six categories below.

Purpose of Performance Appraisals

Starting on the upper right-hand side of the model, we identified that a variety of studies focused on the purposes of performance appraisals as a management tool (Curran, 2002). Oftentimes, performance appraisals are implemented because they serve individual as well as organizational level purposes. Individual level purposes centered around increasing and sustaining employee motivation (Davenport & Gardiner, 2007; Ridder, Piening, et al., 2012), enabling employees to reflect on their work by making work expectations explicit (Millar, 1990) and through formal feedback (Ebrahim, 2005; Selden & Sowa, 2011), and increasing employee learning through development opportunities (Becker et al., 2011; Selden & Sowa, 2011). Moreover, appraisals afford employees the opportunity to influence their own job design (Potter & Smith, 2009; Walk et al., 2014) and provide them with the possibility to comment on performance results (Beem, 2001). Looking from an organizational standpoint, performance appraisals are also used to identify employee's training needs (Ridder, Piening, et al., 2012;

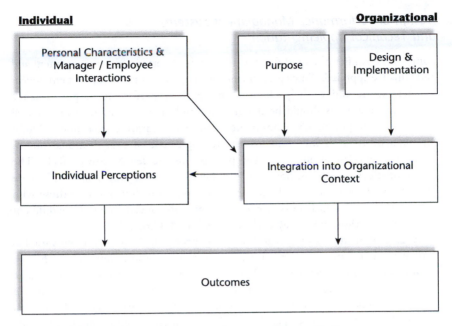

Figure 14.1   Performance management in nonprofit organizations

Robineau, Ohana, & Swaton, 2015), to improve employee job satisfaction (Ridder, Piening, et al., 2012), to reward employees for their performance (Deckop & Cirka, 2000; Millar, 1990; Potter & Smith, 2009; Selden & Sowa, 2011; Wiehe, 1981), to determine the continuation or discontinuation of employment (Deckop & Cirka, 2000; Millar, 1990; Rivas, 1984; Wiehe, 1981), and to function as a tool for quality control (Potter & Smith, 2009).

Some studies discussed the purposes of performance management and performance appraisals in relationship to strategic planning and organization development. For instance, performance appraisals were targeted to facilitate organizational learning (Ebrahim, 2005), to enhance organizational performance and to create a competitive advantage (Potter & Smith, 2009). Similarly, performance management was implemented to cope with rapid growth and to ensure greater accountability (Becker et al., 2011).

While the reasons for implementing performance management systems were diverse, the overall aim was to facilitate organizational success, while being cognizant about the individual employee needs, the potential positive outcomes that performance management has for them and, ultimately, for the organization. Depending on the purpose, organizations might integrate performance management systems differently into the organizational strategy (see below).

Design of Performance Management Systems and Technical Implementation

Some of the studies discussed the specific design of performance management and performance appraisals. Since performance management aims to support employees in their work and to help them improve their performance, performance management systems should be designed around employee motivations as well as factors that potentially demotivate them (Davenport & Gardiner, 2007). Simultaneously, it is important to ensure alignment of organizational intent, managerial enactment and employee perceptions (Selden & Sowa, 2011). The design of effective systems, however, is difficult as human judgments and bias are likely to produce results that do not accurately reflect reality and since those who are evaluating individual performance (most often managers) tend to have different motivations as those who they evaluate (Deckop & Cirka, 2000).

A handful of studies addressed the specific procedures and instruments used as part of the performance appraisal process pointing to the importance of having reliable and valid instruments in place that are able to differentiate performance levels properly (Millar, 1990; Pecora & Hunter, 1988; Wiehe, 1981). Some of the older publications discussed the advantages and disadvantages of (behavioral vs. trait-based) rating scales, checklists, and result-oriented approaches that provide the reader with a toolkit and "how to" advice (Millar, 1990; Pecora & Hunter, 1988). Newer studies continue to mention rating scales as effective tools and the importance of having reliable and valid instruments in place (Becker et al., 2011; Potter & Smith, 2009), but the emphasis lies on the importance of collecting data from co-workers for a more holistic evaluation (Potter & Smith, 2009). Aligned with the trend to a more holistic and process-oriented performance management approach, it seems that the nonprofit field has moved from a rather technical stage to an integrated phase that emphasizes the importance of alignment with and integration into the organizational strategy. Overall, it is expected that the design and implementation of performance management systems impact how these are integrated into the organizational context (see Figure 14.1).

Personal Characteristics and Manager/Employee Interactions

Switching to the left-hand side of the model, an area that has received considerable attention among the reviewed papers are the individual characteristics of managers and employees as well as the interactions between managers and employees that serve as a precondition for successful performance management. Employee intrinsic motivation is the most salient personal characteristic and related to fairness perceptions of (Deckop & Cirka, 2000) and positive attitudes toward (Helmig et al., 2008) performance appraisals. To increase the performance appraisal and performance management experience, managers' skills have been identified as another important predictor (Davenport & Gardiner, 2007). Particularly, their communication skills and goal-setting strategies ensure proper implementation of performance management systems (Curran, 2002; Davenport & Gardiner, 2007; Potter & Smith, 2009). As both managers and employees engage in the performance management process, a considerable amount of studies have looked at the relationship and interaction between these two groups. Employees indicate a more positive evaluation of performance appraisals if they have the opportunity to evaluate their leaders (Helmig et al., 2008), if the communication between managers and employees is open (Becker et al., 2011; Curran, 2002; Pecora & Hunter, 1988), and if feedback occurs in regular intervals (Becker et al., 2011; Curran, 2002).

The employee-manager relationship seems to be key when looking at the quality of performance appraisals, whereby this relationship is not unidirectional but works in both directions. Ultimately, it is expected that personal characteristics as well as manager-employee interactions impact the individual perceptions of performance management and influence how these systems are integrated into the organizational context.

Individual Perceptions Toward Performance Appraisals/Performance Management

Mirroring previous research in the for-profit context (Farndale & Kelliher, 2013; Kuvaas, 2008; Nishii et al., 2008; Nishii & Wright, 2008), employee and manager perceptions of the performance appraisal process have received some attention in the nonprofit context as well. Positive attitudes toward performance appraisals are generally related to individual and organizational level antecedents as well as outcomes (Helmig et al., 2008). These relationships are particularly salient if employees perceive possibilities for personal growth (Helmig et al., 2008), if they are satisfied with how they were treated during performance appraisals (Becker et al., 2011; Curran, 2002), and if this treatment is perceived to be fair (Deckop & Cirka, 2000; Helmig et al., 2008). Otherwise feelings of discomfort, anxiety, dislike, and hate are likely to surface among managers and employees alike (Becker et al., 2011; Curran, 2002; Millar, 1990; Wiehe, 1981) potentially leading to active resistance to the performance appraisal process (Rivas, 1984). Whereas these feelings are common among both managers and employees, Helmig et al. (2008) find that managers tend to be more positive toward performance appraisal systems as compared to their employees. Managers in other studies, however, tend to be concerned about the additional time commitment that a thorough performance appraisal process constitutes (Becker et al., 2011; Deckop & Cirka, 2000). Corresponding to Nishii and Wright (2008), nonprofit scholars observed differences between employee and managerial perceptions of performance management tools (Beem, 2001; Selden & Sowa, 2011). Following Ridder, McCandless Baluch, et al. (2012), it is likely that employee perceptions will subsequently influence organizational level outcomes, and, therefore, indicate the importance of paying attention to employee and manager perceptions of performance management systems.

Integration into Organizational Context

The role of performance appraisals and/or performance management in relation to the wider organizational context has also attracted some recent research attention and can be divided into operational and strategic aspects. Operational aspects that are essential on a day-to-day basis include transparent communication of the performance appraisal goals and the process of performance assessment (Helmig et al., 2008), possibilities for employee participation in the process (Davenport & Gardiner, 2007), and the buy-in of senior management and immediate managers into the goals and processes (Becker et al., 2011). However, scholars caution the feasibility of these aspects as there might be other, more immediate, issues that require managerial attention besides performance management, especially if it is not tightly integrated into the strategy of the organization (Selden & Sowa, 2011).

Strategic aspects have a long-term focus and aim toward a consistent integration of performance management into the organizational strategy. An alignment to the organizational mission and culture is especially important; scholars particularly emphasize the driving force of the mission, which oftentimes serves as a guide for the development of performance management practices (Becker et al., 2011; Curran, 2002). Some studies refer to the specific integration into strategic human resource management (Guo et al., 2011; Ridder, McCandless Baluch, et al., 2012; Rodwell & Teo, 2004, 2008) or high performance work systems (Robineau et al., 2015; Selden & Sowa, 2015), while highlighting the fit between the HR function and the organizational strategy. For instance, Guo and colleagues (2011) propose a strategic HRM Index consisting of 13 core HR practices. Performance management was reflected in two of these practices through the evaluation of employees through multiple performance assessment strategies and the provision of opportunities for systematic employee feedback. When surveying 229 nonprofit organizations, the authors, however, find that performance management related practices were less likely to be implemented in practice than others (i.e., using the organizational mission to attract employees). Studies looking at performance management as a stand-alone practice emphasize a similar fit to the organizational strategy (e.g., through strategic planning) to achieve competitive advantage (Becker et al., 2011; Curran, 2002; Davenport & Gardiner, 2007). The research evidence in the nonprofit field to date points to the importance of an integration of performance management into the organizational strategy in order to provide it with legitimacy and to emphasize the long-term focus needed to achieve sustained organizational performance.

As indicated earlier, performance appraisals fulfill a variety of purposes. These purposes might vary in their implementation depending on the underlying HR architecture in nonprofit organizations. HR architecture is defined as a coherent human resource management system consisting of internally consistent practices (Becker & Huselid, 2006). Four prevalent types have been identified in the nonprofit context: administrative, motivational, strategic, and values-based (Ridder & McCandless, 2010). Nonprofits applying an administrative HR approach tend not to implement performance appraisals (Ridder, McCandless Baluch, et al., 2012); those nonprofits with a motivational approach to HR use performance appraisals as a tool to identify employee needs and to increase employee motivation (Ridder, Piening, et al., 2012), organizations with a more strategic orientation towards HR tend to conceptualize performance appraisals as strategic investment (Ridder, Piening, et al., 2012), and organizations with a values-based approach align performance appraisals with other HR practices to form specific bundles that will help to achieve the organizational mission.

Given this evidence, the specific HR architecture influences the value given to performance appraisals and, thus, impacts individual and organizational level outcomes (as discussed below). Ultimately, then, the particular use of performance appraisals along with other HR practices leads to differences in both individual and organizational performance (Ridder, Piening, et al., 2012). Therefore, it is important for organizations to be reflective about the individual HR practices offered as part of their HR architecture and the influence on subsequent outcomes.

Outcomes

A fair number of studies investigated the relationship between performance management/performance appraisals and subsequent outcomes. Besides serving as an antecedent, employee intrinsic motivation has also been identified as an individual-level outcome (Davenport & Gardiner, 2007; Millar, 1990; Potter & Smith, 2009). In particular, motivation is likely to increase if employees hold positive attitudes toward performance appraisals (Helmig et al., 2008) and if the process is perceived to be fair (Deckop & Cirka, 2000). Employee retention and voluntary turnover form a second category that received considerable research attention. Findings, however, are inconclusive. Selden and Sowa (2011) find a significant relationship between employees' perceptions of the performance management process and intentions to stay as well as levels of voluntary turnover in the organization. Similarly, Becker et al. (2011) identify increased levels of turnover for dissatisfied employees after a new performance management system was initially implemented. Contrary, Selden and Sowa (2015) find no relationship between performance appraisals and voluntary turnover, but caution the importance of the quality of implementation and the influential role of employee perceptions during the appraisal process. Scholars have also focused on increases in individual and organizational performance (Becker et al., 2011; Rodwell & Teo, 2004, 2008). For instance, data collected from nonprofit executives indicate a positive relationship between perceptions of performance appraisals and organizational performance (Rodwell & Teo, 2004, 2008). Scholars also identify links to other outcomes such as organizational commitment and quality of collaboration with colleagues (Helmig et al., 2008), job satisfaction, enjoyment of work, job commitment, and intentions to stay (Selden & Sowa, 2011), as well as less uncertainty and more collaborative problem solving (Potter & Smith, 2009).

Conclusion

Our aim in completing this review was to contribute to a better understanding of the current research on performance management and performance appraisals in the nonprofit context. We searched the literature and identified 22 articles published in academic journals over a time span of 35 years (1980–2015). First, we noticed that the articles fell into four distinct sets: (1) those focusing on performance appraisals as a stand-alone technique; (2) those looking at performance management as strategic tool to assess employee performance; (3) those integrating performance appraisals into human resource management strategies; and (4) those whose main focus was not on performance appraisals/performance management but discussed aspects pertaining to either in relationship to other organizational constructs. In a subsequent step, we inductively reviewed all articles. By going back and forth between the articles, we identified six categories: Purpose of performance appraisals, design and implementation of performance management and performance appraisals, personal characteristics and manager/employee interactions, integration into the organizational context, individual perceptions, and individual and organizational outcomes. Based on these categories, we built a model that illustrates the relationship between these categories (see Figure 14.1) as emerging from the articles and provides an overview of the current research on performance management/performance appraisals in the nonprofit context.

We particularly want to highlight two findings. First, over time, performance appraisals have become more integrated into performance management or human resource management strategies. Whereas some earlier works focused on practical aspects of performance appraisals ("how to do it?"), most of the more contemporary research focuses on performance appraisals in relation to distinct sets of antecedents and outcomes ("what is the significance?"). Second, this review shows that the individual actors (employees, managers) and their interactions as well as the organizational context are important determinants of individual perceptions of performance appraisals and performance management systems. Operating on multiple levels, it seems, requires multilevel approaches to the study of performance management and performance appraisals.

A few other observations are worthy of elaboration. Given the number of research articles that we discarded during the analysis phase (n = 86), we can say that performance management—at least how we conceptualize it in this chapter— is not a widely researched field in the nonprofit context. When discarding articles that did not fit our definition of performance management, we realized that there is no uniform way in which the term performance management is used in the nonprofit research literature yet. For instance, performance management was used in relationship to organizational performance, effectiveness and account- ability; concepts that mainly operate on the organizational level. Here, scholars defined performance management as "a specification of the processes that gener- ate firm performance and hence a specification of how management decisions can control firm performance" (Speckbacher, 2003, p. 268). We also noticed the language that scholars used in the articles originates in the for-profit context (e.g., inputs, accountability, effectiveness, efficiency, strategy). As such, research in performance management follows the overall trend of mirroring policies and procedures of for-profit companies (Maier, Meyer, & Steinbereithner, 2014). The trend of becoming more businesslike might be eventually harmful to nonprofits' ability to efficiently and effectively provide services while still maintaining a bond to civil society (Eikenberry & Kluver, 2004).

As indicated earlier, the relationship between employees and their managers seems to influence the perceptions of performance appraisals and the evaluations thereof. But the relationship between managers and employees is by no means unidirectional, since employees value being able to evaluate their manager (Helmig et al., 2008). Therefore it is striking that the nonprofit literature to date is relatively silent when describing the characteristics of the two-way relationship between leaders and followers, or the quality of leader-member exchange (LMX), a construct that is widely researched in the for-profit context (Graen & Uhl-Bien, 1995). Similarly, with the exception of Deckop and Cirka (2000), perceptions of justice and trust between managers and employees have not been the center of attention in the nonprofit research on performance appraisals, but have been widely discussed in the for-profit context (Erdogan, 2003). These would be important areas for future research (especially focussing on the leader-follower dyad) that nonprofit scholars might want to consider.

A variety of research methodologies were applied across the 22 papers (see Table 14.1). Six papers were conceptual in nature, 5 were qualitative, 7 used quantitative methodologies and 4 studies were based on mixed methods. We noticed several shortcomings across methodological categories. For instance, some of the qualitative papers do not adequately report data collection procedures and data analysis strategies. The quantitative papers tend to base their findings on small sample sizes (range: 22–228), achieve varying, mostly low, response rates (range: 18%–42%), use scales with questionable psychometric properties (e.g., low reliability) and most of the research uses only one source of data for information gathering. Moreover, it was surprising to notice that only one study was based on longitudinal research (Deckop & Cirka, 2000), even though most of the scholars claim causal effects between performance appraisals and/or performance management and individual and/or organizational outcomes. Furthermore, we were intrigued by the fact that there currently is no multilevel research on performance management in nonprofits, despite the importance of individual perceptions. Given the lack of methodological rigor, the lack of longitudinal research and multilevel approaches, we are currently not able to fully disentangle the causal mechanisms between antecedents, performance appraisals/performance management, and outcomes. Since performance management is mission critical and the "most important system link between employee performance and organizational performance" (Akingbola, 2015, p. 189), we echo others (Selden & Sowa, 2011) and conclude that there still is a lack of comprehensive research in the context of nonprofit organizations. Based on our evaluation, we especially encourage future research: (1) to replicate previous findings while ensuring the application of statistical and methodological rigor; (2) to utilize longitudinal research approaches; and (3) to specifically consider multilevel dynamics between employees and their manager within and across nonprofit organizations.

Future research could also investigate the differences in HR architecture in relationship to the implementation of performance appraisals, especially related to a potential variation within nonprofit subsectors and organizational size. Moreover, as we were not able to identify studies that looked at the prevalence of performance appraisal or performance management systems as currently used in the nonprofit sector, future studies might investigate the extent to which these practices are used and how they are implemented to help further clarify the importance in contemporary nonprofit practice.

Recent performance management scholarship in the for-profit context addressed the importance and feasibility of narrowing the gap between academic research and practice (Aguinis, 2009b). Aguinis (2009b) particularly argues that performance management systems can only be used effectively and efficiently by practitioners, if performance management is viewed as more than just an annual administrative necessity, but regarded in alignment with other HR strategies and the overall organizational goal. Similar to the for-profit context, performance management systems are rarely used in the nonprofit sector (Selden & Sowa, 2011; Walk et al., 2014) or fall behind in importance when comparing to other HR practices (Guo et al., 2011). Overall, we seem to know a lot about performance management/performance appraisal techniques from the general literature, but do not have a sufficient evidence base on how effective these are in the nonprofit context. An increased dialogue between nonprofit researchers and practitioners might help to find feasible approaches to implement and subsequently evaluate performance management systems.

Most nonprofit organizations are highly reliant on their workforce as they constitute the main potential for competitive advantage (Akingbola, 2006; Frumkin & Andre-Clark, 2000), scholars and practitioners might therefore put more attention to performance management as it relates to providing employees with a supportive structure that allows them to contribute their full potential to the organization. However, even though we acknowledge the benefits of performance management, we would like to caution that over-engineering of job roles and responsibilities might limit individuals' autonomy in the workplace (Schwartz, 2015), thus, potentially inhibiting proactive employee behavior (Wrzesniewski & Dutton, 2001).

Discussion Questions

1 Have you had experiences with performance appraisals? How would you evaluate these?
2 Given that nonprofit employees are predominantly motivated intrinsically, what would be good incentives in your opinion?

3   How can nonprofit organizations ensure that employees perceive performance management systems in general and performance appraisals in particular as beneficial and valuable tools and not just as another requirement dictated by HR?

References

*part of the review sample.

Aguinis, H. (2009a). *Performance management*: Pearson Prentice Hall Upper Saddle River, NJ.

Aguinis, H. (2009b). An expanded view of performance management. In J. Smither & M. London (Eds.), *Performance management: Putting research into action* (pp. 1–43). San Francisco: Jossey-Bass.

Aguinis, H., Joo, H., & Gottfredson, R. K. (2011). Why we hate performance management—And why we should love it. *Business Horizons, 54*(6), 503–507.

Akingbola, K. (2006). Strategy and HRM in nonprofit organizations: Evidence from Canada. *International Journal of Human Resource Management, 17*(10), 1707–1725.

Akingbola, K. (2015). *Managing human resources for nonprofits*. London: Routledge.

Becker, B. E. & Huselid, M. A. (2006). Strategic human resources management: Where Do we go from here? *Journal of Management, 32*, 898–925.

*Becker, K., Antuar, N., & Everett, C. (2011). Implementing an employee performance management system in a nonprofit organization. *Nonprofit Management & Leadership, 21*(3), 255–271.

*Beem, M. J. (2001). Fundraising in the balance: An analysis of job performance, appraisals and rewards. *International Journal of Nonprofit and Voluntary Sector Marketing, 6*(2), 164–171.

Cawley, B. D., Keeping, L. M., & Levy, P. E. (1998). Participation in the performance appraisal process and employee reactions: A meta-analytic review of field investigations. *Journal of Applied Psychology, 83*(4), 615–633.

*Curran, C. (2002). Performance management: A help or a burden to nonprofits. *Journal for Nonprofit Management, 6*(1).

*Davenport, J. & Gardiner, P. D. (2007). Performance management in the not-for-profit sector with reference to the National Trust for Scotland. *Total Quality Management & Business Excellence, 18*(3), 303–311.

*Deckop, J. R. & Cirka, C. C. (2000). The risk and reward of a double-edgedsword: Effects of a merit payprogram on intrinsic motivation. *Nonprofit and Voluntary Sector Quarterly, 29*(3), 400–418.

Den Hartog, D. N., Boselie, P., & Paauwe, J. (2004). Performance management: A model and research agenda. *Applied Psychology, 53*(4), 556–569.

Devanna, M. A., Fombrun, C. J., & Tichy, N. M. (1984). A framework for strategic human resource management. In N. M. Tichy, C. J. Fombrun, & M. A. Devanna (Eds.), *Strategic human resource management* (pp. 33–55). New York: Wiley.

Devaro, J. & Brookshire, D. (2007). Promotions and incentives in nonprofit and for-profit organizations. *Industrial & Labor Relations Review, 60*(3), 311–339.

*Ebrahim, A. (2005). Accountability myopia: Losing sight of organizational learning. *Nonprofit and Voluntary Sector Quarterly, 34*(1), 56–87.

Eikenberry, A. M. & Kluver, J. D. (2004). The marketization of the nonprofit sector: Civil society at risk? *Public Administration Review, 64*(2), 132–140.

Erdogan, B. (2003). Antecedents and consequences of justice perceptions in performance appraisals. *Human Resource Management Review, 12*(4), 555–578.

Farndale, E. & Kelliher, C. (2013). Implementing performance appraisal: Exploring the employee experience. *Human Resource Management, 52*(6), 879–897.

Fletcher, C. & Perry, E. L. (2002). Performance appraisal and feedback: A consideration of national culture and a review of contemporary research and future trends. In. N. Anderson, D. S. Ones, H. K. Sinangil, & C. Viswesvaran (Eds.), *Handbook of industrial, work and organizational psychology, Volume 1: Personnel psychology* (pp. 127–144). Thousand Oaks, CA: Sage Publications Ltd.

Frumkin, P. & Andre-Clark, A. (2000). When missions, markets, and politics collide: Values and strategy in the nonprofit human services. *Nonprofit and Voluntary Sector Quarterly, 29*, 141–163.

Graen, G. B. & Uhl-Bien, M. (1995). Relationship-based approach to leadership: Development of leader-member exchange (LMX) theory of leadership over 25 years: Applying a multi-level multi-domain perspective. *The Leadership Quarterly, 6*(2), 219–247.

★Guo, C., Brown, W., Ashcraft, R., Yoshioka, C. F., & Dong, D. (2011). Strategic human resource management in nonprofit organizations. *Review of Public Personnel Administration, 31*, 248–269.

★Helmig, B., Michalski, S., & Lauper, P. (2008). Performance management in public & nonprofit Organisationen. Empirische Ergebnisse zum Teilaspekt Performance Appraisal. *Zeitschrift für Personalforschung/German Journal of Research in Human Resource Management, 22*(1), 58–82.

Kuvaas, B. (2008). An exploration of how the employee-organization relationship affects the linkage between perception of developmental human resource practices and employee outcomes. *Journal of Management Studies, 45*(1), 1-25.

Lee, C. (2006). Feedback, not appraisal. *HRMagazine, 51*(11), 111–115.

Levy, P. E. & Williams, J. R. (2004). The social context of performance appraisal: A review and framework for the future. *Journal of Management, 30*(6), 881–905.

Maier, F., Meyer, M., & Steinbereithner, M. (2014). Nonprofit organizations becoming business-like a systematic review. *Nonprofit and Voluntary Sector Quarterly*, 0899764014561796.

★Millar, K. I. (1990). Performance appraisal of professional social workers. *Administration in Social Work, 14*(1), 65–85.

Nishii, L. H., Lepak, D. P., & Schneider, B. (2008). Employee attributions of the "why" of HR practices: Their effects on employee attitudes and behaviors, and customer satisfaction. *Personnel Psychology, 61*, 503–545.

Nishii, L. H. & Wright, P. (2008). Variability within organizations: Implications for strategic human resource management. In D. B. Smith (Ed.), *The people make the place: Dynamic linkages between individuals and organizations* (pp. 225–248). Boca Raton, FL: CRC Press.

★Packard, T. (2010). Staff perceptions of variables affecting performance in human service organizations. *Nonprofit and Voluntary Sector Quarterly, 39*(6), 971–990.

★Pecora, P. J. & Hunter, J. (1988). Performance appraisal in child welfare: Comparing the MBO and BARS methods. *Administration in Social Work, 12*(1), 55–72.

★Potter, J. A. & Smith, A. D. (2009). Performance appraisals and the strategic development of the professional intellect within non-profits. *International Journal of Management in Education, 3*(2), 188–203.

Pynes, J. E. (2013). *Human resources management for public and nonprofit organizations* (4th ed.). San Francisco: Jossey-Bass.

Ridder, H.-G. & McCandless, A. (2010). Influences on the Architecture of Human Resource Management in Nonprofit Organizations. *Nonprofit and Voluntary Sector Quarterly, 29*(1), 124–141.

*Ridder, H.-G., McCandless Baluch, A., & Piening, E. P. (2012). The whole is more than the sum of its parts? How HRM is configured in nonprofit organizations and why it matters. *Human Resource Management Review, 22,* 1–14.

*Ridder, H.-G., Piening, E. P., & McCandless Baluch, A. (2012). The third way reconfigured: How and why nonprofit organizations are shifting their human resource management. *Voluntas: International Journal of Voluntary and Nonprofit Organizations, 23,* 605–635.

*Rivas, R. F. (1984). Perspectives on dismissal as a management prerogative in social service organizations. *Administration in Social Work, 8*(4), 77–92.

Roberts, G. E. (2003). Employee performance appraisal system participation: A technique that works. *Public Personnel Management, 32*(1), 89–98.

*Robineau, A., Ohana, M., & Swaton, S. (2015). The challenges of implementing high performance work practices in the nonprofit sector. *Journal of Applied Business Research (JABR), 31*(1), 103–114.

*Rodwell, J. J. & Teo, S. T. (2004). Strategic HRM in for-profit and non-profit organizations in a knowledge-intensive industry. *Public Management Review, 6*(3), 311–331.

*Rodwell, J. J. & Teo, S. T. (2008). The influence of strategic HRM and sector on perceived performance in health service organizations. *International Journal of Human Resource Management, 19*(10), 1825–1841.

Schwartz, B. (2015). *Why we work.* New York: Simon & Schuster.

*Selden, S. C. & Sowa, J. E. (2011). Performance management and appraisal in human service organizations: Management and staff perspectives. *Public Personnel Management, 40*(3), 251–264.

*Selden, S. C. & Sowa, J. E. (2015). Voluntary turnover in nonprofit human service organizations: The impact of high performance work practices. *Human Service Organizations: Management, Leadership & Governance, 39*(3), 182–207.

Speckbacher, G. (2003). The economics of performance management in nonprofit organizations. *Nonprofit Management & Leadership, 13*(3), 267–281.

Thomas, S. L. & Bretz Jr, R. D. (1994). Research and practice in performance appraisal: Evaluating employee performance in America's largest companies. *SAM Advanced Management Journal, 59*(2), 28.

Twomey, D. F. & Feuerbach Twomey, R. (1992). Assessing and transforming performance appraisal. *Journal of Managerial Psychology, 7*(3), 23–32.

*Walk, M., Schinnenburg, H., & Handy, F. (2014). Missing in action: strategic human resource management in german nonprofits. *Voluntas: International Journal of Voluntary and Nonprofit Organizations, 25,* 991–1021.

*Wiehe, V. R. (1981). Current practices in performance appraisal. *Administration in Social Work, 4*(3), 1–11.

Wrzesniewski, A. & Dutton, J. E. (2001). Crafting a job: Revisioning employees as active crafters of their work. *Academy of Management Review, 26*(2), 179–201.

Part III

Emergent Challenges in Nonprofit Human Resource Management

15

Interchangeability of Labor

Managing a Mixed Paid and Volunteer Workforce

Allison R. Russell, Laurie Mook, and Femida Handy

Introduction

A strong tradition of volunteerism is one of the defining characteristics of the nonprofit sector. Nonprofit organizations are more likely than other organizations to recruit and utilize volunteers, often alongside paid staff. But the involvement of volunteers brings about a unique set of human resource management challenges and raises questions about the best way to manage a diverse paid and unpaid workforce. How should an organization go about finding the optimal balance of paid and volunteer employees? Which tasks should be delegated to volunteers, and which reserved for paid staff? How can nonprofit managers foster positive and productive relationships and avoid conflict between paid staff and volunteers? In times of financial hardship, tensions can arise if paid staff see themselves being replaced by volunteers; when, if at all, is such replacement optimal?

The answers to these questions vary considerably by country, by service domain, and by organizational characteristics. Although many types of nonprofit organizations involve volunteers, from hospitals to human services, from arts to advocacy, organizations utilize volunteer hours differently in the production and delivery of their services. The number of hours contributed by volunteers, and the types of tasks reserved for them, are dynamic and often undefined—or, perhaps, defined too broadly (Handy, Cnaan, Brudney, Ascoli, Meijs, & Ranade, 2000). In some organizations, volunteers take on a central role as essential personnel, delivering services to clients and serving in managerial roles, while in others, volunteers support the work of paid staff. Most nonprofits rely on volunteers for governance. For example, in the United States and Canada, nonprofits are required to make use of a voluntary board of directors for governance as a condition of getting nonprofit status. But the function of the board members fluctuates greatly from organization to organization in terms of time commitment, involvement in other organizational activities, and interactions with paid staff. Some boards are hands on, while others meet at regular intervals and make policy decisions only. Regardless of these differences, nonprofit organizations that choose to utilize paid staff and volunteers face the challenge of managing volunteer-paid staff interchangeability, and of deciding how to optimize their workforce.

This chapter focuses on the topic of volunteer-paid staff interchangeability in the context of nonprofit human resource management (HRM). In reviewing the extant literature, this chapter both describes the factors that influence the development of a mixed nonprofit labor force and highlights some common challenges nonprofit managers face in managing their diverse human resources.

The Economics of the Nonprofit Labor Force

Why Have a Volunteer Workforce? The Legacy of Volunteerism in the Nonprofit Sector

According to the Corporation for National and Community Service, roughly one quarter of the adult population in the United States volunteers at least once per year (Corporation for National and Community Service, 2013). In Canada, this rate is approximately 44% of the adult population, as reported by the 2013 General Social Survey on Giving, Volunteering, and Participating (Turcotte, 2015). Often, volunteers are called upon specifically in times of financial hardship to fill a critical gap in the organization, performing daily administrative and programmatic tasks required to keep the organization open. But in many cases, volunteers fulfill roles that would be inappropriate or not feasible for paid staff, such as serving on boards of directors, acting as mentors to youth, visiting with the elderly in hospitals and nursing homes, and many others (Ellis, 2010; National Council of Nonprofits, 2016). Although cost considerations is one of the most frequently cited reasons for continuing to involve volunteers, nonprofits find volunteers valuable in other ways as well; for example, volunteers act as a link between the organization and the community that it exists to serve or as a signal of the nonprofit's legitimacy (Pynes, 2011). For some nonprofits, the social networks and community ties forged by their employment of volunteers can be just as valuable to their missions as the possibility of cost savings as found in a study of hospital volunteers (Handy & Srinivasan, 2005).

Because they do not get paid for their labor, volunteers are often thought of as "free." However, nonprofit organizations incur several costs as a result of their use of volunteers, including administrative costs, recruiting and training costs, and the cost of space and materials devoted to volunteer tasks (Mook & Handy, 2011). Likewise, volunteers also face costs as a result of their decision to volunteer, including transportation, childcare, and the opportunity cost of foregone earnings or leisure time. Thus, as Handy and Brudney (2007) point out, "Volunteer labor is best used when the net-benefits of using volunteer labor are positive to the organization, and the net-costs to the volunteer are minimized" (p. 2).

The costs and relative productivity of volunteers as compared with paid labor vary according to the type of volunteering utilized by the organization, from service learning or mandated volunteering; short-term or episodic volunteering; virtual volunteering; and long-term or traditional volunteering (Handy & Brudney, 2007). Decisions about how many and which type of volunteers to involve in organizational activities must therefore be weighed carefully by non-profit managers looking to maximize the benefits of their volunteer programs and minimize the overall costs of production both to the organization and to the volunteers.

What Is Interchangeability?

Interchangeability refers to the extent to which nonprofit organizations exchange paid and unpaid labor in their workforce. The degree of interchangeability in a given organization depends on various considerations, such as mission of the organization, management strategies, cost of operations, and workplace regulations regarding the use of volunteers (Handy, Mook, & Quarter, 2008). As these considerations fluctuate over time, the optimal mix of paid and unpaid employees will also change. Ultimately, it is a question of economics: "The use of labor, volunteer or paid, will depend on its productivity, its price, and other available substitutes . . . . Organizations will eschew volunteer labor as its price increases . . . and turn to substitute inputs with lower prices" (Handy, Mook, & Quarter, 2008, p. 2). Thus, the concept of interchangeability introduces a much greater degree of complexity to nonprofits' decisions to employ volunteers than the classic characterization of volunteer labor as "free" would imply.

In many cases, nonprofit organizations choose to substitute volunteers for paid staff, such as in times of financial constraints. However, they may also choose to substitute paid staff for volunteers in an effort to professionalize their labor force (Handy et al., 2008; Lipsky & Smith, 1993). But interchangeability does not refer only to a decision by nonprofit organizations to replace paid staff with volunteers, or vice versa, based on cost considerations. As volunteers can be either substitutes for or complements to paid staff, interchangeability may also involve more complex and nuanced decisions about how to structure the workforce of an organization to support the continued presence of volunteer employees whose work plays a unique but integral role in the day-to-day operations of the organization. For example, hospital volunteers perform a distinct function that is separate from—but also complementary to—the work of paid staff; these volunteers cannot be interchanged easily, but are integral to service delivery (Handy & Srinivasan, 2005; Hotchkiss, Fottler, & Unruh, 2009). A study conducted by Haski-Leventhal, Hustinx, and Handy (2011) at Ronald McDonald House also found volunteers took on several specific roles that supported, but did not supplant, the work of paid co-workers, and in the absence of volunteers, the

273

services, such as their "guest chef" program, were not offered through replacement by paid staff.

Thus, an examination of the phenomenon of interchangeability, and any efforts to optimize the mixture of paid and unpaid staff in an organization, must consider that the two do not always serve as perfect substitutes in every case. Handy et al. (2008) highlight in their work that it is an open question whether volunteers substitute for or complement paid staff, and to discern this relationship, consideration must be paid to the nature of the service, the organization's mission, union regulations, and other factors.

Modeling Interchangeability: A Look at the Existing Literature

Recognizing the practical importance and complexities of managing a mixed workforce, scholars have begun to explore the factors that contribute to the interchangeability of paid and unpaid staff in nonprofit organizations. In a survey of over 600 Canadian nonprofits, Handy et al. (2008) found that interchangeability between volunteers and paid staff was not unidirectional and in some cases happened in both directions in the same organization, at the same time. For example, 25% of organizations surveyed reported volunteers replacing paid staff, and over 50% indicated paid staff had replaced volunteers. The former case occurred primarily as a result of budget cuts and fiscal constraints, whereas the latter case arose when a growth in funding enabled professionalization of the staff—a trend the authors found carried over not only to paid staff but also to volunteers, who were called upon to perform increasingly complex and sophisticated roles as the organization professionalized. Organizations reporting interchangeability in both directions offer evidence to suggest some nonprofits switch back and forth between volunteers and paid staff, indicating the two types of labor may be complementary of one another in certain settings. The authors used two case studies of Canadian hospitals to corroborate these findings; however, although about 68% of nonprofits indicated some interchangeability took place, they also reported the phenomenon pertained to only about 12% of all organizational tasks.

To test the generalizability of Handy et al. (2008), Chum, Mook, Handy, Schugurensky, and Quarter (2013) conducted a second survey of over 800 Canadian nonprofits employing both volunteers and paid staff to examine the extent and direction of interchangeability between paid staff and volunteers. Overall, 80% of respondents reported some degree of interchangeability. As consistent with prior findings, the authors found evidence that interchangeability occurs in both directions, with 29% of organizations surveyed reporting replacement of volunteers with paid staff, and 22% reporting replacement of paid staff with volunteers. Perhaps most importantly, Chum et al. (2013) found several variables act as significant predictors of the extent and direction of interchangeability, including organizational size, field of activity, and factors contributing to organizational stress. In the latter case, organizational stress can produce interchangeability in either direction: a shortage of paid employees, a sudden increase in new tasks, and cost considerations can all contribute to interchangeability from paid staff to volunteers, while a shortage of volunteers, budget fluctuations, and certification and skill levels required for task completion can lead to interchangeability from volunteers to paid staff. Moreover, the authors found that increasing workloads due to organizational growth contributed to interchangeability in either direction, suggesting the direction and extent of interchangeability depend significantly on each organization's specific approach to human resource management in times of transition or stress (Chum et al., 2013).

In examining the phenomenon of interchangeability, the organizational perspective is overwhelmingly the focal point of scholarship. However, in an effort to understand more fully the nature of interchangeability at the individual level occurring in both nonprofit organizations and other sectors, Mook and her colleagues (2014) randomly surveyed 2,100 Canadian volunteers to obtain their perspectives on whether or not they had replaced, or were replaced by, paid staff in their host organizations. Findings suggest about 11% of volunteers surveyed had replaced paid staff, while almost 8% reported being replaced by paid staff. Volunteers infrequently reported a permanent replacement, with only 3% indicating they had permanently replaced a paid staff member, and only 2% reporting a paid staff member had permanently replaced them. Responses on interchangeability were influenced somewhat by the service domain of the organization, the size of the organization, and the skill level of the volunteers. For instance, the authors found that larger organizations (with more than 50 paid staff) were less likely than smaller organizations to replace paid staff with volunteers, and that organizations in the domain of health services were the least likely to replace volunteers with paid staff. Additionally, Mook et al. (2014) noted that higher-skilled volunteers were more likely to report replacing paid staff and vice versa, suggesting skill level may influence the extent of interchangeability between paid and unpaid employees. Overall, their findings were consistent with those of previous studies (Chum et al., 2013; Handy et al., 2008). The authors write:

> [T]he fact that both of these practices [i.e. interchangeability in both directions] were reported and not at dissimilar rates may suggest that nonprofit organizations, in particular, view their human resources, whether paid or unpaid, as interchangeable, and move these human resource components about according to organizational need.
>
> *(Mook et al., 2014, p. 81)*

Both Chum et al. (2013) and Mook et al. (2014) identified religious organizations as examples of nonprofits with high levels of interchangeability in both directions. A study of the roles of paid staff and volunteers in faith-based programs carried out by Netting, O'Connor, Thomas, and Yancey (2005) provides additional evidence. According to Netting et al. (2005), a shared faith and commitment to a religious mission contributed to frequent and significant overlap between the roles of volunteers and the roles of paid staff among the organizations surveyed. Likewise, they report a high instance of internal interchangeability, as many volunteers later assume paid positions in the agency. The authors conclude, "We are discovering that [in these cases] it is almost impossible to separate out paid staff and volunteer roles" (Netting et al., 2005, p. 199). It is possible that the relatively small size of many religious organizations may also contribute to the higher rates of interchangeability described in these studies (Chum et al., 2013; Mook et al., 2014). This indicates that certain factors such as the mission of the organization, and the size of the organization, and the nature of the services provided influence the rates of interchangeability, nevertheless, the potential for interchangeability imposes a complexity of human resource management unseen in organizations that use only paid labor or only volunteers.

Optimizing the Nonprofit Labor Force: Determining Nonprofit Demand for Volunteers

Because many nonprofit organizations utilize both paid and unpaid labor, nonprofit human resource management involves complex decisions about how to manage a diverse workforce, and how to ensure all staff—whether paid or volunteer—contribute to the mission of the organization. These decisions relate in part to the economics of interchangeability, and the question of how many volunteers and paid staff to recruit to maximize production of services. The answer to this question depends on a variety of factors and considerations that are particular to each organization. As a result, we still lack a principle for optimizing the levels of paid staff and volunteers in an organization.

Nevertheless, a growing body of literature has begun to look at the composition of the nonprofit labor force from the lens of economics, and from the perspective of the organizations themselves. In the past, the framing of nonprofit demand for volunteer labor was oversimplified, with the implication that because volunteer labor is a "cheap" alternative to paid labor, nonprofits will choose to take on as many volunteers as are offered or supplied in the market (Handy, Mook, & Quarter, 2006). If this assumption were true, then nonprofit demand for volunteer labor would equal the supply of volunteer labor available to them, determined by individuals who are willing to offer their time and talent as volunteers. This assumption also encouraged the literature to continue to focus on the volunteer supply perspective, and the conditions that encourage individuals to serve as volunteers in the nonprofit sector.

However, economists in the field of nonprofit studies began to take a closer look, and the resulting research "challenges the assumption that organizations are willing to use all the volunteer labor available to them" (Handy & Srinivasan, 2005, p. 1). As Emanuele (1996) argued, volunteer labor is not free, therefore nonprofit organizations will make choices about how many volunteers to use based on cost considerations, resulting in a "downward sloping demand curve for volunteer labor" (p. 195). This implies that the number of volunteers an organization uses will depend on the costs incurred to the organization for using volunteers. These costs involve recruiting; training, retaining, and rewarding their volunteers—in general costs involved in HRM for volunteers. These costs are not insignificant, if volunteers are not managed well or are unsatisfied they can vote with their feet and leave with little cost to themselves, but significant costs to the organization.

The higher the cost of volunteers to the organization, the fewer they will use, which is implicit in the downward slope of the demand curve. Using survey data from the Urban Institute's Nonprofit Sector Project, Emanuele (1996) found evidence to support the presence of a consistent, downward sloping demand curve for volunteer. This lends evidence to the fact that nonprofits' choices about how many (and which volunteers) to use depend on the costs of using volunteers and these costs are both direct and indirect costs; the latter can vary whether or not volunteers act as substitutes or complements for paid labor. In their review of economic research on volunteering, Govekar and Govekar (2002) highlight the findings from Emanuele (1996) and call for additional research on nonprofit demand for volunteers. The authors contextualize the issue in terms of welfare reform and the increasing prevalence of "third party government," that is, the provision of public goods and services by non-governmental organizations, especially nonprofits (Brinkerhoff, 2002, p. 19). Arguing for the importance of focusing on the challenges and choices nonprofit organizations face in determining the composition of their labor force, they write, "We cannot simply assume that nonprofit organizations will use all the volunteer labor that is available. If the government is going to transfer more responsibility to nonprofit organizations, it is important to understand the limits of such transfer" (Govekar & Govekar, 2002, p. 44).

Handy and Srinivasan (2005) investigated the question of nonprofit demand for volunteers more closely in a study of hospital volunteers. Using the work of Emanuele (1996) and others as a point of departure, the authors model the demand curve for volunteer labor. The costs of providing services include three critical factors: the productivity of volunteer labor, the cost of volunteer labor, and the cost of available substitutes for volunteer labor (i.e. paid labor). They write, "[W]e expect the utilization of volunteer labor to be positively influenced by its productivity and negatively influenced by its costs" (Handy & Srinivasan, 2005, p. 4). Thus, in cases where volunteers act as substitutes for paid labor, a nonprofit may choose to interchange paid staff for volunteers, or vice versa, depending on the relative costs of each input. The authors' empirical evidence supports the existence of the downward sloping demand curve for volunteer labor, but they also find that organizations' decisions to use volunteer labor is based on their belief that volunteers bring something unique to the table that may not be supplied by paid labor alone: a "link to their communities" (Handy & Srinivasan, 2005, p. 12). Again, these findings point to the complex relationship between the roles of paid and unpaid staff in nonprofit organizations, and offer insight into why nonprofits continue to use volunteer labor: Despite the challenges of managing a more diverse workforce, nonprofits also stand to gain greater perspective on the communities that they serve from working with volunteers who live within that community, in addition to the possibility of experiencing greater savings on the costs of labor inputs.

To continue to develop the model of nonprofit demand for volunteer labor, Handy, Mook, and Quarter (2006) expand the focus from one service area (hospitals) to a survey of 661 Canadian nonprofit organizations from various domains. They argue that because of the prevalence of volunteers, and the widespread historical legacy of volunteerism in the nonprofit sector, the decision about the type of labor to use—whether paid, unpaid, or some mixture of both—is a critical one faced by the majority of nonprofit organizations. The authors find not only that organizational age is a positive and important predictor of demand for volunteers but also that nonprofits utilizing volunteer labor do not view it as a simple substitute for paid labor. Instead, "they [nonprofit organizations] see positive indirect benefits over and above the direct tasks performed" by the volunteers and "are prepared to spend resources to manage them efficiently" by putting in place professional management for volunteer resources, just like they do for other human resources (Handy et al., 2006, p. 34–35). As nonprofits age and become more entrenched in the communities around them, they therefore may continue to seek out volunteer labor, and perhaps at an even higher rate than before, as increased financial stability makes it possible for them to hire volunteer managers and other staff to support their volunteer programs even more effectively.

As stated above, volunteer labor is not free, neither for the organization nor for the volunteer. Handy and Mook (2011) investigate the specific costs of volunteering from both the individual and organizational perspective and weigh these costs against the benefits of volunteering. They argue a cost-benefit analysis of volunteering is critical for organizations to make the most informed decisions about how much volunteer labor to utilize. Because organizational demand for volunteers is a function of the costs of volunteers and other factors (Handy & Srinivasan, 2005), both costs and benefits of volunteering should be considered to measure the cost of volunteer labor as an input in the production process. These costs and benefits will vary according to the roles volunteers perform and the type of volunteers utilized (Handy & Brudney, 2007). If the costs exceed the benefits of volunteering and if paid labor acts as a cheaper substitute for volunteer labor, then nonprofit organizations will be less likely to choose volunteer labor as an input.

Ultimately, nonprofit managers must make economic decisions about the best use of labor in their organizations. These decisions involve whether or not to use volunteer labor, how much volunteer labor to use, and the role of nonprofit labor in the organization. They also consider the relationship between volunteers and paid labor, and whether the two are complements, substitutes, or both, as well as the extent and direction of interchangeability. Taken together, these factors contribute to an understanding of how nonprofit human resources develop distinctly from other sectors. In the next section, we turn to a discussion of common challenges associated with interchanging paid and volunteer labor in the context of nonprofit human resource management, as it would be unwise to ignore the negative aspects of interchangeability, such as tensions that may arise between volunteers and paid labor.

Confronting the Challenges of Managing a Mixed Workforce: Interchangeability in the Context of Nonprofit Human Resource Management

Because so many nonprofit organizations use both volunteers and paid staff, many nonprofit managers will confront the challenges of managing a mixed workforce. These challenges could involve many aspects of human resource management, including team building, skills development, and employee motivation for both paid staff and volunteers. Other chapters in this volume describe many of these challenges in detail; in this section, we focus on the specific challenges that may confront organizations that engage in the interchange of paid staff and volunteers.

Volunteers and Paid Staff: Comrades or Competitors?

Interchangeability of paid and unpaid staff may provide nonprofit organizations with a flexible approach to human resource management (Mook et al., 2014). However, nonprofit managers should be aware of possible tensions between volunteers and paid staff, especially in organizations with frequent and high levels of interchangeability. Paid staff may view volunteers as potential competitors for their positions, and vice versa, resulting in an atmosphere of mistrust and compromising organizational goals. Likewise, in organizations with a strong union presence that also utilize volunteers, human resource managers may also be required to consider the legal implications of interchanging paid staff with volunteers (Handy et al., 2008). The limitations of what volunteers can and cannot do in unionized environments is often outlined in collective agreements.

Regarding paid staff perceptions of interchangeability, Brudney and Gazley (2002) reported no evidence of perceived antagonism or competition between paid staff and volunteers in a longitudinal study of the integration of the Service Corps of Retired Executives (i.e. volunteers) into the activities of the U.S. Small Business Administration. Although their study focused on a public sector agency, the findings challenge the assumption that an influx of volunteers will be viewed in an inherently negative manner by paid staff at existing agencies and programs. In the case examined by the authors, volunteers were looked at favorably by paid staff, and the longitudinal analysis showed that the volunteers' presence corresponded with a growth in paid employment in the agency (Brudney & Gazley, 2002, p. 549). Their findings indicate that in some scenarios, a growth in the volunteer workforce at an organization may contribute to a growth in overall employment—a net positive for both paid and unpaid staff.

From the volunteers' perspective, however, results have differed. For instance, Milligan and Fyfe (2005) reported feelings of concern among volunteers in local human service organizations in Glasgow, Scotland, who felt "pushed out" and "disempowered" by the increasing professionalization and bureaucratization of voluntary associations (pp. 427–428). In their study of volunteers' perceptions of interchangeability, Mook et al. (2014) reported about 18% of volunteers who had been replaced by paid staff on either a permanent or temporary basis felt their replacement was either unfair or very unfair. By contrast, only 7% of volunteers who reported they had replaced paid staff felt this replacement was unfair or very unfair.

Taken together, these findings suggest perceptions about interchangeability vary among different groups in an organization's workforce and may be favorable or unfavorable, depending on who benefits from the change and a host of other factors. As Netting, Nelson, Borders, and Huber (2004) suggest, "[The] level of resistance [in the relationship between paid staff and volunteers] will vary, depending on cultural norms" (p. 86). For instance, nonprofits that simultaneously celebrate and clarify the roles of both paid staff and volunteers, and which provide volunteers with the same avenues for voicing concerns to management as paid staff, may have more success addressing and alleviating any tensions that arise. Likewise, Rogelberg, Allen, Conway, Goh, Currie, and McFarland (2010) report paid staff perceptions of volunteers vary according to workload and overall levels of employee stress, such that tensions between the two groups may be exacerbated by times of transition. Because the interchange of paid staff and volunteers in either direction could arguably be identified as a significant transition for a nonprofit agency, employee concerns, whether founded or unfounded, and their potential impact on organizational performance must be considered in discussions of nonprofit human resource management.

Interchangeability as Part of Human Resource Management

Despite the challenges associated with managing a mixed nonprofit labor force, many scholars have highlighted the numerous benefits of volunteering for both the volunteer and the organization. For example, nonprofit organizations that utilize both paid staff and volunteers may enjoy added value to the price of labor, as well as a competitive advantage. The integration of paid staff and volunteers increases workforce diversity and enhances organizational skills and knowledge (Liao-Troth, 2001). According to Akingbola (2013), "Volunteer participation . . . increases the quality and diversity of the human resource pool. Nonprofits that are able to effectively deploy these operational resources . . . will facilitate coproduction of outcomes" (p. 220). Interchangeability as a concept represents the very real practice in which nonprofits engage to build a more productive and cost-effective labor force, given the unique forms of social capital available to them, and given resource constraints. This flexibility allows the organization to react quickly and ensure that their work is not disrupted.

To improve productivity, mitigate tensions, and cut costs, nonprofit managers must be willing and able to look closely at their volunteer programs to assess the relationship between paid and unpaid staff, as well as the function and costs of volunteers. An honest assessment of the costs and benefits of volunteer programs may lead nonprofit managers to conclude that volunteers are not being used effectively, or that they are costing the agency too much money (Handy & Mook, 2011). In cases where paid staff and volunteers act as substitutes for each other, interchanging a poorly organized or inefficient volunteer program by a program run by paid staff may be beneficial for improving service delivery and promoting the organization's mission. However, because of their unique contribution to nonprofit agencies, volunteers are viewed frequently as complements to, rather than substitutes for, paid labor (Studer & von Schnurbein, 2013).

In many cases, paid labor cannot deliver the same benefits as volunteers, even when they provide similar services. This finding is well illustrated by Haski-Leventhal et al. (2011) in their research on the multidimensional impact of volunteers for the Philadelphia Ronald McDonald House (PRMH). They write:

> Volunteers ... gave financial and in-kind donations to PRMH. Volunteers ... were goodwill ambassadors ... and sent positive signals to donors and others on the trustworthiness of PRMH. PRMH thus received human, in-kind, and financial resources, as well as publicity that aided in fundraising in the community ... They help create a better image of the organization and the community.
>
> *(Haski-Leventhal et al., 2011, pp. 156–157)*

Thus, it is often not viable, or advisable, for nonprofit organizations to abandon their volunteer programs, even if they could afford to replace the services using paid staff. Ellis (2010) suggests we ask the question "Why do we want volunteers?" in considering whether or not to involve volunteers in the organization (p. 27). If the answer is "because we do not have sufficient resources (money, staff or whatever) to do our job without the help of volunteers," then their use *should* be questioned (Ellis, 2010, p. 13). If, on the other hand, volunteers bring unique benefits to the organization, then volunteer involvement is appropriate.

Increasingly, scholars of volunteer administration and nonprofit human resource management have encouraged nonprofit managers to approach volunteer management in the same way they would approach the management of paid staff. For instance, Brudney and Meijs (2014) argue, "preparing job descriptions for volunteers, matching volunteers' interest and capabilities to unpaid organizational positions, training and orienting volunteers, and having policies and procedures" for volunteer programs could both clarify volunteer and paid staff roles in the agency and improve the outcomes of volunteer programs (p. 297). These steps could also provide nonprofits with a better understanding of how their volunteers and paid staff complement one another, and under what circumstances they may be substituted, if necessary. Similarly, the strategic human resource management approach for nonprofit organizations described by Guo, Brown, Ashcraft, Yoshioka, and Dong (2011) could be applied to all nonprofit employees, including paid staff and volunteers.

Brudney and Meijs (2014) argue that to manage volunteers most effectively, nonprofit managers must first consider whether volunteers perform similar roles to paid staff, or whether their functions are distinct within the organizational structure. By recognizing and clarifying the roles of all employees—whether paid or unpaid, permanent or temporary—nonprofit managers position themselves to maximize the benefits of a diverse workforce, allay staff concerns, and make the most informed decisions about the interchangeability of their paid and unpaid staff.

Conclusion

The interchangeability of paid staff and volunteer labor is an emerging topic in nonprofit studies as more and more organizations in all sectors rely on a mixed pool of human resources, from volunteers to unpaid internships. To the extent that human resource managers must make economic decisions regarding the development and management of a diverse workforce, interchangeability also impacts the study of human resources and the ways in which organizations go about maximizing their productivity and minimizing the cost of labor inputs.

The scholarship reviewed in this chapter highlights the importance of examining the phenomenon of the engagement of volunteers in the nonprofit sector not only as a function of an individual's willingness to contribute uncompensated time to an agency but also as a function of the relationship between paid and unpaid labor, the availability of substitutes and complements, the mission of the organization, the prevailing benefits of a mixed labor force, and the costs of labor. Together, these factors contribute to a nonprofit's demand for volunteers and, consequently, the extent and direction of interchangeability between paid and unpaid staff in their workforce.

Discussion Questions

1   What are the benefits and challenges of working with a mixed labor force?
2   Why might nonprofit organizations interchange paid staff and volunteers?
3   How do economic considerations about labor inputs, volunteers, and paid workers overlap with decisions and challenges related to nonprofit human resource management?
4   How do labor union policies impact decisions about interchangeability?
5   What benefits do organizations receive from professionalizing their volunteer management strategies?
6   When should an organization not incorporate a volunteer labor force?
7   If an organization incorporates volunteers, can it be argued that they are exploiting people?

References

Akingbola, K. (2013). A model of strategic nonprofit human resource management. *Voluntas, 24*, 214–240.

Bingle, B. S., Meyer, C. K., & Taylor, A. (2013). Nonprofit and public sector human resource management: A comparative analysis. *International Journal of Management and Information Systems, 17*(3), 135–162.

Brinkerhoff, J. M. (2002). Government-nonprofit partnership: A defining framework. *Public Administration and Development, 22*(1), 19–30.

Brudney, J. L. & Gazley, B. (2002). Testing the conventional wisdom regarding volunteer programs: A longitudinal analysis of the Service Corps of Retired Executives and the U.S. Small Business Administration. *Nonprofit and Voluntary Sector Quarterly, 31*(4), 525–548.

Brudney, J. L. & Meijs, L. C. P. M. (2014). Models of volunteer management: Professional volunteer program management in social work. *Human Service Organizations: Management, Leadership & Governance, 38*, 297–309.

Chum, A., Mook, L., Handy, F., Schugurensky, D., & Quarter, J. (2013). Degree and direction of paid employee/volunteer interchange in nonprofit organizations. *Nonprofit Management & Leadership, 23*(4), 409–426.

Corporation for National & Community Service. (2013). *Volunteering and civic engagement in the United States*. Available at: www.volunteeringinamerica.gov/national

Ellis, S. J. (2010). *From the top down: The executive role in successful volunteer involvement*. Philadelphia: Energize, Inc.

Emanuele, R. (1996). Is there a (downward sloping) demand curve for volunteer labour? *Annals of Public and Cooperative Economics, 67*(2), 193–208.

Farmer, S. M. & Fedor, D. B. (1999). Volunteer participation and withdrawal: A psychological contract perspective on the role of expectations and organizational support. *Nonprofit Management & Leadership, 9*(4), 349–367.

Govekar, P. L. & Govekar, M. A. (2002). Using economic theory and research to better understand volunteer behavior. *Nonprofit Management & Leadership, 13*(1), 33–48.

Guo, C., Brown, W. A., Ashcraft, R. F., Yoshioka, C. F., & Dong, H. K. D. (2011). Strategic Human Resources Management in nonprofit organizations. *Review of Public Personnel Administration, 31*(3), 248–269.

Hall, M., de Wit, M. L., Lasby, D., McIver, D., Evers, T., & Johnston, C., et al. (2005). *Cornerstones of community: Highlights of the National Survey of Nonprofit and Voluntary Organizations*. Ottawa: Statistics Canada.

Handy, F. & Brudney, J. L. (2007). When to use volunteer labor resources? An organizational analysis for nonprofit management. *Vrijwillige Inzet Onderzoch, 4*, 91–100.

Handy, F., Cnaan, R. A., Brudney, J. L., Meijs, L. C., Ascoli, U., & Ranade, S. (2000). Public perception of "who is a volunteer": An examination of the net-cost approach from a cross-cultural perspective. *Voluntas, 11*(1), 45–65.

Handy, F. & Mook, L. (2011). Volunteering and Volunteers: Benefit-Cost Analysis. *Research in Social Work Practice. Research on Social Work Practice, 21*(4), 412–420.

Handy, F., Mook, L., & Quarter, J. (2006). Organisational perspectives on the value of volunteer labor. *Australian Journal on Volunteering, 11*(1), 28–36.

Handy, F., Mook, L., & Quarter, J. (2008). The interchangeability of paid staff and volunteers in nonprofit organizations. *Nonprofit and Voluntary Sector Quarterly, 37*(1), 76–92.

Handy, F. & Srinivasan, N. (2005). The demand for volunteer labor: A study of hospital volunteers. *Nonprofit and Voluntary Sector Quarterly, 34*(4), 491–509.

Haski-Leventhal, D., Hustinx, L., & Handy, F. (2011). What money cannot buy: The distinctive and multidimensional impact of volunteers. *Journal of Community Practice, 19*(2), 138–158.

Hotchkiss, R. B., Fottler, M. D., & Unruh, L. (2009). Valuing volunteers: The impact of volunteerism on hospital performance. *Health Care Management Review, 34*(2), 119–128.

Liao-Troth, M. A. (2001). Attitude differences between paid workers and volunteers. *Nonprofit Management & Leadership, 11*(4), 423–442.

Lipsky, M. & Smith, S. R. (1993). *Nonprofits for hire: The welfare state in the age of contracting.* Cambridge, MA: Harvard University Press.

Mesch, D. J. (2010). Management of human resources in 2020: The outlook for nonprofit organizations. *Public Administration Review, 70*(1), 173–174.

Milligan, C. & Fyfe, N. R. (2005). Preserving space for volunteers: Exploring the links between voluntary welfare organisations, volunteering and citizenship. *Urban Studies, 42*(3), 417–433.

Mook, L., Farrell, E., Chum, A., Handy, F., Schugurensky, D., & Quarter, J. (2014). Individual and organizational factors in the interchange of paid staff and volunteers: Perspectives of volunteers. *Canadian Journal of Nonprofit and Social Economy Research, 5*(2), 65–85.

Mook, L. & Handy, F. (2011). Volunteering and volunteers: Benefit-cost analyses. *Research on Social Work Practice, 21*(4), 412–420.

National Council of Nonprofits. (2016). Can board members be paid? Available at: www.councilofnonprofits.org/tools-resources/can-board-members-be-paid

Netting, F. E., Nelson, H. W., Borders, K., & Huber, R. (2004). Volunteer and paid staff relationships. *Administration in Social Work, 28*(3–4), 69–89.

Netting, F. E., O'Connor, M. K., Thomas, M. L., & Yancey, G. (2005). Mixing and phasing of roles among volunteers, staff, and participants in faith-based programs. *Nonprofit and Voluntary Sector Quarterly, 34*(2), 179–205.

O'Connell, B. (1996). A major transfer of government responsibility to voluntary organizations? Proceed with caution. *Public Administration Review, 56*(3), 222–225.

Pynes, J. E. (2011). *Effective nonprofit management: Context and environment.* Armonk, NY: M.E. Sharpe.

Ridder, H. G. & McCandless, A. (2010). Influences on the architecture of human resource management in nonprofit organizations: An analytical framework. *Nonprofit and Voluntary Sector Quarterly, 39*(1), 124–141.

Rogelberg, S. G., Allen, J. A., Conway, J. M., Goh, A., Currie, L., & McFarland, B. (2010). Employee experiences with volunteers: Assessment, description, antecedents, and outcomes. *Nonprofit Management & Leadership, 20*(4), 423–444.

Studer, S. & von Schnurbein, G. (2013). Organizational factors affecting volunteers: A literature review on volunteer coordination. *Voluntas, 24*, 403–440.

Turcotte, M. (2015). Volunteering and charitable giving in Canada. Available at: www.statcan.gc.ca/pub/89-652-x/89-652-x2015001-eng.pdf

16

Managing Human Resources in International NGOs

Carrie R. Oelberger, Anne-Meike Fechter,
and Ishbel McWha-Hermann

Introduction

The "associational revolution" and the ongoing proliferation of nonprofits translates to increasing numbers of individuals working within the third sector across the globe (Salamon, 1994). International aid is a multi-sited, multi-level phenomenon that cannot be fully understood based on how it appears in any one location or particular level (Gould, 2004). The "aid industry" includes both long-term international development work that attempts to address structural inequalities like poverty, corruption, or environmental degradation, as well as shorter-term humanitarian relief work that serves communities in need following natural or civil disasters (Hancock, 1989; Van Rooy, 1998). The industry exists largely in lower-income contexts, and is comprised of individuals from a wide range of occupations (e.g. education, agriculture, health). Aid is carried out through non-profit, non-governmental organizations (NGOs) that range in size from small community-based organizations (CBOs) to multi-national international NGOs (INGOs), both secular and faith-based, as well as multilateral and government agencies (e.g. United States Agency for International Development [USAID], the United Kingdom's Department for International Development [DFID]) and for-profit companies (e.g. Chemonics, Development Alternatives Incorporated).

Within the spectrum of NGOs, INGOs represent the most transnational aid organizations, and are the focus of this chapter. INGOs are formal organizations with operations in more than one country, the majority of which are headquartered in the United States or Western Europe, and which work on projects within lower-income contexts. Examples of INGOs include Oxfam, CARE, and Save the Children. This chapter focuses in particular on the human resource management (HRM) issues INGOs face, especially with respect to the diversity of the INGO workforce. The most obvious dimension of staff diversity is nationality, but as we will explain, employment status also varies considerably between international staff and national staff, as well as between those with at-will employment, multi-year contracts, short-term consultants, and interns/volunteers. As this chapter illustrates, a key challenge for HRM in this sector arises from the fact that nationality and employment status do not always map onto other relevant dimensions, such as experience, local and linguistic knowledge, and pay. This chapter sheds light on some of the fissures and tensions arising from this situation, which have implications for both employee motivation and successful implementation of INGO work.

The term "expatriate" describes staff working outside their country of origin, but is often used in a limited way to refer to European or American workers who are employed on international-level contracts with commensurate salaries. It is useful to bear in mind that within the aid workforce, a key distinction is made between those who are "national staff" (that is, employed in their passport country on "national" contracts) and those who are considered "international staff" (that is, originating outside of the country where they work). In the context of INGOs, international staff may include workers from the wider region, such as Kenyans working in Sierra Leone, or from other parts of the Global South, such as Brazilians working in Mozambique. We utilize the terms "national staff" and "international staff" within this chapter. Furthermore, effective management demands an understanding that the positionality and experience of employees is not easily captured by these formal classifications.

Such fuzziness of categories also holds for other central concepts in this chapter. For example, as discussed below, "headquarters" often refers to an office located in the United States or Western Europe, and "field" to a "Southern," "developing," or "lower-income" country. In the context of middle-income countries such as India, however, headquarters may well be in the capital city, while the field is defined as geographically remote, rural areas. It is important, therefore, to be alert to internal differentiations within a category—such as the poorer parts of a country's population in contrast to its urban middle class—to avoid overly simplistic perceptions of both the national workforce and recipient groups. Furthermore, such nuanced understandings help identify the variable and heterogeneous motivations of INGO employees across multiple differentiations, not only national and international staff, but also volunteers, interns, and contract-hired consultants. Across all categories, while the desire to support resource-poor populations is often present (either from a sense of solidarity or personal experience), this may be combined with professional career aspirations. For international staff, it may also include the desire to live and work abroad in culturally diverse contexts (Fechter, 2012; Roth, 2015), while members of the national workforce may need to make a livelihood in countries that often lack a diversity of formal employment options. As suggested above, however, belonging to a particular national or employment category does not imply a fixed set of motivations or interests.

This chapter provides an overview of the role of INGOs in international aid and, specifically, the human resource considerations for those organizations.

We first provide a historical overview of organizational approaches to international aid provision, focusing on the division of knowledge within the sector, where the work occurs, and how it occurs, with a focus on the division of labor. The second part of the chapter then highlights the specific human resource considerations for INGOs, with attention to challenges with staff selection, the complicated nature of compensation, perspectives on performance management and professional development, the delicate nature of staff well-being, and the intricacies of managing staff with frequent travel and expatriation.

INGOs and International Aid

History

The current organizational and institutional structure of international aid originated in the aftermath of World War II, when major multilateral agencies involving three or more countries, such as the International Monetary Fund and the World Bank, were established to carry out reconstruction. World society scholars have also noted the ideological underpinnings of international aid are rooted in this period, when a world culture emphasizing progress and justice was on the rise, contributing to a rationalizing discourse about international aid (Chabbott & Ramirez, 2000). As reconstruction ended and the Cold War period began in the 1950s, international aid organizations turned their efforts towards the Global South, otherwise known as the "developing world" (Gardner & Lewis, 1996). Since that time, a growing number of faith-based and secular NGOs have participated in international aid, with well over 35,000 NGOs involved in international development and relief efforts today (Lindenberg & Dobel, 1999; UIA, 2008). This blossoming of NGOs has been accompanied by two simultaneous processes: one of *professionalization*, i.e. the increasing formal structuring of these organizations (Bromley, 2010; Chabbott, 2003; Hwang & Powell, 2009) and another of *localization*, i.e. an attempt to shift the design of activities from international actors to those within the local context. In addition to these two processes of differentiation, INGOs are being challenged by three interrelated sets of changes in the external environment: (1) economic globalization; (2) the reform of foreign aid; and (3) the evolution of NGOs indigenous to the developing world (Edwards, Hulme, & Wallace, 1999). As a result, some scholars claim INGOs defend social change values at the same time they operate inside a framework that drives an increasingly formalized, professionalized field further into the marketplace (Edwards, 1998).

INGOs are also subject to more general trends affecting the entire global landscape of work. Our analysis of international aid is rooted within the understanding that contemporary work across all industries is increasingly technical, transnational, and temporary (Oelberger, 2014). Work is increasingly scientific and professional, focused on abstracted, portable technical solutions (Habermas, 1970). This portability of skills combines with processes of globalization to result

287

in a transnationally transferable workforce increasingly accustomed to bridging geographic distance with both physical travel and technology (Dicken, 1998; Levitt & Jaworsky, 2007; Schiller, Basch, & Blanc, 1995; Waldinger & Fitzgerald, 2004). Given the portable nature of work commitments, work relationships are also increasingly temporary, with short-term contracts prevailing over career-length organizational commitments (Barley & Kunda, 2006; Barley & Kunda, 2011; Kunda, Barley, & Evans, 2002). Taken together, these features result in a highly mobile, portable modern workforce within a structure of work that favors connections with occupations and skills over connections with organizations and places.

Division of Knowledge

Within international aid, a variety of knowledge and skills are necessary to plan, manage, and implement complex work. Prior to professionalization, this need was predominantly filled by American or European staff who took on generalist roles. The cost of air travel prohibited frequent international flights, and even until the new millennium the ability to communicate by phone or email was extremely limited, resulting in isolated staff who were largely based "in the field" (i.e., within country offices). With rising professionalization, skilled "national" staff, born and raised in the country in which they are working, began undertaking pivotal roles within local, national, and (eventually) international organizations. Their labor costs far less than that of international staff, they often have better cultural and linguistic knowledge, and they make inroads into assuaging the criticism of international aid as white and neocolonial (Escobar, 1994).

The involvement of international staff, however, has not declined. On the contrary, their participation has both grown and shifted (Comoretto, Crichton, & Albery, 2011). Rather than employing international cultural experts familiar with a particular region, aid organizations increasingly hire international staff based on their technical expertise (e.g. scientific or legal expertise) for short-term contracts to design technical solutions to social problems (Moke & Stoll, 2010; O'Flaherty & Ulrich, 2010; Walker, 2004; Walker & Russ, 2010). International staff are largely represented within headquarters positions, doing technical or managerial work that can be applied across geographic settings. They use internet technology, smartphones, and frequent travel to support programs around the globe. Headquarters positions often have leadership responsibilities for communication with donors, as well as providing financial, administrative, and technical support to field offices. Rather than posting international staff in the field for long periods of time, organizations are more likely to use short-term consultancies, trainings, workshops, and visits in order to convey information from the central artery to the field. Against this backdrop, only a few international staff continue to be field-based, often in managerial roles as country directors, or grant writers who remain in one position for three or four years before moving on to another assignment. International staff also work within INGOs on volunteer contracts through volunteer-sending organizations like United Nations Volunteers, the British Voluntary Service Overseas, the United States Peace Corps, or independently through direct relationships with the organization. These volunteer or internship positions are often support or advisory roles, sometimes to facilitate the process of localization, and other times to assist with a particular project or strengthen skills in a particular area.

Recent scholars have argued that international aid has moved beyond the traditional dichotomy of Western international staff and staff native to the Global South. Rather than the conventional North-South axis of development partnership, a distinct and potentially impactful model is that of South-South cooperation (Chisholm & Steiner-Khamsi, 2009; de Renzio & Seifert, 2014). This concept is based on the assumption that Southern actors, including emerging donors and residents of the "BRICS" (Brazil, Russia, India, China, and South Africa), are able to relate differently and more effectively to INGO clients than traditional Northern donor staff. This belief is partly based on a sense of shared colonial history, greater social and political mutual understanding, and Southern solidarity (Mawdsley, 2014). The extent to which these assumptions are justified and produce improvements in aid delivery remains to be seen.

Place of Work

In light of these trends, critics have discussed the relative distance between international staff and the "field," geographically as well as culturally and linguistically. Kothari (2006), for example, notes how the colonial officers of the past often possessed greater cultural and linguistic knowledge than contemporary development professionals, whose periods of stay in a particular place are often much shorter, and thus whose familiarity with the social context is less extensive than their colonial-era predecessors (on the role of cultural knowledge, see also Pottier, Bicker, & Sillitoe, 2003). It has been argued such distance may have detrimental effects on the conceptualization and delivery of aid. As one possible antidote, some have proposed "immersions," that is, short periods in which aid workers are exposed to the living conditions of the resource-poor communities they aim to support (Irvine, Chambers, & Eyben, 2004). The underlying rationale is that first-hand exposure to the realities of poverty provides aid workers with a renewed sense of urgency, as well as a better understanding of the problems they seek to solve. Immersions have traditionally been advocated for international staff who may rarely leave their office in the United States or Western Europe, but could easily be argued to be useful for country nationals who have lived a middle-class lifestyle in their country's capital, with little understanding of what life is like in the rural areas where many projects are based. While immersions have been implemented by some agencies (e.g. ActionAid, 2010), it remains to be seen to what extent these remain a symbolic rather than a substantial exercise (Fechter, 2012).

The issue of distance from the field, and its effects on aid work, has been articulated especially in relation to humanitarian crises and conflict zones.

Collinson and Duffield (2013) point out that the tendency towards a "bunkeriz-ation" of aid has significant implications for the way aid is carried out in these high-risk contexts. Such a bunkerization is a response to the increased insecurity faced by aid agencies and their staff operating in volatile environments. It becomes manifest in the higher prevalence of fortified aid compounds, for example, as well as in 'remote management' practices. Among other challenges, however, such distance can lead to a less-informed workforce whose analysis and decision-making may be impaired as a result of their remoteness from the affected popula-tions. Furthermore, they argue being spatially separated as well as heavily guarded—often by private security firms—weakens social relations between aid workers and local communities, leads to mistrust, and ironically may actually contribute to a lack of security for the workers (Autesserre, 2014). In addition, such "bunkerization," especially where it provides security measures for inter-national but not national staff, reinforces structural inequalities between staff categories. Such a "dual security" system becomes particularly visible in the context of emergency evacuations, prompting the question of whose lives are considered more valuable. As Bettina Scholz discusses in the case of Médécins sans Frontières, the organization does not always fulfill the moral obligations to its national staff that may be expected of them. While international staff are often committed to informally ensure the safety of national staff, in many instances, such as fleeing Rwanda or Darfur, national staff are left behind, to be massacred at the hands of local militia (Scholz, 2015, p. 123).

The concept of mobility, then, is a key lens through which hierarchies among differently categorized aid workers become visible, not just by employment type, but also by nationality, ethnicity, personal migration history, education, and international status. Warne Peters (2013) highlights that some aid workers, in her case, in Angola, who may be employed as "local" staff, may have a complex personal migration and education history, and therefore might strategically present themselves as "international" or "expatriate" in some contexts and as "local" or "national" in others. Presentation allows them to manage perceptions of their expertise, conveying cosmopolitan or local knowledge respectively. Some research also suggests that international workers on a "national" contract, including volunteers, might be better positioned to build relationships with local colleagues and communities, and in turn might facilitate more effective aid outcomes (Devereux, 2008; McWha, 2011).

International staff may also experience malleable categorization related to their positionality and mobility, especially in light of varying definitions of the "field" where they work. Oelberger's (2014) study of international aid workers found that international staff who are "in the field" may feel just as disconnected from their project beneficiaries as those working in headquarters positions in the United States. For example, Ajay is an Indian citizen on an international contract who is technically "field-based" in the urban setting of Lilongwe, Malawi, but his daily interactions are all with other office-based staff. He often feels just as disconnected from the "actual work on the ground" as headquarters staff based in Washington, D.C. might feel. Therefore, when he speaks about going "to the field," he may be referring to travel in remote villages. By contrast, when Julie, a headquarters-based employee of the same organization, speaks about going "to the field," she may be traveling to Bangkok, Thailand, for meetings with staff based in that office (Oelberger, 2014). The work of INGOs occurs across all of these settings: U.S.-based headquarters, urban offices around the world, and more remote, rural offices where projects are based. As a result, INGO staff are located across these various locations, with patterns within the division of labor. It is to this topic that we now turn.

Division of Labor

Within international aid, there are a multitude of types of workers and a hierarchy of tracks. At the top of hierarchy are managerial and policy advising positions. Second in line are technical positions, increasingly including those with methodological training, expertise in monitoring and evaluation, and the ability to conduct experimental analyses. Third in line are those with operations, logistics, or middle-management skills. Finally, at the bottom of the hierarchy are those with geographic, linguistic, or cultural expertise. Importantly, this hierarchy overlays with typical expertise of international versus national staff, in effect conferring greater value to international staff.[1] McWha (2011) found the labels given to workers (volunteer, consultant, expatriate, and local) were implicitly underpinned by power and status, wherein expatriate workers were at the top of the hierarchy with the most respect and status, consultants next, still with status but less respect, then volunteers, and locals at the bottom. These perceptions held regardless of the professional experience the workers brought to the assignment.

Mirroring the overall rise in the use of consultants and contractors in modern work (Barley & Kunda, 2004), many leading INGOs have reorganized to include outsourcing, subcontracting, and short-term organizational positions as key features of international aid staffing (Stubbs, 2003). With the rise in these practices, international aid workers avoid the emotional commitments to other people, communities, projects, and places that develop with long-term work, focusing on service delivery, rather than partnership. Initial research in this area notes that long-held, trust-based partnerships remain vital for development, and that the contract-based relationships implicit in consultancies make this trust more difficult to achieve (Fowler, 1998). Moreover, the impact of these practices on both the private lives of aid workers, as well as the organizations in which they work, remains understudied. Following global trends towards contract relationships, it will be interesting to investigate the future impact of this reorganization towards an increasingly technical and decreasingly relational approach to the work.

Alongside professionalization and the increasingly technical and temporary nature of the work, the "international" component of "international aid" is simultaneously becoming "nationalized" and "transnationalized," representing a bifurcated approach to the human resourcing of international aid. Nationalization refers to the increasing practice of delegating contextualized knowledge to national staff with appropriate local linguistic skills, as well as possessing international linguistic skills and the necessary formal training to act as intermediaries between projects and donors. This practice is an attempt to respond to the critique of aid work as being externally driven, and even neocolonial. It is crucial to note that cultural knowledge is undervalued and underpaid when it is embodied by national staff, in the same way that many professions have become undervalued and underpaid with feminization (Bolton & Muzio, 2008). Moreover, national staff are often members of the elite within their country, posing an additional challenge of overcoming social class barriers while they strive to assist communities without the nuanced knowledge of local culture, power dynamics, and politics necessary to do so.

Parallel to this nationalization, international aid has also been transnationalized as international staff take on shorter-term technical assignments overseas. The projects are accomplished through two main routes: expatriation (and repatriation), and frequent international travel. Both relocation and work-related travel influence the personal lives of aid workers, as they bring both their personal and professional selves with them to other continents.

HRM Considerations for INGOs

Given the context of international aid work just outlined, organizations working in this sphere face numerous human resource (HR) issues, issues which are different from organizations operating within the domestic nonprofit sector, for example within the United States or Europe. One of the key differences is the multitude of different staff within INGOs from a variety of cultural, economic, and social backgrounds. These different workers bring their own expectations, support needs, and personnel challenges, which HR managers need to balance. These personal differences interact with another challenge: the context in which they work—typically categorized as resource poor, often high-risk, and sometimes dangerous. In this section we review some traditional aspects of HRM within the context of INGOs, illustrating various ways that the HR decisions of INGOs can impact their workforce.

The international HRM (IHRM) literature discusses the distinction between universalist and contextualist paradigms, the former advocating a standardized global approach to HRM, and the latter arguing for adaptation to local context and conditions (for more discussion on the distinction, see Sheehan, Fenwick, & Dowling, 2010). However, the majority of IHRM research has been undertaken within the for-profit, often "Western-style" context of multinational corporations, with the result that much of what is known about IHRM may be inapplicable to the NGO context. We caution INGOs against (1) applying principles of IHRM that have been developed in the context of multinational corporations; (2) applying concepts that have been developed in higher-income countries; and

(3) assuming that HR systems that function well at headquarters, or in one country office, will transfer seamlessly into another. Instead, in this chapter, we encourage INGOs to find a way to balance global standardization with consideration of local contexts and the reality of working in a complex nonprofit setting.

Investing in HRM structures can be a source of tension for INGOs. Many NGOs have low budgets and are therefore constrained in their ability to invest in sophisticated HRM. Often there is a challenge for NGOs around how to use limited funding, with the understandable desire to invest in service delivery and "getting the job done" rather than in a strategic function of the organization. As a result, HRM is often interpreted as dealing with everyday personnel issues, rather than as an important component of developing human capital in line with the long-term vision of the organization (Brewster & Lee, 2006). That said, large, well-resourced INGOs are more likely to have a commitment to HRM structures. CHS Alliance (formerly People in Aid) and Association for Human Resource Management in International Organizations are two umbrella organizations that assist INGOs in developing effective HR practices.

Staff Selection

It is critical for INGOs to be able to attract and recruit the best talent. However, this is a complex process. Project sites are regulated by different legal compliance frameworks, and there may be complications depending on whether staff are hired under a national or international contract. International staff can be recruited on national contracts, and, though perhaps less common, national staff can be recruited on international contracts. Some research suggests that recruiting comparatively highly-paid international staff has the potential to undermine the skills of national staff, and may lead to capacity stripping, i.e. a reduced feeling of empowerment and belief in one's skills to do the job and an increased dependency on outside assistance, rather than capacity building, which many would argue is a fundamental goal of INGOs (Carr, McWha, MacLachlan, & Furnham, 2010). In response, some organizations have aimed to recruit locally, or at least regionally (e.g. see, for example, the Catholic Agency for Overseas Development). It is essential that HR managers reflect on the context in which these jobs exist, ensuring the desired competencies and behaviors are appropriate for the culture and context of the role.

Compensation

Compensation is closely related to the issues underpinning staff selection. The challenge here is balancing the need to compete with other INGOs for talent with the desire to adapt to local contexts. INGOs commonly use a dual salary system in which national and international staff are tracked onto different pay scales. Typically, the international pay scale is benchmarked globally, with various added benefits (e.g. extra compensation for workers in high-risk zones or private

293

school tuition for accompanied posts in "family-friendly" areas). By contrast, the local pay scale is benchmarked within the national market, and is therefore much lower. This system is highly divisive, and perpetuates a perception of international staff as experts and locals as novices, when in reality national workers often hold considerable institutional knowledge, as well as contextual knowledge of the area in which they are working.

The dual compensation system is often justified with the claim that high salaries are needed to attract talent internationally. However, research suggests that it is not uncommon for colleagues with similar qualifications and experience to work in similar roles, the only difference between staff being country of origin and compensation. This has been found to be demoralizing for national staff, and possibly also international staff (Carr, McWha, MacLachlan, & Furnham, 2010). Some INGOs have begun to explore different pay systems, such as pay for performance, unified regional pay scales, and single pay scales with some additional benefits for international staff based on need (see for example, WaterAid, ActionAid, and other members of CHS Alliance's Fair Pay Forum). Still other INGOs have applied the principles of localization to their compensation structures. In this approach, international employees can earn an international salary for a limited length of time, at the end of which they can either choose to move to another country office, or to remain where they are, but under the national salary scale. This approach continues to prioritize the technical, temporary, and transnational approach to international aid work.

The dual compensation system can negatively impact relationships among staff. Good relationships are essential for capacity building initiatives specifically, and aid organizations more generally (Eyben, 2006; Girgis, 2007; McWha, 2011), and feelings of injustice and unfairness tend to result in disengagement, dissatisfaction, and potentially turnover (often returning home, for international staff) (Carr, McWha, MacLachlan, & Furnham, 2010). For national staff, global mobility is often constrained by citizenship, and organizational turnover is often not an option given socioeconomic circumstances. As a result, there is some evidence that counterproductive work behaviors such as "moonlighting" (e.g. taking a second job), or practices that may be viewed by outsiders as "corrupt," are a response to feelings of injustice (MacLachlan, Carr, & McAuliffe, 2010). In a review of moonlighting and corruption within the public health sectors of lower- and middle-income countries, Ferrinho & Lerberghe (2002) suggest that individual coping strategies such as absenteeism (including as a means to enable moonlighting), under-the-counter payments for "free" services, drug use, and other seemingly "corrupt" behaviors, are a response to the significantly lower salaries afforded to national workers.

Moreover, research suggests national workers play a key role in the socialization of international workers, a process that ultimately contributes to the success or failure of the international assignment (Toh & DeNisi, 2007). Socialization occurs when international staff arrive at the site of their new assignment, and this is a crucial time for adjustment to the national context. The efforts of national staff to help international staff to adjust may be very important, and national workers' feelings of unfairness regarding a dual salary system can reduce these socialization efforts and may undermine the international assignment (Toh & DeNisi, 2005). Careful design of rewards systems is therefore crucial not only for the engagement and empowerment of national workers, but also for the success of international assignments.

Performance Management and Professional Development

Performance management is particularly challenging for organizations working across national and cultural boundaries. The impact of culture on performance appraisal has been well documented (e.g. Vance, McClaine, Boje, & Stage, 1992; Fletcher, 2001). Different countries and cultures define good performance in different ways, based on proclivities including power distance, uncertainty avoidance, and therefore, horizontal and vertical individualism-collectivism (Hofstede, 1980; Triandis & Gelfand, 1998). As a concept, performance management originated in the United States, and at a very basic level it may not be appropriate in the context of other countries (e.g. countries that are highly collectivist). The issue becomes even more complicated when individuals from multiple countries are employed in one office. Managers should question whether a formal, standardized performance management system is appropriate given cross-national differences in what is considered good performance, as well as cultural biases in responses to rating scales, such as avoiding extreme ratings or choosing all ratings above the scale's midpoint to "save face" (Hui & Triandis, 1989).

HR managers should also consider ongoing training an integral part of performance management. Within the INGO context, there is a keen need for training in cross-cultural diversity and urgent response to humanitarian disasters. Much training is outsourced to organizations like RedR, International NGO Training and Research Centre (INTRAC), Bond, and others. Training is important for improving the quality of service delivery, as well as maintaining safety, preventing accidents, and avoiding cultural conflicts (Chang, 2005). There are also entrenched issues concerning the language capacities of international staff. Though critics have long bemoaned the lack of local language skills of the majority of international staff, in practice, language training has never been particularly emphasized or enabled by sending agencies. Given the availability in many aid contexts of capable local translators and assistants, it appears that such skills have in practice usually been considered expendable by aid institutions, notwithstanding any lip service paid to their importance.

The continued relevance of cultural differences to development has received substantial attention in academic research, if not necessarily in development practice. Yet, differences between INGO staff (both international and national) and "clients" (often referred to as "aid recipients" or "beneficiaries") have also been framed in other terms. For example, Rossi (2006) reminds us not to "compartmentalize" aid workers and recipients into separate worlds of knowledge, arguing for much greater overlap. Further, Heaton-Shrestha (2006) points out while there may be significant differences between national staff and clients that run along the lines of class as well as an urban/rural divide, national staff may still pride themselves on being able to "mix" much better with local clients than international staff can due to language, culture, and national identity.

In the context of these differences, engagement between INGO staff and clients has been considered central to successful aid delivery (Eyben, 2006). This concern has underpinned the "participatory approach," which holds that clients of INGOs should be significantly involved in program design and implementation. However, the paradigm of participation and the ways in which it has been applied may already be based on an inherently paternalistic approach to development (Baaz, 2005), and therefore the approach has often failed to live up to its democratic promise.

Staff Well-Being

While traveling for work or living overseas, staff experience a blurring of the physical domains that separate work from home life (Shaffer, Kraimer, Chen, & Bolino, 2012). In addition, technology bridges the domains such that personal news can easily arrive at work, and work demands can punctuate what was traditionally considered leisure time. This breakdown of traditional boundaries between work and home results in increasing inter-role influence across domains. The impact of work-family conflict is increased in international work arrangements, which often involve some combination of physical relocation away from one's social support network, intensive travel, and long hours. In such cases, the boundaries between work and home become blurred and there is often disruption of traditional family roles, causing increasing stress (Caligiuri, Hyland, & Joshi, 1998). Taken together, these features interfere with aid workers' personal lives and often result in poor physical and mental health. Given the overlap between gender and family roles, this work-life conflict is especially acute for women (Harris, 2004). As such, research has shown that in addition to formal organizational support, informal support, such as when employees have a sense that their manager and the broader organization is concerned with their healthy personal life, is important for success in HRM (Grant-Vallone & Ensher, 2001).

The accumulated effects of working in a range of cultural and social environments, including high-risk locations, may significantly affect engagement, job satisfaction, and turnover among INGO staff (e.g. Korff et al., 2015). As Roth (2015) and others note, the aid sector is characterized by a considerable rate of burnout and dropout. As a result, HR practitioners are beginning to address the issue of staff well-being (see also Bjerneld, 2009 and Pigni, 2014), joining broader efforts including initiatives by agencies such as CHS Alliance, InterHealth, and the Headington Institute. Well-being is particularly important in environments where the physical safety and security of staff is endangered (Fast, 2014). While the sector previously tended to classify employee stress as "post-traumatic stress disorder," it has now been recognized that stressors encompass a much wider spectrum than witnessing conflict and violence among clients. Awareness has emerged only recently, for example, of sexual harassment and violence experienced by, but also carried out by, staff from INGOs and multilateral agencies. Appleby (2010) documents the experience of sexual harassment among female international staff in East Timor at the hands of other international staff, as well as locals. As Csaky (2008) shows, the issue of child sexual abuse by United Nations Peacekeepers is only very slowly being recognized, let alone addressed. In relation to safety and security, as in other areas, a particular sensitivity to gender-related issues is therefore mandatory (Wille & Fast, 2011).

More generally, even though the paradigm of "gender and development" has been a key component of many aid initiatives over the last few decades, the pervasive focus on clients has somewhat occluded issues of gender-related policy and practice among INGO staff. While there have been calls by practitioners for INGOs to "get their own house in order" by promoting gender equality among staff as well as in client-facing programs, relatively little academic attention has been paid to these issues (see, however, de Jong, 2009, for the particular positionality of female staff in Northern INGOs; Eyben & Turquet, 2013 on feminist bureaucrats; and Fechter, 2015 on the relevance of gender among "development people" more generally). One interesting question arising from this context is whether female INGO staff, in their capacity as "internationally mobile professionals," may benefit professionally and personally from the increased mobility that their work entails. There are indications that the availability of (often female) domestic workers in the countries where they are posted, as well as the flexible nature of consultancy work, for example, enables dual-career households, combining professional opportunities with raising a family for both male and female staff (Fechter, 2013).

Travel and Expatriation

Efforts to situate projects within the world's poorest regions, and staff them with highly educated workers, necessitate a significant level of staff mobility and travel. National staff are often based in large cities, and frequently travel within the country and region to visit their INGO's projects. Simultaneously, staff based in Western headquarters will often travel to various international locations, both in the urban capital as well as occasionally to more rural project settings. Both shorter and longer trips are pursued for a number of reasons, including accountability, monitoring and oversight, assessments and evaluations, training and skills transfer, trouble-shooting or problem-solving, and filling staffing gaps. Maintaining a travel portfolio is crucial for continued advancement in the international aid world. Individuals who do not "get out" on a regular basis are branded as "disconnected." Given the evolving nature of the sector, international staff maintain a career advantage through their technical specialization and geographic flexibility.

Travel and expatriation are a prime mechanism by which professional and personal domains intersect and conflict. For national staff with families, it is often difficult to find jobs for both individuals in rural areas, so families are apart, often for long periods of time. Alternatively, families may live together in national capitals, but must travel frequently to rural areas for work. For international staff, similar processes are in play, though the distances between "home" and "work" are often greater. International staff engage in cycles of expatriation (and repatriation) as well as frequent international travel. For both national and international staff, relocation and travel dually influence home life and professional life as staff move both their personal and professionals selves simultaneously between geographic spaces (Harvey, 1997). Travel and expatriation can therefore pose additional challenges to staff well-being.

Conclusion

Strong HRM is pertinent to all organizations within the global development and humanitarian relief sector, from the largest INGOs to the most local CBOs. This chapter has provided an overview of the context of INGO work, including the history of international aid work, its division of knowledge, division of labor, and physical context. Moreover, the chapter has illuminated how these features impact both traditional aspects of domestic HRM (e.g. staffing, compensation, well-being, and training), as well as features that are more common in an IHRM context (e.g. travel, expatriation, and pay discrepancies). These concerns are all the more complex given the innumerable cultural and national differences across the various countries in which a single INGO works. The resulting HR considerations in global workforce management are influenced by myriad features of both the external environment, broadly, as well as the internal environment of the organization. We emphasize that it is the complexity involved in operating in different countries and employing people from different national and cultural backgrounds that differentiates INGO HRM from domestic nonprofit HRM, more than any major differences between the HR activities performed (Dowling, Festing, & Engle, 2008). Moreover, as international aid moves more fully into a transnationalized and nationalized model of workforce constitution, these issues will continue to evolve and change. As managers and employees wrestle with continuing global challenges, a responsive, strategic, and thoughtful approach to HRM is crucial to ensure the well-being and performance of staff and the fulfillment of their organizations' crucial goals.

Discussion Questions

1   What are the differences between a community-based organization (CBO), a non-governmental organization (NGO), and an international non-governmental organization (INGO)? How would staffing look similar or different across these organizations?

2   What types of knowledge are necessary for international aid work? How would you engage in staff selection to ensure you had all the necessary skills for a particular project?

3   Define the key actors working within the international aid sector, e.g. international and national, long-term contract, short-term consultant, and intern/volunteer. How clear are these different categorizations and what are the areas of overlap between different categories? Given that these categories are related to the type of contract an employee is offered, how would you categorize a Kenyan national working in Rwanda or a Chilean national working in Peru?

4   Explain the processes of professionalization and localization within the NGO sector.

5   Consider the practical and ethical issues facing HR managers when designing a reward system for an organization with offices in multiple countries. Design a compensation system for a small office in Krong Bavet, in eastern Cambodia near the Vietnam border. They have hired: (1) a single 60-year-old director from London; (2) a 34-year-old technical advisor who is from Vietnam with her husband and two children; (3) a 23-year-old Cambodian civil engineer from Phnom Penh; (4) a 42-year-old Cambodian project manager who is living apart from his wife and children, who are based in Phnom Penh; and (5) a 31-year-old woman from Krong Bavet, who acts as office administrator.

6   You are an HR manager at a medium-sized INGO with offices in 14 countries. Your organization employs mostly national staff, but some senior management roles in each country office are currently filled by international staff. Design a system for staff well-being, considering the varying needs of different staff members.

Note

1   The most critical analysis of the professionalization of international aid work argues that scientization of the sector is a rebranding attempt, so that those who have invested their lives in this industry can finish careers that would otherwise hold little opportunity to transfer to another industry. The reaction is in line with the research on threatened employment due to immigration trends, and with Michels' (1911 [2009]) analysis of social change organizations.

References

ActionAid. (2010). *Immersions: Making poverty personal*. ActionAid.

Appleby, R. (2010). 'A bit of a grope': Gender, sex and racial boundaries in transitional East Timor. *PORTAL Journal of Multidisciplinary International Studies*, 7(2).

Autesserre, S. (2014). *Peaceland: Conflict resolution and the everyday politics of international intervention*. New York: Cambridge University Press.

Baaz, M. E. (2005). *The paternalism of partnership: A postcolonial reading of identity in development aid*. New York: Zed Books.

Barley, S. R. & Kunda, G. (2006). Contracting: A new form of professional practice." *The Academy of Management Perspectives, 20,* 45–66.

Barley, S. R. & Kunda, G. (2011). *Gurus, hired guns, and warm bodies: Itinerant experts in a knowledge economy.* Princeton, NJ: Princeton University Press.

Bjerneld, M. (2009). Images, motives, and challenges for western health workers in humanitarian Aid. Dissertation, Uppsala University. Acta Universitatis Upsaliensis.

Bolton, S. & Muzio, D. (2008). The paradoxical processes of feminization in the professions: The case of established, aspiring and semi-professions. *Work, Employment & Society, 22*(2), 281–299.

Brewster, C. J. & Lee, S. (2006). HRM in not-for-profit organizations: Different, but also alike. In H. H. Larsen and W. Mayrhofer (Eds.), *European Human Resource Management* (pp. 131–148). London: Routledge.

Bromley, P. (2010). The Rationalization of Educational Development: Scientific Activity among International Nongovernmental Organizations. *Comparative Education Review, 54,* 577–601.

Caligiuri, P. M., Hyland, M., & Joshi, A. (1998). Families on global assignments: Applying work/family theories abroad. *Current Topics in Management, 3*(3), 313–328.

Carr, S. C., McWha, I., MacLachlan, M., & Furnham, A. (2010). International-local remuneration differences across six countries: Do they undermine poverty reduction work? *International Journal of Psychology, 45*(5), 321–340.

Chabbott, C. (2003). *Constructing education for development: international organizations and education for All.* London: Routledge.

Chabbott, C. & Ramirez, F. O. (2000). Development and education. *Handbook of the Sociology of Education, 89,* 163–187.

Chang, W. (2005). Expatriate training in international nongovernmental organizations: A model for research. *Human Resource Development Review, 4*(4), 440–461.

Chisholm, L. & Steiner-Khamsi, G. (2009). *South-South cooperation in education and development,* Cape Town: HSRC Press.

Collinson, S. & Duffield, M. (2013). Paradoxes of presence: Risk management and aid context conditions and individual characteristics on aid worker retention. *Disasters, 39*(3), 522–545.

Comoretto, A., Crichton, N., & Albery, I. (2011). *Resilience in humanitarian aid workers: Understanding processes of development.* LAP LAMBERT Academic Publishing.

Csaky, C. (2008). *No one to turn to: The underreporting of child sexual abuse among aid culture in challenging environments.* London: Overseas Development Institute Report.

De Jong, S. (2009). Constructive complicity enacted? The reflections of women NGO and IGO workers on their practices. *Journal for Intercultural Studies, 30*(4).

De Renzio, P. & Seifert, J. (2014). South–South cooperation and the future of development assistance: Mapping actors and options. *Third World Quarterly, 35*(10).

Devereux, P. (2008). International volunteering for development and sustainability: Outdated paternalism or a radical response to globalisation? *Development in Practice, 18*(3), 357–370.

Dicken, P. (1998). *Global shift: Transforming the world economy.* New York, NY: Guilford Press.

Dowling, P., Festing, M., & Engle, A. D. (2008). *International human resource management: Managing people in a multinational context.* Bristol: Cengage Learning.

Edwards, M. (1998). NGOs as value-based organizations: Does the reality fit the rhetoric? In D. J. Lewis (Ed.), *International Perspectives on Voluntary Action* (pp. 107–127). London: Earthscan.

Edwards, M., Hulme, D., & Wallace, T. (1999). NGOs in a global future: Marrying local delivery to worldwide leverage. *Public Administration and Development, 19*(2), 117–136.

Escobar, A. (1994). *Encountering development: The making and unmaking of the third world.* Princeton, NJ: Princeton University Press.

Eyben, R. (Ed.). (2006). *Relationships for aid*. Sterling, VA: Earthscan.

Eyben, R. & Turquet, L. (2013). *Feminists in development organisations: Change from the margins*. Rugby: Practical Action Publishing.

Fast, L. (2014). *Aid in danger: The perils and promise of humanitarianism*. Philadelphia: University of Pennsylvania Press.

Fechter, A.-M. (2012). 'Living well' while 'doing good'? (Missing) debates on altruism and professionalism in aid work. *Third World Quarterly, 33*(8), 1475–1491.

Fechter, A.-M. (2013). Mobility as enabling gender equality? The case of international aid workers. In T. Bastia (Ed.), *Migration and inequality*. London: Routledge.

Fechter, A.-M. (2015). Development people: how does gender matter? In A. Coles, L. Gray, & J. Mornsen (Eds.), *Routledge handbook of gender and development*. London: Routledge.

Ferrinho, P. & Van Lerberghe, W. (2002). Managing health professionals in the context of limited resources: A fine line between corruption and the need for moonlighting. Unpublished manuscript.

Fletcher, C. (2001). Performance appraisal and management: The developing research agenda. *Journal of Occupational and Organizational Psychology, 74*(4), 473–487.

Fowler, A. F. (1998). Authentic NGDO partnerships in the new policy agenda for international aid: Dead end or light ahead? *Development and Change, 29*(1), 137–159.

Gardner, K. & Lewis, D. (1996). *Anthropology, development, and the post-modern challenge*. Chicago: Pluto Press.

Girgis, M. (2007). The capacity-building paradox: Using friendship to build capacity in the South. *Development in Practice, 17*(3), 353–66.

Gould, J. (2004). Introducing aidnography. In J. Gould (Ed.), *Ethnographies of aid: Exploring development texts and encounters*. International Development Studies Occasional Paper.

Grant-Vallone, E. J. & Ensher, E. A. (2001). An examination of work and personal life conflict, organizational support, and employee health among international expatriates. *International Journal of Intercultural Relations, 25*(3), 261–278.

Habermas, J. (1970). *Toward a rational society: Student protest science and politics*. Boston, MA: Beacon Press.

Hancock, G. (1989). *Lords of poverty: The power, prestige, and corruption of the international aid business*. New York: Atlantic Monthly Press.

Harris, H. (2004). Global careers: Work-life issues and the adjustment of women international managers. *Journal of Management Development, 23*(9), 818–832.

Harvey, M. (1997). Dual-career expatriates: Expectations, adjustment and satisfaction with international relocation. *Journal of International Business Studies, 28*, 627–658.

Heaton-Shrestha, C. (2006). 'They can't mix like we can': Bracketing differences and the professionalization of NGOs in Nepal. In D. Lewis & D. Mosse (Eds.), *Development brokers and translators: The ethnography of aid and agencies*. Bloomfield, IN: Kumarian Press.

Hofstede, G. (1980). Motivation, leadership, and organization: Do American theories apply abroad? *Organizational Dynamics, 9*(1), 42–63.

Hui, C. H. & Triandis, H. C. (1989). Effects of culture and response format on extreme response style. *Journal of Cross-Cultural Psychology, 20*(3), 296–309.

Hwang, H. & Powell, W. (2009). The rationalization of charity: The influences of professionalism in the nonprofit sector. *Administrative Science Quarterly, 54*, 268–298.

Irvine, R., Chambers, R., & Eyben, R. (2004). Learning from poor people's experience: Immersions. *Lessons for Change no. 13*. Brighton: Institute of Development Studies.

Korff, V. P., Balbo, N., Mills, M., Heyse, L., & Wittek, R. (2015). The impact of humanitarian context, conditions and individual characteristics on aid worker retention. *Disasters, 39*(3), 522–545.

Kothari, U. (2006). Spatial practices and imaginaries: Experiences of colonial officers and development professionals. *Singapore Journal of Tropical Geography, 27*(3).

Kunda, G., Barley, S. R., & Evans, J. (2002). Why do contractors contract? The experience of highly skilled technical professionals in a contingent labor market. *Industrial & Labor Relations Review, 78,* 234–261.

Levitt, P. & Nadya Jaworsky, B. (2007). Transnational migration studies: Past developments and future trends. *Annual Review of Sociology, 33,* 129–156.

Lindenberg, M. & Dobel, J. P. (1999). The challenges of globalization for northern international relief and development NGOs. *Nonprofit and Voluntary Sector Quarterly 28,* 4–24.

MacLachlan, M., Carr, S. C., & McAuliffe, E. (2010). *The aid triangle: Recognising the human dynamics of dominance, justice and identity.* London: Zed.

Mawdsley, E. (2014). Human rights and south-south development cooperation: Reflections on the "rising powers" as international development actors. *Human Rights Quarterly, 36,* 630–652.

McWha, I. (2011). The roles of, and relationships between, expatriates, volunteers, and local development workers. *Development in Practice, 21*(1), 29–40.

Michels, R. (1911 [2009]). *Political parties: A sociological study of the oligarchical tendencies of modern democracy* (E. C. Paul, Trans.). New Brunswick. NJ: Transaction Publishers.

Moke, M. & Stoll, S. (2010). Professionalization of Humanitarian Action. In M. Moke & A. Zwitter (Eds.), *Humanitarian action facing the new challenges,* vol. 61. Berlin: BWV Verlag.

Oelberger, C. R. (2014). Private lives and public service: Role negotiation, career paths, and the microfoundations of institutional norms. Doctoral dissertation. Stanford University.

O'Flaherty, M. & Ulrich, G. (2010). The professionalization of human rights field work. *Journal of Human Rights Practice, 2,* 1–27.

Pigni, A. (2014). How to prevent burnout in aid work. WhyDev: www.whydev.org/how-to-prevent-burnout-in-aid-work/

Pottier, J., Bicker. A., & Sillitoe, P. (2003). *Negotiating local knowledge: Identity and power in development.* London: Pluto.

Rossi, B. (2006). Aid policies and recipient strategies in Niger: Why donors and recipients should not be compartmentalized into separate "worlds of knowledge". In D. Lewis & D. Mosse (Eds.), *Development brokers and translators: The ethnography of aid and agencies* (pp. 27–50). Sterling, VA: Kumarian Press.

Roth, S. (2015). *The paradoxes of aid work. Passionate professionals.* New York: Routledge.

Salamon, L. M. (1994). The rise of the nonprofit sector. *Foreign Affairs, 73,* 109–122.

Schiller, N. G., Basch, L., & Szanton Blanc, C. (1995). From immigrant to transmigrant: Theorizing transnational migration. *Anthropological Quarterly, 89,* 48–63.

Scholz, B. (2015). *The cosmopolitan potential of exclusive associations: Criteria for assessing the advancement of cosmopolitan norms.* Lanham, MD: Rowham and Littlefield.

Shaffer, M. A., Kraimer, M. L., Chen, Y.-P., & Bolino, M. C. (2012). Choices, challenges, and career consequences of global work experiences a review and future agenda. *Journal of Management, 38*(4), 1282–1327.

Sheehan, C., Fenwick, M., & Dowling, P. J. (2010). An investigation of paradigm choice in Australian international human resource management research. *The International Journal of Human Resource Management, 21*(11), 1816–1836.

Stubbs, P. (2003). International non-state actors and social development policy. *Global Social Policy, 3*(3), 319.

Toh, S. M. & DeNisi, A. S. (2003). Host country national reactions to expatriate pay policies: A model and implications. *Academy of Management Review, 28,* 606–621.

Toh, S. M. & DeNisi, A. S. (2005). A local perspective to expatriate success. *Academy of Management Executive, 19*(1), 132–146.

Toh, S. M. & DeNisi, A. S. (2007). Host country nationals as socializing agents: A social identity approach. *Journal of Organizational Behavior, 28*(3), 281–301.

Triandis, H. C. & Gelfand, M. J. (1998). Converging measurement of horizontal and vertical individualism and collectivism. *Journal of Personality and Social Psychology, 74*(1), 118–128.

Union of International Associations. (2008). *Yearbook of International Organizations.* www.uia.org/yearbook.

Van Rooy, A. (1998). *Civil society and the aid industry: The politics and promise.* New York: Earthscan.

Vance, C. M., McClaine, S. R., Boje, D. M., & Stage, H. D. (1992). An examination of the transferability of traditional performance appraisal principles across cultural boundaries. *MIR: Management International Review, 32*(4), 313–326.

Waldinger, R. & Fitzgerald, D. (2004). Transnationalism in question. *American Journal of Sociology, 109*, 1177–1195.

Walker, P. (2004). What does it mean to be a professional humanitarian? *The Journal of Humanitarian Assistance: 14.*

Walker, P. & Russ, C. (2010). Professionalising the humanitarian sector: A scoping study. *Enhancing Learning and Research for Humanitarian Assistance.*

Warne Peters, R. (2013). Development mobilities: Identity and authority in an Angolan development programme. *Journal of Ethnic and Migration Studies, 39*(2), 277–293.

Wille, C. & Fast, L. (2011). Aid, gender and security: The gendered nature of security events affecting aid workers and aid delivery. In *Security Insight* www.insecurityinsight.org/files/Security%20Facts%202%20Gender.pdf

17

Managing Generational Differences in Nonprofit Organizations

Jasmine McGinnis Johnson, Jaclyn Schede Piatak, and Eddy Ng

Introduction

Ensuring employees are satisfied with their jobs, committed, and engaged to the organizations for which they work are some of the most salient issues facing managers today. Despite a large amount of research describing the importance of managing all employees with strategic human resource practices, there have been increasing concerns about managing employees across all generations. For example, a number of popular press articles (Alsop, 2008; Lancaster & Stillman, 2009) bemoan the difficulty managers will likely face managing Millennials (individuals born between 1980 and 1995) who have different work values than previous generations, technology preferences, and ideas about work–life balance that are divergent from Baby Boomers (individuals born between 1946 and 1964) and Generation X'ers (individuals born between 1965 and 1979). Yet, many managers continue to grapple with how best to manage employees of all generational groups and many lack knowledge about whether or not learning about generations makes any difference in the workplace. Additionally, very little research on managing across generations is being conducted specific to the nonprofit sector (exceptions include Kunreuther, Kim, & Rodriguez, 2008; McGinnis, 2011; McGinnis Johnson & Ng, 2016; Ng & McGinnis Johnson 2015), and nonprofit managers may believe research on generations does not apply to them because nonprofit employees are inherently different from employees in other sectors.

In this chapter, we present a selection of theoretical and empirical research on work values within and across generations, describing the similarities and differences. We also summarize existing research specific to managing Millennial nonprofit employees. We then describe a strategic human resources (HR) approach to managing nonprofit employees of all generations and conclude by offering additional resources for those interested in managing Millennials in the nonprofit sector.

Work Values and Attraction to Nonprofit Work Across Generations

In nonprofit research, there have been many investigations of the relationship between an individual's work values (relatively stable preferences or needs around particular values in an occupational setting) and an individual's choice of occupation (e.g., Ng, Schweitzer, & Lyons, 2012). This is largely because nonprofit employees are willing to 'donate' their labor (Leete, 2001) and accept lower wages for comparable work performed in other sectors, since they receive some benefits from a nonprofit job consistent with their work values. This idea has been explained by person/environment fit or person/organization fit (Schneider, 1987).

Person/environment and person/organization fit models theorize that all employees have preferences for different work values. Individuals will select occupations and sectors that are congruent with their work values and provide the work-related rewards they prefer (Lyons, Duxbury, & Higgins, 2006; Ros, Schwartz, & Surkiss, 1999). Researchers group work values into several categories; extrinsic (the external rewards employees accrue from work, such as pay, security), intrinsic (the rewards employees accrue from work that are related to the nature of the job, such as interesting, challenging work), altruistic (a desire to help others, such as making a contribution to society, importance of social justice), social (relations with supervisors, coworkers, and others, such as coworker relations, a fun place to work), and prestige (status, influence, and power, such as prestigious work; employer is leader in the industry) (De Cooman, De Gieter, Pepermans, & Jegers, 2009; De Graaf & van Der Wal, 2008; Lyons et al., 2006). Wright and Christensen (2010) find that when employees work in occupations consistent with their work values, they will have higher job satisfaction and greater organizational commitment (Wright & Christensen, 2010).

However, there are mixed findings in empirical research regarding the work values of employees that self-select into the nonprofit sector (Devaro & Brookshire, 2007). On one hand, a subset of research finds nonprofit employees prioritize the intrinsic and altruistic values of the nonprofit sector (Benz, 2005; Kim & Lee, 2007). Consequently, nonprofit employees self-select into occupations that are found in the nonprofit sector because they receive intrinsic and altruistic rewards from the overall nature of nonprofit work (Faulk, Edwards, Lewis, & McGinnis, 2012). Since the nonprofit sector, as compared to for-profit and public sector organizations, places greater importance on the intrinsic and altruistic benefits of work, as opposed to extrinsic rewards such as pay or promotion opportunities, individuals who prefer these work values will self-select into the nonprofit sector (De Cooman et al., 2009; Lee & Wilkins, 2011). Studies confirm these findings, noting that nonprofit employees have work values inherently different from employees in other sectors. Lyons et al. (2006) find that nonprofit employees value career advancement less than their for-profit counterparts, which is also supported in Hansen et al.'s (2003) and Devaro and Brookshire's (2007) research on nonprofit employees. Studies of nonprofit employees paid overtime (Lanfranchi, Narcy, & Larguem, 2010) find that this reduced job satisfaction because the extrinsic rewards did not match the work values of nonprofit employees.

Moreover, studies of the pay differentials between comparable employees in the nonprofit sector and other sectors provide some evidence that nonprofit employees value extrinsic rewards less than employees of other sectors. Pay differentials between nonprofit and for-profit employees tend to show small, but statistically significant wage penalties for nonprofit employees, which again demonstrate that nonprofit employees may have different work values than employees in other sectors (Benz, 2005). For example, Onyx and Maclean's (1996) study of nonprofit professionals found that pay was not a significant predictor of why employees changed jobs, and in this study, 34% of the job changes nonprofit employees made resulted in a reduction in salaries. Moreover, 70% of the employees that changed jobs left because of a promotion or opportunity to gain new skills (Onyx & Maclean, 1996).

Contrary to these studies, other research has found that the work values of nonprofit employees may be more complicated than simple explanations of a desire for intrinsic and altruistic benefits (Chen & Bozeman, 2013). For example, some studies indicate that turnover in the nonprofit sector is consistently related to extrinsic rewards, specifically compensation (McGinnis Johnson & Ng, 2016; Mobley, 1982). In Issa and Herman's (1986) study of 26 nonprofit executives, although none selected low pay as the primary reason they were leaving, 88% indicated that pay was the second reason they were leaving their nonprofit positions. Brown and Yoshioka's (2003) research suggests that nonprofit employees' dissatisfaction with pay may override the intrinsic and altruistic benefits nonprofit employees expect to receive from their nonprofit employers.

For a subset of the nonprofit workforce, Millennials' compensation may be even more of a prominent factor in understanding work behaviors. Studies of Millennials in the nonprofit workforce (McGinnis, 2011; McGinnis Johnson & Ng, 2016) find that Millennials are more likely to leave their job due to low compensation. McGinnis (2011) found that across for-profit, public, and nonprofit sectors, nonprofit industries have the highest proportions of employees with graduate degrees, but nonprofit employees receive the lowest returns to graduate education. Likewise, McGinnis Johnson and Ng (2016) found the sector-switching intentions of Millennial nonprofit managers were predicted by an employee's pay and education. Therefore, concerns have emerged that previous human resource strategies based on the expectations that nonprofit employees may donate their labor in exchange for intrinsic and altruistic benefits from nonprofit work may not be consistent with the new generation of young, nonprofit leaders. In fact, a 2008 Ready to Lead study surveyed a sub-sample of young, nonprofit leaders, and many young leaders were concerned, not just about staying in their nonprofit job, but committing to the nonprofit sector due to low compensation (Cornelius, Corvington, & Ruesga, 2008). A 2011 TIAA-CREF Institute and Independent Sector study similarly found that young, nonprofit leaders were concerned about their ability to retire if they stayed employed in the nonprofit sector (TIAA CREF/Independent Sector, 2011). In light of this emerging research, nonprofit human resource scholars and practitioners must become more knowledgeable about the generational differences in work values. The differences and similarities in work values across generations are critical to understanding other topics such as an employee's organizational commitment, job satisfaction, and eventual organizational performance.

Generational Differences and Work Values

Smola and Sutton (2002) first established a link between generational differences and work values, which leads to differences in desired work outcomes. Their early findings suggest Generation X employees report less loyalty to the employer, are less committed to work, but are impatient to be promoted. However, as the workers age, they are more likely to express greater work centrality. Since the Smola and Sutton study, a number of other studies have also documented generational differences across personality and work values (see Ng & Parry, 2016 for a review).

Twenge, Konrath, Foster, Campbell, and Bushman (2008) examined 85 samples of college students between 1979 and 2006 and concluded that self-esteem and ego are on the rise. In another study, Gentile, Twenge, and Campbell (2010), examining high school and college students between 1988 and 2008, and the authors noted that 18% of the students in 2008 reported perfect self-esteem scores. Twenge and Campbell (2001) had earlier commented that the rise occurred during their high school and college years. The rise in self-esteem and narcissism levels has led to more individualistic behaviors among the younger generation in the workplace. Westerman, Bergman, Bergman, and Daly (2011) found high levels of narcissism among students to be related to job entitlement. As a result, organizations and employers are seeing a rise in unrealistically high expectations, a constant need for feedback and praise, and increasing turnover with successive generations when their needs are not satisfied (Ng, Schweitzer, & Lyons, 2010; Twenge & Campbell, 2008). Indeed, a number of studies have documented shifting work values—arising out of personality shifts—from one generation to another with workplace implications.

Work values are important because they can be indicative of the career preferences and types of work individuals prefer. In general, four work values are commonly studied in generational research: extrinsic (e.g., pay and benefits), intrinsic (interesting, challenging work), social (relations with coworkers, supervisors), and altruistic (e.g., helping behaviors) values. Twenge, Campbell, Hoffman, and Lance (2010) compared different work values across Baby Boomers,

Gen Xers, and Millennials and found that Millennials value extrinsic rewards more than Gen Xers and Baby Boomers. Hansen and Leuty (2012) examined work values across the Silent Generation, Baby Boomers, and Gen Xers, and found that Gen Xers emphasized compensation and job security, while the Silent Generation emphasized status and autonomy. Twenge, Campbell, Hoffman, and Lance (2010) also found that Millennials reported lower altruistic values than older generations. Ng and Parry (2016) conducted a comprehensive review of generational differences in work values and concluded that younger generations—particularly for the Millennials—do tend to exhibit a strong preference for extrinsic values and rewards, while the older generation of workers tends to prefer the intrinsic aspects of work. There was no evidence that Millennials espoused stronger altruistic values than preceding generations.

Of note, Krahn and Galambos (2014) found that Millennials value extrinsic rewards more than Gen Xers, and have stronger job entitlements (an expectation of a well-paying job with rising levels of education). As a result, Millennials have high expectations for pay and benefits and rapid advancement (Ng et al., 2010). This high level of expectation may be attributed to the high self-esteem and strong sense of entitlement fostered by a highly involved parenting style (Hill, 2002). Millennials' preference for high pay may be especially concerning for nonprofit organizations, given that, as an industry, nonprofits pay less than the public and for-profit sectors (Faulk, Edwards, Lewis, & McGinnis, 2012). An overemphasis on good pay and benefits by younger generations may lead to prospective employees self-selecting themselves out of nonprofit jobs and leaving when they are dissatisfied with their pay relative to their for-profit and public sector counterparts. Brown and Yoshioka's (2003) study found that even when employees are attracted to an organization because of its mission, being dissatisfied with pay may explain why they leave an organization—again demonstrating that what attracts an employee to an organization is not always the same factor that explains an organization's ability to retain them (Cornelius & Corvington, 2012).

In another study, Twenge and colleagues (2010) reported the desire for greater leisure time (with corresponding decrease in work centrality) and better work/life balance increases with younger generations, suggesting that the workers today are less committed to work than the Baby Boomers. Indeed, research studies have found that Baby Boomers more strongly espouse a "live to work" attitude, while younger generations tend to emphasize a "work to live" attitude (Gursoy, Maier, & Chi, 2008). The emphasis on leisure over work may be attributed to the younger generation of workers witnessing how Baby Boomers were downsized out of their jobs despite having significantly invested their lives into work (Ng et al., 2010). Moreover, as the younger generation begin their own families and negotiate parental care, they are more likely to demand greater work/life balance (Bianchi & Milkie, 2010). In this regard, nonprofit employers may do well in appealing to younger workers, as they can offer more flexible work arrangements (Ben-Ner & Ren, 2013; Kalleberg, Marsden, Reynolds, & Knoke, 2006) to accommodate greater life demands.

Additionally, despite popular beliefs that the younger generation displays concerns for the environment and expresses strong desires for meaningful and fulfilling work (cf. Ng et al., 2010), Twenge et al. (2010) reported the desire to help others among Millennials was no higher than previous generations. In another study, Chen and Choi (2008) reported that Millennials, in fact, score the lowest on altruistic work value compared to previous generations. Leveson and Joiner (2014) found that Millennials were, in fact, willing to trade off social responsibility for greater extrinsic rewards such as pay. Ertas (2015) reported volunteering hours—a behavior strongly associated with nonprofit employment (Piatak, 2015)—is also on the decline with younger generations. This is a cause for concern, as nonprofit organizations rely on public service appeal and donative labor to attract employees and volunteers (Einoff, 2015). Therefore, it should come as no surprise for Millennials to trade off social responsibility concerns for extrinsic rewards when asked to make job choice decisions (Leveson & Threse, 2014). These studies raise concerns about how nonprofits can continue attracting and retaining Millennials, a growing and important segment of the workforce.

Understanding the Challenges and Opportunities of Millennials' Work Values

Over the past two decades, competition for funding, a focus on performance metrics, and increased complexity in service demands have led to a growing reliance on professional staff to manage programs and run complex nonprofit organizations (Hwang & Powell, 2009; Park & Word, 2012; Smith & Lipsky, 1993; Suarez, 2009). This is a change from the composition of the workforce just 20 years ago, when the average nonprofit worker had some college education and most worked part-time (Preston, 1989). Currently, the average nonprofit worker is employed full-time and has a graduate degree (McGinnis, 2011).

However, Millennial nonprofit employees are also different from previous generations of nonprofit employees as they also hold higher proportions of Masters Degrees, Professional Degrees, and Doctorates than their counterparts in the for-profit and public sectors (McGinnis, 2011). Although statistics indicate young people are attracted to nonprofit work, there are concerns as to whether this commitment to the sector will be sustained due to questions of whether they are satisfied with compensation practices in nonprofit organizations (Brown & Yoshioka, 2003; Cornelius, Corvington, & Rusega, 2008; Cornelius, Moyers, & Bell, 2011; McGinnis Johnson & Ng, 2016). Moreover, there are few indications the average nonprofit organization has any strategic human resources strategy or practices (Guo, Brown, Ashcraft, Yoshioka, & Dong, 2011), so questions about how benefits, promotion opportunities, and other extrinsic benefits affect the likelihood Millennials are satisfied in their nonprofit jobs remain unanswered.

Until a few decades ago, scholarly research supported the notion an employee's choice to work in a particular sector was a permanent decision. For example,

Onyx and Maclean found that sector switching was rare in their 1996 study of nonprofit employees. Nonprofit employees tended to change jobs frequently (an average of 3.6 positions over 10 years), but most remained employed in the nonprofit sector. Yet, 20 years later, McGinnis Johnson and Ng's (2016) study of Millennial nonprofit employees found that compensation was the most significant predictor of sector-switching intention for Millennial nonprofit *managers* (even controlling for different benefit packages). This echoes concerns raised in popular press articles that Millennial employees are difficult to manage because they are interested in rapid advancement and compensation that is not proportionate with their abilities or skills (Ng et al., 2010).

One of the ways the preferences Millennials have about their career advancement may affect nonprofit managers is in their job mobility, or the movement of an employee from one job to another. Lyons et al.'s (2012, 2015) theory on job mobility across generations predicts a combination of factors explain the differences in the turnover or sector-switching intentions of Millennial employees. These factors include: (1) structural factors in the economy; (2) individual work values; and (3) decisional factors, such as a preference for mobility and norms about careers.

On one hand, structural factors in the broader economy have created a growing sense of sector agnosticism, where all generations of employees no longer feel they can only 'do good' in the nonprofit sector. Employees can pursue publicly-oriented missions in the for-profit sector through corporate volunteerism or various social enterprise initiatives (Cornelius et al., 2008; Lee & Whitford, 2008; Rose, 2013; TIAA CREF/Independent Sector, 2011; Tschirhart, Reed, Freeman, & Anker, 2008). A higher proportion of Millennial nonprofit employees are sector agnostic when compared to other generations. Several studies find that sector switching is very common for young, nonprofit employees, who often begin their careers in the nonprofit sector but later switch to other sectors (Chetkovich, 2003; Tschirhart et al. 2008; Piatak, 2012). Furthermore, graduate education constantly reinforces the transferability of skills across sectors, and as more Millennials enter the nonprofit workforce with graduate degrees, they may be more sector agnostic than previous generations (Mirabella & Young, 2012; McGinnis, 2011).

Decisional factors such as norms about career paths may also explain the greater propensity for Millennial nonprofit employees to leave their jobs or sector switch when compared to other generations. Employees across all generational cohorts believe there are costs (advancement and salary) to organizational commitment and do not intend to remain loyal to one employer. However, Millennials feel especially comfortable changing jobs frequently and consider lateral moves an important part of their career trajectories (Lyons et al., 2012, 2015). Lyons et al. (2012) found that Millennials changed jobs more frequently than Generation Xers, arguing "specifically, Millennials averaged 2.59 job changes when they were between the ages of 20 and 24, which was significantly greater than the 1.28 job changes for Xers, 1.39 changes for Boomers, and 0.60 job changes for Matures at the same age" (p. 343). The propensity of Millennials to change jobs more frequently is also confirmed in Lyons et al.'s research. Dries et al.'s (2008) investigation of five generations' career satisfaction and a meta-analysis of 16 cross sectional studies also found that organizational commitment decreased with each generational cohort (Cohen, 1993).

The mobility of Millennials was also found in research specifically focused on nonprofit organizations. Onyx and Maclean (1996) found young nonprofit workers tended to change jobs more frequently. Building on both a growing sense of sector agnosticism and the changing nature of careers, we suggest that Millennial nonprofit employees are more likely to leave their jobs when a nonprofit organization's human resource strategy does not consider the work values Millennials hold—which include but are not limited to—a greater desire for increased compensation, advancement opportunities, flexible schedules, or leisure benefits they desire.

Using Strategic Human Resource Management Practices to Manage Across Generations

Despite the different work values across generations, we suggest awareness of these challenges, along with a commitment to strategic human resource practices (SHRM), can ensure a high performing nonprofit organization with engaged, committed, and satisfied employees. SHRM aligns personnel management with the organization's goals rather than viewing human resource management as a separate organizational function. By taking a strategic approach, nonprofit organizations can assess their environmental context and plan for the future in pursuing their mission. SHRM can help nonprofits be proactive rather than reactive in recruitment and retention efforts.

The human resource management environment for nonprofits is challenging, as nonprofits are accountable to their funders and external and internal stakeholders to fulfill their missions. At the same time, the nonprofit sector is similar to other sectors, as a majority of nonprofit organizations' budgets go towards employees' salaries and benefits (Pynes, 2013). As a result of limited budgets, nonprofits have tended to use volunteers and hired employees who are willing to accept lower wages because they have a commitment to the mission of the organization or helping others. However, the nonprofit sector is both growing in numbers and evolving with different technologies and different organizational forms (social enterprise, benefit corporations, impact-investing firms). Therefore, recruitment efforts will need to focus on a new set of skills (Mesch, 2010) and improving compensation levels (Faulk, Edwards, Lewis, & McGinnis, 2012). The nonprofit sector can no longer solely rely on intrinsic motivation and commitment to helping others, especially as emerging research suggests this is not enough to recruit and retain the next generation of nonprofit employees, i.e. Millennials (those born between 1980–1995) and Generation Z (those born after 1996) (Ng & McGinnis Johnson, 2016).

Regardless of sector, SHRM practices can increase organizational performance (Pynes, 2013; Rodwell & Teo, 2004). SHRM practices and high performance work systems have been linked to both real and perceived measures of performance (Delaney & Huselid, 1996; De Prins & Henderickx, 2007). However, few nonprofits have human resource management specialists (Ban, Drahnak-Faller, & Towers, 2003), and most neglect to align organizational strategy with human resource management (Akingbola, 2006). Existing studies indicate that some nonprofits are more likely to adopt a strategic approach than others. External factors, such as funding, competition, and demographic changes, shape a nonprofit's human resource management approach (Walk, Schinnenburg, & Handy, 2014). Larger, more technologically advanced organizations that use independent contractors are more likely to adopt a SHRM approach, as are younger, educational organizations that do not have dedicated human resource staff (Guo et al., 2011).

Researchers have developed a typology to distinguish the human resource approaches that different nonprofits adopt based on the human resource and strategic orientation of the organization (Akingbola, 2013; Ridder, Baluch, & Piening, 2012; Ridder & McCandless, 2010; Ridder, Piening, & Baluch, 2012). Nonprofits with an administrative focus imitate practices from the for-profit sector without adapting them to the nonprofit context and view employees as a cost to minimize. Nonprofits with a strategic focus view employees as an asset to meet organizational goals, but may neglect the needs of the employees. Nonprofits that focus on employees emphasize organizational commitment and retention with benefits that support a work-life balance. Lastly, nonprofits with a value-driven focus tend to struggle to meet the diverse demands of internal and external stakeholders. Each of these approaches has implications for the main areas of a nonprofit's human resource approach—the recruitment and retention of employees. Schneider's (1987) attraction-selection-attrition framework conceptualizes that people apply for jobs that match their interests, organizations hire employees who are compatible with the organization, and employees leave when they no longer fit. Below we discuss this theoretical concept within the context of managing across generations for nonprofit organizations.

Recruiting and Retaining Nonprofit Employees with Traditional Methods

Nonprofits currently face the pressing challenge of recruiting and retaining effective employees. Studies have found people are often attracted to work in a nonprofit because of their identification with the organization's values and mission (Brown & Yoshioka, 2003; Kim & Lee, 2007; Word & Carpenter, 2013). Since mission attachment is an important aspect of nonprofit work, nonprofits rely more on social networks of current employees in recruitment efforts (Ben-Ner & Ren, 2013). However, an individual's fit with an organization may not be sufficient for retention. For example, Brown and Yoshioka (2003) found mission attachment helped with retention of younger, part-time employees, but "the intrinsic motivations run thin as full-time employees earn salaries that appear noncompetitive to other organizations" (p. 14). Similarly, Kim and Lee (2007) found that nonprofit employees sense of mission attachment did not hold when employees were dissatisfied with pay and/or career advancement opportunities. Nonprofit organizations should recruit people who believe in the organization's values and mission, which enhances employee satisfaction, attachment, and motivation, but this may not be enough to overcome dissatisfactions to retain employees (Herzberg, 2003). Despite the importance of mission attachment, nonprofit employees are less committed to their organizations than for-profit employees (Goulet & Frank, 2002). Retention is a serious issue, especially among younger nonprofit employees (Mann, 2006; Johnson & Ng, 2015; Ng & McGinnis Johnson, 2016).

Nonprofit employees have long been viewed as noble do-gooders willing to accept a lower wage because the work is more important than their salary (Lee & Wilkins, 2011; Leete, 2001, 2006; Mirvis & Hackett, 1983). In this sense, nonprofit employees are willing to 'donate' a portion of their time in order to have fulfilling work. Handy and Katz (1998) even argue, "the need for such self-selection is particularly important in nonprofits because they are not subject to the usual checks and balances imposed by shareholders on for-profits" (p. 259). However, people may leave the nonprofit sector in pursuit of higher wages (Lewis, 2010; McGinnis Johnson & Ng, 2016), and the nonprofit sector can no longer rely on employees to accept a lower wage (Brown and Yoshika 2003; Faulk et al., 2012). Nonprofits should move beyond the view that employees are a cost to be minimized to view employees both as an asset in pursuing the mission and as employees in need of organizational support.

Alternatives to Traditional Models of Retention

Nonprofit organizations have limited financial resources to compete with for-profit sector salaries (Frumkin & Andre-Clark, 2000) and have to legitimize compensation decisions to stakeholders, such as funders, volunteers, and the media (Akingbola, 2013b; Brandl & Güttel, 2007). In addition, pay-for-performance systems are rarely used because of both the relevance of the extrinsic reward with the potential for crowding-out effects and the difficulty of ensuring knowledge, control, and measurement of organizational goals (Theuvsen, 2004). Performance-based pay may thwart the motivation of nonprofit employees that are intrinsically motivated. In addition, nonprofit goals—much like those in the government—are more difficult to measure than goals in the for-profit sector (Perry et al., 2009). Brandl and Güttel (2007) found nonprofits with a competitive environment and freedom to formulate strategic goals were more likely to implement pay-for-performance systems, but also highlight several functional equivalents, including increased autonomy or flexible work hours.

Besides relying on the mission attachment and the nature of the sector, nonprofit organizations can pursue other human resource management strategies to retain employees. Nonprofit employees attracted to the mission and value of the organization expect a work environment that matches those values and gives them the opportunity to contribute to the mission (Quarter, Sousa, Richmond, & Carmichael, 2001; Schepers, 2005). Training helps align employee skills and values to the organization and is vital to ensure transfer of knowledge from one generation of employees to the next (Pynes, 2013). Increased unionization of nonprofit organizations is largely due to employee frustration with the work environment not matching the values and mission (Akingbola, 2013a). In order to sustain individuals' motivation that draws nonprofit employees to work in the organization, nonprofits must create and sustain a work environment that matches their organization's values and mission to retain these employees.

While nonprofit employees tend to value work that makes a difference and contributes to society (Lyons et al., 2006; Tschirhart et al., 2008), they also value responsibility, opportunities for advancement, and work-life balance (Leete, 2006; Park & Word, 2012). Mastracci and Herring (2010) found higher proportions of women in full-time and mission-critical positions in the nonprofit sector than the for-profit sector, which they credit to transparent, inclusive human resource management practices. Nonprofits are more likely to use self-directed work teams and offline committees than for-profit organizations (Kalleberg et al., 2006). In the nursing home context, nonprofits delegated more decision-making authority to their nurses than for-profit homes (Ben-Ner & Ren, 2013). Nonprofit organizations are beginning to take more of a SHRM approach by providing transparency and giving greater autonomy to employees. Nonprofits can compete with for-profit organizations by creating an inclusive and equitable work environment. Nonprofits can do so by creating transparent and inclusive, team-oriented organizational cultures to ensure all employees have a voice and equal opportunities for career advancement.

Nonprofit organizations also tend to offer more work-life benefits than the for-profit sector (Barbeito, Bowman, & Inc, 1998; Pitt-Catsouphes, Swanberg, Bond, & Galinsky, 2004). While smaller nonprofits may not be able to compete with for-profit sector wages, they can compete by getting creative with employee benefits. Some benefits bear no costs to the organization, such as allowing employees to take their pets into the office or allowing for casual dress days. Smaller organizations, those with 50–99 employees, are more likely to allow employees to work at home occasionally, take breaks at their discretion, and tend to family or personal needs during the workday without loss of pay, compared to large organizations with 1,000 or more employees nationwide (Matos & Galinsky, 2014). Smaller nonprofit organizations unable to compete with high salaries can offer employees greater flexibility and work-life balance.

Nonprofits also have the advantage of being able to use volunteers to diversify the human resource management pool and save costs. Handy, Mook, and Quarter (2007) find the interchangeability of employees and volunteers is a function of the organizational demand and volunteer labor supply, where the importance of employees to the organization's mission is relative to the availability of volunteers who can substitute for a permanent workforce. Organizations should anticipate the reaction of staff members if they are to use volunteers to replace paid employees, and nonprofits should work with employees to establish the parameters of any volunteer program (Pynes, 2013). To ensure volunteers and employees see one another as allies rather than competitors, volunteer programs should have a specific purpose and volunteers should have clearly delineated responsibilities. In examining government organizations, using volunteers in place of employees may be seen as unethical and may result in the loss of volunteers (Brudney, 1990). The nonprofit sector is also becoming more professionalized (Salamon, 1995; Weisbrod, 1998), and paid staff is likely to replace volunteers rather than the reverse. Nonprofits became more bureaucratic as they partnered with government to provide public services in the 1980s and 1990s (Smith & Lipsky, 1999) and have become more professional in recent decades adopting business practices (Hwang & Powell, 2009). Correspondingly, the nonprofit sector has a greater need for professional employees with a wide variety of skills, especially when faced with increased demand and/or fewer resources. The evolution of nonprofits highlights the need to recruit and retain the next generation of nonprofit employees to provide these technical skills.

Practical Implications/Advice for Nonprofits and Nonprofit Leaders

Despite research suggesting that nonprofits should provide an egalitarian work environment that matches their values and mission, nonprofits' dependence on resources from external organizations often limits this strategic approach to human resource practices. Funding organizations often require specific human resource practices, such as training, for funding to be granted (Akingbola, 2004). Funding organizations also place limits on the amount of funding that is allowed to go towards administrative costs. Many organizations report funders wanting funds to be used for direct services rather than overhead for infrastructure (Wing et al., 2005) or administrative staff (Ban et al., 2003). However, nonprofit organizations that are part of a national affiliate often have additional support through the sharing of best practices or access to a national human resource system (Ban et al., 2003). Due to changing revenue sources, human resource management practices vary depending on whether funding is available for certain staff positions, reliance on project-based funding for contract employees on a contingent basis, or requirements for specific policies or practices. We offer several suggestions that can work for nonprofit managers, who must manage both within and across generations.

- Implement a strategic human resource management approach that aligns with the organization's mission, not only to enhance organizational performance, but also to retain employees by creating a work environment that matches the organization's mission and values.

- When possible, offer more competitive salaries, as it is not feasible to rely on mission attachment alone.
- Ensure that all employees have some idea of how they can advance within the organization.
- Be transparent and inclusive with human resource management practices. Give employees the opportunity to voice their opinions in order to gain buy-in.
- Give employees autonomy in their jobs. Allow them to accomplish goals without specific instructions on the process, unless they ask.
- Provide supervisors training on giving employees feedback and recognition, outside of the annual performance review.
- Be creative with benefit options. Many benefits can be offered to employees to provide a greater work-life balance and to illustrate that the organization is supportive of its employees that have little to no costs. For example, some nonprofits will pay for lunch so that employees can develop mentor/mentee relationships. Others will pay the cost of the employees' national association dues.

While these recommendations focus on the recruitment and retention of Millenials, who have high expectations for pay, benefits, and opportunities for advancement (Ng et al., 2010), a SHRM approach can help nonprofits in the recruitment and retention of employees across generations. By linking the management of human resources with the management of organizational objectives, nonprofits can lay out a strategic plan to recruit and retain employees needed to pursue their mission. Generations may not require distinct working conditions (Yang & Guy, 2006). In addition, the influence of life stages or age-related changes in an employee's career depends on work circumstances (Kafner & Ackerman, 2004). Nonprofit managers should employ SHRM to create a work environment that supports all generations.

The nonprofit sector is growing and becoming more professional, where human resources can no longer rely on the altruism of employees to 'donate' part of their work efforts. For the nonprofit sector to compete with both the government and for-profit sectors, nonprofit organizations need to be strategic in their human resource practices. To recruit the next generation and retain current employees, nonprofit managers should employ SHRM to create opportunities for advancement, a transparent, inclusive work environment, and positions with meaningful compensation, autonomy, and recognition.

Discussion Questions

1   What do you think the biggest challenge is for nonprofits managing a multi-generational workforce?
2   As a member of your generation, what attracts you to a specific job? What would make you want to build a career with that organization?

3 Do you think a multi-generational workforce breeds competition or cooperation? Why? How can managers foster a culture of cooperation and learning?

4 What are some of the ways in which nonprofits can make themselves more attractive as employers to Millennials?

5 How do older generations (e.g., the Silent Generation and Baby Boomers) view the younger generations (e.g., Millennials) and vice versa? What are some of the stereotypes each generation has for each other?

6 What can Baby Boomers and Millennials learn from each other? How can employers facilitate knowledge transfer across the different generations?

7 How would careers change for Millennials and future generations in terms of the types, quantity, and quality of work?

Further Reading

For additional resources on managing across generations, see the following resources:

Carpenter, H. & Qualls, T. (2015). *The talent development platform: Putting people first in social change organizations*. San Francisco, CA: Wiley.

Hamidullah, M. (2016). *Managing the next generation of public workers*. New York, NY: Routledge. *Talent Philanthropy Project: The Talent Philanthropy Project* (#fundthepeople) works to increase the incentives and knock down the barriers to "talent investing" by producing ideas and research, education and training, and practical tools that funders and fundraisers can use within their ongoing work. www.talentphilanthropy.

References

Akingbola, K. (2004). Staffing, retention, and government funding: A case study. *Nonprofit Management & Leadership*, *14*(4), 453–465.

Akingbola, K. (2006). Strategy and HRM in nonprofit organizations: Evidence from Canada. *The International Journal of Human Resource Management*, *17*(10), 1707–1725.

Akingbola, K. (2013a). Context and nonprofit human resource management. *Administration & Society*, *45*(8), 974–1004.

Akingbola, K. (2013b). A model of strategic nonprofit human resource management. *Voluntas: International Journal of Voluntary and Nonprofit Organizations*, *24*(1), 214–240.

Alsop, R. (2008). *The trophy kids grow up: How the millennial generation is shaking up the workplace*. New York: John Wiley & Sons, Inc.

Ban, C., Drahnak-Faller, A., & Towers, M. (2003). Human resource challenges in human service and community development organizations recruitment and retention of professional staff. *Review of Public Personnel Administration*, *23*(2), 133–153.

Barbeito, C. L., Bowman, J. P., & Inc, A. R. and D. I. I. (1998). *Nonprofit compensation and benefits practices*. Hoboken, NJ: Wiley.

Ben-Ner, A. & Ren, T. (2013). Comparing workplace organization design based on form of ownership: nonprofit, for-profit, and local government. *Nonprofit and Voluntary Sector Quarterly*, *44*(2), 340–359.

Benz, M. (2005). Not for the profit, but for the satisfaction? Evidence on worker well being in non profit firms. *Kyklos*, *58*(2), 155–176.

Bianchi, S. M. & Milkie, M. A. (2010). Work and family research in the first decade of the 21st century. *Journal of Marriage and Family, 72*(3), 705–725.

Brandl, J. & Güttel, W. H. (2007). Organizational antecedents of pay-for-performance systems in nonprofit organizations. *Voluntas: International Journal of Voluntary and Nonprofit Organizations, 18*(2), 176–199.

Brown, W. A. & Yoshioka, C. F. (2003). Mission attachment and satisfaction as factors in employee retention. *Nonprofit Management & Leadership, 14*(1), 5–18.

Brudney, J. L. (1990). *Fostering volunteer programs in the public sector: Planning, initiating, and managing voluntary activities.* San Francisco: Jossey-Bass.

Chen, C. A. & Bozeman, B. (2013). Understanding public and nonprofit managers' motivation through the lens of self-determination theory. *Public Management Review, 15*(4), 584–607.

Chen, P. J. & Choi, Y. (2008). Generational differences in work values: A study of hospitality management. *International Journal of Contemporary Hospitality Management, 20*(6), 595–615.

Chetkovich, C. (2003). What's in a sector? The shifting career plans of public policy students. *Public Administration Review, 63*(6), 660–674.

Cohen, A. (1993). Age and tenure in relation to organizational commitment: A meta-analysis. *Basic and Applied Social Psychology, 14,* 143–159.

Cornelius, M. & Corvington, P. (2012). Nonprofit workforce dynamics. In L. Salamon (Ed.), *The state of nonprofit America.* Washington, DC: Brookings Institution Press.

Cornelius, M., Corvington, P., & Ruesga, A. (2008). *Ready to lead? Next generation leaders speak out.* Baltimore, MD: Annie E. Casey Foundation.

Cornelius, M., Moyers, R., & Bell, J. (2011). *Daring to lead.* Retrieved from www.daringtolead.org

De Cooman, R., De Gieter, S., Pepermans, R., & Jegers, M. (2009). A cross-sector comparison of motivation-related concepts in for-profit and not-for-profit service organizations. *Nonprofit and Voluntary Sector Quarterly, 40*(2), 296–317.

De Graaf, G. & van Der Wal, Z. (2008). On value differences experienced by sector switchers. *Administration & Society, 40*(1), 79–103.

Delaney, J. T. & Huselid, M. A. (1996). The impact of human resource management practices on perceptions of organizational performance. *Academy of Management Journal, 39*(4), 949–969.

De Prins, P. & Henderickx, E. (2007). HRM Effectiveness in older people's and nursing homes: The search for best (quality) practices. *Nonprofit and Voluntary Sector Quarterly, 36*(4), 549–571.

Devaro, J. & Brookshire, D. (2007). Promotions and incentives in nonprofit and for-profit organizations. *Industrial & Labor Relations Review, 60*(3), 311–339.

Dries, N., Pepermans, R., & De Kerpel, E. (2008). Exploring four generations' beliefs about career: Is "satisfied" the new "successful"? *Journal of Managerial Psychology, 23*(8), 907–928.

Einoff, C. J. (2015). Millennials and public service motivation: Findings from a survey of master's degree students. Forthcoming in *Public Administration Quarterly*.

Ertas, N. (2015). Public service motivation theory and participation in formal and informal groups: Do Millennials in public service participate more? Forthcoming in *Public Administration Quarterly*.

Faulk, L., Edwards, L. H., Lewis, G. B., & McGinnis, J. (2012). An analysis of gender pay disparity in the nonprofit sector: An outcome of labor motivation or gendered jobs? *Nonprofit and Voluntary Sector Quarterly, 42*(6), 1268–1287.

Friedell, K., Puskala, K., Smith, M., & Villa, N. (2011). Hiring, promotion, and progress: Millennials' expectations in the workplace. *St. Olaf College Working Paper*.

Frumkin, P. & Andre-Clark, A. (2000). When missions, markets, and politics collide: Values and strategy in the nonprofit human services. *Nonprofit and Voluntary Sector Quarterly, 29*(Suppl. 1), 141–163.

Goulet, L. R. & Frank, M. L. (2002). Organizational commitment across three sectors: Public, non-profit, and for-profit. *Public Personnel Management, 31*(2), 201–210.

Guo, C., Brown, W. A., Ashcraft, R. F., Yoshioka, C. F., & Dong, H.-K. D. (2011). Strategic human resources management in nonprofit organizations. *Review of Public Personnel Administration, 31*(3), 248–269.

Gursoy, D., Maier, T. A., & Chi, C. G. (2008). Generational differences: An examination of work values and generational gaps in the hospitality workforce. *International Journal of Hospitality Management, 27*(3), 448–458.

Handy, F. & Katz, E. (1998). The wage differential between nonprofit institutions and corporations: Getting more by paying less? *Journal of Comparative Economics, 26*(2), 246–261.

Handy, F., Mook, L., & Quarter, J. (2007). The interchangeability of paid staff and volunteers in nonprofit organizations. *Nonprofit and Voluntary Sector Quarterly*. Retrieved from: http://nvs.sagepub.com/content/early/2007/10/12/0899764007303528.short

Hansen, S., Huggins, L., & Ban, C. (2003). Explaining the recruitment and retention by nonprofit organizations: A survey of Pittsburgh area university graduates. *University of Pittsburgh, Report to the Forbes Funds/Copeland Foundation*.

Hansen, J. I. C. & Leuty, M. E. (2012). Work values across generations. *Journal of Career Assessment, 20*(1), 34–52.

Hwang, H. & Powell, W. W. (2009). The rationalization of charity: The influences of professionalism in the nonprofit sector. *Administrative Science Quarterly, 54*(2), 268–298.

Herzberg, F. (2003). One more time: How do you motivate employees? *Harvard Business Review, 81*(1), 87–96.

Hill, R. P. (2002). Managing across generations in the 21st century. *Journal of Management Inquiry, 11*(1), 60–66.

Hwang, H. & Powell, W. W. (2009). The rationalization of charity: The influences of professionalism in the nonprofit sector. *Administrative Science Quarterly, 54*(2), 268–298.

Issa, J. & Herman, R. D. (1986). Turnover among nonprofit chief executives: An initial investigation of self-reported causes and consequences. *Nonprofit and Voluntary Sector Quarterly, 15*(3), 54–59.

Johnson, J. M. & Ng, E. S. (2016). Money talks or Millennials walk the effect of compensation on nonprofit Millennial workers sector-switching intentions. *Review of Public Personnel Administration*, 0734371X15587980.

Kalleberg, A. L., Marsden, P. V., Reynolds, J., & Knoke, D. (2006). Beyond profit? Sectoral differences in high-performance work practices. *Work and Occupations, 33*(3), 271–302.

Kanfer, R. & Ackerman, P. L. (2004). Aging, adult development, and work motivation. *Academy of Management Review, 29*(3), 440–458.

Kim, S. E. & Lee, J. W. (2007). Is mission attachment an effective management tool for employee retention? An empirical analysis of a nonprofit human services agency. *Review of Public Personnel Administration, 27*(3), 227–248.

Krahn, H. J. & Galambos, N. L. (2014). Work values and beliefs of 'Generation X' and 'Generation Y'. *Journal of Youth Studies, 17*(1), 92–112.

Kunreuther, F., Kim, H., & Rodriguez, R. (2008). *Working across generations: Defining the future of nonprofit leadership* (32). San Francisco: John Wiley & Sons.

Lancaster, L. C. & Stillman, D. (2009). *When generations collide*. New York: HarperCollins.

Lanfranchi, J., Narcy, M., & Larguem, M. (2010). Shedding new light on intrinsic motivation to work: Evidence from a discrete choice experiment. *Kyklos, 63*(1), 75–93.

Lee, S. Y. & Whitford, A. B. (2008). Exit, voice, loyalty, and pay: Evidence from the public workforce. *Journal of Public Administration Research and Theory, 18*(4), 647–671.

Lee, Y. & Wilkins, V. M. (2011). More similarities or more differences? Comparing public and nonprofit managers' job motivations. *Public Administration Review, 71*(1), 45–56.

Leete, L. (2001). Whither the nonprofit wage differential? Estimates from the 1990 census. *Journal of Labor Economics, 19*(1), 136–170.

Leete, L. (2006). Work in the Nonprofit Sector. In W. W. Powell & R. Steinburg (Eds.), *The Nonprofit sector: A research handbook* (pp. 159–179). New Haven, CT: Yale University Press.

Leveson, L. & Joiner, A. T. (2014). Exploring corporate social responsibility values of millennial job-seeking students. *Education+ Training, 56*(1), 21–34.

Lewis, G. B. (2010). Modeling nonprofit employment: Why do so many lesbians and gay men work for nonprofit organizations? *Administration & Society, 42*(6), 720–748.

Lyons, S. T., Duxbury, L. E., & Higgins, C. A. (2006). A comparison of the values and commitment of private sector, public sector, and parapublic sector employees. *Public Administration Review, 87*, 605–618.

Lyons, S. T., Schweitzer, L., & Ng, E. S. (2015). How have careers changed? An investigation of changing career patterns across four generations. *Journal of Managerial Psychology, 30*(1), 8–21.

Lyons, S. T., Schweitzer, L., Ng, E. S., & Kuron, L. K. (2012). Comparing apples to apples: A qualitative investigation of career mobility patterns across four generations. *Career Development International, 17*(4), 333–357.

Mann, G. A. (2006). A motive to serve: Public service motivation in human resource management and the role of PSM in the nonprofit sector. *Public Personnel Management, 35*(1), 33–48.

Mastracci, S. H. & Herring, C. (2010). Nonprofit management practices and work processes to promote gender diversity. *Nonprofit Management & Leadership, 21*(2), 155–175.

Matos, K., & Galinsky, E. (2014). *National study of employers*. New York: Families and Work Institute.

McGinnis, J. (2011). The young and restless: Generation Y in the nonprofit workforce. *Public Administration Quarterly*, 342–362.

McGinnis Johnson, J. & Ng, E. S. (2016). Money talks or millennials walk: The effect of compensation on nonprofit millennial workers sector-switching intentions. *Review of Public Personnel Administration, 36*(3), 283–305.

Mesch, D. J. (2010). Management of human resources in 2020: The outlook for nonprofit organizations. *Public Administration Review, 70*(S1), S173.

Mirabella, R. & Young, D. R. (2012). The development of education for social entrepreneurship and nonprofit management: Diverging or converging paths? *Nonprofit Management & Leadership, 23*(1), 43–57.

Mirvis, P. H. & Hackett, E. J. (1983). Work and work force characteristics in the nonprofit sector. *Monthly Labor Review*, 3–12.

Mobley, W. H. (1982). Some unanswered questions in turnover and withdrawal research. *Academy of Management Review, 7*(1), 111–116.

Ng, E. S. & McGinnis Johnson, J. (2015). Millennials: Who are they, how are they different, and why should we care? In *The multigenerational workforce: Challenges and opportunities for organisations* (pp. 121–137). Cheltenham: Edward Elgar.

Ng, E. S. & Parry, E. (2016). Multigenerational research in human resource management. In *Research in Personnel and Human Resources Management* (pp. 1–41). Bibgley: Emerald Group Publishing Limited.

Ng, E. S., Schweitzer, L., & Lyons, S. T. (2010). New generation, great expectations: A field study of the millennial generation. *Journal of Business and Psychology, 25*(2), 281–292.

Ng, E. S., Schweitzer, L., & Lyons, S. T. (2012). Anticipated discrimination and a career choice in nonprofit a study of early career lesbian, gay, bisexual, transgendered (LGBT) job seekers. *Review of Public Personnel Administration*, *32*(4), 332–352.

Onyx, J. & Maclean, M. (1996). Careers in the third sector. *Nonprofit Management & Leadership*, *6*(4), 331–345.

Park, S. M. & Word, J. (2012). Driven to service: Intrinsic and extrinsic motivation for public and nonprofit managers. *Public Personnel Management*, *41*(4), 705–734.

Perry, J. L., Engbers, T. A., & Jun, S. Y. (2009). Back to the future? Performance related pay, empirical research, and the perils of persistence. *Public Administration Review*, 69(1), 39–51.

Piatak, J. (2012). Sector switching in good times and in bad: Are public sector employees less likely to change sectors? *APSA 2012 Annual Meeting Paper*.

Piatak, J. S. (2015). Altruism by job sector: Can public sector employees lead the way in rebuilding social capital? *Journal of Public Administration Research and Theory*, *25*(3), 877–900.

Pitt-Catsouphes, M., Swanberg, J. E., Bond, J. T., & Galinsky, E. (2004). Work-life policies and programs: Comparing the responsiveness of nonprofit and for-profit organizations. *Nonprofit Management & Leadership*, *14*(3), 291–312.

Preston, A. E. (1989). The nonprofit worker in a for-profit world. *Journal of Labor Economics*, *65*, 438–463.

Pynes, J. E. (2013). *Human resources management for public and nonprofit organizations: A strategic approach*. San Francisco: John Wiley & Sons.

Quarter, J., Sousa, J., Richmond, B. J., & Carmichael, I. (2001). Comparing member-based organizations within a social economy framework. *Nonprofit and Voluntary Sector Quarterly*, *30*(2), 351–375.

Ridder, H.-G., Baluch, A. M., & Piening, E. P. (2012). The whole is more than the sum of its parts? How HRM is configured in nonprofit organizations and why it matters. *Human Resource Management Review*, *22*(1), 1–14.

Ridder, H.-G. & McCandless, A. (2010). Influences on the architecture of human resource management in nonprofit organizations: An analytical framework. *Nonprofit and Voluntary Sector Quarterly*, *39*(1), 124–141.

Ridder, H.-G., Piening, E. P., & Baluch, A. M. (2012). The third way reconfigured: How and why nonprofit organizations are shifting their human resource management. *Voluntas: International Journal of Voluntary and Nonprofit Organizations*, *23*(3), 605–635.

Rodwell, J. J. & Teo, S. T. (2004). Strategic HRM in for-profit and non-profit organizations in a knowledge-intensive industry: The same issues predict performance for both types of organization. *Public Management Review*, *6*(3), 311–331.

Ros, M., Schwartz, S. H., & Surkiss, S. (1999). Basic individual values, work values, and the meaning of work. *Applied Psychology*, *113*, 49–71.

Rose, R. P. (2013) Preferences for careers in public work: Examining the government-nonprofit divide among undergraduates through public service motivation. *The American Review of Public Administration*, *43*, 416–437.

Salamon, L. M. (1995). *Partners in public service: Government-nonprofit relations in the modern welfare state*. Baltimore, MD: Johns Hopkins University Press.

Schepers, C., De Gieter, S., Pepermans, R., Bois, C. Du, Caers, R., & Jegers, M. (2005). How are employees of the nonprofit sector motivated. *Nonprofit Management & Leadership*, *16*(2), 191–208.

Schneider, B. (1987). The people make the place. *Personnel Psychology*, *40*(3), 437–453.

Smith, S. R. & Lipsky, M. (1993). *Nonprofits for hire: The welfare state in the age of contracting*. Cambridge, MA: Harvard University Press.

Smola, K. W., & Sutton, C. D. (2002). Generational differences: Revisiting generational work values for the new millennium. *Journal of Organizational Behavior*, *23*(SPI), 363–382.

Suarez, D. F. (2009). Street credentials and management backgrounds: Careers of nonprofit executives in an evolving sector. *Nonprofit and Voluntary Sector Quarterly, 39*(4), 696–716.

Theuvsen, L. (2004). Doing better while doing good: Motivational aspects of pay-for-performance effectiveness in nonprofit organizations. *Voluntas: International Journal of Voluntary and Nonprofit Organizations, 15*(2), 117–136.

TIAA CREF/Independent Sector. (2011). Financial security and careers in the nonprofit and philanthropic sector. Available at: www.independentsector.org/financial_security

Tschirhart, M., Reed, K. K., Freeman, S. J., & Anker, A. L. (2008). Is the grass greener? Sector shifting and choice of sector by MPA and MBA graduates. *Nonprofit and Voluntary Sector Quarterly, 37*(4), 668–688.

Twenge, J. M. & Campbell, W. K. (2001). Age and birth cohort differences in self-esteem: A cross-temporal meta-analysis. *Personality and Social Psychology Review, 5*(4), 321–344.

Twenge, J. M. & Campbell, S. M. (2008). Generational differences in psychological traits and their impact on the workplace. *Journal of Managerial Psychology, 23*(8), 862–877.

Twenge, J. M., Campbell, W. K., & Freeman, E. C. (2012). Generational differences in young adults' life goals, concern for others, and civic orientation, 1966–2009. *Journal of Personality and Social Psychology, 102*(5), 1045.

Twenge, J. M., Campbell, S. M., Hoffman, B. J., & Lance, C. E. (2010). Generational differences in work values: Leisure and extrinsic values increasing, social and intrinsic values decreasing. *Journal of Management, 36*(5), 1117–1142.

Twenge, J. M., Konrath, S., Foster, J. D., Keith Campbell, W., & Bushman, B. J. (2008). Egos inflating over time: A cross temporal meta analysis of the Narcissistic personality inventory. *Journal of Personality, 76*(4), 875–902.

Walk, M., Schinnenburg, H., & Handy, F. (2014). Missing in action: Strategic human resource management in German nonprofits. *Voluntas: International Journal of Voluntary and Nonprofit Organizations, 25*(4), 991–1021.

Weisbrod, B. A. (1998). Guest editor's introduction: The nonprofit mission and its financing. *Journal of Policy Analysis and Management, 17*(2), 165–174.

Westerman, J. W., Bergman, J. Z., Bergman, S. M., & Daly, J. P. (2012). Are universities creating millennial narcissistic employees? An empirical examination of narcissism in business students and its implications. *Journal of Management Education, 36*(1), 5–32.

Wing, F., Hager, M., Rooney, P., & Pollak, T. (2005). Paying for not paying for overhead. *Foundation News and Commentary*, May/June: 32–37.

Word, J. & Carpenter, H. (2013). The new public service? Applying the public service motivation model to nonprofit employees. *Public Personnel Management, 42*(3), 315–336.

Wright, B. E. & Christensen, R. K. (2010). Public service motivation: A test of the job attraction–selection–attrition model. *International Public Management Journal, 13*(2), 155–176.

Yang, S. B. & Guy, M. E. (2006). GenXers versus boomers: Work motivators and management implications. *Public Performance & Management Review, 29*(3), 267–284.

18

Diversity and Diversity Management in Nonprofit Organizations

Judith Y. Weisinger

---

di·ver·si·ty (d-vûrs-t, d-) n.: the quality of being different or unique at the individual or group level.

in·clu·sion (n-klzhn) n.: a strategy to leverage diversity. Diversity always exists in social systems. Inclusion, on the other hand, must be created.

United Way's Diversity and Inclusion page at
www.unitedway.org/about/diversity-and-inclusion

Karamu House stands tall in our nation's history as an inclusive institution that served as a common ground for Clevelanders of different races, religions, and social and economic backgrounds, as well as a trusted community resource for local families.

webpages of the Karamu House theater, Cleveland, Ohio:
www.karamuhouse.org/about-karamu-house

Our mission to serve *every* student is part of what makes our tutoring service the best one for *any* student. Simply put, there is strength in diversity, and competitive advantage in knowing how to help *all* students succeed, not just a narrow subset.

webpages of the Aspire Education Project, at tutoring and educational services
nonprofit in the East Bay, California: http://aspireeducation.org/story/

Introduction

The above examples indicate the wide degree with which the term "diversity" is interpreted and used within nonprofit organizations and in the nonprofit sector as a whole. "Diversity" has been variously defined in the management literature to reflect many dimensions of difference, whether cultural, gender-based, racial or ethnic, related to (dis)abilities, and sometimes even personality traits; and "diversity management" has generally referred to how these dimensions of difference can be "managed" for increased organizational performance and effectiveness. For example, Ivancevich and Gilbert (2000, p. 77) define diversity management as "the commitment on the part of organizations to recruit, retain, reward and promote a heterogeneous mix of productive, motivated, and committed workers including people of color, whites, females, and the physically challenged." In practice, more often than not "diversity" is used to mean representational diversity (Weisinger & Salipante, 2005), or the degree to which organizational membership—board, leadership, staff, volunteers—reflects underrepresented or underserved groups in society. Relatedly, compositional diversity (Gazley, Chang, & Bingham, 2010) can include the degree to which the demographic diversity in a nonprofit organization reflects its various stakeholders.

The Hudson Institute's Workforce 2000 report brought to the management forefront a picture of the U.S. workforce as becoming increasing diverse, with its projection that women, immigrants and (racial/ethnic) minorities would comprise two-thirds of new entrants (Johnston & Packer, 1987). The report implored organizations to take seriously how they were going to manage this workforce diversity. Thus, conceptually, diversity was distinguished from equal employment opportunity (EEO), a legal concept focused on leveling the playing field for protected classes through antidiscrimination laws. As such, EEO efforts are compliance-focused while diversity efforts are voluntary. It should be noted here that critical diversity scholars assert that the diversity concept reflects a "re-appropriation of equal opportunities" (Zanoni, Janssens, Benschop, & Nkomo, 2010, p. 9). According to these authors, this re-appropriation involved rhetoric highlighting diversity as positive and empowering, while at the same time obscuring hidden power dynamics, in particular as concerns race, ethnicity and gender, and making these dynamics more difficult to challenge. As discussed later in this chapter, conceptualizations of diversity are rife with tensions and contradictions that pose challenges for "managing" diversity in organizations, including nonprofits.

Despite the conceptual distinction, in practice, diversity and EEO efforts may be integrated within an organization—representational diversity can refer to traditionally underrepresented groups that are the focus of recruitment and retention efforts. But representational diversity dynamics are also contextual. That is, the characteristics that make a nonprofit "more diverse" depends upon how that organization currently "looks." For example, in a predominantly women-centered nonprofit, staffing more men could be considered diversifying the staff. Or, a nonprofit might enhance representational diversity among its volunteers from the local Muslim community, members of which have not historically been involved with the nonprofit and who are not traditionally considered 'underrepresented'. Thus, representational diversity can be quite broad, depending upon the organizational context.

Breadth of representation notwithstanding, author Derwin Dubose (2014) asserts that the nonprofit sector has a "Ferguson problem." For example, Dubose compares the glaring underrepresentation of African Americans in public leadership and in the police force in Ferguson, Missouri—a city that is two-thirds African American—to that in the nonprofit sector. Dubose paints the following portrait of the sector, citing various recent studies, including one by CommonGoodCareers and the Level Playing Field Institute, which highlights the over-representation of whites in the workforce at 82% (Schwartz, Weinberg, Hagenbuch, & Scott, 2016). This is even more pronounced on a deeper dive into the representation:

> The gap in representation is more pronounced in nonprofit governance, where only 14 percent of board members are people of color. Similarly, in specialized functions such as development, less than six percent of roles are filled by people of color.
>
> *(Schwartz et al., 2016, p. 5, citing the Chronicle of Philanthropy, Association of Fundraising Professionals)*

These data are supported by several studies (Peters & Wolfred, 2001 and Teegarden, 2004) which found that between 75% and 84%, respectively, of nonprofits are led by whites, roughly 10% by African Americans, between 3% and 4% by Latinos, and 6.4% by Asians (Peters & Wolfred, 2001).

Similarly, with regard to human service organizations in particular, Mor Barak states: "Human services organizations have traditionally served a wide array of communities with a high representation of diverse, disadvantaged, and oppressed groups. This diversity has not been typically mirrored in the workforces of those organizations" (Mor Barak, 2015, p. 84). Thus, at the basic level of representation, nonprofit organizations are not wholly representative of their clients and communities, at least when it comes to race and ethnicity involving traditionally underserved groups. Further, some areas in the nonprofit sector suffer from a significant underrepresentation of women. The *Nonprofit Quarterly* has reported on this deficit in environmental organizations, where 70% of presidents and board chairs in conservation/preservation organizations are men; and as with museums, the larger the organization, the larger the gender representation gap. In large conservation/preservation nonprofits, 90% of presidents and board chairs are men (Lamb, 2015). Hence, it is clear that, at least with respect to some aspects of diversity—race, ethnicity, gender—U.S. nonprofit organizational membership does not often reflect those being served, nor does it always reflect shifting societal demographics.

While there are other aspects of representational diversity that are of interest to nonprofits, such as socioeconomic status or religion, representation is but one aspect of the diversity challenge in nonprofit organizations, and its over-emphasis is problematic for "diversity management." For instance, a primarily representational diversity view conceals more complex aspects of identity and diversity dynamics by ignoring the role of context and history in an organizational setting, overlooking the role of multiple and intersectional identities, and downplaying the dynamics of inclusion with respect to power, leadership and decision-making. For example, with respect to power dynamics, Linnehan and Konrad (1999, p. 402) suggest that an emphasis on such individual differences dilutes the focus on intergroup inequality, a critical view echoed in the work of Zanoni, Janssens, Benschop, and Nkomo (2010), who state that studying diversity through a social-psychological lens that focuses on "individual discriminatory acts originating in universal cognitive processes" ignores the fact that such acts are contextually embedded, reflecting "historically determined, structurally unequal access to and distribution of resources between socioeconomic groups" (p. 14).

The remainder of this chapter explores these oft neglected diversity dynamics by first briefly summarizing the current academic literature on diversity in non-profits,[1] then examining why these emergent diversity dynamics are critical for understanding and practicing "diversity management" in third sector organizations. I conclude by advancing the notion that diversity management is a long-term, organizational cultural change process involving the notion of embedding the valuing of difference across all of the organization's activities.

The Business Case and the Social Justice Case for Diversity

Scholars have highlighted two major approaches to diversity efforts in nonprofits—the business case and the social justice case. Though these two approaches may be seen as complementary in the voluntary sector (Tomlinson & Schwabenland, 2010), each refers to a different way of framing (whether explicitly or implicitly) diversity and inclusion efforts within an organization. A brief overview of each framework follows.

The business case suggests that it makes practical sense for organizations to diversify for enhanced organizational performance and effectiveness. In nonprofit organizations, this might mean more outreach to underserved or under-represented clients or community members. It could also mean recruiting and retaining more staff, volunteers and board members who mirror the demographics of the local community and clients. Doing so presumably gives the nonprofit an advantage in terms of mission attainment and organizational performance and effectiveness, which can also potentially translate into increased funding. Furthermore, a diversity of ways of thinking about how to do the organization's work is expected to contribute positively to creativity, innovation, and performance in organizations (Cox, 1991; DiTomaso & Thompson, 1988). However, recent research by Fredette, Bradshaw and Krause (2016) found that the appearance of diversity is not necessarily related to enhanced group effectiveness outcomes in nonprofits, specifically creativity, innovation and decision-making. Thus, it is not entirely clear that these presumed diversity benefits always accrue to the organization.

The business case for diversity emerged in the for-profit sector, where diversity is presented as a strategic advantage to organizations, leading to a presumed positive impact on the "bottom line." One business case argument goes something like this: "By tapping into previously underserved markets for our products (or services), and hiring more employees from those communities in service of our goal, we can increase our revenues, leading to a potential increase in our profits." Another such argument is: "By leveraging the different experiences, capabilities and ways of thinking that diverse employees bring to the table, we can improve our organization's innovation and creativity, and our organizational effectiveness, all of which can be developed into a competitive advantage." Thus, in the for-profit sector, the advantages of representational diversity have been clearly articulated and many private sector organizations operate from this premise.

However, empirical research on the link between diversity and organizational performance, as reflected by the business case, has been mixed (cf., Jayne & Dipboye, 2004), although some studies do establish a positive link between diversity and outcomes. For example, McLeod, Lobel, and Cox (1996) found that ethnically diversity groups produced higher quality creative outcomes than homogeneous groups. Within the public sector, Pitts (2009) found a strong relationship between diversity management and job satisfaction, as well as to perceptions of work group performance. A diversity emphasis has also benefitted women's and African Americans' individual managerial advancement (Kalev, Dobbin, & Kelly, 2006).

Interestingly, Leiter, Solebello, and Tschirhart (2011, p. 33) found in their study of association members that their respondents "rarely advocated a business case for diversity" and in fact, some questioned the use of limited organizational resources on diversity and inclusion initiatives. Thus, while the business case is widely accepted, this does not mean that it is a widespread operating principle in nonprofits. In the nonprofit sector, discussion and usage of the business case has been more diffuse. Business case arguments from the for-profit sector should in theory translate to nonprofit organizations, which do not have 'profit' but still have a financial bottom line. However, while the idea that nonprofit organizations should at least mirror their client base, and doing so will be advantageous to the organization is perhaps a generally accepted notion, getting there has apparently been more challenging.

In contrast to the business case, the social justice case for diversity asserts that addressing diversity in nonprofits is a moral imperative. Its focus is on eliminating the oppression of marginalized groups, redistributing power, and reducing exclusion and marginalization. This framework is very prevalent in research on diversity in education, but very rarely invoked in nonprofit management diversity research. This could be due to the fact that many nonprofits are, by definition of their missions, engaged in social justice work, and thus social justice is an implied construct in these nonprofits. The social justice case addresses some of the issues about diversity raised by critical diversity scholars.

For instance, Noon (2007, p. 778) actively argues against the business case, claiming that it has potentially fatal flaws that can undermine social justice. In critiquing the business case for diversity, Noon states:

> The business case relies on an overly rational cost–benefit analysis which tends to assume that inevitably the balance will tip in favour of investing in equality initiatives. The danger is that in some instances this will simply not be the case. The costs… might be judged bys managers to out-weigh the benefits.

So, just as managers can rationalize the benefits of a diverse workplace, they *could* also rationalize its deficits. In focusing on a cost-benefit analysis of diversity efforts, as the business case implicitly does, any focus on remedying inequality experienced by underrepresented *groups* can become obscured; diversity only matters to the extent that it contributes to the bottom line.

In sum, these two approaches to diversity—the business case and the social justice case—reflect different ways of framing the key focus of diversity efforts in nonprofits. A business case perspective looks at individual differences, regards these as positive, and presumes a positive impact of these differences, if appropriately "managed," on organizational performance and effectiveness. On the other hand, a social justice perspective considers group (and intergroup) differences, explicitly addresses power differentials, including differences in resource access and distribution, with the goal of working towards reducing exclusion and marginalization of disadvantaged groups. It is these group justice remedies that are at the heart of the social justice case, as contrasted with the organizational effectiveness remedies at the heart of the business case.

Current Research on Diversity and Diversity Management

Most research on diversity in the nonprofit sector has as its focus representational diversity, and a good number of the extant empirical studies focus on board diversity (see for example, Bernstein & Bilimoria, 2013; Gazely, Chang, & Bingham, 2010; Hatarska and Nadolynak, 2012; Parker, 2007). Other recent studies examine association membership (cf., Coffee & Geys, 2007a, 2007b; Leiter, Solebello, & Tschirhart, 2011), volunteerism or volunteer activity (Berenson & Stagg, 2016; Caldwell, Farmer, & Fedor, 2008; Forbes & Zampelli, 2014; Paik & Navarre-Jackson, 2011; Savelkoul, Gesthuizen, & Scheepers, 2013), team diversity (Perkins & Fields, 2010), accessibility (Rodman & Cooper, 1995), disability (Kirakosyan, 2016); philanthropy (Drezner & Garvey, 2016) and class diversity (Dean, 2016).

Representational diversity efforts are often coupled with inclusion efforts in organizations. Inclusion refers to "the degree to which individuals feel a part of critical organizational processes, . . ." (Roberson, 2006, p. 215) and also "describes which individuals are allowed to participate and are enabled to contribute fully in the group" (Miller, 1998, p. 151). In its broadest sense, inclusion refers to how the talents of all organizational members are effectively leveraged for mission attainment and better organizational performance. Inclusive practices stand apart from—but are also linked to—representational diversity efforts. While representational diversity is preoccupied with increasing the numbers of staff, volunteers, or board members from underrepresented (or underserved) groups, inclusion concerns the ways in which diverse organizational members are included in meaningful ways in the organization's activities.

Roberson's (2006) study's first phase, examining the meanings attributed to "diversity" and "inclusion," found these to be distinct concepts. For example,

> Consistent with popular and scholarly diversity literature, definitions of diversity focused primarily on heterogeneity and the demographic composition of groups or organizations, whereas definitions of inclusion focused on employee involvement and the integration of diversity into organizational systems and processes.
>
> *(Roberson, 2006, pp. 227–228)*

The study's later confirmatory factor phase then found that several practices were factors associated with both "diversity" *and* "inclusion," such as equity/fairness, organization and stakeholder representation, and diversity commitment. She concludes that these findings suggest that organizational practice has perhaps already moved more towards the inclusion aspect of diversity.

In nonprofit studies, inclusion has been the focus of an increasing number of studies (cf., Bradshaw & Fredette, 2013; Brown, 2002; Fredette, Bradshaw, & Krause, 2016). Such studies, however, have typically focused on nonprofit board inclusion, rather than on organizational inclusiveness more broadly. These studies suggest that while inclusive board practices are beneficial, their relationship to representational diversity is not always clear cut.

Moving Beyond Representational Diversity and Inclusion

The preceding discussion has portrayed the research on diversity in the nonprofit sector as being mostly about representational diversity, with increasing attention being paid to aspects of inclusion. But even the dual foci of representational diversity and inclusion may not suffice for effectively working across differences in nonprofits. The interrelationship between diversity, inclusion, and performance can be "nuanced, complex, and at times, tenuous" (Fredette, Bradshaw, & Krause, 2016). For example, Brown (2002) found no significant relationship between the degree of nonprofit boards' inclusive governance practices and minority composition (reflecting five ethnic categories) within the board, though the research team did find a moderate correlation between categorical composition (reflecting various categories including disability, education level, profession) and these inclusive governance practices. An example of an inclusive practice used in one neighborhood development organization was a "formula board," which mandates that 51% of board members be residents who are eligible for the nonprofit's services. Another youth nonprofit had presentations by staff and service recipients at every board meeting. The goal of such practices is to keep the board in touch with the communities being served, and with their clients. The implication of this finding from Brown (2002) is that boards can reflect inclusive governance without being diverse in terms of race/ethnicity. In this sense, though, one might argue that inclusive practices could lead to better representational diversity as such practices could enhance the interest of individuals from underrepresented groups in the nonprofit.

Further, increasingly fluid and complex individual and group identity dynamics will impact diversity and inclusion success. For example, an increasingly multicultural society means that more individuals are identifying as bi- or multiracial or bi- or multicultural. What does this mean in terms of traditional ways of addressing representational diversity? In organizations, accounting for the number of members of traditionally underrepresented groups is more straightforward if individuals identify with a single group (e.g., African American/Black). But what if individuals identify and African-American *and* European? What if someone identifies as a "White Latino"? Who "counts", and who gets to decide who counts? More pointedly, what is it that the organization intends to demonstrate through its accounting of representational diversity?

It is not only racial or ethnic identities that have become increasingly complex, but likewise, many organizations struggle with how to address workplace issues involving gender identity. Witness the dynamics surrounding North Carolina's HB2 law, the so-called "bathroom bill," which requires transgender individuals in schools and public buildings, including nonprofits, to use the restroom (and related facilities like locker rooms) corresponding to the sex on their birth certificate. The bill also bans LGBT antidiscrimination laws, such as the one that was passed by the city of Charlotte. At the time of this writing, a U.S. district judge has temporarily blocked three plaintiffs from having to follow NC's HB2 law at the University of North Carolina, meaning that for the time being, individuals can use the restroom associated with their gender identity. The HR challenges here center in part on what sort of HR policy, if any, should guide nonprofit policy around restroom usage? Heightened rhetoric around fear for personal safety (i.e., transgender men sharing a restroom with cisgender women) seems to advocate for HR 'policing' of the restrooms. However, such a practice would not only be impractical, but also undesirable from an inclusiveness view. Many organizations have addressed this issue through structural changes (e.g., restructured restrooms, including not only gender neutral restrooms but also private (sometimes called "family") restrooms), rather than through establishing new HR policy.

In previous research, with colleagues, I propose a values-focused approach to diversity, wherein people's inherent diversity is recognized as being fundamentally valuable for the organization throughout all its activities (Weisinger, Borges-Méndez, & Milofsky, 2016). Such an approach does not render representational diversity or inclusion meaningless. Rather, it suggests that organizational leaders recognize the limitations of using these approaches exclusively, and broaden the way that diversity is conceptualized and managed in their organizations:

> Recognizing the complex and contextual nature of identities leads us to a perspective that emphasizes recognizing, involving, and serving multiple constituencies as a way of embedding consciousness of diversity in organizational values and in all aspects of functioning
> (Weisinger, Borges-Méndez, & Milofsky, 2016, p. 3)

Three emergent diversity dynamics inform a more nuanced view of an embedded diversity consciousness for nonprofit managers. These are: (1) the context and history in the diversity trajectory of the nonprofit; (2) intersectional and multiple identities; and (3) inclusive practice with respect to leadership, power, and decision-making.

Contextual and Historicity

As alluded to earlier in the chapter, diversity and its management are not one size fits all propositions (Leiter, Solebello, & Tschirhart, 2011). What is diversity-relevant in one organizational setting may be very different in another. Mor Barak (2015) supports this view, discussing how the categories used by the U.S. federal government to measure and track diversity (e.g. White, Asian, Black or African American, etc.) do not capture the complexity of diversity in the United States today and could not be used in any other national context, making them of a little use overall.

Multiple Identities/Intersectionality

Traditional notions of representational diversity stem from the precepts of affirmative action and EEO. However, these concepts do not adequately deal with intersectional identities (Crenshaw, 1989). For example, a Black woman is "counted" as African-American and counted as a woman for representational diversity purposes, but the unique discrimination and implicit bias challenges facing those with the intersectional identity of "Black woman" are obscured. Thus, binary views of identity (e.g., male or female, Latino or European, able-bodied or disabled) force individuals to choose between what they may feel are equally salient aspects of their identity. If discussions of racial prejudice and discrimination are now routinely ignored in organizations, the specific type faced by those with intersectional identities is likely doubly ignored. Further, such intersectionality requires nonprofit managers to have a more nuanced understanding of identities and their roles in the workplace. Similarly, issues related to gender identity and gender fluidity call into question stereotypical ways of dealing with "gender" in the workplace, that is, as a binary construct (he/she). The movement towards gender neutral restrooms in workplaces stems, in part, from questioning traditional notions of gender, and provides an example of how practical solutions be useful in advancing conceptual ideas. In educational settings, the increasing use of gender-neutral pronouns—by giving agency to individuals in terms of how they wish to identify—is another example. For HR practice, these dynamics suggest the importance of opportunities for organizational members to provide ongoing feedback about their concerns; of meaningful avenues for dealing with these concerns (e.g., employee committees); and ongoing training and education about emergent issues impacting organizational diversity and inclusion.

Power, Leadership and Decision-making

A nonprofit organization may have representative membership, but those members may be excluded from critical decision-making processes and leadership opportunities, thus lacking the ability to exercise the power required to effect meaningful diversity-related change. Therefore, an emphasis on inclusion and inclusive practices is warranted with a focus on decision-making. As alluded to earlier, inclusion refers in part to the degree to which those from traditionally underrepresented groups are fully involved in governance and operational decisions in nonprofits (Weisinger et al., 2016). Relatedly, Mor Barak (2014) appropriately defines inclusion in relation to exclusion:

> The concept of inclusion-exclusion in the workplace refers to the individual's sense of being a part of the organizational system in both the formal processes, such as access to information and decision-making channels, and the informal processes, such as "water cooler" and lunch meetings where information exchange and decisions informally take place
>
> *(Mor Barak, 2014, p. 155)*

Even inclusion in leadership positions can be undermined. Take, for example, women's roles on nonprofit boards. Citing a *Washington Post* article, *the Nonprofit Quarterly* states that while 43% of nonprofit boards comprise women, when we look at nonprofits with $25 million or more in income, that percentage drops to 33% (Lamb, 2015). Thus, while women may be seen as being well-represented on nonprofit boards, this tends to be on the boards of small and medium-sized nonprofits.

Effective diversity management means that not only are nonprofits representative of their clients and their communities; not only do they allow the expression of views from those representing these constituencies, but they also share power with these constituencies, providing them with meaningful participation in decision-making and leadership. One key way of sharing power is developing effective board and leadership recruitment practices that broaden the sources of talent for the nonprofit representation. For instance, a nonprofit, depending upon its area, may reach out to affinity groups, professional associations, or various advocacy groups to tap into talent that may not have traditionally reflected their sources. Another is structuring opportunities for various organizational members to provide input on key programs, activities, and goals.

Implications for People Management

This chapter has discussed nonprofit organizations' focus on representational diversity and inclusion, issues therein, as well as their option to frame these diversity efforts using the business case versus the social justice case for diversity. The chapter has also raised important issues regarding emergent dynamics that call into question mainstream notions of diversity and inclusion.

The consequent discussion leads us to consider the implication of these issues and dynamics for the management of diverse people in organizations. Some of these implications are nicely summarized by Leiter, Solebello, and Tschirhart (2011, p. 3) from their qualitative study of diversity and inclusion in membership associations:

- focusing on particular targets
- being sensitive to incremental accomplishments
- taking a long-term view
- having leadership support and . . .
- . . . making programs worthwhile to members who have competing demands for their time and attention
- involving underrepresented groups and powerful stakeholders in programming [Diversity & Inclusion] decisions is likely to be helpful.

Some of these recommendations are consistent with suggestions in our review of diversity research (Weisinger et al., 2016). We concluded that "the diversity concept must move well beyond a managerial approach to include broader social theories . . ." including those related to power, interest conflicts, complex identity dynamics and the structuring of volunteering and work in nonprofits (Weisinger et al., 2016, p. 1).

What this means in practice is that nonprofit organizations need to focus on diversity and inclusion as a *culture change* process—one in which the idea of valuing difference is embedded in all organizational activities. As such, addressing diversity is a *long-term* proposition. It is also one in which difficult but open conversations need to take place about identity, power dynamics, and leadership, as well as about organizational structures and processes and how these impact the effectiveness of organizational work across dimensions of difference. It also means structuring opportunities for organizational members to learn from others (Weisinger & Salipante, 2005), particularly those who are "in the trenches" and more knowledgeable about aspects of working with diverse clientele. In sum, instead of asking whether organizations "are" or "are not" diverse, we suggest an approach wherein the value of diversity and difference is incorporated in an ongoing fashion into all organizational activities (Weisinger et al., 2016, p. 2). From an HR standpoint, an organization can incent staff and leadership to behave in ways that are consistent with stronger diversity and inclusion practice. In this sense, rewards need not necessarily be monetary; having performance review criteria that reflect desired diversity and inclusion behaviors/practices/goals is one way to reward those who are making the necessary changes. Further, ensuring that nonprofit leadership is held accountable for meeting diversity and inclusion goals is another. Researching and implementing diversity and inclusion best practices (e.g., for recruitment, retention, program development) is another way to move towards a culture that values differences.

A recent example of 'walking the talk' with respect to diversity and inclusion comes from the Girl Scouts of the USA (GSUSA). The Western Washington chapter of the GSUSA received a $100,000 donation from an individual whose name is kept private in the news report (D'Onofrio, 2015). The one request the donor added after giving was: "Please guarantee that our gift will not be used to support transgender girls. If you can't, please return the money." The chapter CEO, without hesitation, returned the money, reiterating the GSUSA's mission to serve *every* girl. What might have been a contentious decision was actually then bolstered by an impromptu IndieGoGo.com campaign that raised three times the original donation in just three days. Thus, inclusive practice in this instance was ingrained in the organization's mission and values, and making the short-term decision not to accept a sizeable donation was seen as completely in sync with their inclusive culture, and further, did not comprise the organization's funding but rather enhanced it. One way, from an HR perspective, to 'walk the talk' is via target of opportunity funding and hires. This provides key decision-makers with funding to hire individuals who were possibly not seeking employment at the nonprofit, but whose experience and expertise complement those of the existing staff. Depending upon which aspects of diversity are relevant, this practice provides leadership with more flexibility in recruiting talent.

This aforementioned example from the Girl Scouts is probably rare. And the fact that nonprofit staff members may have been educated on how to work with diverse clients does not mean that they actually have effective skills to do so (Mor Barak, 2015, p. 86; Weisinger & Salipante, 2005) nor to inculcate effective inclusive practices. Thus, it is first imperative that nonprofit organizations first focus on those diversity and inclusion practices that most directly inform its mission and second, on how to best develop the necessary diversity competence among its leadership, board, staff, members, and volunteers who will implement those practices.

Finally, I would highlight Leiter, Solebello, and Tschirhart's (2011, p. 3) conclusion that the associations in their study with a significant emphasis on diversity and inclusion, "share a high level of comfort with change, conflict, and empowerment of others." Thus, even the development of skills involving adapting to change, managing conflict, and devolving responsibility to empower organizational members is an important aspect of the diversity challenge in nonprofits.

Note

1 A recent review of the empirical literature on diversity in nonprofit organizations can be found in J. Weisinger, R. Borges-Méndez, & C. Milofsky (2015). "Diversity in the Nonprofit Sector," Editors' Introduction to the *Nonprofit and Voluntary Sector Quarterly, Special Issue on Diversity, 45*(1), 3S–27S.

Discussion Questions

Answer the following questions using your own nonprofit organizational context (or one with which you are very familiar):

1 How are diversity and inclusion defined within the context of your organization?
2 Do you think the way these concepts are defined impacts how well your organization advances its mission? Why or Why not?
3 What concrete HRM practices might be developed to enhance an embedded diversity consciousness in your organization? That is, what can you do, beyond the routine diversity and inclusion practices, to develop the recognition of difference as a value threaded throughout the organization's work?

Web Resources

1 The Independent Sector has recently a launched an online portal featuring curated content on diversity, equity and inclusion (DEI), including resources to support effective DEI practice: www.independentsector.org/focus_areas/diversity?s=dei%20
2 The Center for Association Leadership, ASAE, offers diversity and inclusion resources at: www.asaecenter.org/resources/topics/diversity-and-inclusion

References

Aspire Education Project. (2016). The Aspire story. http://aspireeducation.org/story/ (accessed October 17, 2016).

Berenson, J. & Stagg, A. (2016). An asset-based approach to volunteering: exploring benefits for low-income volunteers. *Nonprofit and Voluntary Sector Quarterly, 45,* 131S–149S.

Bernstein, R. S. & Bilimoria, D. (2013). Diversity perspectives and minority nonprofit board member inclusion. *Equality, Diversity and Inclusion: An International Journal, 32,* 636–653.

Bradshaw, P. & Fredette, C. (2013). Determinants of the range of ethnocultural diversity on nonprofit boards: A study of large Canadian nonprofit organizations. *Nonprofit and Voluntary Sector Quarterly, 42,* 1111–1133.

Brown, W. A. (2002). Inclusive governance practices in nonprofit organizations and implications for practice. *Nonprofit Management & Leadership, 12*, 369–385.

Caldwell, S. D., Farmer, S. M., & Fedor, D. B. (2008). The influence of age on volunteer contributions in a nonprofit organization. *Journal of Organizational Behavior, 29*, 311–333.

Coffé, H. & Geys, B. (2007a). Participation in bridging and bonding associations and civic attitudes: Evidence from Flanders. *Voluntas: International Journal of Voluntary and Nonprofit Organizations, 18*, 385–406.

Coffé, H. & Geys, B. (2007b). Toward an empirical characterization of bridging and bonding social capital. *Nonprofit and Voluntary Sector Quarterly, 36*, 121–139.

Cox, T. H. (1991). The multicultural organization. *Academy of Management Executive, 5*(2), 34–47.

Crenshaw, K. (1989). Demarginalizing the intersection of race and sex: A Black feminist critique of antidiscrimination doctrine, feminist theory and antiracist politics. The *University of Chicago Legal Forum, 140*, 139–167.

Dean, J. (2016). Class diversity and youth volunteering in the United Kingdom: Applying Bourdieu's habitus and cultural capital. *Nonprofit and Voluntary Sector Quarterly, 45*, 95S–113S.

DiTomaso, N. & Thompson, D. E. (1988). The advancement of minorities into corporate management: An overview. *Research in the Sociology of Organizations, 6*, 281–312.

D'Onofrio, K. (2015). Girl scouts turn down $100,000, continue supporting transgender girls, DiversityInc (July 6, 2015). Retrieved from: www.diversityinc.com/news/girl-scouts-turn-down-100000-continue-supporting-transgender-girls/

Drezner, N. D. & Garvey, J. C. (2016). LGBTQ alumni philanthropy exploring (un)conscious motivations for giving related to identity and experiences. *Nonprofit and Voluntary Sector Quarterly, 45*, 52S–71S

Dubose, D. (2014). The nonprofit sector has a Ferguson problem. *Nonprofit Quarterly,* (December 5): https://nonprofitquarterly.org/2014/12/05/the-nonprofit-sector-has-a-ferguson-problem/

Forbes, K. F. & Zampelli, E. M. (2014). Volunteerism: The influences of social, religious, and human capital. *Nonprofit and Voluntary Sector Quarterly, 43*, 227–253.

Fredette, C., Bradshaw, P., & Krause, H. (2016). From diversity to inclusion: A multimethod examination of diverse governing groups. *Nonprofit and Voluntary Sector Quarterly, 45*, 28S–51S.

Gazley, B., Chang, W. K., & Bingham, L. B. (2010). Board diversity, stakeholder representation, and collaborative performance in community mediation centers. *Public Administration Review, 70*, 610–620.

Hatarska, V. & Nadolynak, D. (2012). Board size and diversity as governance mechanisms in community development loan funds in the USA. *Applied Economics, 44*, 4313–4329.

Ivancevich, J. M. & Gilbert, J. A. (2000). Diversity management: Time for a new approach. *Public Personnel Management, 29*(1), 75–92.

Jayne, M. E. A. & Dipboye, R. L. (2004). Leveraging diversity to improve business performance: Research findings and recommendations for organizations. *Human Resource Management, 43*, 409–424.

Johnston, W. & Packer, A. (1987). *Workforce 2000: Work and workers for the twenty-first century.* Indianapolis, IN: The Hudson Institute.

Kalev, A., Dobbin, F., & Kelly, E. (2006). Best practices or best guesses? Assessing the efficacy of corporate affirmative action and diversity policies. *American Sociological Review, 71*, 589–617.

Karamu House. (2016). About Karamu House. www.karamuhouse.org/about-karamu-house/ (accessed October 17, 2016).

Kirakosyan, L. (2016). Promoting Disability rights for a stronger democracy in Brazil: The role of NGOs. *Nonprofit and Voluntary Sector Quarterly*, *45*, 114S–130S.

Lamb, E. (2015). Women in power—or, not so much: Gender in the nonprofit sector, *Nonprofit Quarterly* (January 21): https://nonprofitquarterly.org/2015/01/21/women-in-power-or-not-so-much-gender-in-the-nonprofit-sector/

Leiter, J., Solebello, N., & Tschirhart, M. (2011). *Enhancing diversity and inclusion in membership associations: An interview study*. Washington, DC: ASAE.

Linnehan, I. & Konrad, A. (1999). Diluting diversity: Implications for intergroup inequality in organizations. *Journal of Management Inquiry*, *8*(4), 399–414.

McLeod, P., Lobel, S., & Cox, T. H. (1996). Ethnic diversity and creativity in small groups. *Small Group Research*, *27*, 248–264.

Miller, F. A. (1998). Strategic culture change: The door to achieving high performance and inclusion. *Public Personnel Management*, *27*, 151–160.

Mor Barak, M. E. (2014). *Managing diversity: Toward a globally inclusive workplace* (3rd ed.). Thousand Oaks, CA: Sage.

Mor Barak, M. E. (2015, April). Inclusion is the key to diversity management, but what is inclusion? *Human Service Organizations: Management, Leadership & Governance*, pp. 83–88. Retrieved from: 10.1080/23303131.2015.1035599

Noon, M. (2007). The fatal flaws of diversity and the business case for ethnic minorities. *Work, Employment & Society*, *21*(4), 773–784. http://dx.doi.org/10.1177/0950017007082886

Paik, A. & Navarre-Jackson, L. (2011). Social networks, recruitment, and volunteering: Are social capital effects conditional on recruitment? *Nonprofit and Voluntary Sector Quarterly*, *40*, 476–496.

Parker, L. D. (2007). Internal governance in the nonprofit boardroom: A participant observer study. *Corporate Governance: An International Review*, *15*, 923–934.

Perkins, D. C. & Fields, D. (2010). Top management team diversity and performance of Christian churches. *Nonprofit and Voluntary Sector Quarterly*, *39*, 825–843.

Peters, J. & Wolfred, T. (2001). Daring to lead: Nonprofit executive directors and their work experience. San Francisco: CompassPoint Nonprofit Services. Retrieved September 9, 2005, from www.compasspoint.org/sites/default/files/documents/Daring%20to%20Lead%202000.pdf

Pitts, D. (2009). Diversity management, job satisfaction, and performance: Evidence from U.S. federal agencies. *Public Administration Review*, *69*, 328–338.

Roberson, Q. (2006). Disentangling the meanings of diversity and inclusion in organizations. *Group & Organization Management*, *31*, 212–236.

Rodman, M. & Cooper, M. (1995). Accessibility as a discourse of space in Canadian housing cooperatives. *American Ethnologist*, *22*, 589–601.

Savelkoul, M., Gesthuizen, M., & Scheepers, P. (2014). The impact of ethnic diversity on participation in European voluntary organizations: Direct and indirect pathways. *Nonprofit and Voluntary Sector Quarterly*, *43*, 1070–1094.

Schwartz, R., Weinberg, J., Hagenbuch, D., & Scott, A. (2016). *The voice of nonprofit talent: Perceptions of diversity in the workplace*. Boston & San Francisco: CommonGood Careers & Level Playing Field Institute. Retrieved from: http://commongoodcareers.org/diversityreport.pdf

Teegarden, P. H. (2004). Nonprofit executive leadership and transitions survey 2004. Research by Mangance Consulting in Collaboration with TransitionGuides, Funded in part by the Annie E. Casey Foundation. Baltimore, MD: Annie E. Casey Foundation. Available at: www.leadertransitions.com/Resources/Survey%202004.pdf (accessed December 10, 2005).

Tomlinson, F. & Schwabenland, C. (2010). Reconciling competing discourses of diversity? The UK non-profit sector between social justice and the business case. *Organization*, *17*: 101–121, doi:10.1177/1350508409350237

United Way of America. (2016). Diversity and inclusion. Available at: www.unitedway. org/about/diversity-and-inclusion (accessed on October 17, 2016).

Weisinger J. & P. Salipante, 2005. A grounded theory for building ethnically bridging social capital in voluntary organizations. *Nonprofit and Voluntary Sector Quarterly, 34,* March, pp. 29–55.

Weisinger, J., Borges-Méndez, R., & Milofsky, C. (2016). Diversity in the Nonprofit and Voluntary Sector. *Nonprofit and Voluntary Sector Quarterly, 45,* 3S–27S.

Zanoni, P., Janssens, M., Benschop, Y., & Nkomo, S. (2010). Unpacking diversity, grasping inequality: Rethinking difference through critical perspectives. *Organization, 17*(1), 9–29.

19

Technology and Human Resource Management in Nonprofit Organizations

Jennifer A. Jones

Introduction

The landscape of technology, though complex, is one of the most important trends a human resource leader in the nonprofit sector can follow. In fact, a recent report by Society for Human Resource Management (SHRM, 2015) indicated technology is one of two primary drivers of change in Human Resources (HR) and that "continuous innovations in technology will fundamentally change the way HR work is accomplished" (p. ii). More specifically, scholars have found that technological innovations have had a notable impact on the processes of recruiting, selecting, motivating, and retaining employees (Pynes, 2013; Stone, Deadrick, Lukaszewski, & Johnson, 2015). For example, technological innovations are expected to lessen the administrative burdens of Human Resources Management (HRM) and to provide a method for leveraging information about the workforce. Assistive technologies also allow greater access to the workplace for individuals with disabilities (U.S. Department of Labor, 1999) and provide for workplace flexibility in the form of telecommuting and virtual volunteering. There is, of course, a shadow side to technology. Even the most advanced technological systems bring issues such as software viruses, privacy concerns, and ergonomic challenges, all of which have important implications for the management and leadership of nonprofit organizations.

This chapter outlines a variety of the ways technological innovations have changed the business of human resources. It exposes the reader to a broad swath of research and, in particular, to the sorts of benefits and challenges technology is likely to pose within the context of managing people in nonprofit organizations. Technological innovations (and their ensuing challenges) may be of particular interest to nonprofit leaders, many of whom operate with slim budgets and all of whom operate within the complex landscape of nonprofit accountability and legitimacy (Ebrahim, 2003; Sloan, 2009). The chapter is divided into two sections. First, this chapter provides an overview of the existing research of technology and human resources. Then, the chapter makes sense of the research in light of the on-the-ground needs of nonprofit human resource leaders. It frames the use of technology within human resources as a leadership challenge and poses three research-based questions practitioners can use to maximize their implementation of technology within the workforce.

For the purpose of this chapter, technology is defined broadly as the use of computers and digital information, including telecommunications devices, to gather, store, retrieve, and circulate information. This definition includes the hardware (e.g. computers, video recorders), software (e.g. email systems, social media platforms, etc.), and technologically-developed products such as online training programs (for more information, see Brown & Charlier, 2013; Cronin, Morath, Curtin, & Heil, 2006; Stone et al., 2015).

Part I: Review of Existing Research

This section of the chapter reviews existing research on technology and human resources. The presentation of this research is first structured around core functions of HRM: to recruit and select, motivate, and retain talented employees and volunteers (Pynes, 2013). Then, it will look at two specific aspects of technology: (1) the influence technology has had—and is having—on the nature of many job positions; and (2) the broader HRM-related challenges and opportunities posed to organizations via social media. This review is not exhaustive; in fact, the aim of this section is to expose the reader to a broad swath of the types of technology-related benefits and challenges encountered by HR leaders in the nonprofit sector, and to offer insight as to how the field is evolving.

Regrettably, much of the research on human resources and technology is focused on the for-profit sector. Less attention is paid to the nonprofit sector; however, the research that does exist suggests technology affects HR functioning in nonprofit organizations and, often, does so in profound ways. For example, as early as 2000, case studies were emerging that documented the use of information and communications technologies by nonprofits to reshape the flow of communication within the office and to reshape both internal and external relationships (see, for example, Burt & Taylor, 2000). Even less research has been conducted that specifically explores the relationship between technology and volunteers. However, it is clear there are myriad ways technology has informed volunteer administration. For example, technology has allowed volunteer orientation and trainings to be conducted online rather than in person, and technology has allowed volunteers to perform services remotely (i.e., virtual volunteering). In fact, as early as 2001, volunteers were using the internet to search for opportunities and, in some cases, to provide services (Toppe, Kirsch, & Michel, 2001). Given the comparative dearth of nonprofit-related research on technology and human resources, this chapter draws from research related to for-profit companies and, where appropriate, makes suggestions as to how it may be applicable to the nonprofit sector.

Recruiting and Hiring

This section discusses some of the implications of technology in the process of recruiting, interviewing, and selecting employees. Considerations for volunteers are also addressed.

Recruiting

Technology has changed the way nonprofit organizations recruit employees and volunteers, beginning with how opportunities are advertised. The printed—and, often, expensive—newspaper advertisement has been replaced with online ads that are often less expensive or, at times, free. These online ads can be posted on newspapers and magazines as well as hiring sites such as Monster.com. There are also a host of job and volunteer posting boards that specifically target nonprofit organizations (e.g., Idealist and Volunteer Match). Community partners such as colleges and universities may also distribute information about job or volunteer opportunities via online posting boards, social media (e.g., LinkedIn groups), and emails to members of their listserve. Many nonprofit organizations also post job positions on their own website and social media sites, thus potentially attracting passive job seekers who care about the organization.

In theory, the primary advantages of digital advertising are lower costs and the ability to reach a broader, more diverse pool of applicants. The proof, however, is not in the pudding. Online recruiting has increased the number of applicants per position and, subsequently, increased the administrative and transaction costs of hiring (Stone, Lukaszewski, & Isenhour, 2005). However, online recruiting strategies have not attracted a higher quality pool of applicants nor have they increased the general diversity of the applicants (Galanaki, 2002; McManus & Ferguson, 2003). Many would-be applicants do not have the technological access or sophistication necessary to conduct an effective online job search, despite a marked growth in the use of the internet among adults in the United States (from 54% in 2000 to 84% in 2015) (Perrin & Duggan, 2015). It is critical that HR leaders bridge these gaps and make strategic efforts to reach a broader swath of potential applicants.

Online recruiting is evolving. Thus far, it has been a one-way communication process that, in most cases, does not allow potential applicants to interact with or ask questions of the organization. This static communication style has been said to "create an artificial distance between applicants and organizations" (Stone et al., 2015, p. 218). Recently, HR departments have begun using social media platforms such as LinkedIn to engage and develop relationships with potential applicants. These strategies are markedly different from traditional one-way communication and are expected to shift the paradigm of recruiting in general (Dineen & Allen, 2013). Future versions of online recruiting will likely focus on developing opportunities for online interaction between the organization and potential employees, and these new strategies will allow both parties to simultaneously woo and vet the other.

Interviewing

Technology has also been adopted during the screening process, including the use of technology-mediated interviews such as video conferencing and telephone interviews. The interview is an important event during which the interviewer is able to assess candidates on job qualifications and other softer areas such as person-ability in regard to organizational fit (Chuang & Sackett, 2005). There is considerable debate in the literature as to whether technology-mediated interviews can adequately replace the in-person interview. For example, telephone conversations tend to be less interactive and spontaneous than face-to-face conversations; however, they can provide a sense of anonymity and help participants feel less self-conscious (Sellen, 1995), which presumably would be appealing to some job candidates.

Video conferencing also has its benefits and challenges. It can provide important nonverbal cues, increase interactivity, and help participants discriminate among speakers (Sellen, 1995); however, such interviews also pose problems of their own. For example, participants in a series of experiments reported feeling "distanced by the video systems and less a part of the conversation" (p. 430). It is also likely that participants on a video call may look at the faces on the screen instead of at the eye of the camera (often just above the screen). These participants may believe they are making eye contact even though it would not appear as such to their listeners. In fact, it could be perceived as though the participant was avoiding eye contact or being evasive.

In short, it is hard to replicate face-to-face conversations. A study of 802 post-interview job applicants selected via a university campus recruitment center indicated that face-to-face interviews may be preferable to video or telephone interviews. Specifically, "face-to-face interviews procured higher (a) perceptions of fairness than telephone and videoconferencing, (b) perceived interview outcomes than videoconferences, and (c) intentions to accept a job offer than telephone interviews" (Chapman, Uggerslev, & Webster, 2003, p. 950). It is recommended that, before selecting an interview medium, an organization consider the financial and staff time costs, industry norms, and the size of the qualified applicant pool. Nonprofit leaders, in general, will want to carefully weigh the costs of face-to-face interviewing. The costs, for example, may be particularly steep for organizations in rural areas (such as a rural health center trying to recruit physicians) or organizations conducting national executive searches; however, the short-term costs of in-person interviewing may yield an overall lower hiring cost if the candidate, as research suggests, is more likely to accept the job offer after an in-person visit.

Selecting

Organizations may use a variety of technology-based tools to help determine which potential applicant is the best fit for the position. These tools can range from a simple test of an applicant's computer skills to more complex assessments. While many of these methods can offer insight into the candidate, there is the possibility these may prematurely limit the pool of candidates. The results of computer-based tests, for example, are affected by gender and racial differences (Wallace & Clariana, 2005) and may reflect demographic variations in computer ability (Perrin & Duggan, 2015) rather than variations in general ability or aptitude. Research thus far has not conclusively indicated whether technological tools for applicant selection are effective in enabling employers to hire a high-quality, diverse workforce (Stone et al., 2015).

HR professionals should proceed with caution when relying on technology-based tools, and take care to interpret the results in light of other data gathered about the candidate throughout the interview process. In the end, assessment tools might provide more insight about the retention and continued motivation of employees than objective evidence about who should or should not be hired. For example, a nonprofit leader might ascertain through an interview that a potential employee is bright and hard-working, but computer-based tests reveal this person is not as proficient in Microsoft Excel as the organization would like. This person might be hired with the understanding that they will be trained in Excel and their performance measured over time.

Retaining and Motivating

Retaining and motivating employees are also core functions of HR (Pynes, 2013). These functions include performance management, compensation, training, professional growth, and job satisfaction. Here, too, technology has influenced HRM in myriad ways. These ways are of particular importance to nonprofit organizations that seek to streamline HRM costs, use professional development as an employee benefit, or increase the number of staff or volunteers.

Performance management

Many companies are using electronic performance management systems (e-PM) to measure employee performance and provide feedback (Hedge & Borman, 1995; Sierra-Cedar, 2015; Sulsky & Keown, 1998). Such systems can track employee performance, monitor employee activity, record formal and informal feedback, and prompt managers to meet with employees as needed (Stone et al., 2015). These systems have the potential to make the evaluation process more efficient and cost-effective (at least for larger organizations), and can be particularly helpful for organizing feedback from multiple stakeholders (see, for example, Bartram, 2004; Bracken, Summers, & Fleenor, 1998).

However, it is important to be clear about what, exactly, is meant by performance: These e-PM systems typically track quantifiable, objective measures (e.g., number of minutes talking to a client on the phone) (Sulsky & Keown, 1998) and are less likely to address critical issues of quality. E-PM may also decrease interaction between employees and supervisors as information that used to be presented face-to-face can now be delivered electronically. These systems may not be suited for capturing the nuances of nonprofit work. For example, an e-PM system may be able to track the number of clients seen by a group of caseworkers, the number of minutes spent with each client, and the types of services and referrals provided by the caseworkers; however, an e-PM will be less likely to track the more subtle variation in caseworkers' performance (e.g., whether a genuine human connection was forged or the extent to which a caseworker encouraged a client to think differently about how they were approaching challenges).

Less is known about employee reactions to electronic performance management. For example, one quasi-experimental study (n = 35; Payne, Horner, Boswell, Schroeder, & Stine-Cheyne, 2009) of one organization, where one group of employees received electronic appraisals and the other group received the traditional pen-and-paper appraisals, yielded mixed results. Employees who received their performance appraisal via an online system reported higher perceptions of supervisor accountability but lower perceptions of the quality of these evaluations. It is possible that increased usage of electronic processes—including practice and creativity on the supervisor's part—will influence future perceptions. In particular, it has been suggested supervisors can use technology such as video conferencing and internal social media to increase connectivity with their employees and, thus, mitigate the challenges posed by e-PM (Stone et al., 2015). Regardless, care should be taken to alleviate what some would suggest can be an incomplete and somewhat dehumanizing review of employee performance. This caution is especially salient for nonprofit leaders, as much of nonprofit work requires what scholars have described as emotional labor, or relational work that requires both emotional engagement and emotional management (Guy, Newman, Mastracci, & Maynard-Moody, 2010). E-PM systems are likely to be ill-suited for the supervision and support of such labor.

Compensation

Many HR departments have adopted e-Compensation systems, which automate payroll and compensation planning, and employee self-service systems (ESS), which allow employees to process routine transactions (such as changing their address or enrolling in benefits) via a web-based system. These systems have been called the "biggest development" in regard to HR technology (Walker, 2001a). They are designed to decrease costs (Gherson & Jackson, 2001) and decrease error (American Payroll Association's 2010 report, as cited in Inc.com 2014). Such systems also "relieve the organization's HR personnel of routine tasks, and allow them to concentrate on more strategic activities" (Konradt, Christophersen, & Schaeffer-Kuelz, 2006, p. 1150). These systems, ESS in particular, are still fairly new, and academic research is not yet conclusive as to their effectiveness (Dulebohn & Marler, 2005; Konradt et al., 2006; Marler & Fisher, 2013). A number of these claims are based on industry reports.

The success of these systems hinges upon employee acceptance and adoption, factors that are influenced by the usefulness of services and ease of use (Davis, 1993; Konradt, Christophersen, & Schaeffer-Kuelz, 2006). The good news is that, at least in one study (n = 517; Konradt et al., 2006), user strain (i.e., employee angst) was negatively related to usefulness and ease of use. In short, HR leaders who adopt software platforms that are directly useful to employees and include user-friendly characteristics (e.g., visually pleasing, easy to navigate) are likely to be more successful. The extent to which successful adoption occurs in the non-profit context will, of course, vary widely. It is likely that larger nonprofit organizations will have an increased capacity to institute such systems and, for these organizations, the investment of money and staff time may indeed lead to employee satisfaction and increased overall efficiency. Smaller organizations, however, will likely find such services to be cost-prohibitive and, unless they can partner with other small organizations, may find themselves unable to compete in this area.

Training and E-learning

Companies are increasingly using technology-based methods to provide employees with on-the-job training (Miller, 2012). Technologically-based delivery methods such as recorded videos, live webinars, and online courses provide a low-cost, flexible, efficient, and convenient alternative to in-person trainings (Salas, DeRouin, & Littrell, 2005; Welsh, Wanberg, Brown, & Simmering, 2003). Online or digital training courses are especially useful for agencies with multiple locations or where the same information must be conveyed repeatedly (e.g., trainings on client privacy, sexual harassment). Such trainings, also known as e-learning, can include organization-wide privacy and safety trainings, department-specific trainings, as well as leadership and management trainings. In a nonprofit organization, these trainings could potentially be offered to both volunteers and paid staff members. For example, the Red Cross offers an online new employee and volunteer training (Red Cross, n.d.). This training is available publicly and also doubles as a low-cost screening tool: Before ever contacting a Red Cross staff member, potential volunteers can view the online orientation and decide whether or not their interests align with the organization's needs.

E-learning requires significant pre-planning and does have its downfalls. Research has revealed concerns related to the start-up costs, the lack of inter-action, and the temptation to equate the company's delivery of information with the individual's understanding of information (Welsh et al., 2003). This latter point is especially important: An instructor in an in-person course can gauge students' understanding of the material by scanning the room for furrowed brows or by asking a few targeted questions. An instructor in an online course must be more creative and systematic in such assessments. Evaluation of technology-based training is, therefore, especially critical. Additionally, it is important that organizations ensure employees understand the relevance of a specific training: Knowledge transfer is related to knowledge gain and, also, trainees' satisfaction with and perceptions of the utility of the training (Alliger, Tannenbaum, Bennett, Traver, & Shotland, 1997; Sitzmann, Brown, Casper, Ely, & Zimmerman, 2008). Of course, any and all of these factors may be influenced by the users' capacity to interface with technology, which must also be taken into consideration.

In general, it is likely that nonprofit organizations will benefit from adopting a blended approach to employee development which combines both in-person and technology-based trainings (Salas, DeRouin, & Littrell, 2005; Stone et al., 2015). Nonprofits should also stay abreast of changes, as e-learning is developing rapidly and organizations may soon use virtual simulations, gamifications, knowledge repositories, and crowdsourcing as vehicles to train employees (Stone et al., 2015).

Technology-related Changes in Employment Opportunities

In addition to influencing many of the functions of HRM, technology has also had a dramatic impact in the types of position available within nonprofit organizations and the sorts of activities for which each position can reasonably be responsible (Pynes, 2013; Saidel & Cour, 2003). The magnitude of changes cannot be overstated. As Kraemer and Dedrick (1997) wrote, access to information can change the location and nature of decision-making, entire job classifications disappear while new ones are created, layers of management are eliminated, organizational politics take on new dimensions, and jobs can become more or less satisfying to workers (p. 100).

In nonprofit organizations, such changes can occur in myriad forms. For example, the implementation of electronic health records has affected the qualifications required of most nonprofit healthcare professionals and, also, either eliminated or fundamentally changed the nature of most medical record jobs. Separately, the use of software (rather than html coding) to develop websites has meant that nonprofit staff members without any computer science background may be asked to develop and publish websites. This next section explores technology-related changes in job functions, the development of new positions, and implications for job satisfaction.

Technology and changes in job functions

Technology is changing many of today's existing jobs (Pynes, 2013). For example, information technology has increased the number of tasks any individual is able or expected to perform. This is true at all levels of the organization. Lower-level employees may have little technology-related education or skills and, yet, may be tasked with what was previously considered higher-order administrative tasks including maintaining spreadsheets and databases, coordinating client transportation, and even developing websites (Saidel & Cour, 2003). There are different ways to think about such changes in job function, and such changes are especially important to consider for long-time employees who may or may not be interested in learning new techniques. In a series of in-depth interviews conducted at three New York-based nonprofit agencies, such task expansion was described by support staff members as both an enriching experience and a stressful increase in workload. Conversely, executive staff members who were traditionally tasked with higher-order decision-making find that technology makes it more efficient for them to complete many of the lower-order tasks—such as writing memos or generating reports—they would previously have assigned to administrative assistants. Executive staff members have reported significant increases in the amount of work they perform and, also, increased stress during the initial learning phase associated with new technology. In short, technology-related changes to job functions may increase the potential productivity of employees but the lived experience of employees should also be carefully managed before, during, and after the change process. Managing the process may be particularly important for nonprofits for which employee turnover is especially costly, such as smaller organizations operating with limited HR budgets or for organizations seeking to retain employees in niche positions (e.g., bilingual physicians in rural health centers).

Technology and New Jobs

In addition to changing the nature of existing jobs, new technologies also frequently lead to the creation of new types of position. For example, nonprofit healthcare companies that accept federal dollars must use Electronic Health Records (EHR) and demonstrate "meaningful use" of such records (HealthIT.gov, n.d.). As a result, a host of technology-related healthcare jobs have been created to help nonprofit organizations transition from paper to electronic records, train providers and support staff, develop meaningful reports and related policies and procedures, and to ensure patient privacy. Similar, albeit somewhat less dramatic shifts have occurred in human service case management, in theater and ticket sales, and other nonprofit uses of technology. As technology takes over much of the mentally and physically repetitive tasks (Pynes, 2013), many positions, such as medical record filers, are becoming increasingly obsolete.

The nonprofit sector as a whole may be well positioned to benefit from the new jobs that are created. This may be particularly useful for HR leaders whose nonprofit organization is not large enough to offer employees long-term career advancement opportunities. As Saidel and Cour (2003) noted,

> Given the nonprofit workforce's willingness to move laterally into more challenging jobs and the difficulty in hiring technologically skilled employees,

nonprofit organizations may be in a better position to use the implementation of new technologies to reward and motivate workers.

(p. 13).

In short, the old job becomes a new job when new technology and technology-related training is added. This would likely have implications for job satisfaction.

Technology and Job Satisfaction

As technology has changed the nature of jobs in the nonprofit sector, it is important to understand how this technology has influenced how workers experience their jobs. In particular, scholars have found that the strategic implementation of technology can, indeed, improve job satisfaction, particularly for nonprofit organizations. For example, the immediacy of technology may provide increased autonomy and a sense of instant accomplishment that Saidel and Cour (2003) argue is difficult to achieve in human services organizations, organizations that are often focused on long-term outcomes. For example, a caseworker will not be able to solve all of their client's issues in one session; but they can indicate via a performance management system what steps they took toward helping the client achieve long-term goals. This checking of the boxes on small tasks (e.g., specific referrals) can provide an immediate sense of accomplishment that helps sustain the employee's motivation over the long term.

As Pynes (2013) has written, many positions in today's nonprofit sector workplace demand a "more educated workforce with advanced knowledge" (p. 414) and, additionally, require continuous training to keep up with the rapidly evolving field. The good news for HR leaders is that technology-related education can be perceived (i.e., positioned) as an employee benefit. In a series of 23 in-depth interviews, Saidel and Cour (2003) also found that continuous technology training can be an enjoyable activity that improves job satisfaction. Such employee development boosts the nonprofit's overall capacity and, at the same time, increases the marketability of the employee for both internal promotion and external advancement.

Nowhere have the changes in technology-related job functions been so rapid as in the arena of social media. Often, entry-level employees find themselves communicating via social media with hundreds, thousands, and sometimes millions of individuals and, in doing so, must operate more like a seasoned communications director than as entry-level support staff. In this complex and evolving landscape, nonprofit HR leaders are struggling to understand and provide adequate leadership.

Social Media and Human Resources

Social media usage among nonprofit organizations has become ubiquitous: 97% of the largest U.S. nonprofits use social media platforms (e.g., Facebook, Twitter,

Instagram) to communicate with constituents (Barnes, 2010). There are numerous HR-related risks to nonprofit social media usage (Cohen, 2013; Palfry, 2010), including risks related to employee and client privacy (Hyman, Luks, & Sechrest, 2011; Jones & Soltren, 2005; Mainiero & Jones, 2013; Rosenblum, 2007), labor law violations (accidental or intentional; Lafe, 2011; National Labor Relations Board, 2013), and brand reputation (McNeill, 2012), particularly when an employee's morally questionable activities become publicly available via social networking sites.

Social media usage by employees can be divided into two categories: job-related and personal (Jones, 2015). The first category, job-related social media activities, takes place in a variety of departments. For example, fundraising staff may connect with donors via LinkedIn; program staff may connect with clients via Facebook; and volunteer administrators may use Twitter to recruit new volunteers. All of these activities have the potential to blur the boundaries of employees' professional and personal lives, especially if work-related online connections are developed via employees' personal social media sites. This blurring is of particular concern to the organization when it involves at-risk clients (such as youth or victims of domestic violence) or high-profile donors (who may maintain a relationship with the fundraising professional even after that staff member has begun working for another agency).

The second category, employees' personal use of social media, can also have unexpected and, at times, serious impacts on an organization. For example, employees may want to access and update their personal sites during work time, and they may connect with one another via social media, even to the extent of "monitor[ing] each other's location on Foursquare before a lunch meeting" (Mainiero & Jones, 2013, p. 187). Alternatively, employees' personal social media posts may get confused with professional social media posts, such as the example of the Red Cross employee who tweeted to the Red Cross' fan base a message about #gettingslizzerd (i.e., drunk) (Wasserman, 2011). The message had been intended for the employees' personal account. Much of this type of blurring between professional and personal boundaries may be considered harmless, but it does open the doors to less-benign interactions, particularly in cases of stalking and sexual harassment. It does not take much imagination to see why HR leaders must pay attention to and attempt to manage the risks involved in employee social media use, both job-related and personal.

One way that organizations manage risk is by adopting social media policies. There is reason to believe that social media policies, in general, are becoming more prevalent (Barnes et al., 2015; Jones, 2012a; Kind, Genrich, Sodhi, & Chretien, 2010). These policies are far more complex than other governance policies such as a whistleblower or conflict of interest statement. The complexity is twofold: First, social media policies have multiple and, often, divergent functions, including to protect employees' rights (see, for example, Lafe, 2011; National Labor Relations Board, 2013) and to manage the organization's reputation (McNeill, 2012). Second, social media is a mercurial and rapidly-evolving phenomenon. New opportunities and new risks are emerging almost daily, and these new risks can potentially render yesterday's policy obsolete.

There is some debate about which department should be responsible for crafting social media policies. A recent study by SHRM (as cited in Leonard, 2012) indicated that an organization's social media policies are often written by one department (e.g., human resources, information technology, senior leadership, or marketing). This process can be problematic, as each department is likely to have its own internal logic and may not fully understand the needs and/or goals of another. For example, a legal department and a communications department may have very different approaches to social media. Additionally, the social media landscape is evolving rapidly and no policy can adequately address risks that have yet to emerge. Therefore, a team-based approach to developing social media policies may be a better way: (1) to ensure the policies are appropriate for the entire organization; (2) to obtain employee buy-in; and (3) to offer a learning environment that develops staff capacities—individually and as a team—to respond to emergent risk (Jones, 2015).

While social media policies may be one of the more complex policies that a nonprofit develops, there is some good news. For many years, nonprofit organizations have operated without the guidance or best practices related to social media policies (see, for example, Hymen, Luks, & Sechrest, 2011). In recent years, however, such guidance is beginning to emerge. Consultants and industry support organizations have developed workbooks and templates to guide practitioners (for example, Idealware, 2012; Jones, 2012b, February 9). Also, scholars and legal experts are (slowly!) producing material that is also helpful, albeit somewhat less digestible (for example, Cohen, 2013; Jones, 2015b). The challenge for nonprofit organizations is to make sense of both academic and practitioner recommendations in light of their own unique circumstances (e.g., risk tolerance, employee expertise, and specific mission) and, also, to recognize that a social media policy must be reviewed and revised on a regular basis.

Part II: Implications for Practice

The remainder of this chapter discusses the implications for the nonprofit sector of the material presented thus far. This is no easy task. The nonprofit sector is extraordinarily diverse in regard to size and type of organization (McKeever & Pettijohn, 2014) and there are multiple permutations of size and type. These permutations have implications for HRM practices (Guo, Brown, Ashcraft, Yoshioka, & Dong, 2011). Therefore, is difficult, if not impossible, to offer comprehensive recommendations on how nonprofits should implement HR-related technology. Instead, this section of the chapter suggests two things: (1) the use of technology in HRM should be viewed as an issue of strategic leadership directly related to the organization's goals; and (2) implementation should be understood as a process of change management. The chapter then concludes with three questions an HR leader might ask themselves and their team. These questions are based on the research presented earlier in the chapter and are designed to help the HR leader to identify and mitigate at least some of the challenges posed by technology.

Strategic Leadership and Technology

The implementation of technological innovations is, at its core, an issue of strategic leadership. Success is not simply a matter of providing a more efficient, user-friendly experience of human resources but, rather, identifying what that improved experience will mean in terms of broader organizational productivity (e.g., employee retention). In short, as Alfred J. Walker (2001b) has written, "The ultimate goal of HR technology is to help the organization meet its business goals and objectives today and in the future" (p. 10). The link between technology and organizational goals must be clear. Specifically, Walker suggests, to be considered successful, HR technology must accomplish the following objectives:

- *Strategic Alignment* [It] must help users in a way that supports the goals of the business.
- *Business Intelligence* [It] must provide users with relevant information and data, answer questions, and inspire new insights and learning.
- *Efficiency and Effectiveness* [It] must change the work performed by the Human Resources personnel by dramatically improving their level of service, allowing more time for work of higher value, and reducing their costs (pp. 3–4).

The connection between technology and business goals offers an interesting challenge for HR leaders in nonprofit organizations. Nonprofits have a unique set of business goals and objectives that cover a number of different stakeholders (Balser & McClusky, 2005; McCambridge & Salamon, 2003). For example, nonprofit leaders must manage relationships with donors, volunteers, clients, community members, elected officials, and employees. These different relationships with different stakeholders are managed by a variety of departments, and each department may include staff with a range of skillsets and technological backgrounds. In short, a nonprofit organization can be an incredibly diverse universe and, in many cases, a microcosm of society. HR leaders, therefore, must take the time to understand the multiple bottom lines of their organization and the specific contexts of each department. *The benefit of technology to these bottom lines and within these contexts must be explicit, clear, and substantial.*

Leadership in Implementation

It has been suggested an effective way to implement HR-related technology is through the lens of change management (Sierra-Cedar, 2015). The change management model was introduced by Julien Phillips (1983) and includes three critical components: a new strategic vision, new organizational skills, and political support. In regard to HRM and technology, the first component, a new vision, is best addressed when HR leaders frame their work in relationship to organizational goals. For example, technological improvements in the employee hiring and/or training processes would logically lead to improved employee retention which, in turn, allows the organization to focus more dollars on programmatic goals. Or, alternatively, employee training in technology may lead to improved job performance: Training employees in electronic health records, for example, may be costly but it may improve the quality of service provided (and, not inconsequently, the organization's billing efficiency). The importance of this connection between HR and the organization's goals cannot be understated.

The second component, new organizational skills, includes on-the-job training, changes in job functions, and the hiring of new positions. These concepts were the focus of much of the research presented in the first half of the chapter, and it became evident that information technology has changed the nature of a number of positions. As Saidel and Cour (2003) found, "it appears everyone in the labor force, regardless of hierarchical level, must now be more of a technician" (p. 12). Changes in job functions extend even into the realm of HRM. It is increasingly important that HR staff members have a good understanding of technology (SHRM, 2015). As a representative from one of the nation's leading HR consulting firms indicated, "HR professionals must develop a proficiency in broad HR applications and their potential delivery systems. They must be able to apply this knowledge to the business-planning process" (p. 5). HR leaders, therefore, must think broadly about the range and types of organizational skills needed to execute their vision, including the skills needed within the HR department.

The final component, political support, is crucial. Research in change management and, also, in the implementation of HR technology suggests it is critical that HR leaders garner internal support at all levels. This includes involving employees and, where applicable, volunteers in the process. For example, scholars Konradt, Christophersen, and Shaeffer-Kuelz (2006) suggest that the involvement of the employees in the planning process should be an essential component of the project, for example by conducting interviews, performing work-flow and working environment analysis, and collecting ideas based on paper prototypes. During the roll out phase, employees should be informed about the project by running an internal marketing campaign (p. 1150).

Additionally, HR leaders can involve employees in the implementation of technology by developing inter-departmental teams, such as those developed to create social media policies (Jones, 2015). Different organizations will require different strategies for pursuing political support but, in general, process of developing internal buy-in is critical for all HR leaders seeking to implement new technologies.

Three Questions to Consider

As described in the first half of the chapter, research suggests that technology can create at least as many problems as it alleviates. A few simple questions can help organizations sidestep at least some of these challenges. Here are three questions worth considering:

Question #1: How Does This Technology Affect Our Staff and Volunteers?

Nonprofit HR departments are unique in that they often work with both paid and unpaid staff. The implementation of any technological innovation must be considered from the perspective of both groups. Employees may have little choice and many will adapt to whatever technological system the organization adopts; however, volunteers can more easily vote with their feet. Each organization will have to assess their particular team and their current (and future) human resources needs to determine the most appropriate role for technology.

Question #2: What Are the Implications for the Quality and Diversity of Our Workforce?

Research indicates that technology may have important and, sometimes, unfortunate implications for quality and diversity (McManus & Ferguson, 2003; Stone et al., 2015). For example, some seasoned medical providers may retire early rather than learn new technologies or highly skilled individuals may not see a job application that is only distributed electronically. Additionally, internet-based recruiting may yield a candidate pool more likely to contain "job-hoppers" than traditional recruiting methods (McManus & Ferguson, 2003). Nonprofit HR leaders should take care to know their particular community and develop appropriate strategies by, for example, broadening where an organization posts paid and volunteer positions. This does not have to be a time-consuming task. Nonprofits with smaller HR departments can ask a volunteer to develop a wide distribution list of media outlets (e.g., community colleges, and ethnic, cultural, and religious publications) and gathering places (e.g., community centers, advocacy groups), and can share that list with HR departments in other small nonprofits.

Question #3: How Does Technology Affect Relationships Among Our Staff?

Technology can accomplish many of the functions previously performed by management, but at what expense? How does a given technology, such as electronic performance management or employee self-service, change the relationships between staff and supervisors or between staff and human resource personnel? If technology decreases the opportunities for meaningful interaction, strategic HR leaders might look for alternative ways to build internal social cohesion. Additionally, HR leaders might work with supervisory staff to develop management styles and strategies that reinfuse humanity into their relationships with supervisees.

Conclusion

Like rocks skipping on water, this chapter has touched upon a number of different ways HRM has been and will continue to be impacted by technology. The first half of this chapter presented a broad swath of research on how technology affects core HRM functions such as recruiting, hiring, retaining, and motivating employees. It also looked at the influence of technology on position descriptions, namely that technology has eliminated now obsolete positions, changed—at least in part—the nature of almost all positions, and created new job classifications. Additionally, the first half of the chapter discussed the HR-related challenges posed by social media. In looking at the research, two things became increasingly clear: Technology is having a profound impact on the functions of human resources, and technological innovation is rapidly posing new challenges.

The second half of the chapter reflected upon the first half and asked, "What now?" It argued that the implementation of technology is, at its core, an issue of strategic leadership that must be carefully orchestrated. Successful leaders will steward all three aspects of Phillip's (1983) change management model: vision, skills, and political support. Appropriate and effective technological innovations can improve job satisfaction, employee productivity, and, also, offer unique professional development opportunities to all involved.

Discussion Questions

1   There are many different ways technology can be used in human resource management. Do some stand out to you as more important than others? Why?

2   Some researchers suggest that external social media platforms (e.g., Twitter, LinkedIn) can be used to develop relationships with job candidates and, similarly, that internal social media platforms can be used to develop relationships between supervisors and supervisees. How could this be accomplished, and what challenges may arise when pursuing such a strategy?

3   It is often difficult to secure funding for nonprofit administrative expenses. How could an HR leader best position their ideas so that the implementation of technology becomes attractive to the CEO and/or to funders?

References

Alliger, G. M., Tannenbaum, S. I., Bennett, W., Jr., Traver, H., & Shotland, A. (1997). A meta-analysis of the relations among training criteria. *Personnel Psychology, 50,* 341–358.

Balser, D. & McClusky, J. (2005). Managing stakeholder relationships and nonprofit organization effectiveness. *Nonprofit Management & Leadership, 15*(3), 295–315.

Barnes, N. G. (2010). Social media usage now ubiquitous among US top charities, ahead of all other sectors, Center for Marketing Research. Available at: www.umassd.edu/cmr/studiesandresearch/ (accessed August 14, 2015).

Barnes, N. G., Lescault, A. M., & Augusto, K. D. (2015). LinkedIn dominates, Twitter trends and Facebook falls: The 2014 Inc. 500 and social media, Center for Marketing Research. www.umassd.edu/cmr/socialmediaresearch/

Bartram, D. (2004). Assessment in organisations. *Applied Psychology, 53*, 237–259.

Bracken, D. W., Summers, L., & Fleenor, J. (1998). High-tech 360. *Training & Development, 52*, 42–45.

Brown, K. G. & Charlier, S. D. (2013). An integrative model of e-learning use: Leveraging theory to understand and increase use. *Human Resource Management Review, 23*, 37–49.

Burt, E. & Taylor, J. A. (2000). Information and communication technologies: Reshaping voluntary organizations? *Nonprofit Management & Leadership, 11*(2), 131–143.

Chapman, D. S., Uggerslev, K. L., & Webster, J. (2003). Applicant reactions to face-to-face and technology-mediated interviews: A field investigation. *Journal of Applied Psychology, 88*(5), 944–953.

Chuang, A. & Sackett, P. R. (2005). The perceived importance of the person-job fit and the person organization fit between and within interview stages. *Social Behavior and Personality, 33*(3), 209–226.

Cohen, A. (2013). *Social media legal risk and corporate policy*. New York: Wolters Kluwer Law & Business.

Cronin, B., Morath, R., Curtin, P., & Heil, M. (2006). Public sector use of technology in managing human resources. *Human Resource Management Review, 16*, 416–430.

Davis, F. D. (1993). User acceptance of information technology: System characteristics, user perceptions and behavioral impacts. *International Journal of Man-Machine Studies, 38*, 475–487.

Dineen, B. R. & Allen, D. G. (2013). Internet recruiting 2.0: shifting paradigms. In K. Y. T. Yu & D. M. Cable (Eds.), *The Oxford handbook of recruitment* (pp. 382–401). New York: Oxford University Publishers.

Dulebohn, J. H. & Marler, J. H. (2005). e-compensation: The potential to transform practice? In H.G. Gueutal & D. L. Stone (Eds.), *The brave new world of eHR: Human resource management in the digital age* (pp. 166–189). San Francisco: Jossey-Bass.

Ebrahim, A. (2003). Making sense of accountability: Conceptual perspectives for northern and southern nonprofits. *Nonprofit Leadership and Management, 14*(2), 191–212.

Galanaki, E. (2002). The decision to recruit online: A descriptive study. *Career Development International, 7*(4), 243–251.

Gherson, D. & Jackson, A. P. (2001). Web-based compensation planning. In A. J. Walker (Ed.), *Web-based Human Resources* (pp. 83–95). New York, NY: McGraw-Hill.

Guo, C., Brown, W. A., Ashcraft, R. F., Yoshioka, C. F., & Dong, H. D. (2011). Strategic human resources management in nonprofit organizations. *Review of Public Personnel Administration, 31*(3), 248–269.

Guy, M. E., Newman, M. A., Mastracci, S. H., & Maynard-Moody, S. (2010). Emotional labor in the human service organization. In Y. Hassenfeld (Ed.), *Human services as complex organizations* (2nd ed.). Thousand Oaks, CA: Sage.

HealthIT.gov. (n.d.). EHR incentives and certification: How to attain meaningful use. Available at: www.healthit.gov/providers-professionals/how-attain-meaningful-use (accessed August 14, 2015).

Hedge, J. W. & Borman, W. C. (1995). Changing conceptions and practices in performance appraisal. In A. Howard (Ed.), *The changing nature of work* (pp. 451–481). San Francisco: Jossey-Bass.

Hyman, J. L., Luks, H. J., & Sechrest, R. (2011). Online professional networks for physicians: Risk management. *Clinical Orthopedics and Related Research*, *470*(5), 1386–1392.

Idealware. (2012). Nonprofit social media policy workbook. Available at: www.idealware. org/reports/nonprofit-social-media-policy-workbook/ (accessed August 14, 2015).

Inc.com. (2014). How to automate payroll. Available at: www.inc.com/guides/2010/12/how-to-automate-payroll.html (accessed August 14, 2015).

Jones, H. & Soltren, J. H. (2005). Facebook: Threats to privacy. Available at: www.swiss. ai.mit.edu/6805/student-papers/fall05-papers/facebook.pdf (accessed August 14, 2015).

Jones, J. A. (2012a). Nonprofit social media policies: Managing risk, maximizing opportunities. Paper presented at the International Society for Third Sector Research, Sienna, Italy, July 10–13.

Jones, J. A. (2012b, February 9). 10 tips for creating a social media policy for your business, Social media examiner. Available at: www.socialmediaexaminer.com/author/jennifer-amanda-jones/ (accessed August 14, 2015).

Jones, J. A. (2015). Developing social media policies: A team learning approach. In H. Asencio & R. Sun (Eds.), *Cases on strategic social media utilization in the nonprofit sector* (pp. 210–236). Hershey: IGI Global.

Kind, T., Genrich, G., Sodhi, A., & Chretien, K. C. (2010). Social media policies at US medical schools. Medical Education Online, 15. Available at: www.ncbi.nlm.nih.gov/pmc/articles/PMC2941429/ (accessed August 14, 2016).

Konradt, U., Christophersen, T., & Schaeffer-Kuelz, U. (2006). Predicting user satisfaction, strain, and system usage of employee self-services. *International Journal of Human-Computer Studies*, *64*, 1141–1153.

Kraemer, K. L. & Dedrick, J. (1997). Computing and public organizations. *Journal of Public Administration Research and Theory*, 7(1), 89–113.

Lafe, S. (2011). Report of the acting general counsel concerning social media cases (Memorandum OM 11-74). Available at: www.nlrb.gov/news/acting-general-counsel-releases-report-social-media-cases (accessed August 14, 2015).

Leonard, B. (2012). Your active role in social media policies. *HRMagazine*, *57*(3), 105.

Mainiero, L. A. & Jones, K. J. (2013). Sexual harassment versus workplace romance: Social media spillover and the textual harassment in the workplace. *The Academy of Management Perspectives*, *27*(3), 187–203.

Marler, J. H. & Fisher, S. L. (2013). An evidence-based review of e-HRM and strategic human resource management. *Human Resource Management Review*, *23*, 18–36.

McCambridge, R. & Salamon, L. M. (2003, March 21). In, but not of, the market: The special challenge of nonprofit-ness. *The Nonprofit Quarterly*.

McKeever, B. & Pettijohn, S. L. (2014). The nonprofit sector in brief 2014: Public charities, giving, and volunteering, The Urban Institute. Available at: www.urban.org/research/publication/nonprofit-sector-brief-public-charities-giving-and-volunteering-2014 (accessed August 14, 2015).

McManus, M. A. & Ferguson, M. W. (2003). Biodata, personality, and demographic differences of recruits from threes sources. *International Journal of Selection and Assessment*, *11*, 175–183.

McNeill, T. (2012). "Don't affect the share price": Social media policy in higher education as reputation management. *Research in Learning Technology*, *20*. Available at: www.researchinlearningtechnology.net/index.php/rlt/article/view/19194 (accessed August 16, 2015).

Miller, L. (2012). ASTD 2012 State of the industry report: Organizations continue to invest in workplace learning. *Training and Development Magazine*, *66*, 42–48.

National Labor Relations Board. (2013). The NLRB and social media. www.nlrb.gov/news-outreach/fact-sheets/nlrb-and-social-media (accessed August 14, 2015).

Palfry, J. (2010). The challenge of developing effective public policy on the use of social media by youth. *Federal Communications Law Journal, 63*(5), 5–18.

Payne, S. C., Horner, M. T., Boswell, W. R., Schroeder, A. N., & Stine-Cheyne, K. J. (2009). Comparison of online and traditional performance appraisal systems. *Journal of Managerial Psychology, 24,* 526–544.

Perrin, A. & Duggan, M. (2015). Americans' internet access: 2000–2015, Pew Research Center. Available at: www.pewinternet.org/2015/06/26/americans-internet-access-2000-2015/ (accessed August 14, 2015).

Phillips, J. R. (1983). Enhancing the effectiveness of organizational change management. *Human Resource Management, 22* (1–2), 183–199.

Pynes, J. E. (2013). *Human resources management for public and nonprofit organizations* (4th ed.). San Francisco: Jossey-Bass.

Red Cross. (n.d.). *Getting started as a volunteer.* Available at: www.redcross.org/support/volunteer/getting-started (accessed November 27, 2015).

Rosenblum, D. (2007). What anyone can know: The privacy risks of social networking sites. *Security and Privacy, IEEE 5*(30), 40–49.

Saidel, J. R. & Cour, S. (2003). Information technology and the voluntary sector workplace. *Nonprofit and Voluntary Sector Quarterly, 32*(1), 5–24.

Salas, E., DeRouin, R., & Littrell, L. (2005). Research based guidelines for distance learning: What we know so far. In H. G. Gueutal & D. L. Stone (Eds.), *The brave new world of eHR: Human resources management in the digital Age* (pp. 104–137). San Francisco: Jossey-Bass.

Sellen, A. J. (1995). Remote conversations: The effects of mediating talk with technology. *Human-Computer Interaction, 10,* 401–444.

SHRM. (2015). The future of the HR profession: Eight leading consulting firms share their visions for the future of human resources. Available at: www.shrm.org/ResourcesAndTools/tools-and-samples/toolkits/Documents/future_of_hr.pdf (accessed August 14, 2015).

Sierra-Cedar. (2015). *Sierra-Cedar 2014–2015 HR systems survey* (17th ed.), Sierra-Cedar. Available at: www.sierra-cedar.com/research/annual-survey/ (accessed August 14, 2015).

Sitzmann, T., Brown, K. G., Casper, W. J., Ely, K., & Zimmerman, R. D. (2008). A review and meta-analysis of the nomological network of trainee reactions. *Journal of Applied Psychology, 93*(2), 280–288.

Sloan, M. F. (2009). The effects of nonprofit accountability ratings on donor behavior. *Nonprofit and Voluntary Sector Quarterly, 38*(2), 220–236.

Stone, D. L, Deadrick, D. L., Lukaszewski, K. M., & Johnson, R. (2015). The influence of technology on the future of human resource management. *Human Resource Management Review, 24,* 216–231.

Stone, D. L., Lukaszewski, K., & Isenhour, L. C. (2005). E-recruiting: Online strategies for attracting talent. In H. G. Gueutal & D. L. Stone (Eds.), *The brave new world of eHR: Human resources management in the digital age* (pp. 22–53). San Francisco: Jossey-Bass.

Sulsky, L. M. & Keown, J. L. (1998). Performance appraisal in the changing world of work: Implications for the meaning and measurement of work performance. *Canadian Psychology/Psychologie Canadienne 39*(1–2), 52–59.

Toppe, C. M., Kirsch, A. D., & Michel, J. (2001). Giving and volunteering in the United States: Findings from a national survey, the Independent Sector. Available at: www.independentsector.org/giving_volunteering (accessed August 14, 2015).

U.S. Department of Labor. (1999). Futurework: Trends and challenges for work in the 21st century. Available at: www.dol.gov/dol/aboutdol/history/herman/reports/futurework/report.htm (accessed August 14, 2015).

Walker, A. J. (2001a). Best practices in HR technology. In A. J. Walker (Ed.), *Web-based Human Resources* (pp. 1–14). New York, NY: McGraw-Hill.

Walker, A. J. (2001b). Creating a business case for your organization's web-based initiative. In A. J. Walker (Ed.), *Web-based human resources* (pp. 131–149). New York, NY: McGraw-Hill.

Wallace, P. & Clariana, R. B. (2005). Test mode familiarity and performance: Gender and race comparisons of test scores among computer literate students in advanced information systems. *Journal of Information Systems Education, 16,* 177–183.

Wasserman, T. (2011). Red Cross does PR disaster recovery on rogue tweet. Available at: http://mashable.com/2011/02/16/red-cross-tweet/#fV3Ht8t5GSqu (accessed November 27, 2015).

Welsh, E. T., Wanberg, C. R., Brown, E. G., & Simmering, M. J. (2003). E-learning: Emerging uses, empirical results and future direction. *International Journal of Training and Development, 7,* 245–258.

20

Conclusion

Toward a Research Agenda for Nonprofit Human Resource Management

Jessica K. A. Word and Jessica E. Sowa

Work is about a search for daily meaning as well as daily bread, for recognition as well as cash, for astonishment rather than torpor; in short, for a sort of life rather than a Monday through Friday sort of dying.

(Studs Terkel)

Introduction

One of the most challenging and rewarding parts of many people's lives is the work they do. While we work to put food on the table, we also work to achieve personal satisfaction and, in the case of those who work in nonprofit organizations, make a difference in the world, to know we have had an impact. This book approaches work and the management of it in the nonprofit sector from the belief that work is important and critical to individuals, organizations, and the communities they serve. The importance of work in the nonprofit sector is related to the nature of the sector itself. The nonprofit sector more than any other sector is concerned with the "commons" or the things we share and do together as a society apart from pure market rationality (Lohmann, 1992). Work for many in the nonprofit sector is about more than simply performing a job to receive a wage. The aim of this book and much of the scholarship discussed in this volume seeks to improve the ability of organizations to retain, motivate, and engage employees, but also to assure work in the nonprofit sector serves a broader purpose and is meaningful for the employees, nonprofits and the communities they serve.

This volume has attempted to capture the state of the field in terms of the research on human resource management (HRM) concerning the nonprofit sector. As many of the authors have stated, much of the information and research available is limited and in the beginning stages of development. We still have work to do as a community of scholars and practitioners to capture the full complexity of what it means to work in the nonprofit sector and how to manage the human resources of the nonprofit sector effectively. However, these early efforts already show a great deal of promise in terms of their ability to positively impact the development of theory and practice. This chapter begins by exploring some of the fundamental differences in terms of work in the nonprofit sector as a whole, and then returns to the challenges raised in the introduction and throughout this work. We then conclude with a brief review of the work presented in this volume and outline directions for future research. While this book is a comprehensive treatment of the state of HRM research in the nonprofit sector, we hope it is the beginning of a long and continuing conversation on how to strengthen the HRM capacity and make the work meaningful, rewarding, and as professionally managed as possible for those who dedicate their lives to the service of others and society in the nonprofit sector.

The Importance of HRM in Nonprofits

The examination of the issue of human resource management for nonprofits is a timely one with increasing questions in the sector about defining and identifying the impact nonprofit organizations have on our communities. The HR function, while traditionally thought of as payroll, record keeping, and benefits administration, has broadened to be much more important to the success of organizations and, for nonprofits, their ability to deliver on their missions. This shift is one in which organizations focused on performance see human resources as critical to executing strategic initiatives and assuring they have the correct staff in place for those strategies to be successful (Benedict et al., 2008). Again, to connect back to themes raised earlier, people are the critical ingredient for a nonprofit to develop high performance; the resource-based view emphasizes a nonprofit's human capital as central to its competitive advantage. To make sure they have a steady stock of this human capital, in particular, the need for better management of human resources in the nonprofit sector is driven by the need to ensure organizations can compete for and keep the talent they need to be successful. In particular, the work of Jasmine McGinnis Johnson and Eddy S. Ng (2016) points to challenges in retaining Millennial managers and those with advanced degrees when pay is too low. This finding suggests that additional attention needs to be paid to the factors that attract and retain nonprofit workers. As the nonprofit workforce grows in depth, breadth, and demographic complexity, the time is now to improve how we manage this workforce.

Millennials and Gen Xers now make up the largest groups in the labor force (Fry, 2015). The importance of these workers to the current and future of nonprofit organizations cannot be understated. These two generations, along with being the largest groups in the labor force, are also some of the most highly educated workers due to rising education attainment levels. The need to retain and attract these workers early in their careers is underscored by the research on sector choice, which suggests early career experiences and preferences shape where an employee will work throughout their career (Tschirhart, Reed, Freeman, & Anker, 2008). This highlights the need to act quickly to improve human resource management and compensation for nonprofit workers or face long-term deficits in the ability of nonprofit organizations to compete especially as older workers the sector retire (Landis-Cobb, Kramer, & Milway, 2015). If the nonprofit sector is to deliver on the promise of the growth of the last 40 years, the sector needs to take steps to professionalize how its workers are managed, including the smallest, grass-roots nonprofits, to ensure that those who choose to work in the nonprofit sector will not leave to pursue their careers elsewhere.

Qualities of the Nonprofit Workforce and the Sector

One of the main themes that resonated in the study of nonprofit human resource management is the unique challenges and assets of organizations in this sector. The challenges include the unpredictability of many of the resources in the sector such as revenue, due to instability in fundraising and grants, the range in size and complexity of organizations, which challenges the ability to develop recommendations for better management practices, the wide variety of work undertaken in the sector, with so many different types and forms of employment, and the changing roles and availability of volunteers. Paired with these challenges come some of the more unique assets of the sector, which includes the broad support that many organizations enjoy because of their strong ties to the community and the ability to appeal to employees, donors, and volunteers not just in terms of economics but also in terms of altruism (Grønbjerg & Paarlberg, 2001). These challenges and assets are part of what make the nonprofit sector distinct but these qualities require researchers and managers to think differently about these organizations and how to apply their skills to findings solutions to better serve nonprofits and communities. We will now explore some of the characteristics of working in the sector and how they shape the need for future research.

In particular, many of the authors in this volume have highlighted the involvement and importance of volunteers and the work they perform in nonprofit organizations as unique. The voluntary nature of the nonprofit sector remains one of the most rewarding, and challenging, aspects of managing in nonprofit organizations. It asks managers to work with people who are so passionate about the work they do not need to be paid but, because of their status, their service is often less stable and more sporadic than that of paid employees (Cnaan & Handy, 2005; Lammers, 1991). However, the management of volunteers presents distinct advantages and limitations in terms of the management of human resources. As Jeffrey Brudney and Hayley Sink in Chapter 12 discuss, volunteer management until recently has been largely discussed as a one-size-fits-all approach for nonprofit organizations. There is a great need to more closely examine the factors that impact the effectiveness and necessity of volunteer management practices and under which circumstances different aspects of volunteer management can and should be applied. When a nonprofit organization has a sizeable portion of staff who are donating their human capital and therefore are not motivated by extrinsic rewards, careful attention to how these staff are managed and motivated is critical to the organization. This research by Brudney and Sink will help volunteer managers better adjust the universal model to the needs and resources of their organization.

While managing a volunteer staff raises a particular set of questions for a nonprofit, another distinct issue in the sector is the challenge of managing paid staff alongside volunteers. While volunteers and employees both choose to work for a variety of reasons, managing these two sources of labor and talent side by side can at times cause difficulties for both managers and employees. The interplay of paid and volunteer labor was explored in Chapter 15 by Allison Russell, Laurie Mook, and Femida Handy. This chapter illustrates that one of the remaining challenges for researchers is to more closely examine how the interaction between volunteers and staff contribute to or detract from the engagement of volunteers. This chapter also emphasizes the need to examine the trade-off inherent from mixing paid staff and volunteers in the production of nonprofit goods and services. Future research on volunteer management and HRM in nonprofits needs to further investigate the interactions between these labor forces and the possible interactions in terms of productivity, engagement, and the culture of organizations.

Another aspect often documented in the literature and noted by observers of the sector are the characteristics of the nonprofit workforce itself. The individuals who seek to work for and create nonprofit organizations are often described as different in terms of their motivation and engagement at work (Lee & Wilkins, 2011; Leete, 2000; Park & Word, 2012). These workers are often pointed to as more altruistic or motivated to serve a cause bigger than themselves. However, little comparative data exists that truly examines differences between workers across the public, nonprofit, and for-profit sectors of the economy. Most of the research that addresses these differences only looks comparatively across two sectors and excludes the third. Collection of comparative data about individuals who self-select into these sectors can begin to unpack the extent to which theories, such as the donative labor hypothesis (discussed in more detail by Beth Gazley in Chapter 2), are indeed correct about the qualities of nonprofit workers and the organizations they serve. As mentioned earlier, if people do self-select into the sector and early sector choice has an influence on individuals' career paths, we need to better understand what drives people to enter the nonprofit sector first, so we can keep them here and make this a rewarding life-long professional path.

While the sector has grown over time and more individuals are making their careers in the nonprofit sector, some particular HRM challenges remain unaddressed. Unlike many areas of the U.S. economy, the nonprofit sector as a whole tends to include more women than men. Despite the higher than average representation of women in the nonprofit labor force, issues of fairness and equality still persist. The 2016 GuideStar Nonprofit Compensation report, which examined 990's for 96,000 nonprofit entities, found that compensation for female executives still lagged behind their male counterparts, with the gap being the most pronounced measuring 23% at nonprofits with budgets from $2.5 to $5 million dollars (Wyland, 2016). The report also highlighted the fact that few women lead large nonprofit organizations, despite their prevalence in the workforce. The prominence of women in the sector and the often noted pay disparities between nonprofit wages and those in the public sector mean additional research needs to be conducted to examine the role of gender on the nonprofit wage gap (England, 2005; Leete, 2000) and also the role of gender on the evolution of the sector as a whole. In the area of human resources, the role of gender in terms of attracting and keeping talent also needs to be more fully investigated since some research has suggested women are more attracted to nonprofit work because they are more altruistic in nature (Themudo, 2009).

Another aspect of the nonprofit sector that influences the management and development of human resources is the relatively limited size of most nonprofit organizations. As discussed by John C. Ronquillo, Annie Miller, and Ida Drury in Chapter 3, nonprofit organizations currently employ approximately 1 in 10 Americans but the majority of these organizations have relatively few employees. Their relatively small size overall makes it difficult to devote sufficient resources to the management, training, and development of staff. This is especially true given that most nonprofit organizations lack a staff member devoted to human resource management (Guo, Brown, Ashcraft, Yoshioka, & Dong, 2011). For scholars, this means we need to focus our efforts on developing research and theory to apply to smaller organizational settings with fewer HR specialists and more generalists to increase the relevance of this work to all nonprofits.

Directions for Future Research

The nonprofit sector has come a long way. The sector has grown significantly in the past 40 years in the United States and is the main career path for many who are interested in making a difference in their communities. As documented in Chapter 16, by Carrie Oelberger, Anne-Meike Fechter, and Ishbel McWha-Hermann, the power of nonprofits is not limited to the United States—nonprofits are a global force for change, but with that growth remains many management challenges. While more education programs are started every year to train those working in the nonprofit sector and more scholars dedicate their attention to improving our body of knowledge on how the sector does and should operate, we still have work to do.

Many of the limitations of our understanding of the issues surrounding HR in the nonprofit sector are the result of data limitations. The limitations on the availability and quality of the data to study nonprofit organizations are a well-documented and ongoing issue for nonprofit researchers (Grønbjerg, 2002).

Many of the existing data resources stem from data collected by a few government sources including: the federal Internal Revenue Service, state-level data available from State Attorney Generals and Secretaries of state, the federal Department of Labors Bureau of Labor Statistics data, and other archival data sources. The use of these data sets poses challenges for all nonprofit researchers since these data sets were designed for administrative purposes and not for research purposes. This means data must be collected by individual researchers with limited ability to create random samples to gain a representative sample of nonprofits or their employees. Progress is being made in this area (see the work of the Center on Nonprofits and Philanthropy of the Urban Institute and GuideStar), but gathering systematic data on management in the nonprofit sector is a Herculean task.

Additionally, further complications with these data sources ensue because of the failure of many data sources to have specific categories or coding for nonprofit organizations. For example, the Bureau of Labor Statistics collects data on employers through the Quarterly Census of Employment and Wages, which includes most employers in the United States. However, the data is designed to look at employment by industrial classification and does not include coding of organization by type, so both nonprofit and for-profit hospitals fall under the same category within the data. The only way to then identify nonprofit organizations in this data set is to match the data to IRS data sets, which are often somewhat dated by the time they are released. This means the research and analysis into the management of human resources by nonprofit organizations are likely missing many newer and smaller organizations.

Additional issues are faced in creating information relevant for researchers and practitioners across the entire nonprofit sector. The diversity of the nonprofit sector has long been a challenge for nonprofit researchers. We are not just comparing apples and oranges in the nonprofit sector—we are examining the whole fruit basket. As discussed above and in Chapter 3 by John C. Ronquillo, Annie Miller, and Ida Drury, most of the organizations in the nonprofit sector are relatively small, creating an issue in terms of the availability of data and the collection of new data from organizations that represent the sector as a whole. In particular, one of the challenges is collecting data from these smaller nonprofit organizations, which tend to respond at a lower rate to surveys or are simply excluded from data collection (Hager, Wilson, Polack, & Rooney, 2003).

In part, small organizations are often excluded because of the limited availability of data on these organizations from the IRS. Organizations with gross receipts less than $200,000 and assets below $500,000 are only required to file a 990 EZ and organizations with less than $50,000 in gross receipts are only required to file the 990-N or E-postcard, both of which contain fewer data fields afforded for research. The limited data on small organizations makes it more difficult to research management issues that challenge newer and smaller organizations. These include areas examined in this book such as training and development as explored by Toby Eagan in Chapter 13 and recruitment and selection challenges for small organizations as raised by Rikki Abzug in Chapter 6.

Another limitation of the use of the 990 for the study of human resources in the nonprofit sector is the very small amount of information it contains that pertains to management and employment. Currently, the form only collects data on "key employees" or those making in excess of $150,000 in compensation annually. Since this excludes most nonprofit employees, the IRS 990 form is usually just the starting point to identify organizations for researchers interested in nonprofit HRM issues. Even as a starting point it limits the ability of nonprofit researchers to select organizations based upon number of employees for sampling. Limitations in this data make it more difficult to answer questions raised in Chapter 9 by Sally Selden as to how well nonprofits examine their compensation practices, whether they consider questions of equity in setting their salaries and whether they adopt compensation practices designed to promote high performance in their nonprofits.

The lack of consistent data sources also makes it difficult to study organizations over longer time frames. As the nonprofit sector grows in importance and professionalization, we need to understand the dynamics behind this growth for HRM and ensure it follows a productive path. While a great deal of social science research employs cross-sectional data analysis, this approach limits the ability of researchers to more fully examine the causal mechanisms between human resource issues and other outcomes of interest such as organizational performance or outcomes in the community. For example, a recent work by Erin Melton and Kenneth Meier (2016) used multi-year data to examine the link between public sector human resource functions and organizational performance. Their analysis focuses on outcomes for public schools and found that the size and scope of the HRM function needed to change as the goals of the particular school district changed. The type of nuance demonstrated in this analysis would not have been possible had it not been for multi-year data. We need to be able to apply similar analysis techniques as the nonprofit sector grows and changes. This analysis not only demonstrates the need for multi-year data but also the need to examine models that avoid one size fits all approaches to the study of HRM, models that can be tailored to particular nonprofit contexts, such as those discussed by Hans-Gerd Ridder and Alina McCandless Baluch in Chapter 5 and Jeffrey Brudney and Hayley Sink in Chapter 12. Small organizations and those heavily reliant on volunteers will likely need models that adapt to their needs, goals, and available resources. However, knowing that to be true and showing it are two different things—we need more longitudinal data to make the case for investing in nonprofit HRM capacity to foster its growth and professionalization.

One of the unique challenges of examining the impact of HRM on nonprofit success is the difficulty in defining and measuring successful outcomes because of the abstract nature of nonprofit missions (Sawhill & Williamson, 2001). This lack of a universal measure for successful outcomes makes examining the impact of HRM across organizations more challenging. As noted by Marlene Walk and Troy Kennedy in Chapter 14, human resource management and performance appraisal are meant to contribute to the overall success of organizations. However, the limited ability to examine the impact of performance appraisals and other HRM strategies across organizational settings and missions limits the ability of scholars to examine their role in the success of organizations. Walk and Kennedy further point to the need to be cautious in the adaptation of performance appraisal research to both practice and scholarship on nonprofits since ultimately these organizations have different aims.

Chapter 2 by Beth Gazely, Chapter 8 by Heather Carpenter, and Chapter 11 by Kunle Akingbola all point to the need for additional research about how best for managers to balance the competing needs of organizations while at the same time engaging, motivating, and retaining their employees. These challenges are heightened by resource constraints on nonprofit overhead and the pressure to "do more with less" often present in the sector (Lecy & Searing, 2015). However, this focus on doing more with less often limits the ability to effectively manage nonprofits and forces organizations to cut corners in terms of the management and development of employees. While in the short term these trade-offs may lead to cost savings, these savings are likely unsustainable and can impact both the quality of the work done and the ability to maintain and engage employees. The challenge for researchers is to demonstrate the link between these trade-offs in terms of employee engagement and retention and the quality of outcomes for the sector and communities.

A key issue in HRM across sectors is how best to manage diverse staff in an organization. In Chapter 18, Judith Y. Weisinger explored the issue of diversity not just from the traditional frame of representation of diverse groups but also drawing upon perspectives in social justice, power and identity dynamics, and interest conflicts. Examining diversity from this perspective challenges researchers and practitioners to think of diversity and inclusion in new ways that engages the culture of our organizations. The challenge to rethink diversity in the sector also presents new research challenges where scholars must think beyond traditional examinations of looking at head counts in terms of diverse groups and instead investigate the changes diversity brings to organizations for the betterment of staff and the organization.

The examination of the unique qualities of staffing for international NGOs by Carrie Oelberger, Anne-Meike Fechter, and Ishbel McWha-Hermann in Chapter 17 also point to trade-off and difficulties in managing diverse paid staff in an international setting. This examination points to how different employee expectations and cultural differences can shape the nature of the relationships between NGOs and employees. Their work points to a need to better understand the challenges involved in cross-national staffs and the ethical issues such as equity and staff safety inherent in such endeavors.

In Chapter 7, Yeonsoo Kim's examination of succession planning for nonprofit organizations points to the need to better investigate models of succession planning and management suited to the nonprofit setting. As often pointed out, the smaller size of nonprofits limits the resources that these organizations have to devote to such efforts and the attention and resources staff can devote to these efforts.

However, the dependence of nonprofit organizations upon others for resources makes them particularly susceptible to changes in leadership, which suggests the need for careful planning around leadership development and succession. If these challenges are to be dealt with for the nonprofit setting, additional research needs to be conducted about how best to tailor succession planning to smaller organizations in the nonprofit sector. It is likely with the looming retirement of many Baby Boomers across the workforce this research will be valuable not only to small nonprofit organizations but also small businesses.

Related to the issue of succession planning and management is the issue of training and development for nonprofit organizations. In Chapter 13, Toby Eagan examined the current practice and research concerning the training and development of the nonprofit workforce. He found that overall both the research and practice of training and development were underdeveloped, particularly when it came to smaller and less well-established organizations. His review pointed to the need for both researchers and nonprofit leaders to frame training and development of staff as part of the process for organizational learning and strategy for organizations. As practice in this area advances, researchers will need to investigate the link between resources invested in these strategies and broader organizational performance and the role of these actions in recruiting and retaining staff.

Joan Pynes, in Chapter 10, examines the role of labor relations in the nonprofit sector and points out labor relations may become an increasing concern from both researchers and practitioners due to increased unionization in growth areas of the nonprofit sector. These growth areas include fields such as healthcare, legal, education, and research (Desilver, 2015). This might mean some of the larger organizations in the nonprofit sector such as universities and hospitals may face additional management challenges due to unionization, including recent movements by college athletes and graduate students to unionize. This points to the opportunity for scholars to extend existing lines of investigation concerning labor relations in the for-profit and government sectors into nonprofit research, particularly in healthcare and other highly professionalized portions of the nonprofit sector.

In terms of the evolving nature of HRM in the nonprofit sector, Jennifer Jones's examination of the impact of technology in Chapter 19 also poses some interesting questions and challenges for the nonprofit sector. In particular, her work suggests technology will impact the ability to recruit and retain staff and volunteers since many find adaptation to new technology difficult and many diverse groups access technology differently or are shut out from it. It is likely technological change will drive many aspects of HRM especially in terms of how we communicate with and recruit volunteers and employees.

The need for additional research and attention to the development of HRM in the nonprofit sector is clear. However, the reason to do this goes beyond the interests of scholars. Scholars and those in the field need to always keep in mind the importance of employees in terms of our ability to serve society and the missions of nonprofit organizations. Failure to fully employ the resources and potential of staff means further losing ground in terms of addressing society's most pressing issues and allowing for continued suffering and struggle for the most vulnerable in our communities. It means the important work of nonprofits may be less effective than it could be, more costly in terms of time and money, and ultimately could lead many to lose faith in the sector to provide answers and services. It could mean the loss of valuable talent needed to find new paths forward in the nonprofit sector as those employees go elsewhere in search of meaningful work and supportive workplaces.

References

Benedict, A., Lockwood, N., Esen, E., & Williams, S. (2008). HR's evolving role in organizations and its impact on business strategy. Society for Human Resource Management. Available at: www.shrm.org/ResourcesAndTools/tools-and-samples/toolkits/Documents/HR_27s%20Evolving%20Role%20In%20Organizations.pdf

Cnaan, R. A. & Handy, F. (2005). Towards understanding episodic volunteering. *Vrijwillige Inzet Onderzocht, 2*(1), 29–35.

Desilver, D. (April 17, 2015). Job categories where union membership have fallen off most. Fact Tank: News in the Numbers. Pew Research Center. Available at: www.pewresearch.org/fact-tank/2015/04/27/union-membership/

England, P. (2005). Emerging theories of care work. *Annual Review of Sociology,* 381–399.

Fry, R. (2015). Millennials surpass Gen Xers as the largest generation in the US labor force. fact tank: News in the numbers. Pew Research Center. Available at: www.pewresearch.org/fact-tank/2015/05/11/millennials-surpass-gen-xers-as-the-largest-generation-in-u-s-labor-force/

Grønbjerg, K. A. (2002). Evaluating nonprofit databases. *American Behavioral Scientist, 45*(11), 1741–1777.

Grønbjerg, K. A. & Paarlberg, L. (2001). Community variations in the size and scope of the nonprofit sector: Theory and preliminary findings. *Nonprofit and Voluntary Sector Quarterly, 30*(4), 684–706.

Guo, C., Brown, W. A., Ashcraft, R. F., Yoshioka, C. F., & Dong, H. K. D. (2011). Strategic human resources management in nonprofit organizations. *Review of Public Personnel–Administration, 31*(3), 248–269.

Hager, M. A., Wilson, S., Polack, T. H., & Rooney, P. M. (2003). Response rates for mail surveys of nonprofit organizations: A review and empirical test. *Nonprofit and Voluntary Sector Quarterly, 32*(2), 252–267.

Lammers, J. C. (1991). Attitudes, motives, and demographic predictors of volunteer commitment and service duration. *Journal of Social Service Research, 14*(3–4), 125–140.

Landis-Cobb, L., Kramer, K., & Milway, K. (2015) The nonprofit leadership development deficit. Available at: https://ssir.org/articles/entry/the_nonprofit_leadership_development_deficit

Lecy, J. D. & Searing, E. A. (2015). Anatomy of the nonprofit starvation cycle: An analysis of falling overhead ratios in the nonprofit sector. *Nonprofit and Voluntary Sector Quarterly, 44*(3), 539–563.

Lee, Y. J. & Wilkins, V. M. (2011). More similarities or more differences? Comparing public and nonprofit managers' job motivations. *Public Administration Review, 71*(1), 45–56.

Leete, L. (2000). Wage equity and employee motivation in nonprofit and for-profit organizations. *Journal of Economic Behavior and Organization, 43*(4), 423–446.

Lohmann, R. A. (1992). *The commons: Perspectives on nonprofit organization and voluntary Action*. San Francisco, CA: Jossey-Bass.

McGinnis Johnson, J. & Ng, E. S. (2016). Money talks or millennials walk: The effect of compensation on nonprofit millennial workers sector-switching intentions. *Review of Public Personnel Administration, 36*(3), 283–305.

Melton, E. K. & Meier, K. J. (2016). For the want of a nail: the interaction of managerial capacity and human resource management on organizational performance. *Public Administration Review*.

Park, S. M. & Word, J. (2012). Driven to service: Intrinsic and extrinsic motivation for public and nonprofit managers. *Public Personnel Management, 41*(4), 705–734.

Sawhill, J. C. & Williamson, D. (2001). Mission impossible?: Measuring success in nonprofit organizations. *Nonprofit Management & Leadership, 11*(3), 371–386.

Themudo, N. S. (2009). Gender and the nonprofit sector. *Nonprofit and Voluntary Sector Quarterly, 38*(4), 666–683.

Tschirhart, M., Reed, K. K., Freeman, S. J., & Anker, A. L. (2008). Is the grass greener? Sector shifting and choice of sector by MPA and MBA graduates. *Nonprofit and Voluntary Sector Quarterly, 37*(4), 668–688.

Wright, B. E., Manigault, L. J., & Black, T. R. (2004). Quantitative research measurement in public administration and assessment of journal publications. *Administration & Society, 35*(6), 747–764.

Wyland, M. (September 14, 2016). GuidesStar issues new nonprofit compensation report. *Nonprofit Quarterly* . Available at: https://nonprofitquarterly.org/2016/09/14/guidestar-issues-new-nonprofit-compensation-report/

Index

Please note that page references to non-textual content such as Figures will be followed by the letter "f" in italics, whereas those for Tables will be followed by the letter "t". References to Notes will contain the letter "n" followed by the Note number, while references to Web Resources will contain the letter "w". "HRM" stands for "Human Resource Management", while "HR" represents "human resources".